WITH GRATITUDE

to

The Board of Trustees of Spelman College
whose creation of an endowed chair in independent study
brought the SIS Oral History Project into existence

The Department of Psychology
whose decision to make us a part of their family
brought many talented and capable young scholars into SIS

and

Eighteen African Women of Wisdom
whose memories make this volume a sacred text

Volume I

For their early and sustained support, we are indebted to Joyce King, Pauline Drake, Flo Roberts, Cynthia Spence, Myra Burnett, Kai Jackson, Jamila Canady, Victoria Durant Gonzales, Eloise Alexis, Taronda Spencer, Angela Allen, Lorraine Mencer, Wanda Polite, Mary Elias, Velma Royster, Tomika DePriest, Yvonne Jackson, Mary Edmonds, Alicia Smash, Geneva Baxter, Helen Catron, Fleda Jackson, and Ama Sarong. We want to give special thanks to Trisa Long Paschal, whose enthusiasm charted funding waters for us; Shirley Toland and Fatemeh Shafiel, whose teaching and scholarship enriched us; and Barbara Boone, whose unconditional and always-assistance gave us a smooth start. Most of all, we are indebted to Audrey Forbes Manley, whose vision, support and leadership as President of Spelman College brought SIS into existence.

Volume II

We could not have completed Volume II without the support of friends of SIS named above and new friends to whom we express our gratitude: LaConyea Butler, Evelyn Chisholm, Angela Watkins, Sharon Washington, Bill Ransom, Furery Reid, Franita Ware, Romas Mills, Zadie Long, Nakia Threadgill, Bonnie Tidwell, Dan Buscelli, Faye Milner, Janice Martin, Joyce McKay, Jocelyn Jackson, Jennifer Jackson, Tuere Bowles, David Organ, Carolyn Hart, Josephine Smith, Helen Threatt, Jackie Daniels, and Joyce Farmer. We are indebted to Kim Hughes, who, in a few short months, put this volume on a fast track to completion, and to Virginia Floyd, who made us global and richer in many ways. We give our most special thanks to Beverly Daniel Tatum whose enthusiastic support as President of Spelman College made it possible for SIS to grow deeper roots in the Spelman soil of leadership.

Their Memories, Our Treasure

Conversations with African-American

Women of Wisdom

VOLUMES I-II

Edited by

Spelman's Independent Scholars

Yomi Adesanya
Gianna Brown
Jalylah Burrell
Takkara Brunson
Shaekeira Bryan
Wanda Cannick
Jamie Chatman

Natane Eaddy
Mia Everett
Bemnet Fantu
Shayla Griffin
Taneya Gethers
Shacara Johnson
Brandi Lee
Kira Lynch

AeuMuro Lake
Danielle Phillips
Lauren Teague
Hatshepsitu Tull
Radia Turay
Michaela Warren
Lindsay Young

and

SIS Founding Director

Gloria Wade Gayles

The SIS Oral History Project
Spelman College
350 Spelman Lane, SW
Atlanta, Georgia 30314

Printed in the United States of America

Cover Design by Jamine Moton
Photography by Tommy Burns

2nd Printing (2008) Layout Design by
Jamine Moton, Kimberly James, Gabrielle Wood,

1st Printing was made possible by support from The Emily Winship Scott Foundation,
the Arthur J Davis Vinings Foundation, and The Ford Foundation

2nd Printing (2008) was made possible by support from AARP
and the Dogwood City Chapter of LINKS, Inc.

In keeping with the vision of SIS, this volume uses an age-sensitive font.

ISBN 0-9748565-0-9

CONTENTS

WISDOM SO GENEROUSLY GIVEN

Where is the knowledge we have lost in information?
Where is the wisdom we have lost in knowledge?

T.S. Eliot

Though these lines were written more than fifty years ago, they still resonate with power, describing the dilemma of the Information Age. Today's youth have grown up with easy access to an abundance of information, delivered at the touch of a keypad with lightning speed. But does that information translate into knowledge or the deep understanding that might be described as wisdom. Will today's facts yield tomorrow's wisdom? As an educator, I often reflect on this question, recognizing the important role that our colleges and universities must play to prepare the next generation of leaders. There are difficult decisions to make in our increasingly complex world. How do we adequately prepare our students for wise, ethical and responsible leadership? How do we create the opportunities for reflection, integration, and application of ideas that lead to greater self-knowledge and social understanding that help students gain perspective and a greater recognition of the interdependence that necessarily exists within communities? What curricular and pedagogical strategies will lead us to the cultivation of wisdom? If wisdom is our goal, how can we be more intentional in our practice to facilitate its emergence?

I imagine that there might be many good answers to this question, but I can think of no better way than to expose young people to those whose lives embody the principle of wisdom, to ask our students to step away from the instant transmission of facts to listen to the slow unfolding of an elder's life story. To hear firsthand about the choices one has made in the face of challenge, or the steadfastness of faith in response to adversity is to be given a glimpse of wisdom in the making. When Dr. Gloria Gayles conceived of the idea of bringing Spelman College students together with older women who had been, and still are, leaders in their communities, she created a context for important ntergenerational dialogue and set powerful pedagogy in motion.

This collection of narratives is the fruit of that dialogue. More than just words on a page, these narratives are the tangible manifestation of gracious hospitality as teacher and student sipped tea and studied photos, the evidence of thoughtful reflection as memories were shared and lessons were learned, the documentation of wisdom imparted. We owe tremendous gratitude to the elders who were so willing to share their stories with the young women whose lives may have initially seemed worlds apart from their own, and to the students and their guide, Dr. Gloria Gayles, who have now through their work made these narratives available to us. May we too learn from the wisdom of their experience so generously given.

Beverly Daniel Tatum
President of Spelman College

AN EDITORIAL EXPLANATION

This book represents more than 144 hours of interviews Young Scholars conducted with African American Women of Wisdom who mentored them in the SIS Oral History Project. This number does not include the countless hours devoted to seminars, community lectures, research, travel, conferences, writing, transcribing, editing, and proofreading. During the stipulated period of research, each Young Scholar conducted at least four one-hour interviews with her Mentor. In several instances, Scholar and Woman of Wisdom bonded so well that the number of interviews was increased to five and the length to two hours—in two instances, to three. When transcribed, the collective interviews with each Woman of Wisdom averaged thirty pages, a length exceeding space and cost limitations of this volume. For that reason, we edited and excerpted the collective interviews; collapsed them into individual narratives, called "Stories of Wisdom," and submitted the narratives to Women of Wisdom for their review and approval In several instances, we changed the order of the questions asked, but we left the elders' responses unchanged. Weaknesses of any kind should be attributed solely to SIS and not in any way to the remarkable gifts of the Women we honor. Tapes of all interviews excerpted in this volume are located in the archives of SIS in LEADS at Spelman College.

Gloria Wade Gayles
Founding Director of SIS

It was a misty Friday morning in March 2003 on the observation deck of a ferry that my sister scholars and I watched graceful seagulls guide us to Sapelo Island, our second research trip of the academic year 2003-04. I believe the sea gulls were the spirits of our African ancestors and our individual family members giving us their approval and their blessing for our work in the SIS Oral History Project. While we were on this historic island, we began our research on Gullah culture by conducting the first of several interviews with Mrs. Cornelia Bailey, considered by many to be the griot of Sapelo. We toured the island, and we watched the sun rise over the Atlantic Ocean. Sapelo was a transformative experience for all of us. We returned to Spelman with an eagerness and a determination to bond with and learn from African American Women of Wisdom who were our mentors in the SIS project.

We did not see sea gulls when we traveled from campus to the homes of our mentors, but I have no doubt that the ancestors were guiding us. I believe they were pleased with the durable bonds we were developing with African American Women of Wisdom and with the conversations that made every interview a rich learning experience. For two years, we have been on a journey of research and growth. The volume you are holding in your hand is the "destination" toward which we have been traveling. It contains life stories from interviews we conducted with African American Women of Wisdom who were our mentors in SIS during the academic years, 2001-02 and 2002-03.

A two-semester independent, interdisciplinary and intergenerational learning experience, SIS is open to students across all majors. In SIS, we enhance our critical writing and critical thinking skills. In weekly seminars, we share our research, sharpen our skills and grow in knowledge about oral history. In addition to learning sessions with the SIS faculty mentor, we are privileged to lectures by guest scholars. This year, 2002-03, the scholars included a gerontologist, two oral historians, a museum curator, an archivist, and a physician-researcher in traditional knowledge. The first semester in SIS focuses on research and interviewing. The second semester focuses on transcribing and editing.

Our research as Young Scholars is not limited to the City of Atlanta. During the academic year 2002-03, we traveled to Sapelo and also to Newtown, Georgia. It was in Newton that we developed relationships with African American Women of Wisdom who have struggled, and continue to struggle, against environmental racism. We were accompanied on the trip to Newtown by Dr. Fatemeh Shafiei, a Spelman faculty scholar of environmental justice, and by Dr. Gloria Wade-Gayles, the SIS faculty mentor. On the Sapelo trip last year, we were accompanied by Dr. Shirley Toland, a Spelman faculty scholar of Diasporan literature; by Dr. Virginia Floyd, a physician-scholar of traditional knowledge; and by our SIS faculty mentor. During the spring semester of this academic year, 200304, we will return to Newtown and to Sapelo, and three of us will journey with Dr. Virginia Floyd to Benin, West Africa. The research we conduct on these three trips will be included in Volume III of Their Memories, Their Treasures.

The stories included in this, our first volume, were created from interviews we conducted with Women of Wisdom in Atlanta who served as our mentors during the academic years 2001-2003.

They grew up in rural farm communities or in urban areas; lived in housing projects or in middle class communities; and were born into families with three children or families of thirteen children. They worked as professional secretaries, caterers, receptionists, social workers, domestics, cooks, nurses, school teachers, high school counselors, journalists, college professors, school administrators, entrepreneurs, notary publics, artists, preachers, theologians, published scholars, and community activists.They birthed daughters or they adopted daughters. They range in age from seventy to ninety-five. All of them now reside in the South. All of them are remarkable women. Clearly, with such a diverse group of women, we expected different stories, and yet we discovered that, at the very core of this difference, there are commonalities about belief in family and community, education and integrity, resistance and change and, most of us, in our future as leaders. All of us heard the same message from our mentors: "You are special, and you must achieve." Their memories supplement our learning at Spelman College. Their memories are our treasure. Their stories are texts we must read, again and again. That is why all Young Scholars "genuflect" to the Women of Wisdom! This volume is our way of honoring them and sharing with others the wisdom they shared with us.

Danielle Phillips
Young Scholar 2001-2003

A TRIBUTE TO MRS. JUDIA MAE FERRELL
THE WISEST OF THE WISE

In the first year of its existence, the SIS Oral History Project was blessed by the participation of an African American Woman of Wisdom who would become known as "The Wisest of the Wise": Mrs. Judia Mae Ferrell. Not only was Mrs. Ferrell, at ninety-three, the oldest woman in the first group of African American Women of Wisdom, she was also the first woman to say "yes" to our invitation to participate in the project. The story about her gifts to SIS is worth telling.

Mrs. Ferrell received the letter of invitation barely two months after she had buried her daughter, Dr. Joyce Clark, a Spelman graduate and the mother of a Spelman graduate. Under the circumstances, she had every reason to decline the invitation. Understandably, all of us were reassured, and grateful, when Mrs. Ferrell agreed to be a Woman of Wisdom in the SIS Oral History Project, our first and our most elder of honorees. However, the realization that academic projects have been known to exploit people in the interest of scholarship gave me a gnawing sense of disquietude. That is why, as I drove Lindsay Young, the SIS mentee, to her first interview with Mrs. Ferrell, I searched for the right words that would rescind the invitation in a way that would not offend Mrs. Ferrell.

We rang the doorbell. Mrs. Ferrell answered almost immediately. She was expecting us. She greeted us with maternal warmth, invited us to make ourselves comfortable in her living room, and began to tell us how much she missed Joyce. Mrs. Ferrell's grief was palpable. We listened, interrupting only to say that we understood and that we marveled in her strength. At an appropriate moment in the conversation, we informed Mrs. Ferrell that we could postpone the interviews until next year. "This is the year," she told us, explaining that this is what Joyce would want and adding, "Joyce has her hand in this." How could she say no to an experience that came from God and from Joyce? "But am I worthy?" she asked. "Am I worthy?"

I was not present when, in subsequent weeks, Lindsay interviewed Mrs. Ferrell, but Lindsay's reports in SIS seminars confirmed what I knew what happen. Mrs. Ferrell opened her home and her heart to Lindsay, and Lindsay made bonding with Mrs. Ferrell central to her learning experience at Spelman College. I believe Lindsay was the only SIS student early in the program who attended Sunday worship with her mentor. The bonding between Lindsay and Mrs. Ferrell was exemplary of the intergenerational experience SIS wanted for each Young Scholar. At the first annual SIS banquet held in April 2003 in LLCII Auditorium at Spelman College, Mrs. Ferrell testified, in the tradition of her faith, how much comfort SIS had brought her during her period of grief. She was strengthened by her attendance at SIS activities, by conversations with Lindsay, and, of course, by her faith. "I always wanted to be somebody," she told Lindsay, and she was becoming somebody through the project. But she asked, "Am I worthy?"

Through this volume and our efforts to incorporate in our lives many of the values that sustained her, we hope SIS can be worthy of the bounteous wisdom Mrs. Judia Mae Ferrell has given all of us.

MRS. JUDIA MAE FERRELL

Greenville, Georgia
Teacher and Entrepreneur

My father was a small farmer, and my mama's people were big farmers. We would get up early in the morning to work on the farm. Sometimes we would say, "Papa, it's cloudy. We can't work on the farm." And he would say, "God is tending to His business, and we are going to tend to ours." I didn't like working on the farm. I was glad to get away to be what I wanted to be, and that was a teacher.

EXCERPTS OF INTERVIEWS WITH MRS. JUDIA MAE FERRELL
Conducted by Lindsay Young

YS: Are you a native of Atlanta?

JF: No, I was born in Merriwether County, where President Roosevelt would visit. You know he was crippled, and he would come up to Merriwether County for the water. You know, it's called Warm Spring. That's where I was born. In Merriwether County. My father was a farmer.

JF: He grew vegetables and corn and cotton.

YS: Really? Did you work on the farm?

JF: Oh yes. All the children did. We planted and cultivated and gathered, what we call harvested, and we sold in the nearest county. My father owned his own farm.

YS: So, he was not a sharecropper?

JF: Oh, no! He owned his own farm. Now it was not a big farm, but it was his. Yes, my father owned his own farm.

YS: Did many Blacks in Merriwether County also own farms?

JF: Oh yes! My father was a small farmer, but some people were big farmers. My mama's people were big farmers. I know about the country. [laughter] We would get up early in the morning to work on the farm. Sometimes we would say, "Papa, it's cloudy. We can't work on the farm." And he would say, "God is tending to his business, and we are going to tend to ours." [Laughing] So, you know what that meant?

YS: It meant you worked.

JF: I didn't like working on the farm. Not at all. Oh, not at all. I was so glad to get away from there I didn't know what to do. I was so glad to get away to be what I wanted to be, and that was a teacher.

YS: How many children were in your family?

JF: Twelve. My mama gave birth to twelve children. I was the third child and the first girl.

JF: You see, after me, Mama had nine children, and I worked very hard to help the family. I started cooking when I was twelve. I would get up early in the morning and start cooking just to help out, you know.

YS: Did your parents ask you to do that?

11

JF: No, they didn't. I saw the need. Mama was having baby after baby. I'd say, "Lord, she's gonna have another baby." So, I saw the need, and I helped her. We had a cousin who would bring enough food to last for a few days, but I helped out a lot.

YS: Did your mother deliver in a hospital?

JF: Oh, no. All of the babies were born at home. My great grandmother was a midwife, and she delivered all the babies except my sister Doris. I helped Mama with Doris.

YS: You were like a midwife?

JF: Well, yes. You could say that. When Doris was born, my great grandmother Lucy, the one I told you about who was the midwife? Well, she was dead. There was another woman, a Mrs. Fortune, who helped with deliveries, and Papa went to get her, but the baby came before he could get back home. Mama told me what to do. I didn't feel too comfortable, but I knew the baby was coming. I did everything Mama told me and when the baby was delivered, I separated her from Mama.

YS: Did you cut the cord?

JF: Oh no! I didn't do that, and Mama didn't ask me to. That's what I meant when I said I separated the baby from Mama. When Mrs. Fortune came, she cut the cord.

YS: Were you home when your mother gave birth to the other children?

JF: Oh yes and I never heard Mama cry out, except one time.

YS: Were you frightened?

JF: No. It was a natural thing, you know, for a woman to have a baby at home. I never thought about Mama dying. My father was at all the deliveries except the last one, which I told you about. He was always with my mother. I told my daughter Gwen the other day that men nowadays aren't like my father. He was always with my mother. Now Papa wasn't a house man. He wasn't that, but he was there when Mama needed him. He liked sports and he would always go, you know, to see sports and sometimes she would get upset with him because he would stay too long. Papa would ask her forgiveness. He would say, "Baby, I'm sorry." He was the one who would give in. He was quick to acknowledge wrong and quick to ask for forgiveness.

YS: I sense that you are like that, Mrs. Ferrell.

JF: That's what people say about me, and I think, yes, I'm like that. If I have wronged you, I ask for your forgiveness. That's in my bloodline. My father loved my mother. He gave the oldest son my mother's maiden name. Jackson. That was my mother's maiden name. Papa was an unusual man.

YS: Is there a story associated with your name?

JF: It came from my great grandmother. I have her name. She died when she was a young married woman. I don't know whether I was born or not. Maybe. Maybe not. Her name was Judith and that's where I got my name.

YS: What else do you know about your great grandparents? Were any of them in slavery?

JF: We have our family reunions (which we haven't had in several years), and my daughter would go to the archives. That's how I know a good bit about my family. She went to the archives here and looked up when we were brought and she looked up the records. I know my great great grandmother was White. She looked up the record and found that we had always owned land. Way, way back we owned land and stuff like that. My great grandmother was brought here as a slave and she came here on a White horse with her master, and she had a red apple. That's in the archives. She was a doctor. A midwife. I know she was White. Lucy Jackson. She married a Jackson. His name was Bill or Willie. Think his name was Bill. Now, I saw her and I have seen some of her children, but I never saw her husband. I know that she was brought here as a slave.

YS: Tell me about the relationship between Black people and White people in Greenville..

JF: We had some White people. But I didn't have anything to do with them. There wasn't a lot of them. Just a few. I would see them all lined up going to school. My sister Adele got along with them real well. You know she talked to them like I am talking to you. But, really, we weren't around White people that much. We stayed close to our community. It was a small community, but it had everything we needed.

YS: Did you hear about any incidents of racial violence taking place in Merriwether County?

JF: Well, yes, but our parents didn't expose us to talk about it. They protected us. We stayed close to home and when we were together . . . or when the children were around . . . they just didn't talk about White people. Now I do know there was a family in Merriwether County called the _____ and they were mean to Black people. Everybody knew that. And I do remember hearing about a lynching, but we just didn't talk too much about that kind of thing. We lived between home and church and school. That was our world. The church was Black. The school was Black. And everybody in our community was Black. And when you think about it, things are no different now. It's really not. When I went to get my teaching material, the superintendent had me to know that he liked me.

YS: The superintendent was White?

JF: Yes, and he had me to know that he liked me. Same thing with the riding postman. I ignored them. I didn't even tell my friends. But I never went to the superintendent's office alone after that. I protected myself. You know, it's always been that way. They've always gone after Black women.

YS: Tell me about the school you attended in Merriwether County.

JF: We had one school, and there was more than one class in a room. I liked school. I liked school because I always wanted to be a teacher. The teacher would tell us not to be a zero and I never wanted to be a zero. You know, a taxi driver from home. Well, he was driving a taxi here in Atlanta, but he came from Merriwether County. He brought a passenger near here, and when he saw this house, he asked the passenger who lived there and the passenger, one of my neighbors, told him my name and told him I was from Merriwether County. Well, you know what that taxi driver said? He said, "Judith Mae always did want to be something." [laughter] And that's true. That's one of the reasons I like this book you students are doing because it's nice to know where people come from. If we could just trace back to the roots of every person, we'd have more understanding and we'd see what they really wanted to be. I like what you are doing. I like this book because I'm being somebody.

YS: You are a very special woman, Mrs. Ferrell.

JF: I thank you for saying that.

YS: Did you know of any girls in your community who became pregnant out of wedlock?

JF: Yes, more than one, but they were good girls. They were good girls.

YS: How did the community treat them after they became pregnant and how did the community treat the boys who were the fathers? I don't know that they did anything to the boys, but I remember they turned one of the girls out of church

YS: Turned out of church? What does that mean?

JF: That means she couldn't be a member. Couldn't attend church. The trustees had a meeting and they turned the girl out of church.

YS: How did you feel about that?

JF: I thought it was cruel, and it is not what Christ would have done. Didn't he say let the ones who have no sins cast the first stone and not a stone was cast. I thought it was cruel what the church did to that girl. She was such a good girl.

YS: The church had a great deal of influence on the lives of people in Merriwether County.

JF: The church was all we had.

YS: Tell me about dating experiences in Merriwether. Where did you go on dates and at what age did your parents allow you to begin dating?

JF: Well, we went to school functions. That's all. We didn't party or anything. And we went to picnics. And, oh yes, we went to BTU. That was in the evenings on Sundays. It was for the young people at church.

YS: You didn't go to any dances?

JF: No, we didn't do that. The first dance I went to was when I was an assistant teacher, and I didn't know how to act. And let me see now. You asked me about when I started dating. Well, I was seventeen, maybe eighteen. No, I was seventeen. My first boyfriend was a boy named Glen Mitchell. He went to school with me. It was a one-room school and we had one teacher.

YS: Were you the first daughter in the family to get married?

JF: No, the third daughter was the first one. Adele. A-d-e-l-e. She married in Greenville and they lived with her mother-in-law, her husband's family. When we would go there, we would eat! His mother was a good cook, and her husband was a butcher, so he would deliver stuff to his mother and she could cook!!!! She taught my sister how to cook. Now Adele can cook!

YS: When you were growing up, what were you told about husbands and wives and the role of the wife in the marriage and the role of the husband in the marriage?

JF: I think- -and this is kinda old-fashioned - - my husband's mother didn't encourage him to do housework. This is my belief in her. I think where strength is, it should be used. Some of us have strength in one area and some of us have strengths in another. And when I gave a toast to my second granddaughter, I told them that I hope they would use their strengths and weaknesses to enhance each other. I think that makes for a good marriage.

YS: Were you raised to think that way?

JF: Life taught me that. But I'll tell you what my father said. When he married, he thought his wife should pick up his clothes and wash them and do all the things like that. He read in the Atlanta Constitution where some writer . . . I know this was a hundred years ago . . . said, "Your wife is not your slave. She is your help mate." And so he wouldn't let Mama do anything else for him. You won't find many men like that. But I remember him saying that. I'll be 93 next month. I remember him saying that when I was just a little girl. He was a lecturer. He'd just talk sometimes.

YS: I'd like to know how you met your husband? Did he grow up with you in Merriwether County?

JF: No, but that's where I met him. Every August, we had a revival and this time James drove up from LaGrange and that's when I met him. We courted for about a year and a half and then we married. We married in Odessa. That's here in Merriwether County. You know my husband never let me live in an apartment. When we first married, he took me to a house he had built over on Lena Street. He was a house builder. He was a contractor, a building contractor. He was very smart. My neighbor said he was before fifty years before his time. Fifty years before his time. He went to night school here in Atlanta. James was the one who took me to Wheat Street. He was from LaGrange, and he came here and joined Wheat Street. When I met him, he carried me to Wheat Street Church. I have been there ever since. At first, I didn't like Wheat Street.

YS: You didn't like it?

JF: No, I thought it was . . . . Well, my children started coming and I said, "James, I don't want to go to that church. It's too big." We had a couple of churches around here, you know, but he insisted that we go to Wheat Street. I don't know any other church in Atlanta, but any church I go to, I can get a message. Sometimes it's in the sermon. Sometimes it's in a song. I always leave feeling that I can go a little farther.

YS: How would you describe a good minister?

JF: I think a good minister practices what he preaches. His life speaks so loud that nobody can hear what he says in words. Tithing. I believe in tithing, but I don't tithe. I believe that God will make a way for us. God has put so many things in my life and so many good people like you and Dr. Gayles and so many of my neighbors and of course people at my church.

YS: What do you think about the big churches that are now on television?

JF: I think some of them are just feathering their own nest, but some are very sincere. Now I do believe this: the church has been unkind to women. For a long time, women couldn't preach in the pulpit and they still can't in some churches. I don't think that's right.

YS: When you moved from Greenville to Atlanta, you probably had to make an adjustment to living in the city.

JF: Greenville was what we called the country. I came here when first got married, and it was so hard for me to get used to. I would tell my sister who had stayed home. I would say, "It's just so noisy up here. I wish I was down there with all the kids." It was quiet in the country. But I'm all right where I am. My husband built this house and we've been here every since. All four of my children were born here. Yes, he built this house.

YS: Do you know the year?

JF: 1950. In '50 something. '52 or '53. I married in '34. No, I married. Wait. I have to get my dates together. I married in 1938. My first child was born in 1941. And Gwen was my first born.

YS: I'd like you to talk to me about your relationship with your children.

JF: We were close. I was close to all of my children. We did everything together. We cooked. We cleaned. We did the yard. We picked pecans. That's a pecan tree out there. I will give you some before you leave. We did things together. I married in Greenville, Georgia. I think I told you that, and I was teaching at the time. My husband built a house in Atlanta. He was always that kind of man. And he took me dancing to Lena Street. He continued his night school and finished night school. And all four of my children were born there. We stayed there about until he built this house.

YS: Tell me about your experience with childbirth.

JF: It was an ordeal for me. Painful in every way. I tell you. Really an ordeal. But all of them were natural born. None were caesarean. All my babies were what we call natural birth. A year and seven months after I had Gwen, I had Joyce, my second daughter. Gwen was very studious and Joyce was outgoing. I had to take a little more time with Gwen than I did with Joyce. And what I gave Gwen, I didn't have to go through the same thing with Joyce because they were together. They were pals and I was the mother and whatever I said, they did. And then James came after about two years after Joyce.

YS: Gwen, the oldest was studious. Joyce was outgoing. What about Harriet, your youngest daughter? Was she spoiled?

JF: Yes, ma'am! Harriet is spoiled. You see, it was a long time before she was born. Four years after James, she was born.

YS: So she really was the baby.

JF: You know it.

YS: What are your proudest memories as a mother?

JF: When my daughters finished high school and when Joyce got her Ph.D.

YS: I admire the strong way you are handling your grief.

JF: I think about Joyce a lot. I have tears sometimes. The sermon today centered around death and how it affects you. A lady in the Bible handled death like I did when Joyce died. Can't think of her name. She's not as prominent as Ruth and Naomi, but she was a different kind of woman. I can't call her name, but I know it just as I know yours. You know, you are so smart. Well, Rev. Borders was pastor for thirty years and his wife was really a pastor's wife. I said I would write these things down so I wouldn't take up your time.

YS: Oh, you aren't taking up my time. What about the sermon made you think of Joyce?

JF: I should have taken notes. First, he told us about how he got an email that one of his best college friends passed. He was in his thirties. How disappointing life can be when you dream dreams and things don't go as planned. He said to remember at the time of climax God is there. You don't have to be old to die. It was very encouraging. He didn't want to preach, but God called him. When Joyce became ill, she went to lots of doctors but there was nothing they could do. You know, she went to college, married, had kids, and saw them through college. She saw it all. Church helps me to get through the hard times. And I do other things, too?

YS: What other kinds of things do you do?

JF: Well, I read. I have this one book, "God is Enough." A lady gave it to me, and it has helped me so much since my daughter died.

YS: Do you read it everyday?

JF: Just when I feel like it. You know how it is. Sometimes you are in the mood to read .....
      sometimes you just want to mediate.

YS: Is that your favorite book?

JF: That is my favorite book.

YS: What other books do you like to read? I know you said that you like to read the Bible.

JF: Yes, I read that. I read a commentary that goes along with the Bible. Well, I read the newspaper sometimes.

YS: You have come through hard times in your life, but you remain strong. How have you done it?

JF: I just do what needs to be done.

YS: Is that the attitude that led you to open the nursery? How did you decide to?

JF: Well, that's where we were. When Harriett was born, her father was building on this street. He would take care of her.

YS: There weren't any daycare centers?

JF: He took care of her. He would take her along when he got his building materials. He just took care of her because she was dependent. She couldn't walk or anything. He was building houses on this street at that time so it was easy for him to keep her. But after he started going other places, it wasn't so easy. I said, "Well, if I can work at Wheat Street in a nursery." I knew I had plenty of room. And I knew that I lived in a very respectable community. So I decided. That's how I got my own nursery. I had several years of experience in the Wheat Street nursery. When he couldn't see after her anymore, I came home and opened my own nursery. started with three children and then I got up to sixteen. I never had over eighteen.

YS: Was it hard working from your home?

JF: It was easy to be at home working because my husband was a contractor. Being at home meant I could take his calls and still do my work.

YS: How many years?

JF: I just stopped around ... I stopped it in '80. That's thirty years. About thirty years. Yea, I retired at the nursery, then I retired here.

YS: Some women are afraid to do what they want to do. They seem afraid to be all that they can be. It seemed that you never had that problem.

JF: That's true.

YS: I want to know who gave you that confidence?

JF: Well, you know, no man is an island, so you can't do anything by yourself. You know people say, "Didn't nobody help me, didn't nobody help me." But I had help from my oldest children, Gwen and Joyce. I had help from James, who was in the service at that time. And I had outside help, when it was necessary. I have always worked, honey. I mean, I have always worked, and I'm working now. Anytime you cook and keep house, you are working.

YS: Right. Definitely.

JF: I wash and fold, but I don't iron anymore.

YS: Mrs. Ferrell, the one thing that you always talk about when we get together is your faith and the fact that you were reared in a God-fearing home. Do you have a favorite Biblical story?

JF: I like the story about Jonah running from God. Jonah wanted to keep right on. But God had him preach to the people. So I think the same thing that happened in those days happen now. We have to listen to God. And I am a strong believer in His word. I couldn't have made it through what I am going through if I didn't have my faith. I believe we can do all things through Christ who strengthens us. And I believe there is good in everybody. Every color. Every race. I just believe all of us were made by God. He gave us all something.

YS: You haven't told me what it's like to be a grandmother.

JF: Oh it is beautiful. It is so nice. It's one of the best feelings I ever had. You think about them so much and you wonder how they are being treated. It's just good to be a Grandmamma. [Laughter]

YS: No one would believe you are ninety-three, Mrs. Ferrell, because you are so very active.

JF: You know, it's up to you. If you don't move, you can't move.

YS: I like that: if you don't move, you can't move.

JF: That's right. You have to move even when you don't feel like it. It's not always pleasant for me to do the things I do and not always without pain, but I continue to do. I see a need, and I think I can make life a little better by doing as I do. You know when I went to the doctor this week, he asked me what did I think about a living will. And I said that I wanted to make one. I don't know how I'm going, but I do know we leave when God is ready for us. I don't feel like I used to feel. But I keep moving. And I know that God has a hand in every person's life. I've had my tough times, but I've been blessed. This book is a blessing. I get a chance to share the life I've tried to live. Not for put-on or fun. It's just me. And you asked me to talk about my life. You have given me joy.

MRS. DIANA ANDERSON

Tate Springs, Tennessee
Teacher, Artist, and Boy Scout Leader

Traveling the mountains was a way of life for us and, yes, it could be scary at times, but also beautiful. Sometimes when we would go up the mountains, we would be so high we could see the tops of clouds and we could see hairpin curves in the road.

EXCERPTS OF INTERVIEWS WITH MRS. DIANA ANDERSON
Conducted by Radia Turay and Yomi Adesanya

YS: I have been looking forward to this interview, Mrs. Anderson, since you prepared dinner for all of the students in SIS. I'd like to begin with your description of the city in which you were born.

DA: Well, I was born in Tate Springs. It was a small country town in Tennessee. Well, it wasn't really a town. It was more of a resort with mineral water, you know, and there were six Black families in the town. We were surrounded by Whites. Our neighbors were White, and we were in between. There was a farm behind our property. The people who lived there were White, and the people on the right side were White. In the next house, the people were Black. Along the highway, there was a White family and they owned a lot of land in the area. . . People came to Tate Springs to get hot baths. Most of them stayed in a large hotel back in the mountains. That's where everybody worked really. It was a resort hotel and the hot bath treatment was done by German doctors. The water in the area tasted awful. Actually, it tasted like sulfur. But drinking water came from drilled wells, so it did not taste or smell like the sulfur springs. The spring water that was used for those baths contained sulfur. I remember once my sisters and one of our neighbors went up into the mountains and we saw the springs come up. They were yellow bubbling springs in a large shallow area.

YS: Oh, that must have been nice. Were your parents the first in your family to live in Tate Spring and did your grandparents live there?

DA: I didn't know any of my grandparents, but I know that my mother's parents lived in Tennessee and my father's parents lived in South Carolina. I know how my mother got to Tate Springs. . . . She was raised by my uncle. His name was James Jennings, but we called him Uncle Jim. My mother's parents died when she was a young girl and it was Uncle Jim, my mother's uncle, who took her in. In fact, he built the house in Tate Springs for my mother and my father. He worked at the hotel—really it was a resort—and because he worked there, he was able to buy land in the area. I'm sorry that I didn't ask questions about this. There was a main highway in Tate Springs and Blacks owned land all along that highway.

YS: I want to tell you, Mrs. Anderson, that you are the first African American I have met who grew up in the mountains. Were they beautiful?

DA: Oh yes! The mountains were very beautiful, especially in the spring and in the winter. Sometimes you could hardly see the top of the mountains because the clouds were low. My family lived on one side of the mountains, and my sister taught school on the other side. I remember the sharp hairpin curves we had to travel to get from our house to her school. In the winter, the far side of the mountain would be very icy. One winter, I had a very scary experience traveling on those roads. The roads were so icy that we had to get out of the car, park it on the drive-out spot of the mountains, and walk from the top down.

That was scary, scary. When we got to the bottom, the back of our legs ached. Before we arrived, one of my sister's students—the oldest student—had built a fire in the school so that we could be warm. He carried us to his grandmother's house and that's where we spent the night. Traveling the mountains was a way of life for us and, yes, it could be scary at times, but also beautiful. Sometimes when we would go up the mountains, we would be so high we could see the tops of clouds and we could see hairpin curves in the road. Do you know about feuding mountain families, the Hatfields and the McCoys?

YS: Feuding? No, we didn't study them in Sierre Leone.

DA: [Laughing] They were two mountain families who were feuding for a long, long time. When we would leave the highway and travel to the school where my sister taught, we would pass relatives of the Hatfields and the McCoys and they would say, "Here comes that-ar teacher."

YS: Were these high mountains?

DA: Oh yes. Very high. And water seeped out of the rocks and, of course, in the winter, the water would freeze. In autumn, there was a myriad of colors in the mountains. There were all kinds of trees. Elm, oak, pine. And wild flowers and, of course, streams. I remember swinging on vines over ravines, and that was so much fun. I don't know what the vines were called, but they were strong enough to carry our weight. We would hold on to the vines and swing over ravines. It was very dangerous, but it was a lot of fun.

YS: How many sisters do you have and do you have any brothers. Would you give me their names and also the names of your parents?

DA: My mother's name was Ida Jennings and my father's name was Walter Mattison. There were five children: William, Lela, Cecil, Hazel and myself. There are only two of us left. I was the last child. My brother was the oldest. He was about eleven years old when I was born. There were two years between everyone else, and nine years between my sister and me.

YS: Is there a story associated with your name?

DA: My mother read a love story in a true romance magazine about a woman named Diana, and she just liked the name. Back then, you didn't run into many Dianas, Black or White. I like my name. Children at school and even relatives called me Dee, but my father always called me Diana. I said that once in the presence of my husband and from that time on, he never called me Dee.

YS: Tell me about going to school in Tate Springs.

DA: I was born in Tate Spring, but we moved to Morristown when the Tennessee Dam Authority bought the property in the area, and that was in 1935. I remember because it was my first year in high school. Water backed up, and people had to leave their farms.

Some people moved to other places, but we moved to Morristown, which was only twelve miles from Tate Spring, and that's where I grew up. That's where I went to elementary school and to high school? My high school was really a college high school, somewhat like a junior college because there was a negotiation between the city of Morristown and the Methodist College. The high school was small, very small. There might have been as few as ten to fifteen students in my class. Whites went to a different elementary school and a different high school. We really did not come in contact with Whites our age, but neither did my children and they grew up in Atlanta. They didn't have contact with Whites because they were in Black schools. They went to Douglass High School. But my children had White teachers, and I taught with White teachers after desegregation. What was interesting about Morristown is that the Black college was the only college in the city and as a result there were very few Blacks in Morristown who didn't finish at least two years of college. There were White teachers and Black teachers in Morristown during my time in high school. We lived in segregated communities, but there never were any problems between Whites and Blacks that I know of. Blacks were in their community, and Whites were in their community

YS: You didn't hear about any acts of racial violence? About lynchings? About the KKK? Wasn't it founded in Tennessee?

DA: Nothing of that sort happened in Morristown. In fact, I don't think I was aware of the KKK until I came to college.

YS: I have some idea of how Blacks were treated, but what about Black women? What kinds of jobs did women hold and what kinds of restrictions did they live with?

DA: Most of the schoolteachers were women. There were no jobs other than domestic or cafeteria jobs for Black women. Let's see now. What about the railroad? Morristown was the connection point for trains going to North Carolina and Virginia, but I don't think Blacks were employed by the railroad.

YS: Would you paint a picture for me of your Morristown neighborhood: the houses, the church you attended, stores, neighbors . . . ?

DA: The homes were small and most of them were family-owned with more yard space than we find in the average home today. Many people had flower and vegetable gardens. Most of the streets were paved. There were small churches and grocery stores, and we were able to walk from where we lived to everywhere in Morristown—to school, church and shopping. All of our activities centered around the school and the church and, of course, everybody in the immediate neighborhood went to all of the activities: plays, games, proms. We really didn't come into contact with Whites because when we went to these different activities, all of the people were Black.

Family life was very dear to us because we did fun things together. We learned to make candy and cookies. We would pop popcorn with the neighbor's children. I remember that there was a large family with about eight children who lived in the neighborhood, and we played at their house one weekend and at my house the next weekend. Family life was very dear. Holidays were particularly fun. We decorated trees and made wreaths together.

YS: Did you attend church as a family?

DA: My father didn't go to church with us because he was working as a waiter in Tate Spring, but my mother and my sisters and I attended church every Sunday. We were Methodists. You know that was during the Depression, but we didn't know we were poor. We didn't go without, but I remember I had to be very careful with my shoes because we couldn't afford to buy new pairs. I had play shoes and dress shoes. As a matter of fact, it was the Depression that made us move to Morristown.

YS: What do you mean?

DA: Well, in Tate Spring, we had to drive to school. But in Morristown, we could walk to school. Having to drive cost money and during the Depression, money was not easy to come by. My mother was very skillful and so she was able to manage even during this time. She made all of my clothes.

YS:.   What attracted you to Spelman?

DA: Well, I went to Knoxville College for one year and a friend of mine persuaded me to go with her to Spelman. And my first year at Spelman, I lived in what was then Bessie Strong. The only person on campus when I arrived at Spelman was a person from Toronto, Canada. Her name was Jean. We became roommates and we've been friends ever since.

YS: Did your parents bring you to Spelman or how did you travel?

DA: No, my parents didn't bring me. A friend and I came together because, you see, Knoxville is not that far from Atlanta, and Morristown is close to Knoxville. We rode the train.

YS: Was it segregated?

DA: Of course! Everything was segregated at that time. But we weren't bothered about that because the train was filled with students. At that time, you know, you didn't pay much attention to segregation. You had your own car, you know. That was in the forties. Let's see. It was early forties. That's when I came to Spelman.

YS: And I've heard about the rules, the rules, the Spelman rules.

DA: Yes, we had plenty of them, but [the rules] didn't bother me because I didn't go there to run around. Hardly anybody went to Spelman for that reason. The rules didn't bother me because where was I going after five o' clock in a city where I didn't know anybody? Sometimes we would go downtown in a group.

YS: I'd like to hear what it was like shopping at the famous Rich's and the famous Macy's.

DA: Blacks and Whites shopped at both stores, but Macy's was called Davidson's then. We went into stores, but not the restaurants. That was a different matter altogether. We couldn't go into restaurants downtown and that's why there were sit-ins, you know, to desegregate public places. That was in the sixties here in Atlanta.

YS: It must have been really frustrating to live in a segregated city.

DA: Well, you went where you had to go for whatever you had to do. You knew what the laws were and one person alone wasn't going to buck the law and that was the way it was. But, back then, Blacks didn't have the jobs they have now. The educated ones were teachers, lawyers, doctors . . .

YS: I didn't know there were Black physicians back then.

DA: Oh yes! There were Black doctors here in Atlanta. There were Black businesses all along MLK and on Auburn Avenue there were businesses and dentists and markets. Oh there was so much on Auburn Avenue. Hotels. Restaurants. Nightclubs. Black banks. Black insurance company. All of them were Black owned and Black operated. You know MLK is not like it was. Then it was Hunter Street, not MLK.

YS: I have heard that before the sixties, the Black community was close. People knew one another, people spoke, and, you know, they were close.

DA: Well, I've never lived in a neighborhood where I didn't know or get to know the neighbors, and they didn't know you. Everybody spoke and said "Hi, how are you today," and that sort of thing. You weren't afraid to talk to people and kids could play in the streets or play in the yards without fear of harm. You just weren't afraid for your safety. You weren't afraid to go to the parks. Washington Park was the one Black park then. Mosley Park was on MLK Well, it was Hunter Street then, but we couldn't go there. It was only for Whites. And when Blacks started moving out into MLK and that whole area became Black, Mosley Park was open to us. Hunter Street, now MLK, was a main thoroughfare with many Black businesses: a real estate office, a drugstore, a movie theatre. So, we didn't have to worry about going downtown. And over on the other side of town, over on Edgewood (I think it was Edgewood), there was another theatre. And Paschal's was on MLK. Clark students live in the hotel at Paschal's now, but at first it was a restaurant. The Paschal Brothers had a little shop across the street from where it is now. They were famous for their fried chicken sandwiches. Then they built the building that is there now, and Paschal's just became a big business. There was a place called La Carousel, and that's where integration on this side of town really took place and nobody ever knew it. There were outstanding entertainers at La Carousel and Whites came. That had to have been in the fifties. Oh dear. I moved here in fifty-three, and it was there before then. Whites would come into the Black neighborhood, and they would go to La Carousel. Nothing was ever said about it.

26

YS: I want to go back to when you were growing up in Morristown and ask you how parents explained Jim Crow to their children.

DA: I imagine parents told their children, "You don't go to this theatre; you go to that theatre." I think kids then were just happy doing what they did with one another on familiar ground. The only time that many children got to go or even wanted to go downtown to the stores was at Christmas, Easter or vacation. And here in Atlanta, there were areas of town with a lot of small stores that carried good quality goods and those stores were crowded with Blacks. Do you know where the Marta lines cross downtown?

YS: Five Points?

DA: Not really Five Points. Closer back this way, where old Rich's used to be. The Federal Building's there now. Well, there were a lot of little businesses in that area. McCrory's was an old five and dime store that carried nice things. And there was Walgreens, which is coming back to Atlanta now. The Booterrie was in that area. Every child I know got shoes from the Booterrie. There was a dress shop, called Dianne, and people could get nice things there, less expensive than clothes at Rich's or Davidson's. There was a place called Highs and another store called Green's. Blacks could go into those shops and get what they wanted and be satisfied. All along on Broad Street and Forsythe Street there were shops filled with Blacks.

YS: And schools were segregated, of course.

DA: Of course! When I finished Spelman in 1947, I worked at C.W. Hill, an elementary school that had once been a school for White children. I don't know where Black children were going to school before Hill was opened to us. I don't know.

YS: And Douglas was the high school for Blacks?

DA: No, Douglas didn't exist then. There was Washington High School and there was another school across town. I can't think of it right now. There was only one Black high school at first and then there were two. The school I taught at was in the area we now call Midtown. Do you know where the Civic Center is? Well, right on that plot is where I taught. That's where the school was located. It had been a vocational school for Whites, but it became a school for Blacks because there were so many Black people in the area. It was an old building. No books. No teacher's guides. When they turned the school over to Blacks, they cleared everything out. They brought in old desks with seat parts messed up. Not a one of the desks had a bottom. I worked there for four years and then I just got sick of the situation. That's when I left Atlanta and went to Raleigh, North Carolina, and I taught there for two years. By the time I came back to Atlanta, schools here had improved.

RT: I loved the last time we were together. We were so laid back and, you know, you were telling me a lot of stories and I just enjoyed it so much .

DA: [speaking to Yomi] So, you are driving tonight?

RT: Yes, she is

DA: [speaking to Radia] Then, Dr. Gayles does not have to pick you up tonight?

RT: No. We can take our time. Dr. Gayles knows that Yomi is with me and she's probably glad because Dr. Gayles does not do night driving very well. [Laughter]

DA: Now I am going to pour you some tea.

RT: You are so kind, Mrs. Anderson. Thank you. I know you go to the Senior Center to take art classes, which is one of the reasons you are never home during the day. [Laughing]. Tell me about the Center.

DA: The Darnell Senior Citizen Center. It is on Fairburn Road right off Collier. It's sort of a new facility. I imagine it's three or maybe four years old. The Center is named after Council Woman Emma Darnell's mother. There are as many as twenty-three classes or more a week. I am often not home because I am at the Center.

RT: I would like to know what you consider to be the most pressing problem in our nation today.

DA: The war. The war that we are in. Another pressing problem is unemployment. So many people are losing jobs. I am also concerned about the behavior of our young people. They are unruly at home and at school and I think we lost control over our children when we started thinking, "Don't inhibit the child."

YA: I think a very big problem with the society today is lack of respect for elders. That is shocking to me because where I'm from (I'm Nigerian, but I grew up in Britain} when someone who is an authoritative figure speaks or an older person speaks, you stop to listen. But here, there's absolutely no regard. I think that is a really big problem in American culture.

DA: So many mothers (let me put more hot water in your cup) are only twelve, thirteen or fourteen years old. It's so sad.

RT: Did you know of any teenager mothers when you were growing up, and did you hear anything about women having abortions?

DA: No. Everybody who went to high school with me stayed in school. Education in our small town was very important. Some of the girls married early, in their teens, but they were married. I don't remember hearing anything about pregnancy out of wedlock or anything about abortion. You know, in a small town, there are some things that everybody knows and other things that you will never know. There are secrets in small towns.

RT: Do you believe more was expected of your generation than of today's generation?

DA: I can't say. I don't know. Generally. I would say yes, but I guess it depends on where you are, the school system that you are in, the community you are in. So many things help mold you into a good citizen, a good person, a good parent. Well, in the average Black family when I was growing up, parents may not have finished high school or may not have gone to college, but they made sure their children did. My mother and father didn't have much schooling, but they saw that five of us finished normal college. I went to college and after college to grad school. What was there for you to do? Teach. If there had been a counselor or some kind of guidance when I was in high school, I would have been in either science or math or art. I would not have chosen home economics as a major. My mother had already taught me home economics and when I finished Spelman, I didn't teach home economics. I taught elementary school, and I loved it. Loved it!

RT: How long did you teach?

DA: Let's see now. When you teach in different states, it's difficult to add up the years. I think I taught for thirty-eight years. I came home when my husband and my sister-in-law had health problems, and I'm glad I did.

RT: I know you are always busy because I can never catch you home during the day or early evening. Sometimes when Dr.Gayles asks me if I have made the appointment for our next interview, all I can say is "Mrs. Anderson is never home." [Laughing] So, tell me, Mrs. Anderson, what are some of your service projects.

DA: The Sunday school Superintendent said to us one day, "Why do you think you are here? What is your job?" I said that all I have done since I was eight years old is serve. I used to read for an old lady. I was in the third grade when I started reading for her and I didn't know how to pronounce all of the words. Right now, I do the bills for a lady who is blind. She did my hair for years. I cooked some things last night to take to her. I also have sole power of attorney for my neighbor, the one next to me. She's in a home, so I have to do everything for her. I've been doing that since about 1987.

YS: You told us earlier how active you have been in Boy Scouts.

DA: Well, yes. I have spent thirty plus years with scouting, and I've stayed with the same troop and pack all these years. I do their banking and whatever else they need. I enjoyed scouting. I am a Silver Beaver. I received the Whitney Young Award, the District Merit, and, actually, all the awards that you could possibly get in scouting and all the pens. Sometimes I forget what they are all for because they all look alike. [Laughing] I have been in scouting for so long I was part of the first woman group to do Wood Badge. That's a level of training that had always been for men and when they finally let women in, I was in the first group.

RT: Mrs. Anderson, I'd like you to tell Yomi what you told me about differences between our generation and your generation.

DA: Well, I am sure people did the same things when I came along that your generation is doing, but the dress was different. We wore sweaters that were down to here and we always had a string of beads and loafers. And we kept our loafers white even in winter. We were very neat. Today, kids wear very expensive clothes, but the clothes are too big for them and girls wear everything that is tight and short.

RT: Yes. I am actually having a problem wearing jeans . Everything is low rise. So you put them on and you are struggling with your shirt so that your mom won't complain about your jeans and then when you sit down, it's just all over .

DA: [Laughing] Older folks would say you are showing your plumber's behind.

RT: Plumber's behind? I never heard that expression.

DA: A plumber is always stooped over and on the ground and naturally his pants go down.

YA: A plumber's behind. Radia, we will have to remember that.

RT: What do you think about Black women of our generation?

DA: Well, let me say I was never too keen on loudness and I have always said that I'm gonna tell whoever will be in charge of my funeral to tell the preacher not to yell and holler. Even though I will be dead, I don't want anyone to be hollering over me.

RT: You think women of our generation are too loud?

DA: Well, I think you are seen too much in public places. In my time, nobody went to a bar, and now it's a common thing. We went to house parties or we went to a nightclub, but we never went alone. We were in groups, maybe three girls and five boys or five girls and two boys. Now girls go wherever they want to go with just another girl. Now you can decide on Friday to get together and go to Florida, maybe three or four of you, just for the weekend. That wasn't the kind of thing we did in my day. But, then, in my day, cars were not that common. Every family didn't own a car or a telephone for that matter. And so, we didn't spend time talking on the phone the way your generation does. Whoever I might want to call might not have had a phone. Times are different. That's all. In my generation, we would always notice whether boys would be mannerable and that would be one of the criteria for going out with a fella. It was a common belief then that girls should not walk on the outside of the sidewalk. The saying was: "She's for sale." And so, we always made sure that we were on the inside and we would look to see if the boy remembered that.

RT: If you could speak to a group of young Black women in their early twenties about being Black women, what would you say to them?

DA: Oh, I would definitely push education. Dream big and work to achieve goals. That's very important. And I would mention some of the things that might interrupt your goals, such as early sex, becoming parents, misconceptions about impregnation, a lot of health issues that sometimes you don't even think about, setting standards for yourself, choosing the right associates. Your friends can pretty much determine the way you go. I would tell you that it's important not only to set a goal, but also to give yourself a timeline. Enjoy your life. Have fun in what you do.

RT: And you have certainly had fun teaching. Tell me about your life since your graduation from Spelman.

DA: After Spelman, I taught for four years in Atlanta and then I went to Raleigh, North Carolina, and taught there for two years. While I was in North Carolina, I married and then I returned to Atlanta and finished my master's degree. I have been here since.

YA: I didn't get your husband's name. Maybe Radia has it from earlier interviews.

DA: Wesley. Wesley Gideon Anderson. We had two children. A boy and a girl.
Wesley Gideon and Anita Louise. My son was named after my husband and my daughter . I don't know why but I just liked the name Anita. I was married seven years before my first pregnancy. My first child was due the first week in December and my mother died the 20th of November. When I learned of her death, I cried so hard that my water broke. Thus, my son was born.

RT: I think you told me that you retired from teaching in order to care for your husband.

DA: I was disappointed with what was happening in schools and that's one of the reasons I was ready to leave. But I left because I was needed at home. My husband and my sister-in-law had health challenges. My husband had glaucoma and he eventually went blind. He didn't die of glaucoma. Of blindness. I think his spirit was just dissolved.

YS: And this is the house in which you lived – in historic Vine City.

DA: Yes, it's quite historic. This community has been pretty stable, but now it's not because the people who owned these houses are dead. Some of the houses are rented out and others have to be redone. We are being bombarded by offers to sell, because the real estate folk are putting up things in this area and all over Atlanta.

YS: What makes you happy?

DA: I don't know. I am not often sad or downtrodden about anything. Right now the freedom to do as I want to, and to do the things that I am doing now at the senior center-- that makes me happy and to see that my children and my grands are happy. Health wise, I've just been really blessed. I've never had anything tragic happen to me. I have just been really blessed.

YS: You are very modest, Mrs. Anderson, because you said nothing about the fact that you are an artist. All of these beautiful paintings on your walls, upstairs and downstairs. You painted them. What does painting do for you?

DA: It's just a thing that I wanted to do, but I didn't have the training for it. I think I should have been trained in the visual arts. That's where my passion is. The training I am getting at the Center provides me an outlet. I like what I am doing and I have made many new friends.

YS: Getting to know you has been a high point of my years at Spelman. I'd like to know what the SIS experience has meant to you?

DA: This experience was really uplifting because I hadn't been with college-age girls or boys in such a long time that it was just wonderful that you showed interest in the stories of elders, especially those from Spelman. The idea and the project activities are fantastic. I am glad to have been invited to participate.

MRS. NADINE BRYANT

Atlanta, Georgia
Computer Student and Cook at Horizon Community Center

I was cleaning this one room and I opened the drawer. A big roll of money was in the drawer, one hundred dollar bills! I slammed it shut. I walked around the room. I went back and looked at it. It was still there. I could see my grandmamma's face telling me, "That's not the way I raised you, Nadine Why didn't you call me?" That was somebody's hard earned money they left. Did I turn it in? Yes, because it was not mine.

YS: Are you ready to start, Ms. Bryant?

NB: Yes, I'm ready.

YS: So let's start at the beginning.

NB: Okay. My name is Z-o-r-a. My middle name is Rutland. My name was Z-o-w-i-e. I changed it from Zowie to Zora. But on my birth certificate it's Z-o-w-i-e. Okay. I didn't want an ugly name with everybody laughing at me. You know, children laugh at your name. They called me "Zowie the Black Wrip." I was in high school when I started putting my name as Z-o-r-a, but my name is Z-o-w-i-e, and I was born April 21st. I was born April 22, 1934, but my mother said I was born April 21st, 1934. So, I have two birthdays. I celebrate two birthdays. In fact, I celebrate my birthday clear on up to Mother's Day. My birthday is in April, right? Mother's Day is in May. In fact, I celebrate from May up to Mother's Day. Then I'm through. Everyday is my birthday.

YS: So your father's last name was Rutland?

NB: My mother's name is [she's deceased] Evelyn Elizabeth Rutland. My father's name was Ernest Phinnzee. Phinnzee. P-h-i-n-n-z-e-e. My name is Nadine. My maiden name before I got married was Nadine Zowie Rutland. Then I got married and my name became Bryant. I got married in January 29, 1957.

YS: Where did you go to school?

NB: Okay. First I went to E. A. Ware School public school. Then I went to a school called Davis Street. It was affiliated with Washington High School. I went there from the seventh to the eighth grade. Then I graduated from the eighth grade and went to Booker T. Washington High. I graduated in 1952. My grandmamma raised me. I lived with my mother, but she was, you know, out of town working. My grandmother raised me up. At that time, we didn't have much. My grandmother's name was Beulah William Boyd. My grandmother, that's who raised me. My mother was sixteen years old when she had me. So, my grandmother raised me. My grandmother went to the third grade, but she was a very smart lady. My grandmamma was a proud woman. A very proud woman. And so, at Washington High School, they had a program called . . . . Well anyway, we could work. We could work and go to school after we got into the eleventh grade. Yeah, they would get us jobs.

YS: What kind of jobs?

NB: Some people worked in offices and some people worked in homes. Our teacher was named Ms. Annabel Hatcher. And I 'm trying to think. Did she go to Spelman or did she go to Clark? But anyway, her name was Annabel Hatcher. She was a very fine lady. She was over the program. I went to work for a lady called Halle Brooks. She was a professor over at Atlanta University. I cleaned up her house and different things like that. Then after that I got married, I still went to her house to clean up for her after school. Yeah, I graduated. Oh, yeah. I graduated, and then that's when I thought I wanted to marry. Everybody else was getting married. Everybody! Some people went to college and some didn't. Some friends I know just preferred to work. A lot of people just worked because some families weren't able, at that time, to send their children to college. A lot of people got scholarships. It was about who you knew. Yeah. I finished high school. My grades were average. I wanted to be a nurse and so I went some to a school called Beaumont School of Nursing. It was on Boulevard Avenue. At that time, Black people didn't have nursing schools to go to. Finally, we could start going to Grady. They were teaching nursing out at George Washington Carver Vocational School, but at that time I was married. That's when I found out I was pregnant. I was married but I still wanted to be a nurse.

I had three kids. We didn't know anything about birth control.I first knew about the pill when I had my third child. See, they didn't tell Black women about birth control until a later date, a real later date. I found out about the pill from the nurse who did the follow-up exam after my third pregnancy. I thought that I had it made, you know. Thought that if I was taking those pills that I wouldn't have anymore children. But, anyway, I'm proud of my kids. I have six children.

At that time, you think that's all you're supposed to do. Have children. Really. Then further on down the line, you learn better and better. You learn more and more about yourself, your body, a lot of the things I didn't know, even when I was a girl. I want to tell you something, but I want you to . . .

YS: You want me to turn off the tape recorder?

Tape is turned off.

NB: My grandmamma worked at a laundry. People would bring her clothes and she would fold sheets and use a presser. That's what she did, and she would come home at 3:30. That's when she got off at that laundry. She would come home and cook.. My grandmamma taught me how to wash. We had a big bench in the back yard, and we had three tubs. The tin tubs were covered with a big board to keep out dirt and leaves. When it rained they'd take the covers off the tubs and let them fill up with the rainwater. But meanwhile we still carried a tin bucket and filled the tubs up with it. We had a pot, a big iron pot. I got that pot right now, an iron pot. Yeah, I have a big pot. And they'd have what you call a stick. It was a long stick, a real long stick. And it's end was flat, like a paddle. You know, like they have them paddle boats? That's what we would stir the clothes with. And my grandmamma made her own soap. What you call lye soap? As years went by, they still made soap but they graduated. They started putting Cheer in with the soap. Yeah. I watched them. Yeah. They used meat grease, fat grease, bacon and stuff like that. They put it in a pot and poured what you call lye, Red Devil Lye, in there. They stirred in so much water. Then they started putting that lye in there again, and they stirred it 'til it was boiling. That's when they started adding Cheer to it. Come out just as pretty. I got some soap right now. I got some at home. We were using Octagon soap, too. Octagon. They still sell it. You know, Dr. Gayles told you about that. I still use that soap. I wash my face with it. It's the best soap, baby. It suds my face real good and then I have to shave. See all these hairs on my face. You know, when you get older, you get this. Well, I rinse off the soap and I put witch-hazel on my face. What you call astringent is nothing but witch-hazel with something smelling good put in it. Do you use a rag on your face? Don't put a rag on your face. Just wash with your hands and soap and water and then rinse your face. Don't put a rag on your face. You know, the washrag. Wash with your hands.

YS: So Octagon was the only soap on the market?

NB: Yeah, it was, but then we found out about Life bar soap. Black folks started using Life, and then they had another soap called PNG. It was a bar of white soap about that big. You were doing something if you had that PNG soap. We didn't have anything else. Then finally, it came to Palmolive soap. A green soap. They still make Palmolive soap. I got to get these things and show you. Now let me get back to the washing. You would soak the clothes in one tub with the soap. The next step was to rinse, and the last step was called bluing. It was in a little blue box about like that. They poured some in the last water. That's what you rinsed with. After you rinsed, you had clothespins and you had a line. The clothes got hung out on the line. Oh, white clean! I mean we washed things with a rub board. I've got two rub boards right now. Rub board. You get on the board and wash your clothes like this. I don't know if there is still one in that room n there. Anyway, I'm gonna get one and show you. I got two.   And that's not all. We used Argo Starch. You've seen starched clothes, haven't you? Okay, my grandma would sprinkle the clothes that evening, and the next evening start ironing. We had what you call smoothing irons, a smoothing iron. It was like a iron. Yeah, I got one. And we would put charcoal in this little bucket. It would get red hot. That's where you do your ironing from, that bucket. You would sit your iron on the bucket, and it would get red around there. Yes, I was doing something. To me, I was doing well.

YS: Considering all the work you had to do after school, did you have a good childhood?

NB: Sure. I was never hungry, and I think I looked good. My grandmamma made my clothes. She sewed, yeah, on the sewing machine. If she didn't feel like it, I would mash the peddle for her while she sewed, using a Singer Sewing Machine. She made them, and she bought me things, too. Shoes and clothes like that, but she made so much. . . . A lot of people then bought flour. A twenty-five pound bag of flour was about this high. The flour bag came in all kinds of colored material or white material. They would take that material, after emptying the bag, and wash it. Then they would use that material to make clothes. They would make dresses and things. Nice. Real nice. We had pillowcases, too. Sometimes my grandmamma would sew on Saturday. But we definitely went to church on Sunday. Know that now. Yes. They did nothing like that on Sunday. You didn't wash on Sunday like these people do now. We went to church. We'd go to Sunday school at about 9:30. Then you'd stay for service. You didn't come back home. You went to church and you ate dinner there, yeah, in the basement of the church, and you stayed for BTU. That was something like Sunday school, but it was a little heavier studying. You know, you'd learn more about the Bible. And my grandma would stay until 6:00 BTU. Then we would go home. I knew we were gonna stay at church all day. When I got on up in high school, I was still going to church. Yeah, I didn't stray away till I called myself grown. You know? Grown.

YS: What was the most important lesson you learned in your childhood?

NB: I've learned a lot. And one thing is common sense. Common sense means a lot. Oh, yes it does. As they used to say "mother wit." You've heard that word? It means, if you're a mother you know things. You can sense things, and you can use those things. You can learn how to treat people. You can learn how to understand folks. Some say, "Oh, she ain't got no kinda mother with." They are talking about a lady that doesn't have any wisdom, someone who hasn't learned anything from the world. Yeah, that's what they say. Sometimes you might hear people say, "Oh, that mom ain't got no kinda mother wit." Or, they say, common eyes, or like common sense. That means a whole lot.

You know what I'm talking about. Okay. Some people say I can talk. I believe I can go anywhere and talk with anybody. I don't care how much smarter they are than me. I say, you sit and listen and you will learn a lot. Oh yes, learn a lot. That's one thing. But, otherwise, I think my life has been good, and I'm proud of my children. I have six children. I have six grandchildren, two boys and four girls. They all went to school. Some went to college and some went to the army. You got it? You want me to tell you about my girls and my boys?

YS: Yes. I would like to hear about your children.

NB: All of my girls did good for themselves. One finished Clark. One went to Atlanta Junior College. One went to Merritt Business College on Peachtree. It was open at that time. And, my baby, she started working for Jewish people. My oldest girl got a scholarship from Betty Crocker. My second girl got a scholarship from HUD. HUD, H-U-D. It was housing, HUD, housing. She got a scholarship to attend Clark. She majored in business administration. She graduated. My oldest girl graduated from Atlanta Junior College. My oldest son went to the army. I got two boys and four girls. My baby boy didn't go to the army. He works at Journal and Constitution. They all live right around me. I have six grandchildren. I'm proud of my six little grandchildren. Yes. Overall, I think I have a good life. We had hard times. We had good times. You learn to deal with the hard times. I'm proud of my life.

You want me to tell you about some of the hard times? Okay, you know during the 60's Martin Luther King was fighting for civil rights. Well, before that, it was really a mess. I remember I was doing domestic work. Black people took the trolley cars to work. Sometimes the White people would spread out and sit almost to the back of the bus so that we would have to stand up. If a White person wanted to sit down, we had to stand up.

This is after we had worked in these people's houses all day. Do you hear me? Look, instead of sitting up in the front, they would sit in the back. They were not thinking about us. They would sit like one in every other seat to each seat to keep us from sitting, and the bus would be empty, almost empty. Maybe there would be five people or so on the bus and we still had to stand up. But we worked hard all day. We were domestic workers going to clean people's houses. Oh, we had to ride the bus and things. Yes. Women. I told you. There were plenty of domestic workers. We would go to White folks houses and clean up, cook for 'em, raising the children. We were helping them with the children and everything, and we still had to get up on that bus and stand.

YS: Did you ever want to protest?

NB: For what! So the cops could lock you up? Or so the conductor could ask you to get off the bus? You knew, it'd be a mess. We would talk about them real bad. Oh, yes. Not while we were on the bus, though. We would talk about how we had to stand up and all that. They wouldn't pay us any attention. Well, some of them would act so ugly. Just sitting. One time the conductor told this man, "No, you gon' have to come up to the front and let those ladies sit down." And the man was so mad he said, "What you mean?" Oh, he wanted to get all ugly. The women were looking at him. He got up and moved up. I mean he was all the way on the back seat, too. There were seats up in the front. What were we gonna do about it?

YS: So how did you feel about the bus boycott?

NB: Wonderful. Wonderful. I was so proud. They made a movie about Rosa Parks. They filmed it over where I live in the West End. I'm telling you, there are some stories to be told. How Black people had to stand up after we worked hard all day. Say, you got off work at 3: 30 p.m., all you could see were Black women catching the bus. We were all coming down from these big, rich sections out past Buckhead, and we knew the drivers. Intelligent White people, like office workers, would be riding the bus and they would sit up front. They didn't act ugly. It was just those uneducated White people who wanted to act ugly. You see what I'm saying. They'd get on the bus and sit in the back, you know, just because they could do it. It was ugly just because they could do it. Now what would you call that?

YS: I call it unfair.

NB: And you are right. We worked for these people all day long. Sometimes you had to bring your children because you didn't have anybody to keep them. So, your children and their children are playing together and eating together and stuff, oh yeah. Yes! My grandmother worked for this doctor, and my oldest girl used to go to work with my grandmamma all the time. His name was Dr. Toole. My daughter would even go out of town with them. Yeah, they would take her so that she could be with their children. That's how they kept my grandmother, by taking my daughter, too. Yes, it was some hard times. But, as far as, like food, you might not have what you want, but you wouldn't be hungry. We had a garden: tomatoes, corn, peppers, collards, cabbage, turnip greens, sweet potatoes, Irish potatoes, lettuce. Yes, and then my granddaddy had hogs. We also had chickens. We were never hungry. Now, we might not get all that was fine, but we had chickens. You didn't have to buy eggs, and we had a big garden. We would kill the hogs at a certain time in the winter. Then people in the neighborhood would all come together at my house, and when the neighbors killed a hog, we all went over to their house. We'd just go to different places like that. During that time, when my grandmamma was alive, we shared with our neighbors. You wouldn't let that family go hungry. Oh no! In the whole neighborhood we didn't let anyone go hungry.

YS: In my neighborhood, we don't know anybody. We know their names, but we just say "hi" and "bye" from the door.

NB: That's the way it is now.

YS: Is that the way it is for you now, or do you still know your neighbors?

NB: I know two of my neighbors. I live in a nice neighborhood. The grass is green and the streets are clean. It's a nice neighborhood. I live down from the Shrine of the Black Madonna, over on Cascade.

YS: You live in what is called The Flat?

NB: Yes, they call it The Flat because it's the flat part of the street. You see, it's an intersection, but the way we got that house is a good story. I was living in Herndon Homes. I used to live in Vine City, over by the Dome. At that time, I had my children and my grandmother. We stayed on Thurman Street, in Herndon Homes. We stayed in the projects, but the projects were good for people. Oh, you lived well in the projects. They didn't have mess like tearing up the yards and all that crazy stuff. They didn't have people hanging all out the windows and all that kinda stuff. You had to go down to the office and pay a fine if you did something like that, and the children didn't walk on the grass. They did not tear up those projects, okay? It was nice. Thurman Street was where my grandma lived. I was raised on that street.

YS: Why did you decide to move?

NB: Well, see, the city bought out all of that area. So, they got houses for us. They let you go pick out your own house, and they paid. So, I got a real-estate man and he showed me all kinds of houses. See, that's when Black people started buying houses out this way. Only White people used to live in the West End, baby. Sears & Roebuck was up there. We moved in our house in 1972. Yeah, it was in the 70s when HUD started buying the houses. That's when they tore down those projects. They built apartments and things, but they paid for our house. When I first got the house, it was paid for, but keeping up the house cost money. That's how I got in debt. I was trying to keep the house up. The furnace had to be changed. Those houses had been over there for a long time, and all of those old trees made it hard when you had to have your yard dug up to replace old piping.

But, I did what I had to do to keep my house. It was funny because Black people used to work for folks over where we stayed in the West End.

YS: Did the Whites move out as the Blacks moved in to West End?

NB: Yes, some did move, but some stayed. Some of the White people didn't move, and now they're coming back. Yes, in all the areas. Fine with me. I didn't do anything to those peoples. They are not bothering me. That's fine. They're all coming back to town. They moved out, way out, but now they're coming back into the city. And that's why you have to keep your house up and everything. The only problem is that they're going up on taxes now. You may have got your house for about fifteen thousand dollars. Now that price is between sixty and ninety thousand dollars. It's because of all the fixing up in the neighborhood. They have fixed up those houses real, real well.

I call all new houses they're building in these subdivisions "wind breakers." If a strong wind comes, it will blow them down. [The houses} aren't strong. They are using sawdust wood to build them. Like those apartments right here. This used to be the projects. Did you see those beautiful apartments? They were projects. But they tore all that down and filled it all with windbreakers. What you call that, right there on Martin Luther King Avenue? If that ain't a windbreaker, what do you call a windbreaker? Hard wind could come and pull it up and away.

YS: Tell me about Vine City. What was it like when you lived there with your grandmother?

NB: Well, at first we lived in a place near where the Dome is now. Back in those days, they called that area the Light then. I guess I was about four years old when we moved to Vine City. I lived on Thurman Street. I went to school in Vine City, and I got married in Vine City. Here. This is where I was raised up on Thurman Street. We could walk to school. It wasn't far from Washington High School. We didn't have buses. There was no riding on buses to get to school. We walked. We all walked to school back then. It wasn't no where to walk. I mean it was real nice. You know, you would meet up with your friends and walk to school. Sometimes we would all go to the movies and stuff like that. Now there's one thing my grandmamma did not play: you did not go to the movies on Sunday. No. I wanted to go, but my grandmamma didn't play that stuff, girl. It was about six of us girls that lived in the same neighborhood. We were friends and everything. We all walked to school together, and our families knew each other. One family looked out for the other. When my grandmamma worked, one of the other mothers would look after me, and whatever she said for me to do, I had to do. If I got out of line, she would tear my backside up. My grandmamma wouldn't say a word, either. In fact, when she came home, I'd get another whooping. Everybody was your mother. You did what they said to do. You did not talk back, no. Oh no, like these children are doing now. Have you seen how kids stand around looking in grown people's face? I knew better than to stand up and look at grown people in the eye. No, you did what the neighbors said.

YS: Sounds like you lived in a community where people protected one another.

NB: That's right. We looked out for each other. They helped you and you helped them. When I got home from school, my grandmamma would be at work and I knew to pull off my school clothes and then put on my play clothes. I didn't wear my Sunday clothes or Sunday shoes during the week. I put on one outfit on Monday. Then I'd wear another dress on Tuesday. On Wednesday, I'd wear the same dress I wore on Monday. I knew better than to get dirty playing in my school clothes. You see, my grandmamma made my slips and things. My slips. You know? Like under slips and things? My grandmamma made them. Yeah, I told you about that white material came from the flour sack. She would bleach that material. She would wash it and bleach it. Then she would make under slips, but things started to change when the war came. We started living better. World War II changed our lives.

YS: In what way?

NB: My uncle went to the army. He told the Army to send his allotment to my grandmamma, and my grandmamma was working at the physical plant making tents. Many Black people got on up when the War was going on because they started working. They were making a little change then, you know. At that time, a lot of Black people got up on their feet. But you know we made it even before the War. You learn to live with the poverty, as they called it at that time. I didn't call it poverty, because we had food. We raised our food. Some people didn't have anything. There were Black folks that didn't have anything and had a lot of children. Ten or fifteen children. Maybe they didn't have as much as we had at that time. That's the reason I said people helped each other. You know what I'm saying? If your mama had ten children, she would send and ask my grandmamma for some greens. She didn't say, "Sell me some greens." She said, "Send me some greens." You see what I'm saying? They would do that with no problem. What else you want me to tell you? Now, I told you a lot. What I got to talk from now?

YS: How old were you when you got married?

NB: Was I twenty-one or twenty-two? I think I was twenty-one. Yes. I met my husband on the trolley. We were teenagers. We would ride to the river, get on the trolley, and go from one end to the other. At one point, this gang of boys got on the bus, got on the trolley. They were laughing and they were talking. I guess they picked us out, or we picked them out. I picked out my husband. I liked him. Yeah, he lived out in that area. Yeah, it was a group of girls. Yeah, he looked at me and I looked at him. . . .

If a boy liked you, he would have to see you in church. When I was going to church, we'd start Sunday morning and stay at church all day. You stayed from Sunday school to church to the choir, and you stayed in BYPU. It was nothing. It was the same thing like Sunday school, and they tell you what to study for the next Sunday. I got so tired. All day long you stayed at church. We had food to bring to church. I joined that church. I remember when I joined the church. I was thirteen years old. I got baptized. I thought I was . . . Oh, you couldn't tell me nothing.

YS: You were baptized at age thirteen.

NB: Yeah, when I was thirteen years old. One Easter they asked me if I was saved, I said, "Yes." At that time, I thought I was. But as far as my first boyfriend, he was at church, see. I had one at church, but you're around grown people all the time. You're never seen alone, oh no! Girls stay together. Boys stay together. You can look at them, laugh, and be in Sunday school class with them. That was okay. When we got out of church, my grandmother would be waiting on me to get out. She would stay, too. So children would stay busy at church all day.

YS: When did you have your first real date?

NB: When I was sixteen years old. That's the first time she let me. It was a group of girls and a group of boys. We all had to stay on my front porch. Maybe the girls would be up the street. We could laugh and talk together, but as singles.

YS: Tell me how you met your husband.

NB: I met my husband after he had gone to the army and come back. We dated maybe about three or four years. We had to go to the movies. We would group together and go to the movies. The boys would be waiting on us at the trolley stop. I remember tricking her, tricking my grandmamma.

YS: What did you do?

NB: To trick her? Oh, she thought all the girls were going together. As we got older, we didn't have to stay at church all day on Sunday. Oh, especially in the summertime, they let us go to the park. Washington Park is right over here. We used to go to the park, Washington Park. That was the only Black park. Out in Pittsburg they had a park, but we would go to Washington Park. They would let you go, but you just go to look. You didn't swim. They wouldn't let us go swimming. My grandma wouldn't let me swim for a long time, but I tricked her. We went to camp and she didn't know they had swimming there. Hon, I wasn't gonna let her know about that.

YS: Why didn't your grandmother want you to swim?

NB: Oh, that's the way they were. I think it was because my mother was sixteen years old when I was born. I guess my grandmamma wasn't going to let me grow up the wrong way. But I still say, it wasn't growing the wrong way. If God hadn't intended for me to be here, I wouldn't be here. So, I could talk all I wanted, but she didn't see it that way. I told you about the other part didn't I?

YS: What other part?

NB: Turn the tape off so I can tell you.

[Tape is turned off]

NB: So, every time I see that man, it looked like another baby was coming. But, anyway, I'm glad about my six children. I think we did good. When they got bigger, the oldest one could help with the others while I worked. I would work for the Board of Education in the wintertime, and go out to the golf club or something like that in the summer at White people's clubs. Jewish clubs. Sometimes I worked for the Board of Education, cooking. That's my main thing. That's what I like to do, cook. I would work for the Board of Education. First, I did domestic work. At that time, we were making like $2.50 to $3.50 an hour. Back in that time that was a lot of money. I could handle big work, too. One time a friend and I started working down to the Omni. She had a lot of children, too, and she stayed in the project. When we heard about jobs at the Omni, ALL of my children went. Everybody! We all went. They used to laugh at us. "Here comes that momma with all her children." That's right, baby. I'd have my children sweeping, picking up paper . . . You hear me? I raised them to work. You are going to work. Oh yes, you are going to work. I started working when I was thirteen, and they could work, too. They had jobs. Yeah. What else you want to know?

YS: What is this? [pointing to a certificate from a computer class]

NB: Well, you know we are graduating in June from our computer classes. Who would have thought after all this time? I am sixty seven years old and taking up a computer class. In June, we are going to have caps and gowns. I'll let you know when we're doing it. This is our second course. It lasted four weeks and I can't think right now, but next Monday is our last day. I don't know if it's next Monday. I'll let you know. I never thought I would do this. I never would've thought in my, what you say, wildest dreams, that I would be taking a computer class. When we first started, our instructor was Ms. Jones. Every time that virus would come up, I'd say, "Oh no, not me. This virus is fittin' to get on me. No, not me." You know the little signs in the computer. I said, "Oh no, Ms. Jones, I got to go now. Not me. Bye." After I got on in, I'd say, "Oh, Ms. Jones, here it is." I knew they had been talking about the virus on T.V. I thought that thing was going to bother me. I said, "No, Nadine Bryant, you gonna have to stop . " I thought it would come up in my hands and everything. I said, "What about them crazy talking on TV?" I said, "I'm gone!" Then I found out it wasn't like that, but at first they couldn't tell me different. That shows you. Not knowing. I just thought it was a virus that it was going to get you. Anyway, like I said, never in my wildest dreams. What else you want to know?

YS: Whatever you want to share with me about your life.

NB: Okay, let me tell you this. I used to go to the country with my grandmamma when school was out in the summer. We would go to Macon. After work, I would get cleaned up. The White folks were nice to us, but we were still Black. ''You still Black, ain't you? All right then, come around the back door." And Black people would go whimpering around to knock on the back door asking for a dollar. I used to work for a teacher. I would go over and clean her house. She really taught me how to clean. I learned a lot from her, but mostly I learned from a woman I met in the work-study program. Her name was Annerbelle Hatcher. I loved her. She taught me how to write out a money order. She showed me how to pay bills. She showed my grandmamma, too. I worked for her too. I wanted to be a nurse, but I had it in my head that I had to get married. It's like that sometime. I had all my children. Nursing was what I liked, but I didn't make it.

YS: Did you ever volunteer at a hospital?

NB: I have thought about caring for those babies, but I got a tender heart. I can't take it when I know they're not gonna be with us long. You know, working with the AIDS babies. You're rocking the babies but the babies only have two days to live. That's why they need volunteers to come in. They need a lot of folks to go there. Lord, why is the mother on drugs? I guess she just got weak. But we're all on drugs. We're all on legal drugs. Do you go to church? Do you go to the chapel?

YS: No.

NB: Cut that off.

YS: You want me to turn the recorder off?

[Tape is turned off]

NB: My grandmamma used to hit my nose like that to make it flat. She would say my momma had a pretty little nose. You know I felt bad when she did me like that, but that's over now. I've been in this house for twenty-nine years. You got to look at this picture. [Pulling out photo album] See right here this lady. Who is that?

YS: Maya Angelou.

NB: I love her because she inspired me with her books and the way she talks. She's a woman of wisdom. I love her. That lady.

YS: How did you learn about Maya Angelou?

NB: It was before Oprah had her on her program. I can't think of when it was. She was here for something. I had been hearing her on T.V. She's been here. You didn't see her? Then you need to go to the library. You need to go find information about when she came. That's your assignment. That's what I want you to do, and give me a report. That's the lady right there. She's a woman of wisdom.

YS: Who are these men? [Pointing to a picture]

NB: You know about White cowboy, right? Well, there are Black cowboys in Atlanta. They have a ranch here. They ride horses. They have horses that you can rent for little children's birthday parties. They bring you horses and sometimes they come, too. They have lady riders, too. I love it. I love it. Yeah, if I was a young woman, I'd ride one. You hear me? [Laughter]

YS: In this picture, you have on a uniform. Where were you working at the time?

NB: I'm gonna tell you something that happened to me when I was working one day. I worked at a hotel, and I was in cleaning the room. I worked at night. After people checked out, somebody else would come in the room, and it was my job to get the room clean. I was cleaning this one room and I opened the drawer. A big roll of money was in the drawer, one hundred dollar bills! I slammed it back again. I walked around the room. I cut on the T.V. I went back and looked at it. It was still there. Then I sat down and thought about it. I sat up in that room and I prayed for the Lord to tell me what to do. I thought about keeping it. Then I said, "No, that ain't the way I was raised." I thought about my children. I could see my children and me going to jail. I could see my grandmama's face telling me, "That's not the way I raised you, Nadine. Why didn't you call me? Why didn't you call me, because that's not the way." That was somebody's hard earned money that they left. Did I go and turn it in? Oh, you got it. Yes, it was mine. I had quit my other job to sit at home and take care of my grandmamma. She said God's gonna bless you. I'm gonna be blessed, so nobody can tell me nothing.

YS: That's a wonderful story. You have a lovely collection of photographs. While I look through them, I'd like you to tell me about male figures in your life. You told me what you learned from your grandmother. Did you learn anything from the men in your life?

NB: Yes, my uncle who went into the service. He took care of my grandmother and me. I had a very nice stepfather. His name was Frank Chaney. He was good to me. I knew more about him than I did my dad. He gave me my first birthday party when I was thirteen. He bought me my first bicycle. I thought I was tops. He was real nice to me. I learned to ride a bike in about two weeks, I believe. I would just go riding in the neighborhood and go to visit my friends. When I got older, like fifteen, I stopped riding. At that time, usually when you got about fifteen, you were more of a young lady. I didn't want to be riding no bicycle and let those boys see me fall.. Do you know what? Women did not wear pants. It was later on, after the War that they came up with what your generation call "capris". We called them "peddle pushers". They were half way up your leg, right. But these folk talk about some capris. Yeah, they let us wear those. But otherwise, women in my family, we didn't wear pants. When I started wanting to wear pants, it was after the war. Women were working in those factories and things. But otherwise, they didn't wear pants. Everybody would be looking at you, because at that time ladies just didn't wear pants. Not until after the war. We had started wearing shorts. That's a funny thing, how you could wear shorts, but you didn't wear long pants. We had shorts because they had ladies softball teams. Black women were playing softball. In each neighborhood they had little softball teams for the women, as well as, the young children. At Washington Park, we would go out and play ball on Saturday. But you didn't play on Sunday. Now what else you wanna know?

YS: You have been such an extraordinary mother.

NB: Thank you. Yeah. I tried. I raised my children in the housing project, which we talked about, and it was strict. You hear me? Things such as cleanliness were important. You kept up the projects. They didn't have walking on lawns and all that. The projects were well kept. And, like I told you about HUD building-up the area and buying part of Vine City. So, we got a chance to move where I am now, on Willard Avenue; out in the Cascade area. When we first moved there, my grandmother was still living. That's where she died. And my mother was living there, also. My mother passed and the house was left to me. There are two girls with me now. I don't want to live by myself at this point in my life. I am diabetic. And I don't want to stay by myself because with diabetics . . . No way. I don't know what time I'm going to maybe get sick or something by myself. You know, you can be in the house by yourself and nobody can hear you. That telephone isn't any good if you can't get to it. What else you want to know?

YS: Tell me what your six children are doing now?

NB: My oldest daughter works for a Jewish home. She's a dietician. My second girl works for Bellsouth. My third girl works for The Federal Reserve. My fourth girl, baby girl, works in Community Affairs. My oldest son works for KIPS. He fixes trucks. When he was in the army, he was a helicopter engineer. He learned to work on big trailers, too. That's what he likes. And my baby son was working at the Journal Constitution. Now he works for Piedmont Nations Electronics. Yep. Okay, I'm going to tell you about my little grandson. He's an honor roll student. He got a chance to go and take the gifted test. He'll be going to Brown High. He was accepted into the gifted program. Oh, yeah. I have six children and six grandchildren. I'm proud. I'm real proud of my children. I would have liked to go on to be a nurse, but since that didn't happen I think I did real well. I really would have liked to go on to school to be a nurse, but I thought I wanted to be married. But I'm real happy, real happy because I love my children and they did real well.

MRS. HARRIET CHISHOLM

Atlanta, Georgia
Elementary School Teacher and
Charter of Atlanta Chapter of Jack and Jill

They lived in Newnan, Georgia, as husband and wife, away from the plantation, but that didn't sit well with whites in Newnan....You see, Jamie, they were...bothering no one....Can you believe the Court decided that "letting Negroes live together away from the plantation would tend most powerfully to deepen and widen that restless spirit basely attempted to be excited in the minds of slaves...." [Document: Coweta County Superior Court Minutes, 1830]

EXCERPTS OF INTERVIEWS WITH MRS. HARRIET CHISHOLM
Conducted by Jamie Chatman

YS: Mrs. Chisholm, I want to thank you for agreeing to share some of your life stories with me, and I want to begin by asking you if you are a native of Atlanta?

HC: Yes. I was born in Atlanta in my parents' home on Howell Street.

YS: Tell me about your family.

HC: I grew up in what you would call a middle-class Black family. My father was a physician, and my grandfather was the first Black real estate agent in the City. My grandmother on my mother's side attended Atlanta University, and my mother earned a Master's in Social Work at Atlanta University in 1939.

YS: How many children were in your family?

HC: There were six of us. Five daughters--Marie Irwin, Catherine, Helen, Dorothy, and myself—and one son, my brother Herman. Marie Irwin, named after my mother and my father, died when she was an infant. My sister Catharine died six years ago.

YS: What are some of your fondest memories of your father, not as a physician, but as a father?

HC: I know a good way to describe my father. He was a father who had all of his children at heart. He wanted the best for all of us. I remember that he always told us, "You never promise something you can't keep." Sometimes he would be late coming home when he was going to take us somewhere and we'd say, "Daddy, we thought you weren't coming," and he would say, "I promised you, didn't I?" My father never broke a promise to us. He died at the age of ninety-two.

YS: At what age did he retire from practicing medicine?

HC: He didn't retire?

YS: He practiced medicine when he was in his nineties?

HC: Yes. In fact, he had been to the office on the day he died. His office was located on Auburn Avenue, and he had walked to the First Congregational Church to a funeral and stopped at the bank, Citizens Trust, on Piedmont. He might have done one thing that was detrimental to his health. He usually used the side door of the church where there were not many steps, but on this day, he climbed the steps at the front of the church. It was just his time maybe. He was a great daddy and a person very well thought of. Let me get his book.

[Mrs. Chisholm goes into the living room and returns with a very large scrapbook, red in color, that contains pictures, documents, newspaper clippings, letters, cards, and occasional notes. I learned in subsequent sessions that this was one of many such scrapbooks Mrs. Chisholm has put together to chronicle the history of her family.]

HC: This is an article about my father's seventy-one years of service to Atlanta. [She reads from The Atlanta Constitution: March 26, 1981]: "Dr. Nash's death brings an era to an end." At ninety-two, my father was the oldest practicing physician in Atlanta. [turning pages in the scrapbook] This is a letter my grandfather wrote my father. He wrote this when my father asked for my mother's hand in marriage. This is a picture of my parents when they were older. My mother had broken her hip and was using a cane. This is their marriage license. They were married in 1918. And this is her wedding picture. My parents married at home, and my grandmother and my mother made the wedding dress. This is a picture of my father, fifth from the left. This was during World War I.

YS: [reading official document] "First Lieutenant." The President of the United States sent your father this certificate of appreciation?

HC: That's when my father was examining young men for the draft.

YS: So he was a physician in the Army. Where did he attend medical school?

HC: Meharry. He entered right after finishing high school. They could do that then. This is the picture of my parents' first baby, Marie Irwin. She died at the age of two. I don't think any of us realized how much losing her baby affected my mother until we were grown and had children of our own. What she must have gone through to lose a cute toddler. I really believe that was why my mother was so very cautious with the rest of us. [She turns pages in the album] And here is another picture of my father.

YS: Were there any women physicians in Atlanta at the time?

HC: Sure there were! You didn't know that, Jamie?

YS: No.

HC: I had my tonsils removed at a hospital owned by a Black woman, Dr. Georgia Dwellie. The hospital was located on Boulevard. You know, Jamie, we are not aware of some of our history. We seem to think that Blacks didn't have achievements until the 1960's.

YS: Well, in my feminist theory class, in the books we are reading, it seems that women didn't do anything other than stay home.

HC: That's just my point, Jamie, when I say we have lost some of our history. My mother got her Master's degree in the 30's.

YS: Did many women do that?

HC: Not many that I knew, but if you were fortunate enough to be where you were exposed to education, you did. Many people did not have the opportunity, but there was a large group that did.

YS: A Black woman owned a hospital here in Atlanta?

HC: Yes. Dr. Georgia Dwelle. She was not our doctor. Our doctor was Dr. Madison, but we were patients in her hospital.

YS: Your doctor was a man, but a woman doctor owned the hospital? Do you think it was more difficult for a woman to go to medical school then than for a man?

HC: Yes, it was. When my sister wanted to go to medical school, my daddy wasn't gung-ho about letting her go because she weighed only sixty-nine pounds and he knew how rough medical school could be. But my grandfather said, "Let her go." She went. There were five women in her class. Of course the men gave them a fit, but my sister was feisty and she stood her ground and came out on top. She dealt with the foolishness men try to hand you anywhere in life. If you are strong, you don't pay any attention to them. My sister was an excellent doctor. . . She finished medical school in 1945. That was during World War II. Student went to medical school all year round, without a break. My sister finished college in 1942 and medical school in 1945.

YS: Many of the articles we are reading in my feminist theory class are about how women really wanted to work, but they stayed at home. I guess my question to you is, do you think, or was it in the case in your experience, that women were not allowed to do certain things? And what were some of the things women were not allowed to do?

HC: It would be hard for me to respond to that question, Jamie, because, in my environment, everybody was educated. Some women worked, and some stayed home for many and varied reasons.

YS: Are you saying there were no barriers for women?

HC: There were many barriers, Jamie, but it was a matter of money and ability and also a desire for education.

YS: What about getting a job? Did women face barriers?

HC: Yes. Women were limited. Women could teach or work as secretaries, unless they went into a profession. My mother had a Master's in social work, but she did not work for most of her married life. She did social work for about three or four years, but that was after all of us were out of school. I adored my mother.

YS: Tell me about her parenting style. Did she believe in spanking?

HC: My mother talked to us. We very seldom got spankings. She loved us, and there was no need for her to beat us or spank us. We knew that she meant it when she told us to do something. That is not to say she did not punish us. She did. She would punish us by not permitting us to do something we wanted to do. For example, she would not permit us to go on a trip or to a party. That is the way she punished us. She did not believe in spankings, and she didn't have a lot of do-nots for us to obey. You know, I have friends who say their mothers told them they'd better not do this or better not do that. My mother never did say any of that to us. She did more talking through her actions. I think she believed that, because we were her children, we were going to behave as she wanted us to. She was a lady.

YS: What did that mean?

HC: When you are a "lady," you know how to act whether you are around women or men or children . . . and whether you are at church or at a party. Mama expected us to be ladies, and she was our example.

YS: Today, we hear so much about girls having babies out of wedlock.

HC: But children have had illegitimate babies since the beginning of time. Let me share this with you, Jamie. We lived on Simpson Street all my life, and the houses on the street were small brick houses. Tiger Flowers, a retired boxer, lived in a mansion on Simpson, and across the street from his house, in the back, where Herndon Elementary School is now located, was the Crittendon Home. It was a home for pregnant White girls. The way we knew about it was that we would see a nurse with a girl with a fat stomach come down the street. Our mother explained the home to us. The girls stayed there until their babies were born, and then they would give the babies up for adoption. They would hide their pregnancy from White people. You know, while they were at Crittendon, they were supposed to be out of the city, or out of the country.

YS: When Whites came to Crittendon, was that the only time they were in the Black community.

HC: Oh, no. They would ride up and down our streets. They went wherever they wanted to go, but they didn't live in the neighborhood. There was no living together of Blacks and Whites then. Atlanta became integrated in your time.

YS: If Crittendon was for White girls only, what did Black girls do when they became pregnant?

HC: Their grandmothers took them or their mothers kept them.

YS: The grandmothers took care of the babies?

HC: Apparently.

YS: Tell me, what dating was like when you were growing up?

HC: We dated the way you date today, but we didn't have the freedom you have. We could not date during the week because that was a school day. We could only date on the weekend, and the boys had to leave at ten o'clock. One of the mothers worked at the canteen during the War and that gave us a chance to go there. And there was Parish House on Ashby Street, which is now Lowery Boulevard, where we sometimes held dances.

YS: When I was looking at your pictures, you told me that your mother had a lady do your hair.

HC: Yes, there were always people to do your hair. There were hair shops like the ones we have today.

YS: How often did you go, and how old were you when you started getting your hair done? I ask because I didn't get my hair done at a salon until I was older.

HC: We went whenever my mother decided to send us. I don't recall that we had a frequency of schedule for our hair as girls have now, and I really don't know when we started getting our hair done. I am sure we were in elementary school. We went to a lady named Mrs. Campbell, who worked in her home. You see, Jamie, my mother was not about to do four heads. [laughing] I remember that my father would take us to Mrs. Campbell, and we would stay all day because she had to do four heads. Mrs. Campbell would give us a sandwich of butter and sugar, and we hated it. We laugh about that even today.

YS: It's interesting that your father was the one who took you to get your hair done.

HC: We were close to our father, and we had only had one car. He took us to school every day. When we left home, all of us left together with our father. He worked until six o'clock. Sometimes he made house calls in the evening and delivered babies at night. In spite of his demanding schedule, he was very involved in our lives. He cooked breakfast every Sunday. We had the best of breakfasts! We had salmon croquettes, grits and homemade rolls. My mother would make the rolls, and my father always made the croquettes. That was his specialty. Sunday was a special day for my family We went every Sunday as a family to First Congregational Church. It's located on Courtland and Dobbs. I am a third generation member. My grandmother, my mother, and my father were members. I was christened there, and I was married there.

When we were very young, the children in the family did not have to go to church. We went to Sunday School, but not to church. At the time, my grandmother lived across the street from where Martin Luther King, Jr. lived on Auburn Avenue, so we would walk from church to her house, and we would stay there while our parents were in church. But when we were older, all of the children went to church. We knew to get our things ready on Saturday night for church on Sunday morning. If we said, "But I didn't polish my shoes," then we would go to church without our shoes being polished. Staying home from church was not a choice. All of us went, and we loved going.

YS: I'd like to know if the children in the family had to help out in the house. My sister and I have assigned chores, and mine is cutting the grass.

HC: We all had a week when it was our responsibility to do the dishes. The rules were the same for all of us. My mother didn't teach her daughters one thing and her son something different. She didn't give us dolls and give him trucks. I remember that, at Christmas, my brother would say he wanted a doll, and my mother would get him a boy doll. My brother played housekeeping with us. You know, Jamie, many people are afraid little boys who play with dolls are not going to turn out to be men, but that's not the case. My brother is all male. He has five girls. He has a set of twins. I'll tell you this story. When his daughters were at Howard University [three of them went there] and they came home with Afros, my brother said he thought their Afros were reaching ceiling. He did not say anything to his daughters, but that night, when he went to bed, he said to himself, "Heavenly Father, what do I do now?" He decided that it was their hair. If you can't do what you want with your own hair, what can you do? I guess I am sharing this with you, Jamie, to say that I don't think any of us in the family have had parents who said, "You'd better not do this," and I believe this kind of parenting came from my mother.

YS: Would you tell me about fun things children did when you were growing? And I'd like to know if you had a best friend.

HC: We liked to ride bicycles. We would ride or we would walk to Washington Park. We'd go to parties, you know. We loved to play with dolls. We'd dress them and pretend that they were going to school. We loved hopscotch and sitting on the steps playing "May I?" If you didn't answer correctly, you couldn't move up the steps. Little home games. My best friend was a classmate of mine through high school and college. She became pregnant and married early. She is dead now. She and I were opposites: she was quiet, and I was talkative. Our families were very different. She grew up without a mother. Her father married again, and we did not like the lady he married. My friend had three sisters, and all of them are dead except one, and she had one daughter. She was my very dear friend, and I am her child's Godmother.

YS: I know you do a great deal of traveling, and I was wondering whether or not your love for travel started when you were young.

HC: Actually, we did very little traveling as a family. You have to understand, Jamie, that there were five children and, of course, everything was segregated then. Travel was simply not something Blacks could easily do and certainly not with five children

YS: Segregation made it difficult. Would you tell me what it was like growing up in a Jim Crow city.

53

HC: Well, we were aware that there were certain places we couldn't go. We could go into stores downtown, but, at Rich's for example, we couldn't try on hats or gloves and in the shoe department there were only six seats for us. We didn't go to the Fox Theatre because Blacks had to climb up the back stairs, and my mother would not allow us to do that. She protected us as much as she could from having to deal with segregation. Actually, Jamie, that was true of many Black families. You see, Atlanta had a fairly large population of Black professionals who tried to create a world for their children that did not have negative racial experiences. Our parents protected us. We went to Oglethorpe Elementary School, which was Atlanta University's elementary school, and from there we went to Laboratory High on Spelman's campus, from grades eight to twelve. That's where we went to high school, and our faculty was integrated, both at Oglethorpe and at Lab High. I can remember some of the teachers very well: the gym teacher Ms. Dupre; the biology teacher Mrs. Foley; and Dr. Eva Knox, who became a writer of children's books. She taught kindergarten at Oglethorpe Elementary. So, during Jim Crow, we were exposed to Whites and to integration within our educational community.

YS: Did you experience any overt forms of racism?

HC: No, I did not because, as I said earlier, my mother didn't allow us to go where we were not welcomed. Most of our activities took place in the homes of our friends and our parents' friends. We went to Black movie theatres on Auburn Avenue and on Ashby Street. There was a nice theatre on Hunter Street, now M.L. King Boulevard, not far from where we lived. I don't want you to think that I didn't know racism existed. I did, but I didn't face it on a daily basis because my parents didn't let any of us go where we were not welcomed.

YS: Did you ever ride a Jim Crow bus and, if so, did you get upset about having to sit in the back of the bus?

HC: Yes, when we were going to town, we rode the bus, and it was a Jim Crow bus. Blacks sat in the back of the bus. We got on the bus, sat in the back, rode to our destination, and got off. We did what we were required to do. No, it didn't upset me, and it was not pleasant. You don't get upset about everything you can or cannot do, do you? So, when you are growing up in a society that requires you legally to sit in the back of the bus, you just go and sit in the back of the bus. If you want to ride the bus, that's what you do. I was not a fighter. I was not going to be confrontational. For what? To get slapped down by a White person? That could have happened then. When the demonstrations began, I did my protesting on the quiet side in a way that fits my personality. I did not march. I did not do sit-ins or anything like that. I worked in offices. I joined the NAACP and I went to meetings, but I did not participate in any of the protests.

YS: How did you feel when the Movement began?

HC: I thought the Civil Rights Movement was something that needed to be done. I thought it was something that was long overdue. I still become angry when I think about one group of people deciding that they were appointed by God to tell everybody else what to do. I think I get angry even now when they [Whites] look at us as a race that is their enemy.

YS: I'd like to move forward from your childhood to your marriage to your husband. Tell me how the two of you met.

HC: Would you believe I met him at a party at my house? My oldest sister and a friend had done some very good work at Sunday School, and my mother treated them to a party at our house. Each one could bring one guest. Well, a very good friend of mine called some of his friends at Morehouse and invited them to the party. My husband came, and that's when I met him. I wasn't invited to the party, but I was there, and he asked me to dance.

YS: You started dating then?

HC: Yes, and I dated him while I was in high school and while I was at Spelman. He left Morehouse when he was drafted into the Army, into the 99th Pursuit Squadron. That was the first air group of Black men. While he was in the military, he lived in Tuskegee. He wrote my mother and my father a letter asking if he could marry me. My parents gave their approval, but they said I had to finish college.

At the time, I was to live on campus, as all seniors were required to do, and, of course, I went to see President Florence Read. She said, "No, you're not going to marry on September 2nd. You cannot adapt to married life, senior life and college life at the same time. I will tell you what you are going to do. You're going to finish your year and then we'll have a nice wedding after you graduate." And I said, "Really?" I didn't go back to her. My wedding invitation was already being engraved.

YS: Tell me about your wedding.

HC: I had ten bridesmaids. [turning pages in scrapbook] This is my husband's mother. These are his sisters. He had four sisters. The entire family is dead now. Here is the letter my husband wrote asking me to marry him. You know, boys don't do that nowadays. You saw the letter my grandfather received from my father?

YS: Yes. Was that the custom?

HC: It was customary for men to do that.

YS: And this is a letter your husband wrote to your father?

HC: Yes. He wrote more than one letter.

YS: This is so special! He says that he thought he had convinced your parents that he was in love with you. [reading from handwritten letter dated July 4, 1943]: "The close attention I have shown the past four years is ample proof of that. . . ." Wow! "I will do my very best to make and keep her happy."

HC: He kept that promise.

YS: How long after you met your husband at the party were you married?

HC: I met him when I was a senior in high school, and I married him at the beginning of my senior year in college. I left Spelman and transferred to Morris Brown. You see, Jamie, back then, married women couldn't attend Spelman. My parents gave me their approval, and I promised them that I would finish college. I kept that promise. I graduated from Morris Brown, and then I went to Atlanta University for my Masters. It's funny how things sometimes happen. I say that because when I graduated from Atlanta University, President Read gave me my degree. She said, "Well, I didn't get to give you your undergraduate degree, but I get to give you your graduate degree." This is a picture of my husband. Isn't he handsome?

YS: Yes, he is. How old were you when you married?

HC: I had just turned twenty. My birthday was August 7th. I married September 2nd.

YS: Was that the age at which Black women in your generation were getting married?

HC: No. Most women were not getting married at twenty. I was the exception among my friends. I married at twenty, and my husband Charles and I were together for forty-four years. It's been sixteen years since his death. He died in 1986.

YS: You and your husband lived in Tuskegee, but your daughter was born here in Atlanta?

HC: Yes, I didn't want to ride up and down the tracks on a rickety train from Tuskegee to Atlanta pregnant. My daughter Cheryl, our only child, was born here in Atlanta, at Harris Memorial Hospital. It has closed. It was located on Hunter Street, which is now Martin Luther King.

YS: What do you remember about being pregnant?

HC: It was a very happy period. I was never sick.

YS: What do you remember about the delivery?

HC: Pain, pain and more pain. And then joy, joy, joy.

YS: I asked you about a baby story and you said you would think about it.

HC: Well, Jamie, when you are young and you are working and you have a baby and a husband and a house, you miss so many things. I know this to be the case because I saw so much as I watched my granddaughter Hallie grow up. But the story I want to share is about my daughter Cheryl, who is very independent. Even as a young child, she was independent. When she was eight years old, she flew to St. Louis for a summer camp experience. My mother said, "Harriet, you ought to be ashamed to put that child on a plane." I said, "You know she can do it." I said to Cheryl, "I am going to send you money and your return ticket." And she said, "Momma, I can take care of my money and my own return ticket." So I pinned telephone numbers in her pocket book and off she went. She has been going ever since. She is now living in California and working on a degree in clinical therapy. She finished Radcliffe and then went to UCLA, where she earned a degree in teaching film, not making film. But she has made one film. Now she is back out there. She likes California. I would not want to live there. I think it's a great place to visit, but this is home. I like Atlanta. My daughter Cheryl is wonderful. Always has been. She is a marvelous adult, and she has always had a mind of her own. She has always been a reader. She reads incessantly. She is very bright.

YS: How did you explain Jim Crow to her?

HC: She would often say, "I wish we could eat in Rich's in The Magnolia Room." That was a very nice restaurant in Rich's. I think it was on the fifth floor. Very nice. Whenever my daughter would say that, my husband and I would say, "That's right, Cheryl. It would be nice if we could." And she would ask, "What have we done?" And we would say, "We haven't done anything, but this is the law and until they change it, we cannot do anything about it." I would always tell her, "It's not worth you and me getting into trouble about it."

YS: You said that your daughter went to Radcliffe and to UCLA. Where did she go to high school? Here in Atlanta?

HC: No, she went to Northfield School for Girls, a boarding school in Massachusetts.

YS: Was it your wish that she go there?

HC: Yes, because I was not pleased with public schools in Atlanta.

YS: There wasn't a private school in Atlanta she could have attended?

HC: Yes. There was Westminster, but it was segregated. Blacks could not go to Westminster when Cheryl entered high school.

YS: What about the private schools you and your sisters and your brother attended?

HC: Oglethorpe Elementary and Laboratory High at Atlanta University closed down in 1941. But, you know, Cheryl had no qualms about going away to school. She made great friends at Northfield. She traveled with them. Went to Europe with them. She's always been a child who could do her own thinking. I remember when her daddy was going to give her a car. She said, "I can buy a car when I start working." She preferred a trip to Europe. She has traveled widely since.

YS: You mentioned that your daughter was in Jack & Jill. I was in Jack & Jill in Nashville. Tell me what kinds of activities the Atlanta chapter had.

HC: We took the children to Woody Willow. He was a TV personality like "Howdy Doody." Only the White children could go to see him. I remember, one time, we were able to take our children. That was the highlight of our activities. And going to The High Museum was also a highlight. When my daughter was in the 7th grade . . . see that small white vase? She bought one from the High when she was in the 7th grade. She fell in love with museums. She has been to museums all over the world, and she can tell you about all of them. That is her passion, and I think it started when we went to The High. That's when she saw the painting, Whistler's Mother, which was on loan from the Louvre. It wasn't only Jack & Jill that went to the High. I took my third graders there and, of course, I told them about the paintings they would see before we went. They didn't like Whistler's Mother. They told me, "Mrs. Chisholm, she is a mean-looking lady." They also said, "Mrs. Chisholm, my grandmother doesn't look that." Of course I talked to them about the rigidity in her body, about her expression . But, you know, art is in the eye of the beholder. Take symphony for example. I love the symphony. I love beautiful music, but I cannot stand brass. I don't care who performs it or who wrote the composition, brass is not for me.

YS: Your mother played the piano. Did she teach you to play?

HC: All of us took music lessons. My mother loved music. We had a victrola and she would wind it up and put a record on. She loved music, and all of us learned an instrument. We didn't play as well as my mother, but we learned an instrument. You know, Jamie, we as Blacks should have been able to go to the symphony and to the museums. We should have had more choices. I was thinking about that after one of our conversations. We should have had more choices.

YS: I am still in awe that all of your sisters and your brother went to private schools. Could anyone go to private schools back then?

HC: Yes. Anybody could go if they could pay and if they got in, as is the case with schools today. The schools were private, Jamie, but the children of professionals and non-professionals went there. Remember my telling you about Chadwick Homes? That was a home for girls located on Spelman's campus. Some of the children were there because their parents worked all the time and couldn't take care of them. Well, some of the children at Chadwick went to Oglethorpe and Lab High, and they were not treated differently from the children of professional parents. Where did you attend school, Jamie?

YS: I went to a private school. University School. I went there from kindergarten to 12th grade. It was associated with Vanderbilt University.

HC: That is exactly what Lab High was. The same thing. Most of us went straight through and on to Spelman. But one year, during the Depression, when times were very, very hard, we went to a public school. I was in the sixth grade, but I returned to private school and finished in 1940. Finished Lab High. Spelman and Atlanta University took the building back in 1942. My youngest sister went to Washington High School, a public school, because Lab High had been closed and there were no other private school for Blacks in Atlanta. Remember, I told you that was why Cheryl went to Northfield. Her daughter Hallie went to Padeia, which is a private elementary school here in Atlanta, then to Northfield for high school, and from there to Yale for undergraduate studies. So it's been an education thing with my family. My father was intent on all of his children earning degrees beyond the bachelors. You see, he was very poor, and he had to work his way through Meharry. He paid every penny of his education except $50.00. And Meharry wouldn't let him march because of that fifty dollars. So, he asked for a letter that confirmed he had finished Meharry. He needed that proof because he was going into the medical corps in the Army. I think he was very hurt that Meharry would not let him march. My father was determined that all of his children would get an education and that none of them would have to work hard the way he did. He sent all of us to college and to graduate school. My mother got her Master's in Social Work from Atlanta University the year my oldest sister finished Spelman.

YS: Tell me about your life in Tuskegee when your husband was with the . . . What was the name?

HC: The 99th Pursuit Squadron. We lived on the base for a year. We shared an apartment with another couple, and that was great. We went to movies on the base and we shopped at the PX.

YS: Tuskegee was all Black, so you didn't have to deal with segregation?

HC: No, Blacks and Whites lived in Tuskegee.

YS: Describe a normal day for you when you lived in Tuskegee.

HC: My husband would dress in his uniform and go down to the hangars and return to our apartment at 5:00. He was a fine instruments specialist.

YS: When the War ended, what did he do?

HC: He went to the Pennsylvania School of Optometry, and we lived in Philadelphia for four years. That's where the school was located. When he finished school, we moved to Atlanta. My husband worked for an optometrist for a while and then he opened his own office on Hunter Street.

YS: That's when you began teaching.

HC: No, I did not teach until sometime in the 50's. I started in the nursery school at Spelman and stayed there for about three years before going to public schools to teach third grade.

I worked in Atlanta schools for thirty-two years. Before I retired in 1984, I began volunteering at Grady Hospital in the neonatal clinic.

YS: I want to go back to what it was like to grow up in such a professional family. Do you think you were treated special in any way?

HC: You know, Jamie, after you leave, I think about our conversations and the questions you ask me. For example, I thought about your asking me last week how did it feel to have a husband who was the first Black optometrist in Atlanta, to have an uncle who was a dentist, a sister who was a doctor, and an aunt who studied at Oberlin. So, my father was a doctor and my mother earned a graduate degree from Atlanta University. No big deal. I came from a professional middle-class family. That was it. No, I don't think I was treated special in any way. I am not trying to be evasive, Jamie. You see, as I told you last week, we have lost so much of our history. The fact is, Jamie, that Atlanta had a thriving Black middle-class and the people in that class were doing the same kind of things. All the children went to private schools. Let me get this book. It will help make the point about Black achievements in Atlanta. Now this is where my grandmother was born during slavery. In this house. Okay? This is my grandparents' house on Howell Street. My mother married my father in this house. Now, look at the dates on these engraved invitations. They belonged to my grandmother. She was having a masquerade party. The date on the invitation is 1882. Here is another one, printed in 1897. I am showing you this, Jamie, because too many of us think Blacks were not doing any of this back then. [Turns the pages] These are my grandmother's invitations. In the nineteenth century. And this is a 1904 directory of Black Atlanta that belonged to my grandfather. 1904. "Population: 47,000 Blacks; 85,000 Whites." There were Black schools and businesses here in Atlanta. Black people were involved in so many things. They were seamstresses, dressmakers, fashionable dressmakers. They owned their own businesses. Here are ads for grocery stores. A nursery. A jewelry. Here is an ad for Albert Watt's Grocery Store. Watts was a member of our church. Here is an ad for a Black dentist. Dry goods. Caterers. An ice cream store. The Pioneer Drug Store. We need to stop thinking Blacks didn't have anything and didn't do anything until after the Civil Rights Movement.

YS: You mentioned in one of our conversations that Lena Horne is your cousin? Have you ever gone to hear her in concert?

HC: Yes. She came to Atlanta and I went to the concert. She spent ten days with me one Christmas. She has been here several times, and I have gone to visit with her. We talk about twice a month. Lena is my great-grandmother's brother's child. So we are third or fourth cousins. That picture up there on the balcony, on the credenza, was taken when she came to Atlanta during her U.S. tour. When she was interviewed in the Constitution, she said, "I have cousins here, and I would love to meet them. I hope they come to the show. I would like them to come back stage after the concert." And that is what we did. Let's see. That was about twelve years or more ago. I have to look in my book to get the exact year. After the concert, Andy Young and his late wife Jean were back stage, too, and they said, "We just can't wait to see who Lena's cousin is." They were surprised when I said, "Well, you are looking at her." I think Lena is great. Just great. I will never forget when we were in the mall and a man was coming our way. Suddenly, we heard, "Wait! Hold it! Hold it! You are Lena Horne!! And she said, "That's me, honey." People passing by in cars and walking on the street would say, "Lena, is that you?" She would say, "Yup, it's me." Many people at her level of fame would be snobbish, but not Lena. She's just as sweet as can be.

YS: I want to go back to what you said about the house your grandmother was born in during slavery and ask you about other members in your family's history who might have been slaves.

HC: My great-great grandmother, my great grandmother, and my grandmother all on my mother's side lived on a plantation in Newnan, Georgia, owned by Andrew Calhoun. All of them were slaves. My great grandmother took care of Calhoun's children following their mother's death, and Calhoun left her a piece of property in Atlanta with a house on it. She moved to Atlanta to that house, and her brother, Lena's grandfather, moved here also. He opened up a store up in Summer Hill.

YS: Her daughter was your maternal grandmother, the one who went to Atlanta University?

HC: Yes. And her father was a White man named Judge Ezra.

YS: And he paid for your grandmother to go to Atlanta University?

HC: No. Her mother did. Her mother paid for her to go to Atlanta University and that's where she met my grandfather. Her mother's name was Sinai and I have a paper in that first book, which shows that she married Felix Reynolds and her plantation owner let them move off the plantation and live by themselves. They lived in Newnan, Georgia, as husband and wife away from the plantation. But that didn't sit well with Whites in Newnan and so they had to return to the plantation. I have the document, which says something like "It has come to the attention of the court that two Negro people are being allowed to live off the plantation and alone." Let me get the document so that you can read the exact words. [Document is Coweta County Superior Court Minutes, dated 1830]. You see, Jamie, they were living in Newnan, bothering no one, until Whites took the matter to court. Can you believe the Court decided that letting Negroes live together away from the plantation would [reading from document] "tend most powerfully to deepen and widen that restless spirit basely attempted to be excited in the minds of slaves."

YS: When they were living away from the plantation, did they have to work?

HC: Yes. They were probably washing clothes or whatever slaves could do back then. You know, having to move back to the plantation didn't kill my great great grandmother's spirit because she made cakes and sold them and with that money she bought all of her children except one and that one, a daughter, went to New Liberia. We have been trying to trace her, but we have not been successful.

YS: How does it make you feel that your great great grandfather was a White man.

HC: It's a fact in my history. I'm neither happy about it, nor ashamed of it. It's a fact in my history. I don't like it, but I can't undo it. And why should I waste my energy wishing it had not happened? You know, when I was teaching, I would tell the children to be proud of who they are. When they would come to me in tears because someone had called them Black, I would tell them, so your skin is Black. Be proud of it. My skin is lighter than yours but that doesn't make me better than you. It's just a fact in our history as a people.

YS: As a retired school teacher, what is your assessment of schools in Atlanta now?

HC: I am concerned that our schools are focusing too much attention on getting children to pass tests and not enough attention on teaching them how to think. I believe this makes children statistics . You know, what percentage of them passed the tests. This is not peculiar to Atlanta. It is happening all over the nation. That, to me, is very sad. You see, rote work never helps. Memorizing everything is not good. Getting children to think about what they have read, not regurgitating it back-that's education. I say, you can take Little Red Riding Hood and have the best lesson with little children: "Do you think a girl should go skipping in the forest at dark all alone? Would you do it? Why wouldn't you do it? And the children can come up with some great answers. They are not stupid. They just have not been asked to think. "Do you think Little Red Riding Hood will do that again?" "No!" a four-year-old will tell you. "No, that was wrong." You can take nursery rhymes and develop very good lessons.

YS: What do you consider to be your greatest achievement?

HC: I think my greatest achievement is learning who I am. I was never really looking for myself, but I realized for a long time I had not identified myself to myself. I think that, as I have grown older, I have. And I am very happy with that.

YS: Is there a particular quote that you live by?

HC: The one I try to live by is "Do unto others as you would have them do unto you." I think that's so important, and I try awfully hard to do that. I'm not always successful, but I try. I'm imperfect and so it is foolish of me to require perfection of my family, my friends, or people I run into.

YS: You said in one of our conversations that you wouldn't like to be young now because young people have too many choices.

HC: No, I didn't say I wouldn't like to be young. I said, "I wonder how I would be in today's world as a young person with all the choices you have." When I was a child and even a young adult, you didn't have the choices of today's generation. I admire so many of the young people who are able to refine and define what they are about and can march to their own time. I guess I wonder how having so many choices and so much freedom would have affected me. I want to return to something we were talking about last week,

Jamie: your determination to move off campus next year and live in an apartment. But this is your senior year and you have nine months of school before you get your degree. I honestly believe that if you get the apartment and have it furnished, when you are older and look back on your decision, you will ask yourself, "What was I thinking about?" We realize later that things were not as important as we thought they were. Now don't think I wasn't young once, Jamie. Don't think I wasn't impatient. I was not pleased when my mother would say that I could have something the next year that I wanted that year. I am just saying, Jamie, that you need to give careful thought to your decision to move into an apartment in your senior year. It's a funny thing, Jamie, but the more things we acquire, the more we want.

YS: What makes you sad?

HC: Man's inhumanity to man. I am concerned about the war. I know war is war, but somewhere in my heart, I just wish we could do more talking and more negotiating. And I really believe that at one point we'll get a woman President who knows about the pulling of the heartstrings. Who knows about losing a child in war. Women are just more tuned into that, I think.

YS: It's interesting that you mentioned war because I was going to ask you what it was like living through WW II.

HC: The War affected my family in a personal way because my brother was injured in Italy. We stayed concerned about him all the time. He recovered and went back into battle, and he received a Purple Heart.

YS: What makes you happy.

HC: I think I'm happiest when all's right with my daughter and my granddaughter, my friends and family. I try to handle things without being irritable. You know—and I might have learned this late in life--it's the little things that make the big difference. Like calling a sick person to say, "Just thinking about you.:" Those are the things that make me feel real good. That make me happy. I want to be a person who relates well to all situations and circumstances. I'll tell you this, Jamie, anger and negativity can't hurt a soul except yourself. The more you can get anger out of your system, the better off you are.

YS: If you could speak to a group of young Black women in their early twenties about achievement, what would you say?

HC: I would tell them to have a dream, to dare to dream and to believe that they can make their dreams come true. I would tell them that the words, "I can't," shouldn't be in their vocabulary. I would also tell them what I have said to you, Jamie, and that is, "It's not the destination that's important. It's the journey."

YS: What has this experience meant to you?

HC: It has meant a lot to me, Jamie. I don't think I have ever sat down and talked to a young person your age as often and as long as we have talked. It has been an enjoyable and an enlightening experience for me.

MRS. EVELYN DABNEY

Merriwether County, Georgia
Receptionist and Notary Public

No blacks went downtown that day. Somebody had done something, committed a murder, and this boy was the only person they saw down there. They hanged him because they couldn't find anybody else. He was our playmate. He was twelve years old. They called him Boo, but his real name was Whatley. I shall never forget that name because it is in my memory.

EXCERPTS OF INTERVEIWS WITH MRS. EVELYN DABNEY
Conducted by Jalylah Burrell

ED: I want you to know my whole name. It's Evelyn Nesbit Owens Dabney

YS: Okay. Were you born in Atlanta?

ED: No. I was born nine to ten miles from Warm Springs. That's where President Roosevelt used to go to get inthe water. You know he couldn't walk. He's the first president I ever saw. Where my grandmother was living was right by the railroad and he was on the train and when the train passed my grandmother's house, we saw him. And let's see. Warm Springs can't be too many miles from Atlanta. We started school, my sister and I started school down there, but we moved to Atlanta. My mother was a cook. She cooked for Whites. My daddy traveled a lot because he was driving for White people and wherever they wanted to go, he had to drive them. He would move and sometimes it wasn't but for a while and sometimes we would be with him and sometimes we wouldn't. He even worked in the coal mines. But he never took us where the coal mines were, you know, and theren't too many Blacks doing that, but he was one of those who could work in the mines. So, we spent a while in Columbus, Georgia, and then in Jacksonville, Florida. When we came here to Atlanta, I started grade school at what used to be E. A. Ware. It's right at Morris Brown. It was on what was Hunter Street then. Right there near Morris Brown, but I think it's a part of Morris Brown now. And of course I went to Washington. Booker T. Washington High School.

YS: When you said that you graduated from Washington High School, you sounded very proud.

ED: Yes, I am proud. I was in the first graduation class that had over three hundred members from Washington. That was in 1933. Dr. Asa Yancy was valedictorian. Do you know about Booker T. Washington High? It was the first Black high in Atlanta. Before it was built, Blacks went as far as elementary and couldn't go any further because there was no high school. It's in history. M. L. King was graduated from Washington High School. We had three hundred in our graduating class. That was in 1933. Three. Three. Three. 1933 and three hundred graduate. I was proud of that, but I have some sad memories about my graduation.

YS: Sad memories? Why?

ED: I was the first person from my hometown to finish high school. I was the first one and when I graduated, my sister was in the hospital and my mother was with her and my daddy wasn't there, and I was just with friends who took me. You know, like you have a mother or somebody to be in the audience. I had nobody. When I was in the eighth grade, I won the Ever Ready Living Cup in the history contest. I was the first Black to win. I wrote about "Up From Slavery." About Booker T. Washington. On graduation night, I received the living cup. It was silver and they were going to put my name on it, but they didn't. I don't know what happened. I just know that I never got the cup with my name on it. But I was proud that I was the winner in the contest. Everybody was proud. And I was really proud when I graduated from Washington High, the first from my hometown to finish high school. I was proud, but I was hurting because my mom and my daddy couldn't be there. But I had friends who were there.

YS: You said your sister was sick?

ED: Yes, she was. I don't know what happened to her at that time. She's sick right now. But my mother and daddy have gone on. Something happened to my sister and my mother had to be at the hospital on the night of my graduation. Had to be at my sister's bedside.

YS: Is your sister older or younger than you?

ED: She's fifteen months younger than me. I had a brother, but he's gone now. He was the first child. I was the second, and then my sister. My brother's name was Fred A.Owens and he was a barber. A professional barber. My sister's name is Rosa Owens, and she was a nurse. When we came to Atlanta, we were behind, but it seems like I knew more than the other children and I was always up front. In elementary school I was always outstanding in whatever contest or spelling bee they had. Always in first place. I can remember when my mother let me come from there to be with my aunt in Columbus, Georgia because my aunt didn't have children. She was my daddy's sister. We didn't have a telephone. We didn't have a lot of things that they had in Columbus.

YS: How old were you when you went to live with your aunt?

ED: I was nine. I was reading then. I remember writing my mother a letter telling her I wanted to go home. My mother had given me a stamp and she told me to write her if I got dissatisfied. And that's what I did. I wrote her a letter and told her I wanted to come home. The children thought that was funny, me writing a letter and putting a stamp on it. I mean, kids just didn't do that then. I was already reading. I remember my grandmother and my great-great grandmother couldn't read and couldn't write their names. I taught them how to write. Just their names. And I did that when I was nine years old. One night, my grandmother was gonna surprise me. She got in bed and she said "B-A-D. Bed." She thought she was spelling BED, and that was amusing. That was amusing to us.

YS: Did you spend a lot of time with your grandmother and your great-grandmother?

ED: Every chance we could get. I have pictures. Now my brother had the camera, but I started taking pictures of my grandparents. I wish I had them with me now. My grandmother used to wash for White people. They lived on the hill and she would walk up the hill to get the laundry and then she would come down the hill with this thing of clothes on top of her head. I used to wonder if she had a flat head because of the way she carried that thing from the top of the hill down. It was amusing to see somebody as small as she was holding something that big on her head. Honey, it looked so heavy and she held it on the top of her head, but her head wasn't flat. She walked up a hill with it on her head. My grandmother didn't live long, but my great-grandmother lived to be a hundred. When she died, she was one hundred and one.

YS: Did your great-grandmother experience slavery?

ED: Yes, both of them. I guess that's why they couldn't read. Of course, of course that was why they couldn't read. And my, my, my. I don't know about being in the fields like, you know, children would be in the fields and all. I don't know about that. But I know my grandmother washed for White people. That's why she was doing all those clothes. I don't know of my great-grandmother doing anything like that. She lived in this little house by herself. She was a loner. They say after her husband died, she didn't want the kids around her too much because they would get on her nerves. I guess that's the reason. And she smoked a pipe! [laughter] That fascinated me. She would get in her rocker and smoke that pipe. I guess she was concentrating on something, or whatever. There was a sadness about her I guess because I think one of her sons was killed by some of the White folks. I don't know what he had done. Maybe he hadn't done anything, but they said he did. I think that's why she would have those spells of not wanting to be around us.

YS: And your grandmother?

ED: Well, she was just, like I said, she didn't talk very much but she would take care of them White folks' clothes, and that's what she would talk about. She'd take care of White folks clothes and iron for those White folks.

YS: Tell me about the racial make-up of Merriwether Country.

ED: It was a small, small place, and it was a few Black people on this side of the railroad and, you know, up the hill further from us were the White people. But we played with them. And my sister would mess with their hair. I don't know how she could do that. I never messed with nobody's hair, but my sister always did. She said their hair was like . . . I don't know what she said it was like, but I never put my hand in it. I don't know how it was. But we played with them. Yeah, we played with them. See, in this place where we lived, there were only two schools. The White school was, like I said, up on the hill yonder, so we were down by the railroad and I don't know anything about their school, you know, just to see them coming and going.

YS: Were you happy when your family left Merriwether County and moved to Atlanta?

ED: Well, I guess I felt like Atlanta was the place that I should have been and everything was good as far as I was concerned. And let's see, before the ending of high school, I was into this dramatic group. We played at this theatre. It used to be right there at M.L. King, used to be Hunter, and Ashby Street. Well, we lived right across from the theater. It was called the Ashby Theatre. We used to play there and one of the plays we did was "Sophie Spills the Beans." I can't recall what the group was called, but we would play in the theaters and play at churches. We would get a little money and I liked that. Our teacher was a drama professor at Morris Brown and he got most of the money.

YS: You said your family moved to Atlanta when you were nine or ten? That would be in the early 20's. Tell me what kind of work they did when they came to Atlanta.

ED: My father messed around with the Whites. He used to say, "I don't ever want my little girls to work for White folks in their kitchens and stuff like that." He never wanted that. "Never in White folks' kitchen or house. Not my girls." He never wanted us in nobody's kitchen or doing service, you know. So let me let you go.

YS: No. No. I can stay longer. This is really interesting. Go on. Tell me the rest of the story.

ED: Well, like I told you, my daddy would drive for White folks and do different things for them. I found out later he didn't really like them, but they liked him. He'd do grinning and dancing and all. Whatever they wanted done, he would do it. A lot of the fellas worked in the fields, but not my daddy. He never worked in the fields even though his daddy was on this farm. They had other people working on the farm. My daddy never did that kind of thing. Later on, he was a barber and then later on he worked for the government for a long time. Before he got that job, he was working for what used to be a tire place where they sold tires and did mechanical work. They put him on the radio. He would say one little part of a song, "That's why everybody loves Goodrich Silver," and then he'd do his little number. He wrote little poems. I don't know if they gave him fifty-cents for his songs. Later on, he worked at City Hall and he worked part-time. My daddy always had more than one job. Even while he was working downtown, he had a little job running the elevator at night and doing little errands for them and still writing poems and carrying on like that. And they just loved it. The White people just loved it. He entertained. My daddy was an entertainer.

YS: Is that where you think you got your dramatic flair?

ED: I guess. I guess so. Maybe so. I don't know. Maybe so. My daddy always wanted us not to be under "the foot of mean men," not only White men, but, you know, all mean men. He said little girls have a hard time a lot of times with men, and men would take advantage of little girls. I don't know what was the problem, but he knew what he was talking about. We didn't understand it then, but he said, "I don't never want you under the foot of men. I hope God'll let me live to see you grow up." And He did.

YS: Were there incidents with mean men in your community?

ED: Well, I tell you about the thing that was the hardest for us to swallow was our oldest playmate. I told you. It's a little town. This boy would hang around downtown sometimes. But this day we didn't know why we couldn't go to school or nothing because no Blacks went downtown that day. Somebody had done something, committed a murder, and this boy was the only person they saw down there. They kept him a couple of days and the next thing we saw my mother crying and all. They hung that boy. He didn't do the crime, but they hung him because they couldn't find anybody else. That was our playmate. He was twelve years old. I will never forget that. As long as I live, I will never forget that.

YS: Did people talk about it?

ED: Blacks would whisper about it, but they wanted to get away from that place because this was a terrible thing. And of course we hear the word "lynch" now, and it happened and a lot of times the people wouldn't be guilty. But we had a lot of KKK in Merriwether County. A lot of them. And if it was something they didn't like, they'd go into your house and they'd go with Black women and the Black men couldn't do anything. What could they do? Huh? They couldn't do anything. People would whisper when there was a lynching or something and they would tell us, the children, about it later on, but it would be years later, like when we were in our teens. At the time, we wouldn't know what was happening. We'd just be scary, you know? We'd be so scary. We didn't understand it. Only thing we know is that they killed him, but that was a whisper thing. And his mother lived in the house not far from our house and she would just moan. She would say, "Boo didn't do nothing and they killed him." She was a widow. Her husband had passed away. She said he didn't do anything and they killed him. They called him Boo, but his real name was Whatley. I should never forget that name because it is in my memory. I'm forever thinking about how he had to die. It was real sad. Real sad.

YS: And you say that White men could just have their way with Black women?

ED: See, we didn't hear too much about that. I mean, we saw them coming and going, you know. We'd say, "yes sir and no sir" to the White ones even if they were young like us. I remember we would say "yes sir" and "no sir" to the teenage boys, you know. Wasn't that some kind of living when you think about it?

YS: Yes. Yes, it was. When you graduated from Washington High, you went to Morris Brown.

ED: I went just the one semester because financially we couldn't afford it. You know about Bronner Brothers? Well, there was Cannolene Products before Bronner Brothers. See, Mr. Cannon was what Bronner Brothers is today. He wanted some Black girls to go and integrate Kress downtown here in Atlanta. That was a five and dime store. But, I mean, you could go in there. White and Black. But no Black person could work there. Well, Mr. Cannon put some of his products in there and he got three of us. Cannon was a Black man, you know, and he got three of us to integrate Kress. It was me and Margaret Anderson and Peggy Church. Okay. We couldn't ring the cash register at first. For a while, we couldn't. There was a fountain for Whites and a fountain for "colored." So one day Margaret said, "I wanna try that water," meaning water in the white fountain. So she did. She said, "All of it taste the same to me!" You know, white water and Black water. And we couldn't eat there either. We had to bring our brown bags. I don't know what Mr. Cannon got out of it. He got something. He had to get some experience and stuff out of it, but it wasn't long before they were letting Blacks in.

YS: What year was this?

ED: Early sixties, but I wasn't by myself. There were three of us: Margaret Anderson and Peggy Church and me. After that, Mr. Cannon put us in the field. You know, door-to-door selling. I have sold everything from inhalers to, you know, stuff for your scalp and all of that. And I did this radio and television survey. I don't know where they got our names. You had to have a car and you had to be courageous because if you were scared, they wouldn't hire you. These people, they were from out of town. They weren't from Atlanta these White people doing the testing and we did the testing in Lithonia, Hapeville, outside of Atlanta. It was money in that, but some time you would ring a bell and some of the people would say, "Black gal, what you want? What do you want?" and "Get away from my door." If we couldn't stand that, we couldn't work. For so many years, we worked for those people. Doing that survey. They got it working better where you would just be on the phone. But this was from door-to-door for over six year. From door to door. That was a lot of work, but it was fun to us. We enjoyed doing it 'cause we were the only Blacks that were doing it, right here in Atlanta. And, like I said, it was good money. I worked that for over six years.

YS: When did you get married?

ED: Oh I got married early. I got married in '34. A lot of this stuff I did after I got married. My husband went through WWII and at that time I was a volunteer for USO. I don't know if you know about that or not. It was where the soldiers would come and all. The USO. And we would entertain them. You know the 99th. You probably read about them. The Black men? I knew them. They came to the USO. I did more volunteer work there and I won. Let's see now. What did I win? I won something for doing more volunteer work at the USO than any of the other girls. I wanted to go to the WACs. That was "Women's Auxillary." You know. The Women's Army. I thought I was going because, you know, I was doing good, but they examined me and said I had a heart murmur and that's why they wouldn't accept me. Of course that hurt me to my heart because I knew I could do it. I wanted to do it. I had done a lot of things that other Blacks hadn't done.

YS: How did you meet your husband?

YS: Oh my Lord! You don't know anything about boxing. When we were in school, we were just friends, see, and he was trying to be a boxer and there was Sunset Park. That's in our Black history, Sunset Park. There were these boxers, fighters, prizefighters or boxers. Tiger Flowers. I know you don't know about him. I saw him in person. We used to go there, to Sunset Park a lot, and my husband would box a little bit. We were just friends, see, but he introduced me to this man who was a boxer and he was older than me. I wanted to know him real bad. And then one day I was coming down the hill-they called it College Hill-down from Morris Brown and I was skating and one of the skates was messing up and I was scared I was gonna fall and hurt myself. Well, I looked up and there was this man. He caught me. That was a pretty page in my book! Anyway, I told my husband, who was just my friend, about it and then he wanted to start being more than just a friend. And that's how it happened. Oh Lord.

YS: And then, how long after you married was it before he went off to war?

ED: Oh, at first he was at a CC camp. I don't know if you ever heard of that. That's the training that, you know, they did in those days. Money wasn't easy to get to. So they went to this CC thing, this CC training up there from Chattanooga, Tennessee, where people go on special things now. But, anyway, that's where he got in training. He wasn't thinking about going to War then, but he found out that was a good job for him. And from that, he went on, you know, to the service. That was in Chattanooga, Tennessee. Before then, he was driving. What did they call people then? These men, these White men, who would go from place to place selling stuff? Sometimes they would have a Black boy driving for them. Well, that's what he was doing and we went to many places. Sometimes we were at this place or that place for however long it took.

YS: So did you go to New York while he was away in the War? Did you go to New York before you married?

ED: No, we were married when we went to New York. But the thing about the separation was, like I said, I had a nervous breakdown and my husband had disappeared and I didn't ever want to see him again, so I was back with my mama and daddy. And when I went to New York, I couldn't even walk up steps. The first time I ever see my daddy cry was when he put me on the train to New York. While I was in New York, my husband started writing me when he found out where I was and, of course we got back together.

YS: You went to New York when you were ill? Was it that care was better there?

ED: The people at Grady Hospital had given me up. They said I was not gonna live. I can show you a book where they said I had some kind of rare blood disease. I couldn't build red blood. A friend of mine wanted to just try something out in New York and I went and she took care of me. She was a nurse and I met her at a nurse's club meeting and people said we looked alike. We favored each other, and that's when we became friends. She was working at Belleview Hospital in the Bronx and she and her mother took care of me. At the hospital where they treated me, they found out whatever it was. I don't know. Something they gave me brought life back to me. It wasn't my time. I was there like winter all the way 'til the end of must have been September or October. All the year, I might say, until wintertime. Four to six months, and I got better. I got to where I could walk. At first, I couldn't. But I got better and started walking a little every day until I had walked up to the subway. I felt strong, and I wanted to go back to Atlanta. And that's when I came back, all better, and thought I could join the Army and do anything.

YS: So was it a stressful time up there?

ED: No, it wasn't. Everything was good. I don't know. Seems like I was a different person all together. I don't know what it was. It was like a dream almost. It wasn't real. My friend and her mother lived in the Bronx and they were good people. You know, every now and then, you meet somebody who is good. I have worked at the Department of Labor, but you didn't ask me that, did you?

YS: Oh, no, please tell me. Please tell me whatever you want to share.

ED: Okay, I was gonna say, my daddy got sick. He had several strokes. I moved back home to help my mother because it was wearing her down real bad. My daddy was sick for six years and, believe it or not, she died before he did. I didn't expect that. And eighteen months later, he passed. And then I was just, you know, out there. That's what put me with the Department of Labor. From the Department of Labor, I went to the Girl Scouts for a while until I broke my wrist. A few years later I went to Sellers Brothers Funeral Home up there to see someone who had passed, and I saw Juanita, the owner. I said, "Juanita, I need a job." She said, "Evelyn, you don't wanna work for us." She said, "You still scared of dead folks?"

YS: Still scared of what?

ED: Dead folks. She said, "You don't wanna work here?" I said, "Yes I do." For several months I didn't hear anything and then a friend of mine called me one day and said, "Are you working now?" I said, "No, I need a job." She said, "Juanita Stone been trying to find you. She said you wanted a job at the funeral home." And I started working there as a receptionist, and that's where I retired from three years ago. All those people, in and out. So many, many people. That was some experience. So many people. That was my last job.But you would be surprised at some of the things that happen when people die. [laughter] I remember these two women were fighting about a man.

YS: You mean, a man who was dead?

ED: Yes. They were fighting on the stairs and I stopped them because we didn't allow all that in the funeral home. I had a button, see, and I hit the button. Someone came to stop the fighting. The funny thing is that there they were fighting over him and the man wasn't worth a nickel and he was married. [laughter] Seller's Funeral Home. That's where I worked before I retired three years ago. But I'm still a notary. That's when you put your seal on legal papers. Let me show you my seal. I don't know whether that'll help or not.

YS: Yes, just to help me understand. Now how'd you get involved with it?

ED: See, when we first started over thirty years ago, we didn't have to charge but fifty-cents, but, see, now every four years, when we renew it, they go up higher and higher. A lot of retired people come to me and I don't charge them but a little bit. And then sometimes you do a big job, like a lady lost her sister live right down the hallway. I had never met her, but I knew her sister and she had a lot of papers. She said, "My sister's not gonna live and I wanna get you to notarize something for me." I didn't know the woman, but I knew her sister, so I went on and notarized it for her. She said, "How much do you charge?" I said, "Well, just a love gift." I said, "Give me a love dollar or something." That woman gave me $54.00. Yes she did!

YS: Mrs. Dabney, can we go back a little bit? You said your husband left for the War and then you said he disappeared.

ED: I didn't know where he was then because, see, I got sick. I think he got frightened. I didn't know where he was for a couple of years. That was during the time of the War. When I found out that he was in service, I applied for, you know, what you would get as spouse when a husband is in service. That's when we sorta got back together.

YS: You know, I didn't get his name.

ED: John Arthur Dabney. We looked somewhat alike and when we'd go to parties, we would play games on people. Pretend that we were sister and brother. Everybody could dance but him. His feet were too big or something, but every time it came time to dance, I'm up. But we had fun. We had fun. We were married for seventeen years and we divorced and then he married again and I married again. We had drifted apart. He got to the place where he would gamble and he couldn't win. He couldn't win. Well, he was doing it when I married him, but I didn't know it. He would tell me "So and so stole my shoes." I'd be feeling so sorry for him! That was in him, I guess. I'll show you pictures of us next time. We used to look like brother and sister. We had a lot of fun together. I wanted to be married forever, but a tragic thing happened with our son. I don't know. I think that was in me against him.

YS: What happened?

ED: An accident. Yeah. I can't even . . . But he was my . . .

YS: I understand. How did you meet your second husband?

ED: I met him at a prayer meeting, believe it or not. That was the praying-est man I ever saw in my life. I was on the bus one day and he was on the same bus, but I didn't know he was on there. He saw me getting off and then he got off. He said, "I hear you going to do it." I said, "What?" He said, "I hear that you're gonna get married." I said, "Well, you're married." He had married a week or two before. He said, "Don't do it." He said, "Wait a little longer. We can get together." He was married but he said he didn't want me to get married. But I did.

YS: What was your second husband's name?

ED: John.

YS: John what?

ED: John. Just leave it at John. The man had I don't know how many different wives and when my daddy had that thing traced down, I don't know what number wife I was and he hadn't gotten divorced at all. So that is why my daddy had this thing annulled so that I'm still using Dabney. Burns was really his name. Lord, people can play so many games! We were married almost seven months before I learned about the other wives. God has given me nice companions to be with. The last person . . . but he was at his house and I was at mine. He would tuck me in every night, I want you to know. Yes he did! He would have his place and I would have mine. Oh Lord. But I'm still alive and living. Thank God for that. The last time I was engaged, I was living right here. I was engaged to this man for six months. Now wasn't that something? I know I wasn't gonna marry him. He had lost his wife a year before. He lived in Detroit. We had been seeing each other because I have relatives in Detroit. And when he found out I wasn't married anymore, he said, "Mind living in Detroit?" I said, "Yeah, I mind living in Detroit." I said, "I'm gonna stay here living in Atlanta." So he would come down here, you know, to see me. He said, "Be engaged to me for six months. I guarantee you that we'll get married." We didn't get married. We didn't get married. When I knew anything, the man had had a stroke. I don't remember how long he survived, but he passed on. So I told my sister, "I'm not getting engaged to nobody else."

YS: What are some of your happiest memories living here in Atlanta?

ED: I had a lot of happy moments, honey. I don't know what's the happiest or the highest moment. One of the high moments I guess was when we got the house right across the street from Washington High School. We couldn't buy it because we didn't have any money, but we leased it. The house is still there. It had seven and a half rooms. That's where I took care of my daddy and my mother. The trolley went right by our door. My daddy at the time he got sick was working for Gene Talmadge. He used to work for Herman Talmadge's daddy. You know he was a segregationist, but he liked my dad. Daddy conned them to hire him and to give him a whole lot. He used to work for Herman Talmadge's daddy. Gene Talmadge, and he was a segregationist, but he liked my dad. Daddy conned these people to hire him. Daddy had a motorcycle and back then you didn't see many middle-aged Black men with motorcycles. When it got to be rough on mother, that's when I moved back home and I got the house. At one point, both of them were sick and I had them in one room in hospital beds.

I took care of them at home. And I had a lady come once or twice a week to assist me. I strained my back trying to help my mother. That's when the doctor who was waiting on my daddy said to me, "Put your daddy in a home and straighten up yourself because if you don't you're going to . . . " He told me what was going to happen to me. But do you know what happened? My daddy was sick for six years. My mother was sick for almost twelve months and three days. I'm right there with her looking at her when she died. My brother and his wife were there. I had no idea that she was going to die. See, I thought my daddy would leave first, you know. But I had no idea that she was gonna die. I remember I went into the bathroom and got on my knees. I have not shed a tear for her, and I love her better than anything in the world. I have not shed a tear for her.

YS: Why do you think you haven't cried for her?

ED: I don't know. There was this little lady preacher who had come in and out when my daddy was sick, you know, and when she found out about my momma, she got down on her knees. I said, "Get up off your knees." And that's the first time I got a little mean spirited. I said, "Get up off your knees." She said, "Huh?" I said, "Don't do that" because my daddy was still living and my mamma was gone. I called Ms. Abernathy. I don't know if I told you I was a member at Rev. Abernathy's church. So, I called her to find out where Abernathy was. He and King were across seas somewhere, but anyway he came on over here and he talked to my daddy, and my daddy wept and wept. And Daddy told him said, "She didn't need to die. I need to die. I'm the one that need to." He carried on so. I didn't weep. A doctor said to me, he said, "If you don't weep or something, you're going to get into a state of depression." But I didn't have time for weeping. I had to take care of my daddy. Pastor helped. He would come over in the middle of the morning and he would say to my daddy, "Brother Owens, don't you want to go to bed?" And Daddy would say, "Yessir." He loved Pastor so much. The last thing my daddy played on our piano was a solo for Mrs. Abernathy. Pastor would be right down with the demonstrators, but he meant a whole lot to us at the church. You could call on him and he would come. He would get out of his bed and come. Daddy lived eighteen months after Mama died.

I don't have any regrets about my life. Not really. I guess it went like it should have. When I was a little girl, I wanted six girls and six boys. Now that sounds funny, but I did! I wanted children. I wanted to be around kids and play with kids. For so many years, I was working for this photographer out in Macon. I would go from house to house with him making baby pictures. I would get on the floor with the babies. I just liked to be surrounded by kids. I have an adopted daughter and I just love her.

YS: When did you adopt her?

ED: Well, she came to rent a room in my house. This was after I had lost both parents and Rev. Abernathy told me not to live alone in the house and to share my home and put it in the church newspaper. I was called the Poet of West Hunter.

YS: Really?

ED: Yes. I wrote poems for Abernathy. I wasn't involved in the movement, but I wrote poems for Pastor. He would call me the night before something and say, "Evelyn, I need a poem." And I would write it.

YS: And you met your adopted daughter when Rev. Abernathy told you to put an announcement in the church bulletin about your house.

ED: Yes. He told me not to live alone and to share my house with someone, and that's what I did. She came with her husband and she told me that she was six months pregnant and that they probably wouldn't stay past six months. She was living with me when the baby was born and I just love that child. He calls me G-Mama.

76

YS: G-Mama. Does the G-Mama mean Grandmother?

ED: G stands for Good, Great. [Laughing]. God's Almighty Grace. God's Amazing Grace.

YS: Is there something you have wanted to do but you have not yet done?

ED: I can't think of anything. When I was at Grady Hospital, my husband sat at the foot of my bed and read what they had on my chart. That I couldn't build red blood. A lot of people gave me blood. I would like to do that for somebody. That's what I want to do. I want to do for somebody else what so many people did for me. They didn't think I would make it because I couldn't build red blood. You know, when I was working at Seller's, a man came in there and looked at the name on my name plate. Dabney. He said to me, "Didn't you used to be sick and you couldn't use your hand for seven years?" You see, his girlfriend was one of my nurses when I was at Grady. "Are you that Dabney?" I said, "Yes." And then he said, "Excuse, but I thought you died. I swear for God I thought you died." A few years later the man went on to Glory and here I am. It was my crowning achievement to live to be ninety. And I am getting ready for my ninety-first birthday.

YS: What makes you sad?

ED: To know that children are abused and old people, too. Plus to see the young Black people throwing their lives away. When I think about what I went through as a youngster to give them a chance at a better life and they're throwing it away. I'm passing the torch to you. That's what I want to tell them. Take it and run with it. They don't know what that means. All this energy wasted.

YS: What makes you happy?

ED: To put a smile on somebody's face. Get on the elevator and when people say, "Good morning," I say, "What's good about it?" I make them laugh. That's what makes me happy.

YS: What has this experience, our conversations, meant to you?

ED: It has opened some doors that I wasn't paying attention to. It has made me dig a little deeper in my brain and this emphasizes the fact that I know who I am. I know who I am. I don't enjoy some of the things I used to enjoy, but I enjoy life. I am going to live until I die. My mama had a way of telling me when she was happy with something I had done and when she just wanted to tell me she loved me. "She would say, I wouldn't take a pretty for you." That's what I want to say to you: "I wouldn't take a pretty for you."

MRS. DARLYNE KILLIAN

Bremen, Texas
Teacher, Artist, and School Administrator

No excuses. No whining. No half-stepping. I think her philosophy was the philosophy of so many Black people during her time: there are simply no reasons to do anything other than your best. They believed in the old saying, "Put a piece of steel in your back, throw your shoulders back, tilt your chin just a little bit, and keep moving."

EXCERPTS OF INTERVIEWS WITH MRS. DARLYNE KILLIAN
Conducted by Takkara Brunson

YS: Mrs. Killian, I am very grateful for this opportunity to talk with you, and I know that your memories will teach me a great deal about life and achievement.

DK: That is nice of you to say.

YS: Are you a native of Atlanta?

DK: I'm from Texas.. My mother is from Tennessee. She grew up in Nashville and in Chicago. She met my father when he was at the Meharry School of Dentistry in Nashville. She was teaching at Pearl High School at the time. My father was Joseph Donahue Atkinson and my mother was Gladys Lenora Peyton. They married on May 21, 1925 in Nashville at her grandparents' home.My father's parents, Emma Ann Fitch and Harry H. Atkinson, moved to Brenham in the late 1880's and bought property there. It was a little bitty town, the biggest thing between Houston and Austin. Actually, Brenham was a railroad town because of the Southern Pacific and Santa Fe junction. My paternal grandfather worked for the Sante Fe. Well, he worked for both railroads, but mainly for the Sante Fe because that's who paid him. And Brenham is well-known all over the country because that's the home of Blue Bell Ice Cream. The warehouse was no more than three blocks down the railroad tracks from my high school. I remember leaving school during the lunch and walking down the tracks to the warehouse. I practically grew up on Blue Bell Ice Cream. That's why I can't eat it now. [Laughing]

YS: So, you were born in Texas, but your mother was born in Nashville. Is that where her parents were born?

DK: Her father was from the area near Murfreesboro, and his people were from Rutherford County. They lived out in Walnut something. I don't remember the exact name. There is a story in the family about the time a man tried to buy a pony from Great Grandpa— his name was Paden Peyton—and the man said, "All your children can go to school in Nashville." Well, that was not what my great grandfather wanted and so he said, "My children aren't ever going to school in Nashville." Nashville was about thirty miles away, and my great grandfather wanted the children to be close to home. What's interesting is that his wife, my great grandmother Annie Peyton, delivered a lot of babies in Rutherford County. She was a midwife, and her name was Annie Osbourne or Osby [depending on how you pronounce it]. We've done a lot of genealogical research and we have found that both Great Grandfather Peyton and his mother were on The Trail of Tears. But they didn't get any farther than the area around Nashville. They never made it to Oklahoma. My maternal grandparents, DeWitt Peyton and Mary Sabina Johnson Peyton, had eight children, but only seven lived. Half of the children were born in Chicago and half in Nashvilee. My mother was the oldest child, and she was born in Nasvhille. Now Mary Sabina's father, Thomas Wood Johnson, who was my maternal great grandfather, was a Methodist minister and when Fisk was being built, he and his father hauled stones to construct the wall around the school. I guess that's where he learned to read and to write and to do all the things necessary for him to become a presiding elder in the Methodist church. Fisk was the only place for him to go right after War. He used to tell Mama that when they were freed, he couldn't read his name in boxcar letters. I imagine that he helped pay his way to school by hauling stones and helping to build the wall. I'm always proud when I tell that story.

My paternal grandparents were Emma Ann Fitch and Harry H. Atkinson, and they moved to Brenham in the late 1880's and bought property there. Grandma Emma attended Mary Allen College in Crockett, Texas. She and my grandfather sent four children to college.

YS: Most of us are first-generation college graduates, so your family was rather unusual.

DK: Well, my maternal grandmother taught school in East Tennessee, but when the railroad came through, the family moved to Nashville. They lived in Brentwood, which is a fairly well-known suburb of the city. My grandmother rode the train to Nashville. Her brother rode the horse. Both of them attended Roger Williams, which was a Baptist school. My mother attended Walden University, which was located in South Nashville, and she taught in a place called Keeling at Hoffmann-St. Mary Episcopal School in West Tennessee. We had the opportunity to go by the school when I used to take Mama home to Texas during the summer. The school is now called Gaillard Institute. When we visited, we had a long talk with the principal and his wife. During the course of their conversation, the principal's wife mentioned that somebody had put on a big exhibit at the school back in the twenties. Well, that was during the time my mother was at the school, and it turned out that she and a lady named Ms. Butcher were the ones who put on the exhibit.

YS;   Do you have siblings?

DK: I have a sister and a brother. I'm ten years older than my sister, and my brother is two years older than I am. I guess that makes me the middle child, but everyone swears that I act like the oldest child. When I was growing up, I was a tomboy. There were several boys in our neighborhood, but very few girls, so I grew up with boys. When we played ball, in order for there to be two teams, I was chosen to be pitcher. I liked to play ball. I liked to climb trees. In fact, whatever the boys did, I did, and probably better.

YS: Tell me about your neighborhood in Brenham.

DK: We lived diagonal across the street from Methodist College, which was for Whites only. Black people and German Jews lived in the neighborhood. The street was integrated. Several blocks down the street was a cotton mill and let me tell you, there was a lot of cotton at that mill! A lot of cotton! And when they pressed oil out of the cotton seed, that stuff smelled so good! Can you believe that pressing oil out of cotton seed would smell good! People said that if you fed the cotton seed meal to cattle, they would go blind. Brenham was an interesting town of railroad junctions. It was the biggest thing between Houston and Austin. You have to remember that this was the time of shipping by rail and actually traveling by rail. This was the era of "train stations" rather than "airports." What I remember vividly is that Brenham was busy on Saturday with ranchers and farmers who would come to the city and spend the day shopping, or hanging out at the restaurants. The City CafŽ was White. Campbell's CafŽ was Black. It was called The Dew Drop Inn. I think there must be one of those in every Black neighborhood. [laughter] It's funny, but it's just little things that I can remember. I remember when my mama was teaching me to cook—I was only seven years old—she made me write recipes in her book and I spelled skillet s-c-h-i-l-le-t. There were so many German names around that started with s-c-h that I thought skillet started that way, too. Oh, boy.

YS: You started cooking when you were seven?

DK: Yes, my mother taught me to cook when I was seven, and you will find this hard to believe: my dad taught me how to drive when I was about seven. In the garage, on the left side was the first part of our lesson. He painted it on the wall. Then, on the backside, were two other lessons, also painted on the wall. We saw the lessons every time we went into the garage. We learned how to shift gears and how to push that clutch down and shift again. He taught us the rules of the road, which we had to memorize. Back then, there were no blinkers on cars. You had to signal with your arm. Early, on Sunday mornings, he would take us out on Green Vine Road that came out towards Mill Creek. There were a lot of Polish people who lived in that area and Czechoslovakians, too, and they usually came to town to go to church. Once they were settled in church, there wouldn't be any traffic on the road, and that's when we would do our driving lessons. I was barely big enough to touch the accelerator. I knew how to drive when I could barely peep over the windshield of a car.

YS: Tell me what it was like growing up in your family.

DK: Well, during that time we had to do a whole lot of independent living. I mean people had to learn to do for themselves. You didn't have two coins to rub together. If you had money, you were lucky. We had our chickens. We had our garden. Fortunately, there was still a mill in town. We raised enough corn to carry us through the winter. We had to make sure we had dried kernels to take down to that mill. They would grind it. Then you would pick it up. The stuff was so hot you could put a tomato in there and ripen it over night. We kept enough of our corn to have a winter's supply of meal. In fact, we had a winter's supply of many of the foods we ate. Take for instance peas. My grandmother planted black-eyed peas between each corn stalk. When they were dried, she would put them into bags. We had black-eyed all winter. We had lima bean and squash, too. Three or four times a year, we planted turnips and mustards. And we made jelly and preserves from fruits.

YS: Did you participate in any of this work?

DK: Did I!!! All of the children did. When we got out of school, there was not much time to go out to play. You got out and you prepared food for the winter. It got tight around there a couple of times. When my sister was a baby, my parents had to take the telephone out so that they could buy milk. You know, I think about all the millions of people who are out of work. They don't know how to survive. First of all, people don't have a place to plant a little handful of greens. I hate to say this, but it sure seems that this recession is going to be with us longer than was predicted.

YS: You mentioned that there were many farms and ranches in Brenham. Were they owned by Whites?

DK: Not all of them. My daddy's people were farmers. His daddy's people were farmers. As farming became more difficult, prices of crops went down. In fact, my granddaddy's sister Mandy went to sell her cotton one day and the price had gone down to something like two cents a pound. They said Mandy never got over that. My great grandfather Armistead Fitch was the county veterinarian.

YS: A Black veterinarian in Texas! I know there is a story about your great grandfather.

DK: Well, my understanding is that he came from North Carolina and then his folks migrated out West. They were called the Black Indians from North Carolina. They were looking for free land in an area that, at the time, was the Republic of Texas. Those folks came from Tennessee and other parts of the South. You know, I'm still trying to figure out how a handful of folks fought at the Alamo and captured those people and all that territory. California, Arizona and New Mexico—all of that was Mexico at the time. It couldn't have been the United States because the United States, as we now know it, didn't exist. We decided—or "they" decided—that everything below the Rio Grande was Mexican. Everything above it and way out to the Pacific Ocean was American. Girl, we got some tales in this country.

YS: Do you know other stories about that time in our history?

DK: I know the story of those poor folks on the Trail of Tears. Finally, our nation had the decency to put a sign on the Trail of Tears out on Highway I-75. People were moved right out of what is now I-75 North. Cherokee Indians had a newspaper, a written language, and everything. I took Mama up there one time." Cherokees had newspapers, their own language and everything in the area where the Trail of Tears started. The Creeks—now they were in the Macon area—mixed more with Blacks than Cherokees did. When my mother and father moved to Atlanta, she became a chartered member of the African-American Family History Association, and we used to go to meetings all the time. I have done quite a bit of our family history, but, you know, you can devote just so much time to it. I'm at a point now where I either have to get it done or someone else is going to have to do it.

YS: I was wondering whether or not you heard talk about lynchings when you were growing up in Texas.

DK: Well, we heard about lynchings in other places, but not in Texas. You see, we subscribed to the Black papers—The Houston Informer and the Pittsburg Courier and the Chicago

Defender—and that is how we kept up with Black news from across the nation. There wasn't an article about a lynching in Texas, but I remember hearing through the grapevine that a young man was lynched because he had a White girlfriend and she had his child. I think that was when I was in the sixth or seventh grade. The adults didn't do too much talk about racial violence around the children. Do you know about Juneteenth?

YS: Yes.

DK: So, you know that—well, this is what has been handed down in history—slaves didn't know about emancipation until two years after the fact. The story is that Whites got their crops planted before they let the slaves know that they were free. Black people celebrate emancipation all over the South, but in Texas, they don't say the year. Juneteenth was quite a celebration in Brenham—in fact, all over Texas.

YS: I was wondering whether or not your parents gave you any warnings about dealing with Whites.

DK: Not really. You know, my father had Polish patients. And that was in the late thirties.

YS: In Texas in the late thirties? That's really something. Tell me about schools in Brenham?

DK: Well, I remember that my mother wasn't all that pleased with the school system, so I had school at school and school at home. You know, my mother was a pianist. I'd like to say she was a classical pianist, but who during the Depression was going to pay a dollar to hear a Negro woman play Bach, Beethoven and Mozart? She learned some of the music from her mother and she took lessons right after the War—World War I—from a French woman who was quite an accomplished pianist. My mother believed in excellence, and she taught us to set goals and to work toward them. No excuses. No whining. No half-stepping. I think her philosophy was the philosophy of so many Black people during her time: there are simply no reasons to do anything other than your best. And when it came to difficulties of any kind, they believed in the old saying: "Put a piece of steel in your back, throw your shoulders back, tilt your chin just a little bit, and keep moving."

YS: Tell me about the relationship you had with your mother. Were the two of you close?

DK: Until the day we laid her to rest in June 1990! Yes, we were very close.

YS: Do you think she reared your brother differently from the way she reared you and your sister? You know the saying that Black mothers coddle their sons and . . .

DK: My mother believed that everybody should be self-sufficient. She taught my brother how to clean and how to cook and how to sew. In fact, it was my brother, not my sister and I, who helped Mama make her Christmas cakes. And when his wife was ill, he kept the family going. My brother, by the way, was very instrumental in Spelman getting the NASA grant. He recently retired from the Johnson Space Center. My sister was in special education and she is now an interior decorator and a real estate agent. If you could sit us down together, you would hear all of us saying what I have said: that Mama expected the same thing of all three of us.

YS: When it came to dating, too?

DK: Well, everyone just hung together in a group. We were just really good friends. This was the first time since World War I that Americans had gotten involved in a big conflict, and a lot of guys from high school were drafted. There was what was called the draft. It wasn't anything like a volunteer army, and it wasn't for all the men folk. Some weren't drafted because they had flat feet and couldn't do all the marching. Some were declared inept because of some childhood disease like polio. There weren't a lot of guys in our high school class. As the saying goes, "Wars are made by men, but fought by children." Well, that's exactly the way it was.

YS: There were probably other ways that the War affected your life.

DK: Well, yes. You knew that there were things you couldn't get because of the war. And you were always aware of someone who was in active duty or who had been drafted, and so you were concerned. Food was rationed. Gasoline was rationed. Sugar was rationed. Shoes were rationed. Everything was rationed. You understood what that meant. Even if you lived in the city, you found a little piece of land and turned it into a victory garden.

YS: When you think about our nation being at war then and being at war now, what do you see as a difference?

DK: Well, we were pulled into World War II to help save Europe, but that's not the case now. People then believed in the War. Today we have questions about the War. I will be glad when it is over!

YS: I want to go back to your adolescent years in Texas and ask you what adult women taught young girls about starting their cycles.

DK: It's very interesting that you should ask because I was talking about this just the other day with one of my granddaughters. I was telling her about the time Life Magazine carried a feature on pregnancy. My mother was pregnant at the time with my sister, and she gave me the magazine to read. Well, Grandmama Emma had a fit!!! My mother told us the same thing I told my daughter and I now tell my granddaughters: "That's the only thing you have that you have complete control over, and it's not for sale."

YS: I'd like to know about the community's attitude toward pregnancy out of wedlock?

DK: My good friend got pregnant and she and the fellow got married after the baby was born. I didn't know about abortions until I heard girls talking about it at Spelman.

YS: Was Spelman your choice or your parents' choice?

DK: Well, I was really going to Bennett, but my brother was at Morehouse and he said, "If you are going to a girl's school, you might as well go to Spelman." I said, "Okay." And he told me, "You'd better finish in four years." I enrolled here when I was fifteen. Now that's not saying much because there were five of us who were sixteen after school opened. I came [to Spelman] by train, and I came by myself. You have to keep in mind that people didn't travel much during the war. In fact, I barely got here myself. To get from Texas to Atlanta, you had to change trains in New Orleans and you had to know where to change. You had to catch a train at two different stations, and you had to catch a bus to go from one station to the other. It was not a glamorous trip. There were many soldiers on the train. We arrived in the city at one in the morning. It was a very long trip! At no time could we go to the dining car for meals, which is why my mother packed food for me—probably put it in a shoe box: fried chicken and sliced bread wrapped in wax paper. Now when I travel by train, I make it a point to patronize the dining car and as I am sitting there, I say, "Thank you, Dr. Mays for suing Southern Railroad." If he hadn't brought that suit, there is no telling how long it would have taken us to eat in the dining car.

YS: What did you take with you on the train trip to Spelman?

DK: I had my mother's trunk and my brother had painted the Spelman pennant on it. It's still in my basement. It has 1944-1948 painted on it. My aunt from Chicago sent me a beautiful piece of luggage, and luggage was hard to get during the War. And I had a little portable radio that my brother gave me. It was a luxury to have a battery operated radio. I was in good shape. You might find this surprising, but I didn't like Spelman until my senior year. Actually, I tried to go to Xavier, but they didn't have any dorms so my mama said "No". Then she sent my application to Washington University in St. Louis, Missouri. I wish I had kept that letter. They said they weren't accepting Negroes. So my mama said, "Well, you will have to go back to Spelman." I came back to Spelman, but each year I tried to have an excuse to leave. [laughter]

YS: You met your husband when you were a student at Spelman?

DK: Yes. Herty Killian was his name and I remember that he would look at me when we would play ball down where the Fine Arts Building is now located. That was once an open field. Well, Miss Simon was the PE teacher and she would let us play ball in that field. If you hit the ball hard enough, it could reach Clark's campus. I think the veterans had just come back from the War and the Morehouse campus was just running over with men folk. There weren't many men at Morehouse when I arrived in 1944. Anyway, I invited Herty to go to the prom and also to the Valentine's Dance with me. That year the prom was at Morehouse, and we helped the men decorate the gym. Well, as some of my Spelman sisters and I were hauling stuff to the gym, Hertie was sitting on the library steps watching us. I almost broke it off with him for good then. He didn't bother to come down while we were lugging all that stuff. He was sitting up there laughing at us. But, obviously, I didn't break it off. [laughter] When I finished Spelman in 1948 [and there were only sixty-four in my class], we were already discussing marriage. After graduation, I went home—by then my family was living in San Antonio—and learned that my mother was ill. I was offered a job in East Texas, but my father thought I would do better staying at home and helping Mama with my baby sister. While I was home, Herty wrote my parents a letter asking for my hand in marriage and he sent the engagement ring to my father. He asked my father to put the ring on my finger. [laughter] We married a year later, in 1949, in a garden ceremony at my parents' home in San Antonio. We moved to Atlanta after the wedding, and the first house we lived in is the house I am living in now. When Herty died in 1989, we had been married forty-four years, four months and two weeks. I have three children: Billy, Michael and Darnita. Childbirth? I now have three grandchildren—Ebony, Shani and Michael Anthony II and three great grands—Deja, Khala and Calel. They range in age from eight years to six months. So I have plenty of company and lots of joy.

YS: I have been told that you were a pioneer in art education here in the City of Atlanta. I would like to hear about your work in that area.

DK: Well, when my children grew up, I returned to school, and twenty years after earning my bachelor's at Spelman, I earned my Master's in Art Education from the University of Georgia. After forty years in education, I retired in 1992. During those years, I worked at a number of schools in the City—Gate City, Spelman Nursery, Wheat Street, Georgia Avenue, Cooper Street, Coan Middle School, Roosevelt, Murpy, and C.D. Hubert. That's where we had bomb threats all the time. That was during the turbulent time of the sixties.

YS: I know you had many high moments in your work as an art teacher.

DK: Many, especially in my work with Future Studies. I presented the program at the Education Division International Conference of the World Future Society at the University of Houston/Clear Lake, which is next to the Johnson Space Center, and people from all over the world attended. There were only six Black people at the conference, and Mama was one of them. [laughter] The Future Studies program started in 1978. I was fortunate enough to have a principal who thought along the same lines as I did. That was at Sammy E. Coan Middle School [named for a Spelman graduate], which was a pilot middle school for the State of Georgia. My most rewarding work was the development of art curricula for middle schools in the Atlanta system. A group of seventh graders developed a downtown plan that included a people mover which ran from Rich's on for about twelve to fourteen blocks. I think the City was just building the Marta. Three or four years after that, there was an article in the paper about the Marta Five Points Station, which had some of the students' ideas. Another group built a robot about so high . . . maybe about four feet. Another group constructed a medical community center, and everything in the center revolved around curing certain kinds of diseases. Nobody can tell me that a group of Black kids can't think. All you have to do is open the door.

YS: I am sure you had a positive impact on your students. Why do you think art is important?

DK: I think it's quite clear that I love art. I believe that your life is affected by art from the cradle to the grave. You are born from the designs of darkness. All babies aren't breast fed, but they all wear those little soft caps. Babies are affected by the kinds of toys they play with, the kinds of clothes they wear. It goes all the way up to the kind of casket that is chosen as your final resting place. It could be blue, could be mahogany, could be bronze, and it could be rose petal. Somebody had to design it. I love art. I love teaching art. I credit my mother and my father for my love of art. My father did calligraphy, photography and sign etching. I remember that Mama used to make crepe paper flowers, and she never threw the little scraps away. They became my paint. I'd get a little water, get a brush, go on and paint.

YS: What makes you happy?

DK: I don't know. I can be happy with a lot of little things. Simple things. I have been trying to complete legacy paintings and incorporate in them genealogy that can be passed on to my children and grandchildren and nieces. But I haven't gotten a chance to do those paintings. I keep putting them on the back burner. But the backburner is getting closer to the end. As a diabetic and a cancer survivor, I can't push myself the way I once did. What makes me happy? I enjoy being quiet. I enjoy taking pictures. Lots of pictures. Pictures of clouds when I am sitting in an airplane. Pictures of the river. Pictures of the Smoky Mountains.

YS: What makes you sad?

DK: I had gotten to the point where I couldn't cry anymore. I accept death as the cycle of life, and it doesn't make me as sad as it once did. What makes me sad? That so many children never reach their potential. That almost makes me grind my teeth. People ought to be a little more considerate of future generations. We have gotten to be an egotistical and vengeful bunch of people. We have become arrogant and negative and that I can't stand.

YS: If there was one thing you had the power to do for Atlanta's schools, what would that be?

DK: Just one thing? There are so many things I'd like to do. I would like to give every child an opportunity to soar with the eagles. Our kids aren't doing that. You know when my daughter Darnita was in school, I would tell her to soar with the eagles and I would call her Eagle Woman Two because I am Eagle Woman One. That's how I would sign my letters: Eagle Woman One.

YS: I'd like to know what this experience has meant to you.

DK: It has made me focus on the things I want to pass on to my grandchildren. It has made me know that somewhere along the way, I have touched a few lives. It gives me that boost I need to finish the things I plan to do for so long. It makes me feel good about my life. You are not going to see any of my art work hanging in galleries, but You will see something of my artistic work in various places where students I have taught are working and living their lives.

YS: If you were asked to tell Black women of my generation what, for you, was the most meaningful advice you were given when you were our age, what would you tell them?

DK: I would tell them: "Put some steel in your back, throw your shoulders back, tilt your chin just a little bit, and keep moving."

MRS. MABEL KING

Hayworth, Oklahoma
Computer Student at H.J.C Bowden Communiy Center

So my brothers were working on the stock cutter and my mother decided one day, "My two sons are not getting paid what the men are getting paid." And this day, when they were going to work, she said to the owner, "These horses are not moving today." My mother was calling a strike and that was brave because we needed the money. We were so proud of her!

EXCERPTS OF INTERVIEWS WITH MRS. MABEL KING
Conducted by Taneya Gethers

TG: I am really happy that you are my Woman of Wisdom because both of us are from California. Were you born there?

MK: No, I was born in Oklahoma. In a small town called Hayworth. I was born in 1917. My mother was born in Arkansas and my father was born in Louisiana. My mother's name was Elrena Harrell, and my father was Andrew Harrell. They had five children: Andrew, Jr., Ossie, Luther, Arthur Lee, and me, the only girl.

TG: Did your parents meet in Oklahoma?

MK: No, I think they met in Arkansas near the line.

TG: What does "near the line" mean?

MK: The line between Oklahoma and Louisiana. You know, there was a land race to Oklahoma. A lot of Blacks went out there to get land. Some of them traveled by train. Some of them hoboed. They were looking for a better situation out in Oklahoma. They followed the highway. I don't know the whole story. I know that they would ride a day and then rest and then ride again and then rest and then ride again. All of them were going in the same direction, following the highway and going to Oklahoma. That must have been right in the beginning of the 1900's. My father's people were shingle makers and my mother's people were farmers. They had great hopes for my mother. She was going to a Lutheran College, but when they had a bad year on the farm, they didn't have the money to send her to school. Her family had high expectations for my mother because she was the only girl and my father was different. He looked different. He almost looked Indian, and they just didn't think there was a future in allowing him to court my mother. Her brothers—and she had nine of them—got it in their minds that he would NOT get their sister, but her heart was set on him. As it worked out, she married my father against all odds. I don't know the date that they married, but I saw the shoes she wore. They were cute little lace-up shoes, like little boots. I don't know if they eloped. My father took her far from her family and those brothers. He went to Oklahoma. That's where they settled. In Hayworth. And that's where I was born. I was their first child and their only girl.

TG: Do you know whether or not you were delivered by a midwife?

MK: Oh yes! That's how babies were delivered. I remember when families would send for the midwife. Sometimes they would go and get the lady too early and then have to take her back. [laughter] And when it was almost time for the baby to be born, the children would be told to heat the water and when we were very young, we would say, "What are they gonna do with all that water?" [laughter] It was such a mystery for us. I never heard of midwives losing a child. They had no medicine for the mother's pain, and I never heard of midwives losing a child. And after women had babies, they had to keep the shades drawn and they couldn't wash their hair for a whole month.

TG: Take me to your community in Hayworth. I mean, describe it for me.

MK: Farms. Cattle. Hayworth was small. The people there were farmers. My parents and my grandparents farmed the land. We stayed out on the farm and my grandfather would go into Hayworth to get supplies and that would be so exciting for us because he would come back with so many goodies. They farmed sugar cane and corn and cotton, and we had cattle. We would give milk to neighbors. That's how it was with all the farmers. There was a lot of milk and nobody ever went without enough milk for children. Everybody could get the milk.

YS: Was Hayworth an all-Black town?

MK: No. Hayworth was White. That's where the farming people went to be in touch with what you would call their loan officers. Many acres of land would belong to someone and so people would say that they lived on Baldwin land or Grace land and those were the names of the people who owned the land. People who are looking for their families today will ask, "Did they live on Grace land?" People might never see the land owner, but they knew his name.

YS: Did you come in contact with Native Americans?

MK: Oh, yes. After our family migrated to Oklahoma, there were Indian reservations and they were very special. They were considered rich. But no ordinary person could talk to them because you couldn't speak their language. My father, because of his looks and his personality, was allowed to go into the reservation. I remember being parked in a wagon when he left to go into the reservation. I couldn't go. He could go farther into their area to get favors and visit with them. They would always be glad to see him. I remember that it was against the law to take liquor to them. I remember looking across a distance and seeing all these hands going up, welcoming him, reaching out to him. That was a sign of friendship. They would speak with their hands. I remember they had lots of horses. I don't ever remember my father getting a horse from them, but I always remember those hands going up.

TG: Did you work on the farm?

MK: Oh yes. Everybody worked on the farm. And the children were paid to work on the farm and that gave us money for schoolbooks and for clothes. You had to buy everything then. There was no welfare. We were proud that we worked and earned money that would pay for our books. We were so proud. But we couldn't go straight through. Some seasons, we had to work. Boys worked harder on the farms than the girls did. People believed the girls should get an education and so they wanted the girls to go to high school because they believed the woman had to make a good family, a beautiful family. Girls married at eighteen then, but if you got permission from the family, you could marry at sixteen. And some girls did marry at sixteen.

YS: Tell me what your parents stressed most when you were growing up in Oklahoma.

MK: Hard work and the family name. That was important to everyone then. I would say that most people strived hard for a good family name and you just wouldn't dare do anything that would put shame on the family name. They would say, "Be sure to remember not to do anything to shame the family name." It was like a point of sacrifice to the last drop of blood for your family and anyone that did something that shamed the family name, it was like going to prison or something. Family was important, and people took care of older people in the family. Grandparents lived with you and elderly aunts lived with you. You didn't put seniors away back then. They lived in the house with you. And it was important to go to church. Church was everything. We went early on Sunday morning. I wanted to join church in order to be popular and to wear pretty patent shoes, but something kept pulling me back and telling me, "You're not sincere about this." But then, I became sincere. I will never forget the day, the night, I truly gave my heart to God. People delivered me home. I remember bursting into the house and going to Mama and just hugging her face. "Mama, I'm so happy. I really got it." I was between eleven and twelve, and I was really happy.

YS: Tell me what children in Hayworth did for fun and entertainment.

MK: At that time, children younger than twelve usually played around their home with animals. You might have a pony someone had given you and you had pony rides. It was always a treat to visit from one home to another. It was a great honor to be claimed as a friend. To visit was a great treat. Even a walk through the woods to go to visit was a great treat. Rules were laid down: "You must get back before sundown." It was a treat for the friend you visited to say, "I will walk back half way home with you." Then you would get halfway and the friend would say, "Now you walk back half way with me." And you would go back and forth and then you would look at the sun and say, "It's not down yet, it's just red." I remember those games. Children might have a homemade wagon or a sleigh they made on their own or a special tree in the yard and the game was who could climb that tree or who could not. Gathering nuts or selecting the Christmas tree was entertainment. There were no bicycles. Children walked. There was a time when some land owners put brand new fences across some acres that had been open before. You had to go a long way around the area that you could walk through before. Then there was a saying, "Your friendship goes a long way with me." That meant that this fence had been built between us, but you would walk along this fence a long way for a visit. Friendships, neighbors, cousins and aunts were a strong bond. You couldn't be promoted to the next grade until you had all the books required for that grade. A good friend would promise to pass on their books to you so that you could get promoted.

YS: Tell me what you remember most about your mother from your years of growing up in Oklahoma.

MK: My mother had her children when she was eighteen. She was a strong woman who sacrificed for her family. She was small, only 115 pounds, but she was a strong woman.

She was the only girl among ten children. She was a young wife and she was living far away from her original family. They were in Arkansas and she was in Oklahoma. She was lonely and she wanted company. So, my mother accepted me as a friend and also as a daughter. We would talk and share maybe more than some other mothers did because she was young and she was lonely. She had four sons and I was her only daughter, and I was the oldest child. So that's why we grew together, you know, almost kept growing like sisters. All through life when things would be really tough and she would be in tears, she would cry for things that she wished we had. She would tell me what she was crying about. Well, when you are a child and you don't have something, you don't feel it as much as an older person feels it. I grew into becoming the parent. My mother softened up and was like the child. She depended on me to lead her and sometimes to make decisions.

YS: Give me an example of a very important matter she needed your advice on.

MK: A very important matter was when my father had been gone for a few years out in California and he returned to take the children, to do his part. He knew he had not done what he should do. He left the family and moved to California. Let's see. I think I was eleven or twelve. He left the family and went to California. Well, you know, at first Blacks went to Oklahoma for a better life and then some of them went to California. That's what my father did. He moved to California. That was in 1929 or 1930. And after he had been out there for about five years, he came back to Oklahoma to get the children. I was seventeen. All the children went. My mother wanted us to go. There were lots of stories about California being the dream place to go and my mother wanted us to go there. And she wanted me to help her make the decision. My mother said to me, "What do you think about it?" My father was going to take the ones with him that wanted to go and he was not going to force any of us to go but he wanted us to be brave enough to leave home. My mother wanted me to make the decision. And she said, "I won't agree for anyone to go unless you go with them". In the back of her mind she was thinking, "You will be the mother that I want over them." She didn't want to break up the family. She wanted us to stay together. For a couple of days, we did not talk to each other about it. We didn't let the other know what we were thinking. We all just hung around for a couple of days until we all said "Yes" at one time. We had trust that work was better in California. There were jobs in California. There was something to do to make money and right away in the back of our minds, we knew we would work and send for our mother.

YS: That must have been a difficult decision for you.

MK: Well, yes, but it didn't frighten me because our mother had to be working all the time to take care of us and I had shared the responsibility of being the mother, looking after the others. You see, my mother was working and I had to take care of my brothers.

YS: So all of you went to California to live with your father. How did you travel from Oklahoma to California?

MK: My father came with a car and a huge trailer that he had built himself. He was driving something like a Buick. It wasn't new, but everything was in shape to travel by car.

YS: I am guessing that California looked very different to you from Hayworth. When you arrived, did you think you would like living there?

MK: California itself was a dream come true because we had heard so many stories about how wonderful it was there. But it was not. It was far below the dream story of oranges and fruit, but it was not free. Sunshine all the time. That was the really beautiful story we had been hearing. You would have to make that dream come true on your own.

YS: Were things better there for Blacks than they were in Oklahoma?

MK: Better? Well I would say race relations were in progress. You were making your own way. Sometimes you were accepted according to what you were striving for. In California I learned for the first time about a wino, a person who was drunk all day long, who smelled bad and acted crazy. You were in a state where this could happen to anyone if you weren't careful. You could be caught in a rut. You could be what they now call homeless. That was new to me.

YS: Living with your father was probably different from living with your mother.

MK: It was very different. Because we had not lived with our father for four or five years, he didn't want us to be unhappy and want to leave, so he was very busy trying to give us lots of everything that he could. Food and the excitement of entertainment. Movies. Clothing. Friends. Teaching the young men how to drive.

YS: How long did it take you to bring your mother to California?

MK: Let's see. It took about two years because we had seasonal work. We were ranch workers. My father was a ranch contractor. He would drive through ranches and count the acres and come up with how many workers would be needed and then the people who owned the ranches would give my father a contract to find the workers and he would find them and be responsible for them doing their jobs. That's what a ranch contractor did. We did seasonal work. We worked the root season and we worked the cotton season. Everything was about agriculture and so we had to go with the seasons. When the season was in, you tried to live and save a little money.

We were occupying a ranch home when I was living with my mother, and the boys were able to get some work. I remember my mother called a strike one day. She was a small lady but she was very determined and fiery. Her word stood out against the male population. The boys had worked and it was spring time and just before planting time. They used this wheel machine that cut down all the stocks. I've forgotten what they called it, but it was a rolling chopping wheel and it was pulled by one horse. You got a whole day's labor for riding a stock cutter. You would ride up and down the rows and the stock cutter chops up corn or cotton or whatever. So my brothers were working on the stock cutter and my mother decided one day, "My two sons are not getting paid what the men are getting paid." And this day, when they were going to work, she said to the owner, "They are not working today unless you pay them what you pay the men, the grown men." My mother was calling a strike and that was brave because we needed the money. The owner could have said, "Well, you just leave," but he told my mother, "Okay. We'll pay them what we pay the men." We were so proud of her. You think a person might be tall and big and have a big voice and everything to do this, but she was just five feet tall and maybe 120 pounds. We were always proud of her for that.

YS: So you moved to California to live with your father and that's where you met your husband.

MK: Yes. After we had been in California a few years, I got married to Mr. King. We moved into Oakland and Oakland is a city across the way from San Francisco. My husband was a driver for my father. He would drive my father to San Francisco or all around. So, Mr. King was at our house quite often and he would come to take my father places. After a couple of years, we were married. Mr. King was older than I was. My father did not approve at first because he thought there was such a gap between us and that we were so different also. "You're coming from a rural area. You're a country girl. This is a city man. This man knows everything else." What my father thought at first was that Mr. King wanted to take advantage of me. He saw it as an unequal situation. My father pulled me aside and said, "I don't want you to take up with him," and I said, "Well, I won't let you make up my mind how I feel about someone." He respected how I felt. I favored him, Mr. King, because he had been my father's friend, driving him everywhere. They were friends, so it was pretty easy for me to feel friendly towards this person.

YS: May I ask how old you were when you married?

MK: Well, let's see, I am trying to think back. Well, I was twenty-nine because we had harvested and we had sent for my mother in between. I was twenty-nine. My husband was seven years older than I was at the time. My father did not favor the age difference, but I admired Mr. King and I saw him as an educated man. He was a college man and he had won a scholarship to college. He was really something to admire, you know, and I thought he would be ideal to be the head of a household. In those times—from the 30's up until the 40's and World War II—if people had someone in their life a little bit earlier who had been able to go to school and come on up to the college level, you kind of admired them. You thought they were kind of a miracle. And that's how it was with Mr. King. He had come from the South and we were in California. Actually, he came from Atlanta, my husband. This is his home. I married older than most people did because I was taking care of my brothers. I didn't want to leave them. I wanted them to be up on their own and everything. Things turned out pretty well for me and I was the only girl. My father had another wife. We had a stepmother and we adored her and got along with her really well.

YS: You married in California and that's where you started your family?

MK: All of my children were born in California: Steven, Joyce and Kenneth.

YS: How did you feel when you learned that you were pregnant with your first child?

MK: I was just really happy. It surprised me because we were working in the war plants and we were saving our money for a home. We had three checks lying on the dresser that we hadn't cashed. A lot of money came through your hands during the War and there was nothing to buy. Most stores were empty. Markets were empty. They were making war goods. So I was working in war plants and saving my money for a home. There were no men for the jobs and women began working where they hadn't worked before the War. Women worked in shipyards and war plants. The plants never closed. People worked around the clock. I worked in a plant where I did spot welding and I worked with my hands.

YS: Were the war plants integrated?

MK: Yes. When the War came, the War itself had an effect on people. The pressure to get workers automatically put the pressure on bringing in all kinds of people. It was a whole turnover of people coming into the area from all over. The work was not just ship building, but all kind of work that was supporting the War. There was a whole turn over. What we have now as Jeeps were automobiles for the War.

YS: You said you worked with your hands. Tell me what you did.

MK: There were seven different pieces that had to be put in a dish and we would use a tweezer and our feet would push a pedal and a needle would come down and sparks would fly and those pieces would be welded together. Nobody was ever laid off. And we could work time and a half. A lot of money just came through your hands and there was nothing to buy because all that they were making then was war goods. We had saved our money and we said we were going to buy a house and I became pregnant and my husband became very ill. He had to have surgery, so we had to twist our brains and think of what shall we do now? Shall we go ahead and buy the home? Or shall we try to get the surgery? I'm pregnant and if they can prove that you have money, you have to pay instead of going to the county. So we were able to find a doctor and the doctor said, "I will give him the operation and you won't have to pay for the surgery but you'll have to pay for your hospital bills for the baby." So that's the way they divided the money. I was so excited about being pregnant, and I did everything the doctor said do as much as I could. At that time, I still had the skinny frame of a teenager. The doctor gave me vitamins and he asked me to start eating four times a day. I tried to do what he said and I had a huge baby boy, eight pounds and nine ounces. That was in 1945. The delivery was tough, and I thought I was going to die. [laughter] I was in labor for a whole day and a night. I was so weak I couldn't even hold the baby. They just put me to sleep so that I would rest and they came to tell me, my husband and his sister and different ones in the family, that they had seen the baby. I had not seen it.

YS: You didn't have an epidural or anything like that?

MK: They didn't give it to me. They tried to let it go as naturally as they could. I was in perfect health, good health, so they let nature take its course. Before they brought the baby to me, I had seen the little foot print on the paper. I was excited, so excited , but I was too weak to hold it up. I was going to nurse it and I was too weak to hold it up to my breast.

YS: Was your mother in California when you delivered?

MK: Well, we had sent her money to come and she had not come the first season. The next season, which would have been the second year, we sent more money and tickets and things. It was quite a while before we really got her to come. But I had a real close friend who had two children and she knew I had wanted children for so long and finally I was pregnant. She told me a little about pregnancy and about delivery. People held back from telling you about the pain. They didn't want you to panic. My friend told me, she said, "You will have pain and this is probably the worst pain you will ever have." That's as far as she would go. They just didn't want to frighten you when you were pregnant. They just wanted you to go ahead and get through the pregnancy and the delivery as best you can.

YS: Did you return to work and, if so, how long after the baby was born?

MK: Lets see. I started driving after about six months because my husband did not want me to go back to work. I was working in a war plant. I got pregnant while I was working in the war plant and I stopped when I was about six months because I couldn't drive. I was too far out here. And then after the baby came, the War was over and when the War was over, he had the surgery. In three months, he was on his feet again. In three months he was up. Too soon, but he was up. He wanted to get going. We still had the money for the home. So we were deciding where we wanted to buy the home. We did not want to be in a big city so my father was doing contractor and ranch and so we went to the town where my father was. He was in Fresno and we went and bought the home there.

YS: Tell me what race relations were like in California at this time.

MK: Race relations were favorable, I would say, because people were being paid such a high salary and there was such a stress for laborers. To be unfavorable would have been a backward trend. The stress was on paying a lot of money to keep good workers if you could. There was no question about race. The unions came in at that time and you might have a White shop steward. But the unions were against racism.

MK: I've got some few words written in a book here. Let me get it. I don't want to take up your time. I know you have things to do.

YS: No, you wouldn't take up our time.

MK: I know you're supposed to be working

YS: No, we are supposed to be doing exactly what we are doing-having a conversation. So, please take your time. We are thoroughly enjoying your company.

MK: [showing pictures] This is my grandson. That's the prom. This is my granddaughter. These are my daughter's children. This is one of them when they were babies. All during the children's early ages, I was always taking pictures. That's why we have so many of these little snap shots because I was taking pictures always. That's Joyce. This is Jibari, her son. He graduated from, let's see, Morehouse, and I'm going to get my book. [They leave the sitting room and go into the den] This is the den and this is the patio and if you want to sit here, you can. We're just being formal, but we can sit in the kitchen. You're interviewing me. I'm not going to try to interview you. Just because I'm older, I don't want to be bossy. I want to be humble and I am so happy to be working with the Spelman students. Do you have anything special you would like to start out on?

YS: I want you to talk, Mrs. King.

MK: I call this a year of orientation. Of course you know that Joyce is my daughter. Dr. King. Her job has changed. We have always been like Siamese twins joined at the hip. We were joined at the hip and I said that's one mistake we made, that we were so close and we've always been so close. When your children grow up, they are entitled to their lives and a choice of living and going their separate ways. This was a huge project. It was the biggest that ever happened to us. To come to Spelman. When she got selected, we were in New York and in the kitchen: "Oh, do you know what! I got selected to Spelman." And I started dancing in the kitchen and I was saying, "Oh I'm a Spelman mom. I'm a Spelman mom." She's a professor, my daughter, but when we are alone, we are just mom and daughter. You know we just shouted because we were so happy. Then we came here, but I think both of us were totally naive. We knew it was a big project, but we didn't have any idea what it really was. And I still don't really know what it really was. We were in a position to offer our bodies like Aretha Franklin said. Offer ourselves a bridge over troubled waters. You know, just go and lie down and let people cross over. She is so dedicated and she wants to do something great for Black people and this is a Black school. We were just shouting, we were so happy.

Well, the year of orientation is over and we must get busy finding ourselves something to do. I am really devoted to the senior center that I go to. It is like I've been taken in. I've been sheltered. I have found love and I separated the Siamese twin thing. I am not dealing on the past. I am filling this gaping whole in my life. Well, seniors at eighty-six are facing the final chapter of their lives everyday and if they make it another year, they say, "Thank you" for another year. I said I could be gone by now, but I am here, so I told myself to get up and get busy. I want to talk about why I thought we were prepared to come to Atlanta. We are a second generation from Georgia in this family. My husband, the children's father, this was his home, Atlanta. Joyce's first husband, her children's father, was from Atlanta. And so we just love Atlanta people. The men were such gentlemen and they were from the old school with good manners and wearing a suit and a tie. They were trained by mothers. In the hard times when people went out and found work doing whatever they could do, they would come home with the work clothes and work shoes, shower and put on a suit at the end of the day. My husband, Joyce's father, did that. So they were such precious men from Georgia. And we were very happy to come to Atlanta.

I haven't made too many bold steps yet towards my final arrangements. I have a plot paid for in California, I have some funds in New York, I have funds in Atlanta and I have funds in California. So now I should get all these in one place so it won't be difficult for my daughter at my final time. There's a whole list of things to make a choice about, so I'm working on my final arrangements. When I get it all worked out, we may go over it together. We have a whole plot of about twelve people that passed on and they are in Atlanta. And whether I want to be there near them or do I want to be in California. My plot that I have in California is on Skyline Boulevard and when I lived on the coast, it was such a sight seeing spot. When you go there, you can see all up and down the coast and I thought that would be such a wonderful resting place because I loved it so much.

But here I am, more than 2000 miles away from it. I wouldn't want all the problems of sending me all the way back there. I'm working on it. So those are the things that older people work on and I guess they shouldn't put too many things off too far. Then my daughter said maybe I want to go back to New York. I have a lot of good friends, people in the church, but I'm not strong enough to leave her. I'm not strong enough to go to New York and not be with her. So here I am. So the turn of events might change. I don't know. But if something major comes up, I'll call you.

I have something I want to share with you. Live by example. People might be watching you and you don't even know. They could be watching you while you sleep. We talked about losing some battles. In war when the soldiers lose a battle and they find themselves outnumbered, they fall back to their main group to get help. If you find yourself on a board and everyone else votes the other way and you're losing, you get help by falling back behind your own lines. Soldiers fall back to their main group to get help. We fall back to old friends and people that have known us since we were born or even knew our parents before we were born. You can get on the phone and call someone. Fall back behind your own lines. That's a war strategy for winning. So that is what I have to say and if you have anything, I love to talk [Laughing]

YS: And we love to hear you talk. The Atlanta connection is very interesting. Your husband and your daughter's first husband both came from Atlanta.

MK: Yes. And my husband and I brought the children to Atlanta on summer vacations. Every time we came to Atlanta, I put on five pounds. [laughter] We would go to Atlanta and to Virginia. Oh, let's see. Where else did we go? I know we went to the mountains to go hunting with him. On each one of those trips, I put on five pounds because people invite you out. My husband would say. "These people in Atlanta cook, and they'll be so disappointed if you don't eat. When you get invited, you've just got to eat something." So that means you are going to put on five pounds on your vacation trip." My husband would tease me about my weight. He would say to our friends that he had to drive the station wagon (we had a truck and the Chevrolet) because my hips were so large.

99

[laughter] His friends would ask him, "Man, how did you get this young lady? " And they'd ask me, "Well, how did he get you?" I said, "I was a child bride. That's how he got me here. I was a child bride." [Laughing]

YS: When you were talking about weight, I was wondering if they put a lot of emphasis on a woman's weight, on her being thin?

MK: They did not make too much about really really thin. We wanted good health. Your hair shows when you are in good health and a bust, a nice bust. People had to do so much manual work, they really needed the body that would hold up and work. You had nine hours of work and there wasn't a lot of complaining about being real thin. Normally, the Black woman has large bones. You can tell that you are Afro American because of your bone structure. And usually a good strong mother was assurance that she could work, care for the children, nurse the baby, and be a good companion for her husband after she did all that other work. After you did all the washing, ironing, cleaning, caring for the children, driving, night comes and you have got to be a good companion. Usually a lot of times your mood wasn't there because you had spent many hours doing other things. You were responsible for the family, how they look when they go out. White shirts, his suit and everything had to be in good shape. All of your children's things had to be together when they went to school. You were responsible for the gym clothes. Getting all the grass stains out and making everything really White when they are on the team or doing gymnastics. All of those socks, tennis shoes and everything. You were responsible for them being together. Children are not able to see that everything is ready for them on Monday morning. The Black woman can do that. She is equipped to do that. We have said that other races have advantages over Black women because they made more money, or the husband made more money and had jobs when the Black woman's husband did not have a job. But the Black woman copes and she has the magic to do it all.

YS: Is there something you have wanted to do but have not yet done?

MK: I would say that I did part of what I wanted. I had the satisfaction of part of what I dreamed about— being a homeowner. The first step was to have my children graduate from high school. Then we began to search out scholarships and that was almost a dream of a higher standard. Each one of my children became a college person. That was part of my dream. And we did own a home. Owned several.

YS: What makes you happy?

MK: Good health and good relationships with family and friends and living as a Christian.

YK: What makes you sad?

MK: Let me think. The loss of many close relatives and close friends. Unforunate things that happen to them. Of course, things you can't control. You just have to live with it. I try to be inspiring and rise above it. Fear and love teach us a great lesson. Sometimes these things are forced upon us with no choice. My question to you is have you lost anyone close to you to cancer or heart attack? You don't look like you have suffered a day; you look like you've been one of the lucky ones, just blessed with what you've needed to get through.

You know, when you're driving on the highway, you see all the signs to drive which speeds if they're working on the highway. "Slow down" or "This street is closed." The sign tells you. And you can also tell by the colors—green, yellow and red-down. A real policeman waving a flag. So elders have the signs of life— green, yellow, red. So, how are we driving? Are we driving safely, cautiously, or are we lost? I hope our lives would represent love because so often we're suffering from not having love when we have everything else. We have all the money we need. We have clothes and opportunity. But we don't have true love and trust. And so the elders want to give true love, unconditional love. Whatever happens to you, we love you, and you can come and talk about so many things. That's what we really want to do. What do you think?

YS: I agree

MK: I hope what I've shared is helpful. It is truly a pleasure and wonderful to talk with you. I am learning from the students. I am learning from you and I am so proud of you. I just wish you well and I am going to tell you the truth from my heart every time, every time we meet. And as I go around and wait for the next visit, I'll be making notes. You know, the resurrection talks about another life. About going away and being able to come back. I say I'm so happy I lived the Afro-American life first. If I had lived another life and I would have to come back and do the Afro-American life, I wouldn't like that. I'm glad I learned my lessons first.

YS: Do you think that living your life as a Black American first made you stronger, taught you valuable lessons about life?

MK: The Afro-American experience is something that only the person that lived it could understand. The laws that are written down weren't meant for the Afro-American. Take the working woman. The Afro-American woman has to have the children ready for nursery school, hair shampooed, clothing washed, everything sparkling clean. She has to have her house clean to be called a successful mother and she has to be successful on the job. And yet, the Afro-American salary is most times very low. Other races have an advantage over us. The husband worked and earned a nice salary. You know, they have an upward level over us and our little children take a little more time. It takes a little more time to take care of the little Black child's hair. To see that it's braided or however you wear it. To shampoo each night, to clean clothes, to take an extra set of clothing to the nursery school. We have a load to carry. The laws that they give us don't consider how much responsibility we have to carry. And then we have to be a happy couple. That's hard.

YS: That's hard. When I'm writing this chapter and telling your story, how would you like me to describe you?

MK: As a Christian. I became a Christian at the age of eleven. I had lots of relatives that loved me and I was very indebted to them to be what they wanted me to be. That's two grandmothers, my mother, an aunt and uncles, lots of uncles. And as I described our family, we were overcomers, meaning that we overcame so many different setbacks. I would like to be described as what sometimes we call movers and shakers. When things are not working right, we reserve our strength to shake up everything and we don't throw away valuable things. We shake 'em. We throw out the things that are no good and we take the turn around and we keep on trying. We keep on climbing. So I would like to be remembered in that way. As an overcomer. I have been lucky to be a cancer survivor. I'm a surviving heart patient. After raising two generations of children and working in a nursery school raising children, I wouldn't say that I've seen it all, but I've seen a lot and I kind of know what it takes. And I would like to be known as a giver. A person can talk to me and I can forgive them for great injustices because I'd like to represent the Savior as a saver. I'd like to save what is worth saving. That's the way I'd like to be known.

YS: What has this experience meant to you?

MK: It has meant everything to me because I came here by no choice. It was not my choice. I'm in my eighties. I didn't know what to expect. And if we had just a little apartment on campus, I thought I might be placed in a home because people are placed in a home much earlier than eighty. They're placed in a home for convenience. They're placed in a home for popularity sake or esteem. You know, if someone knocks on the door, they'll find a gray old lady just barely walking. So coming here, I plunged into a great depression. It just crept over me. When I found out there was a place for me, I was happy about that. And I was reluctant about senior centers because, you know, it's like they're all the same. I didn't want to take part in just having someone baby-sit me or cook the lunch and I just eat. I wanted more than that. But at the Center, I have found things that have inspired me and lifted me from depression. I felt a new me coming out. You kind of feel like life is like a crab. You've seen a crab. A crab has these big claws and if you have more than one close to each other, they lock these claws and they're hard to separate. So I felt it was a part of life that was like a crab, that was holding on with claws, and I wanted to shake it off. So after I got in here, I was able to shake off the ugly things and begin to do something beautiful. I've been promoted three times in the computer program. I'm going on to word processing. . And I am really doing something that gives me an uplift. The center is called therapeutic. The exercise and the program—everything is supposed to give you choices. I've joined the chorus. I do the computer two days a week and exercise two days a week. And I think I've lost a couple of pounds.

I would like to credit you for being so grateful. I don't know if you're Christian or not, but you have really showed me a loving side. You have been loving and kind and patient with me and you've been so faithful and I've got a big thank you for you.

YS: That's how I feel about you. Even if I have another meeting to go to, you're always so understanding. Being with you has been therapeutic for me. You shared this with me before. Your favorite scripture.

MK: Psalms 118. It says I shall live and not die. That was the missionary program and it appealed to the women. Sometime when you are at the end of your ropes, you can feel like you're about to die. But if your hope is in Christ, you can hold on and say, "I shall live and not die."

MRS. MIGNON LEWIS

Ardmore, Oklahoma
Elementary School Teacher and Recipient of Spelman College
Founder Spirit Award

My great-great grandmother was half-Indian and half-African. She had five children by a White man named McMullan. The youngest of those five children was Bettie McMullan, who married a White man. Bettie is my great grandmother, and she died in February 1929. I didn't know her, but I know about her from our family history. Bettie had fourteen children. Isn't that something?

YS: Good afternoon Mrs. Lewis, I am Brandi Lee and as you know, I am the student in SIS who will be interviewing you this semester for our oral history project. I am very excited about the time we will spend together. I want to begin with biographical information. Are you a native of Atlanta?

ML: No, I was born in Ardmore, a southern town in Oklahoma.

YS: I can't believe this!!! I'm from Oklahoma.

ML: Well, how interesting that a young lady from Oklahoma is interviewing me. You don't speak like you're from Oklahoma.

YS: Really? A lot of people tell me I speak with kind of a southern accent. Where is Ardmore located?

ML: It is located in southern Oklahoma, 100 miles north of Dallas. When I was growing up there, Ardmore was a small town of 15,000 people and, of course, it was segregated. Negroes went to one school, the Whites to another, and the Indians were on the reservations not going to school. How sad. The Indians were not allowed to go to school on their own land.

YS: Yes, we forget that. What did your parents do in Ardmore?

ML: My father, Sevellia Marquette Lackey, was custodian at the post office in Ardmore, and my mother taught school.

YS: Are you an only child?

ML: Oh heavens no! I'm from a family of six children: Lawrence Sevallia, Wynola, Zenobia, Gwendolyn, Mignon, and Mervyn. There are two boys and four girls. The oldest and the youngest are males and the girls are in between. I am the youngest girl. I have a brother who is four years younger than I am. I am the only one of the six children who left the state of Oklahoma to go away to college. And that's a pretty long way, isn't it?

YS: Anywhere in Oklahoma to Atlanta is a long way. Tell me what it was like growing up in a segregated town in Oklahoma.

ML: Actually, Brandi, my parents shielded us from segregated conditions in Ardmore. We had our own entertainment at home with family members and with neighborhood kids. There was one movie theatre for Negroes to attend. Many evenings after all the work was completed, we played dominoes and table tennis. I loved to play with my older brother Lawrence when he was home.

YS: When you spoke to our SIS seminar class, and we really enjoyed you, Mrs. Lewis, you told us about the time your mother said something about not swimming in a pool because it was dirty. Would you share that story with me, please? I want to get it on tape.

ML: Yes. We lived in what was called the north side of Ardmore near the high school where my mother taught, and when we would go downtown, we would have to walk through the park to church and to downtown for shopping. It was a White park. Of course Negroes couldn't go there for picnics or just to be there, but we could cut through the park on our way to church. We couldn't stop in the park. We could walk through the park. We did that on our way to church. We were A.M.E. members. And so, on our way to church, we would pass a swimming pool and I would see all the White children in the pool. I wanted to swim, too, but I was too young at the time to know that I was "different." I asked my mother, "Why can't I swim in that pool? Why can't I go in there?" My mother just kept walking and she caught my arm and she said, "Oh, you wouldn't want to swim in there. The water is dirty." I took my mother's word. Of course I know now that was her way of not saying to me, "You, as a Negro child, are not allowed to swim in that pool." If she had said that, there would have been other questions I do believe. So that was her way of smoothing it over. She said the water was dirty. That was just one of the many, many incidents my mother had to cope with and she dealt with all of them in ways that protected us. There were restaurants in Ardmore, little hot dog stands and chilidog stands and, you know, places like that, but we never considered going to eat in any of them because we had our own garden. We worked in the garden. We planted and harvested vegetables, and we ate at home. There was no such thing as eating out, and that has been to my advantage. I think that has ensured me pretty good health.

My family couldn't afford to eat out anyhow. My mother was concerned about sending six children to college. That was her goal. And I'd like to tell you something interesting, Brandi, just to detour a minute. Not only did my mother have six children of her own, but she helped raise some of her sister's children who lived down in a country town called Atoka and in Atoka, the eighth grade was as far as Blacks could go. My mother's sister had eleven children. My mother would bring them to Ardmore and they would stay with us. So we had a basketball and a football team. [Laughing]

We learned how to live with one another. We learned how to have one bathroom, use it and come out. [Laughing] And you know, Brandi, when my cousins would come to Ardmore, they would bring a croaker sack full of sweet potatoes or a big gallon can of sorghum molasses. In Atoka, they grew corn and they made their own molasses and they had all kinds of fruits. We would go down to the country, sometimes around Thanksgiving, and pick pecans. My grandparents lived down there. They would butcher cows and hogs. My mother didn't like pork. She was a home economics teacher, and she said pork's not good for you. We didn't get to eat bacon at home. I didn't start eating bacon until I came to Atlanta.

YS: You talked about the sting of segregation for Blacks. What about Native Americans? Did you have any interaction with them? How were they treated?

ML: I had deep compassion for them. I don't know why, but I was especially sensitive to what they were dealing with. I didn't understand everything about their lives, but I knew they were not treated like Whites or like Blacks. When the Indians, that's what they were called then, came to town, they would go down a street called Caddo. I see it vividly now. They would come into the city, the way you see it in the movies. They would come in a wagon or on horses, and they would tie their horses up and go shopping. They always walked in a single file. The chief would be at the front, the men after him, and then the women, and at the very rear, the children. I didn't think about it then, but years later I wondered why the children were at the end of the line. They were so unprotected there. Since we lived out in the north side of town, they would have to pass us on their way back to the reservation. One time, when they were leaving town, one of the wagons lost a wheel and rolled onto our land. I remember that my father worked with the Indians to fix the wagon. I can see that very vividly. My parents never took me to see a reservation out of respect for the people who lived there. And I don't know why, Brandi, but when I was young, I felt a sense of kinship with them. I would ask my mother, "Why can't I be a pretty reddish brown? Why can't I have that long good straight hair like my Indian cousins?" She'd say, "Well, God didn't want you to have it. Maybe you didn't know how to handle it." My mother would say things like that. She never really came out and told me that I had hair like my daddy. She had straight hair herself because she was part Indian.

YS: You have Native American ancestry?

ML: My great-great grandmother was half-Indian and half-African. She had five children by a White man named McMullan. The youngest of those five children was Bettie McMullan, who married a White man. Bettie is my great grandmother, and she died in February 1929. I was born October 20, 1928, so I didn't know her, but I know about her from our family history. Bettie had fourteen children. Isn't that something? My grandmother Ozora was Bettie's first born, and she looked completely White. I can recall one time as a young child being ashamed of that. Why I was ashamed, I don't know. Maybe I had succumbed to some of the teasing by children.

YS: How would they tease you? What would they say?

ML: Well, we lived out near the high school and when the kids would be going home, Grandmother Ozora would be sitting on the porch waiting for us. You see, when she came up from the country, she brought sugar cane, vegetables and things like that. She would be sitting on the porch waiting for us to come home from school, and the children would say, "Oh look at that old White lady," talking about my grandmother. They knew I couldn't fight because my mother was a registered teacher. I couldn't do anything at that moment, but I'd get them the next day at school.

Ozora was my grandmother on my mother's side. Now, about the lineage of my father. My father looked more Indian than my mother did. I'll bring a picture of him, too. His father was from Brownville, Texas. Grandfather Charlie Lackey. That was his name. Charlie Lackey had two sons: a boy named Reel and my daddy Sevellia. My daddy was part Spanish, and, actually, he looked more Indian than my mother did. I have been told that his father was African and Spanish. He was a dark man with grey eyes. It is told in the family that that my good solid African ancestry came from my father's grandmother. I have a picture of her. I have all those pictures. I'll show them to you. You can't really see her features, but she was very dark. All I can find on my father's side is my grandfather, Charlie Lackey.

YS: Tell me about your father. Sevallia.

ML: Sevallia Marquette Lackey. He was a real radical and so was my grandfather who would write articles--and that was in the early 1890's--about racism in Texas. Can you believe that? He was radical before there was a movement. You won't be surprised to know that he was run out of Texas because of his inflammatory writing. I think you know about the Black Panthers. Well, if there had been Black Panthers back then, he would have been one. He was a radical, and my father was very much like him when it came to racial matters. Take the library situation for example. Negroes didn't have a library in Ardmore and that was unacceptable to my father, and so he went to the city council—it was called the Chamber of Commerce—and said, "Negroes in Ardmore need a library." Well, don't you know that the Chamber of Commerce opened a library for Negroes. There is a similar story about the recreation center for Negroes. There were several centers for Whites, but not a single one for Negroes. My father drew up a petition for a Negro recreation center and collected enough signatures to give the petition teeth. And the city responded. That was in 1946, the year I finished high school. My daddy was a very special man and I say that, Brandi, because of what he did for Negroes in Ardmore. People respected him as a man of courage and a man of integrity. I must tell you about the time my father went to the aid of a Negro woman who had been insulted by a White man.

YS: I want to hear that story.

ML: As I told you, my father was custodian at the post office in Ardmore and one day—I was very young at the time— a Negro day worker came to purchase stamps five minutes before closing time. And do you know, Brandi, a White employer said to her, "Get out of here, nigger. We are closing." And then he slapped her. My father, by reflex, hit the man and knocked him to the floor. It was unheard of in those days for a Negro to hit a White man and live to tell it. Because my father had earned the respect of White leaders in the city, Mr. Carlock, the bank president, called my mother and said to her, "Mrs. Lackey, you'd better keep Lackey at home for a few weeks until we get this cleared up." We later found out that the White postman who slapped the woman was transferred to a country town in Texas, and my father kept his job.

Well, we are very proud of him. I think I told you that Daddy was from Indian territory. His father, my grandfather, came to Texas, to Dallas, where he met my grandmother. Her name was Willie Lackey, and she was quite a humdinger. [laughter] She was very assertive, very nosey, very pushy and very opinionated. She tried to run the church. They were big time AME people, and my grandmother wanted everything in the church to go her way. She was a humdinger. Let me tell you this about Grandma Lackey, Brandi. When my older sisters attended Langston, she would go to the Black Dispatcher, the Negro paper, and tell a reporter that her grandchildren were visiting her. She wanted that in the paper for everyone to know. My mother didn't like advertising, or bragging. And my sisters stopped visiting Grandma Willie Lackey because they didn't want their names in the newspaper. I guess she was proud that her grandchildren were in college because my father went only as far as the seventh or eighth grade, and I believe he went to Langston. It was the only Negro school in Oklahoma and President Page would admit any Negro who wanted to come to the school to learn. He would give them work. It was somewhat like what Booker T. Washington did in Alabama. President Page said any child who wanted to learn could go to Langston. I don't know what year it became a college, but I do know this: my mother received a certificate in plain sewing from Langston in 1914. That's when she met my daddy. My mother came from a different background, but she saw that my daddy wanted to learn and they kinda fell in love. He was a nice looking man. I have a picture of him when he was in his younger years. I'll bring it with me next time.

YS: I want to hear more about your mother.

ML: My mother received her certificate in 1914 in plain sewing and then she went back to Langston and received another certificate in something else. That was in 1921, but she didn't get her college degree until 1941. In Oklahoma, you could teach with this so-called certificate, and that's what my mother did. She and my daddy married in 1917. My brother was born in 1918 while Daddy was overseas in World War I. My mother married my father in 1917. She got her degree twenty some years later.

YS: I'd like to know more about the genealogy on your mother's side. I want to be sure I have it right.

ML: I can go back four generations on my mother's side. There was a White man named McMullan. I don't have a picture of him, but I do have a picture of his slave mistress. Her name was Rachel, and the story is that he treated her well. They lived in Carroll County, Georgia, but they left there in 1848 and went to Indian territory, which became the state of Oklahoma in 1907, because he thought life would be better for them there. Bettie was born in 1842, she was my great great grandmother, which means that she was about six years old when they left Georgia. She knew all about the Trail of Tears.

YS: Where did they go when they left Georgia?

ML: The story is that he stopped in Lookout Mountain and then he moved on and went to Indian Territory. I think it was called Boggy Ben, but he found out that it was a little too rough there, so he went across the border to Texas and founded the little town of Hillsborough, Texas. We don't have records of when Rachel died, but we know that Bettie was there with her. McMullen's White wife and children lived there.

YS: He had two families? One White and one Black, and they lived together?

ML: Yes. All of them lived in the "big house." I have learned more about the White McMullan family from a book written about Frank, one of the sons. Frank McMullan's Elusive Eden. That's the title. When I read the book, I learned that in 1865 Frank took a band of people to Brazil. This was in 1865 after emancipation. Well, I wrote the man who wrote the book and informed him that I am a distant relative of Frank McMullan. I haven't gotten a response yet, but I wrote him. Now this is quite interesting, Brandi: Frank took one Black man with him to Brazil and that Black man was the only person in the group who prospered.

YS: I want to ask you about your parents' relationship, but you have so much information about your family's history that, well, I want to hear more about that.

ML: Okay. Bettie had fourteen children. My grandmother—her name was Ozora—was the oldest child, and she really wanted to go to college. Now my great grandmother Betty did not go to college, but she had a desire to learn. Bettie was a very smart woman. I say that because she married a wealthy man. If you are gonna have fourteen children, you'd better marry somebody to take care of them. [laughter] Her husband donated money to build Paul Quinn in Waco, Texas. It's in Dallas now. Have you heard of Paul Quinn College?
Well, my great grandfather, Ozora's father, William Guess, was raised by a wealthy White family and he told Bettie that he didn't want the girls going to college, but he was not opposed to the boys going. Three of his sons went and they did well: one became a lawyer, another a doctor. But Papa Guess—that's what we called him—did not want Ozora to get a college education. He said to her, "All you gon' do is go down there and get married." And you know what? She went to college and she did just what he said she would do. She went to Paul Quinn College and she met a man named Clem Beaty and married him. Quinn was first in Waco, but it has moved to Dallas.

YS: Waco, Texas, where the tragedy took place?

ML: Yes.

YS: When you heard about the Waco tragedy, how did you feel?

ML: I felt great pain because Waco is in my family history. I couldn't watch the news and see it as just another city in our nation. I saw it as a place where my ancestors had been. It was tragic. Really tragic.

YS: Ozora and Clem Beaty are your mother's parents?

ML: Yes. They had two children: my mother and her sister Juanita. The family ended up in Oklahoma.

YS: I'd like to hear about dating conventions in Ardmore.

ML: My mother allowed us to date when we reached sixteen, and our dates were rather simple. We would sit in the living and my mother would sit in the dining room with the French doors wide open. When we heard her clear her throat, we knew that it was time for our dates to go home. A date lasted just one hour. We would sit and talk or listen to music. Occasionally, my mother would allow my sister and me to walk to the movies, which cost ten cents at that time. We had to be home by six o'clock when it was still daylight. Really, Brandi, courtship for me was having a boy walk me home from school and carry my books. [laughter]

YS: As far as you can remember, did your mother have one set of rules for your brothers and a different set of rules for you and your sisters?

ML: Absolutely not!!!! There were no gender differences in the Lackey household. All of us washed dishes, all of us worked in the garden, all of us ironed, and all of us learned to cook. My mother had a boys' class in home economics and sewing in 1940. So, in answer to your question, my mother didn't believe in gender differences in her parenting or in her teaching.

YS: That's good to hear. Mrs. Lewis, tell me what you knew about racial violence when you were growing up in Oklahoma.

ML: Well, my parents didn't talk too much about that around the children. They were avid readers of The Pittsburgh Courier and The Black Dispatch, which kept Negroes across the country informed about incidents of racial violence. You know, one of the worst incidents of racial violence occurred in our state, Brandi.

YS: You mean the violence in Tulsa?

ML: Yes. In 1921. Greenwood Street was annihilated. Completely burned to the ground. My parents lived in Ardmore at the time, and not until I was an adult did I learn that my mother had an uncle who tried to save some of the property by passing for White. He was an attorney and because he looked White, he would attend meetings that Whites held and then go to the Negro community to warn them about what was going to happen. You know Tulsa was such a tragedy, and it took place because Whites were jealous of the wealth Negroes had accumulated.

Well, racial violence happened all over the country, not just in Tulsa. One of the worst lynchings in Georgia occurred the year my mother came to Atlanta to work on her master's degree at Atlanta University. That was in 1946 . In June of 1946, I believe. Two men and two women were lynched.

YS: Your father took some real chances in Ardmore when he spoke out and especially when he slapped the White man.

ML: Yes, he did, and we were fortunate that Daddy did not encounter violence. The only explanation I can give for this is that he was respected for his integrity and his courage.

When Daddy passed Whites on the street, he tipped his hat to them, and they would tip their hat in return. Then, too, Brandi, we were one of the more privileged Negro families in Ardmore. We lived in one of the better neighborhoods, and the school principal and two of the teachers were our neighbors. We had lots of land and, actually, we lived in the nicest house on the street. And yet, we were never taught to feel superior to anyone, and that's how I reared my children.

YS: You taught school for many years. Where did you teach?

ML: I taught here in Atlanta at Turner High from 1951 to 1954, and then I moved to California and taught school in Compton. I left California in 1975 and went to Illinois, where I taught in an all-White area. There was no other Black teacher in the school and, you know, Brandi, the White children needed me because they appeared to know nothing about Afro-Americans. So I took the liberty, since I was teaching reading, English, and Social Studies, to enlighten them and their parents, too. Some of the teachers told me they had never been in the company of Blacks, and I thought to myself, "My, you certainly have been limited."

YS: That was a good response to a difficult situation.

ML: Well, let me tell you this, Brandi. This is when my life got interesting. I left Georgia in 1954 and moved to Los Angeles. That's where all my relatives were—my sister, cousins, uncles, aunts, everybody. They moved from Oklahoma to California. Only my mother and daddy stayed in Ardmore, Oklahoma. I had one cousin still teaching at Langston.

YS: So what happened that was interesting?

ML: I met my husband. [Laughing]

YS: I was getting around to that story.

ML: A medical convention was taking place in the city and many people were coming to Los Angeles to attend the convention. My brother and some of my friends came to the convention. Well, I asked a young man who had been to Morehouse, "Do you know any nice Afro American men?" This was 1955. He introduced me to a nice young man named Frederick Gaston Lewis. He was an only child and very special to his family. He came to Los Angeles in June. I met him in August. He got a degree in aeronautical engineering from Ohio State and moved to Los Angeles. He drove from Ohio to California accompanied by his mother and his grandmother. I met him on a Friday night and the following Sunday he came to my church, a Presbyterian church in Los Angeles. I was the organist at the church and that impressed him. He would come by every day after work to see me and, you know, Brandi, I really didn't have time for that much courting because in addition to serving as organist at the church, I was teaching school and also giving piano lessons to three students. After we had been dating for about three or four weeks, I told him, "I really like you, but I can't see you every evening." It hurt his feelings somewhat, but he respected my wishes. We became closer and closer. [laughter] Needless to say,

Brandi, by October, I was engaged. I wanted to travel, go to school and work, but I was in love. We got married on March 25, 1956. In June of '56, he was commissioned to go to jet pilot school in the Air Force. I got pregnant in April, and my first child was born on January 14, 1957. Because my husband was in the Air Force, we lived in a number of places-- Texas, Arizona and Nevada. My husband was a pilot in the Air Force. Actually, he was the only Negro in his class in the squadron T57. He had somewhat of an advantage in flight school because he had previous instruction from Dr. Jackson while he was attending Wilberforce University in Wilberforce, Ohio. He also had an advantage because he was an aeronautical engineer and he knew a great deal about planes.

YS: Did he experience any racial prejudice in flight school?

ML: I'm sure he did, but he never really talked about it. He experienced more when he got out of the Air Force, when he was working in El Segundo, California with scientists and engineers at a company called TRW. And when he was working on his Masters in Aerospace Engineering at the University of Southern California, he experienced racial prejudice. I'm going to share an incident with you about my husband. We were driving around in Indiana one day, going from base to base, and we stopped to get some food. Well, the waitress said, "I'm sorry we can't serve you." This had to be '57, and here my husband was in an Air Force uniform with a bar on his shoulder. He was a lieutenant and we couldn't be served. So I acted up. I said, "You better give us some food." You know, I was selling wolf tickets. The woman served us. Later, my husband said, "I could never do that," and I told him, "You couldn't because you are a Black man. They would come out there after you, but sometimes a woman can do things a Black man can't do." I don't think I told you, Brandi, that my husband was an intellectual. He read all the time. He spent his childhood at Wilberforce College because his father was coach there—County Lewis, a famous coach. So, he grew up in a college environment and his mother encouraged him to read and she let him read whatever he wanted to read. He read all the time as a young child and he kept that up as an adult. Now that he has died, I realize it was a stimulating and exciting marriage.

YS: I want to go back to what you said about starting a family early in your marriage. When you learned that you were pregnant with your first child, were you happy?

ML: I was not too elated, but my husband was simply delighted. You see, he was an only child. Remember, Brandi, I came from a big family. But more than that, I was not ready to start a family because I wanted to spend time with my husband. Actually, I was using birth control, which lets you know that I was not ready to start a family. [laughter] I was newly married and I was twenty-seven years old. During my first pregnancy, my husband and I were living in Malden, Missouri, a small town with a population of 322. He was in pilot school at the time. Well, he wanted his child to be born in a city, not in the country, so I went to Toledo to live with his mother, and that's where my first child was born. I wasn't ready to become a mother, but motherhood has been a joyous experience for me. I have four daughters: Camille, who was the child born in Toledo; Diana, who was born in Ardmore and my husband was on duty in Bentwater, England; Adrienne and Angela, who were born in Los Angeles. My husband was out of the service when they were born and living in Los Angeles. I breastfed all of my children and I potty trained them early.

YS: When you talked with our seminar class, you said that you prefer dark-skinned men. Was your husband dark?

ML: Well, Brandi, when I think about it, I don't fully understand my preference for dark-skinned men because my mother didn't allow us to talk about color in the house. I can remember getting a serious whipping right there in the home economics room where my mother taught because a boy was fooling with me and pulling my braids and I called him a Black fool. He went to my mother, to her classroom, and told her what I had said. She got her yardstick and whipped me right there in the room. I must have been in the 10th grade. My mother never used that word. I don't know why, but all my life I have been attracted to a man who is dark and smooth. I don't know what it is but that's just me. You know what's interesting, Brandi, is that my husband [laughter] wanted a brown-skinned lady. When I was positive and up beat, he would say, "You know you're my good luck piece." I would say, "That's a compliment."

YS: What attracted you to your husband?

ML: I liked my husband because he was articulate and he was intelligent. I don't like dummies. He was comical. Oh, he was comical. He could tell some jokes [laughter] and be very dignified about it. I made another comment to you young ladies and the teacher about relationships between men and women and I think I said something like "You know sometimes the fellas will want to use you." Two girls perked up and they said, "What do you mean, 'using'?" I think I talked a little bit about that, but then we went on to something else.

YS: We were surprised again by your honesty.

ML: Well, I was brought up in that manner. That was the only way that my mother could deal with us. She always told us that women were the strongest people in the world . She told us we could not afford to have a child. It would be a disgrace. She'd tell us not to let a fella touch us. She wasn't the way I tried to be with my four daughters. She didn't try to explain. Also, Brandi, there were things that my mother didn't let us do because she did not want us to experience any stimulation. By stimulation, I mean sexual, of course. I remember she would not let us read Cosmopolitan and True Stories. My mother was trying to show us that we didn't have to let fellas use our bodies. She would tell us, "You know, fellas like the girls that they can't have their way with."

YS: Did you know any girls who got pregnant out of wedlock?

ML: Yes, I knew two who got pregnant when they were teenagers. I was in high school at the time, and I remember one girl's mother wanted to put her out. She was embarrassed that her daughter was pregnant. See, back then, it was simply a disgrace to get pregnant out of wedlock. My mother rescued the girl. She went to a department store and purchased material for a layette and she helped the girl make clothes for the baby, a blanket, gowns, and even diapers. I remember hearing my parents argue about this and my father saying, "Doll, you can't save everybody." My mother said, "But we can't let the girl be put out.".

YS: I'd like to hear more about your mother.

ML: My mother was an interesting lady. She brought me to Spelman when she came to Atlanta to work on her Masters. My mother was determined to get her Masters. She came down here, worked and went to school one summer. By that time, my brother and a woman named Ada Lois Sipuel had filed a lawsuit against the University of Oklahoma.

YS: Your brother filed a lawsuit against the University of Oklahoma? Wow!

ML: Yes, he and a woman named Sickely. Well, they won the suit and so my mother didn't have to come all the way to Atlanta to get her degree. But let me quickly add that my daddy was supportive of her coming to Atlanta for her degree. He may not have liked it, but he didn't complain. I think my mother cleared it with him early. She went to Stillwater, to the Oklahoma State University, where she earned the Masters in 1950. She was sixty five years old at the time. She had that kind of determination. My mother was a remarkable woman. And you know something, Brandi, I believe that's why the six of us, especially the girls, are such take-charge people. You know, we make decisions and set goals and take charge of our lives. My husband understood that about me. He knew that I was going to express my opinions and I think he respected that about me.

YS: Well, we definitely learned that about you when you came to SIS. There was nothing you didn't discuss with us and also we were really kinda surprised at your emphasis on physical fitness. Would you walk me through an ordinary day with Mrs. Mignon Lewis?

ML: My day usually begins with stretching and after stretching, I do yoga. According to what mood I am in, I will play music. I love music, and my husband loved music. From Tina Turner to Bach and Beethoven. I love music. So I play music while I do my stretching exercise and then I go to water aerobics at least three times a week

YS: I know you majored in music at Spelman.

ML: I did my senior recital in organ. I also played the violin, but I sold my violin when I was in Illinois. And I actually don't play the organ anymore because it takes a discipline I'm not willing to give right now. I want to hang loose and be free. If I want to sit in the middle of my cleaning and read a book or listen to a song, that's exactly what I will do. You see, Brandi, I came up in a very disciplined household. I had to get up every morning and work in the garden. Then I had to come in and get ready for school. I had to practice whatever instrument I was learning before I went to school. I played the piano, the clarinet and the saxophone. I had to practice. And on top of that, I played piano for church. That I didn't like, but in those days you did what your parents told you to do. So you see, there is a very valid reason why I am not pursuing any of those musical things. My life now is about enjoyment. I want to hear others play. I don't play cards and I don't like to party. I do not go out because I am widow. I am not a television watcher in the sense of spending hours in front of the television. I watch the Today Show at eight in the morning and programs on the arts and entertainment channels. I dislike watching the news because it's always about something negative that has happened, and I don't go to see movies that are negative. I just don't want to put that into my psyche right now.

YS: Is there anything you have wanted to do with your life that you have not yet done?

ML: I really wanted to be a dancer, but I always thought I was too large and not graceful enough. And I have always wanted to work with young mothers to get them to be strong mothers, but I simply haven't had the time.

YS: Well, Ms. Lewis, you are always doing so much for Spelman. Didn't you receive an award for your dedication to the College?

ML: The Founders' Spirit Award, which is given to an alumna who graduated at least fifty years ago who exemplifies the spirit of the founders of the College. I received the award in 2002. In 1996, I received the Merit Award from the NAASC (National Alumnae Association of Spelman College), which recognizes leadership and assistance in financial aid and recruitment. I am very grateful for both awards.

YS: If you could talk to a group of women in my generation about becoming empowered women, what would you say to them?

ML: I would encourage them to be as intellectual as they can be. Read, read, read. Learn as much as they can about everything. I would also tell them that we women are the ones who set the pace because we are the one who have the children and rear them into adults. We are the mothers and as mothers we can make a difference in our children's lives and, really, Brandi, a difference in the world. I believe that motherhood is one of the most important and empowering experiences a woman can have. Having said that, I would quickly add that motherhood is not the only path for us. It is not the only experience in which we demonstrate our talents and it is not the only experience in which we can make a difference in the world. We can also be powerful women in the work force. In fact, we must be. One of the reasons I think teaching is such a wonderful profession is that it gives us an opportunity to be both mother and teacher. What is more rewarding than those two roles?

YS: What has this SIS experience meant to you?

ML: It amazes me, Brandi, that you young women would want to give your time to talking to older people. This experience has been most uplifting. It added youth to my life. It made me feel young all over again.

MRS. SHIRLEY MCKIBBEN

Blakely, Georgia
Domestic, Student at Metropolitan College and
Recipient of Hope Scholarship

I believe I was a chosen vessel before I was born. . . . God must have had me in training to make me wiser, more loving and kinder than I would have been if I hadn't been a chosen vessel. I have cried about sixty years of my eighty years. . . I was like Jeremiah the crying prophet. I would say, "Why me?" And then God began to speak to my spirit. And I say now, "Thank you for choosing me. Thank you for letting me be worthy."

YS: Mrs. McKibben, I want to thank you for permitting me to interview you for the SIS project.

SM: Well, I am honored that I am in the project, and I welcome you warmly.

YS: I want to begin by asking you biographical questions--where were you born and how many children were in your family and any other information you want to share.

SM: I was born on January 18th in 1920 in Early County, near Blakely, Georgia. B-l-a-k-e-l-y. Blakely, Georgia. But I was born in Early County. That was near Blakely. There were eight children-three boys and five girls-and I was the last. I was the baby, and I was delivered by a midwife and the midwife was my mother's cousin. My father's name was Seymour Harris and my mother's name was Callie Patterson Harris. My father died before I was born. Six weeks before I was born. He was a farmer, a sharecropper, and he died on December 4, 1919. My mother grieved real hard and having no other means of support, she stayed on the farm and continued to farm. She stayed in Early County for five more years after my daddy passed. She had eight children to support and so she continued to farm. In 1926, we moved from the farm into the city, into Blakely, and that's where my mother met Moses Calloway. They married in Blakely and my mother had a son and a daughter from this union.

YS: How did you feel when your mother remarried?

SM: Well, to tell you the truth, I was so little, I really didn't understand, but I think I was happy because the man she married had children and we got along real good. Kids today in step families don't make it. Some of them don't. But back then, it was different. If a woman married a man who had children- - the more, the merrier. The more kids, the less work I'll have to do, you know. [Laughing] We did work together. We were happy and we got along fine. But after three years, the marriage ended, and we moved to another small town called Sasser, Georgia. S-a-s-s-e-r. Sasser, Georgia. Then we moved from Sasser, Georgia, over to a little town called Herod. H-e-r-o-d, Herod, Georgia. By that time, my oldest brother had married and moved to Atlanta and my second oldest brother stepped forward as head of the house. So my mother started to farm again. It was a hard life, a very hard life. Very hard. My father died before I was born. My mother said it was about five weeks before I was born. But she continued to be a sharecropper because she had two sons that were old enough to plow the mules and take care of the livestock. She continued to sharecrop until I was about eight or nine years old. That's when she changed from the country and moved to town and started doing domestic work. At that time, we didn't have laundries like we do now, so what my mother would do was, she would go to different White people's homes and pick up maybe two bundles of clothes from this house and maybe one bundle from the next house. She went about all over the city getting White people's clothes. Then she would bring them home where she would wash them, iron them, fold them up, and then put them up. Back then, there were cotton baskets and when my mother would do the clothes, she would fold them, neatly, and put them in the baskets. And on the weekends, on Friday and Saturday, she would distribute the laundry back to the White people's homes. Maybe she would get, from a large family, maybe she would get a dollar and a quarter per household for washing and ironing their clothes.

She was exposed to winter's cold freezing weather and to hard work all the time, which is why she became ill. The last farmer my mother worked for was _____, and she died on his plantation. She died on March 23, 1934. Luckily, my sister Sarah lived in Blakely, Georgia, which was about seventy-five miles from Sasser. She came to us and made arrangements to have our mother laid to rest. My stepfather was there, but I never really connected to him. I had a longing to know my biological father. It was the most devastating time of my young life. Not to have known my father and losing my mother like that when I was so young, I just grieved and grieved and grieved.

Then we moved to Blakely and my sister was like a second mother to the younger children. She was married and she was a domestic worker. She earned a small salary and it was barely enough to support all of us: myself, a brother who was nine and a sister who was five. I couldn't continue in school because I was needed to help support the younger ones. So, I started doing domestic work. That's why I stopped school. To help with the family.

YS: Tell me about some of your experiences as a domestic worker in Blakely.

SM: Well, I worked for a White man named _____and he was the only White doctor in Blakely who would treat Black people. Well, we were called colored then. His wife was bedridden and couldn't be left alone. I stayed with her six days a week for fourteen hours a day. I didn't have any certain time to leave. I left when he said, "You can go now." I made $1.25 a week. Sometimes I went to work on Sunday if he played golf. I had to go there to keep the wife because she couldn't be left alone. Domestic workers were just property. Back then White people, all they wanted, was a piece of toast, or a scrambled egg, or a soft boiled egg, and two strips of bacon and a cup of coffee. So they hired me and paid me a dollar and a quarter a week. I would give my older sister the dollar and a quarter. There were six of us in all. Times were hard, but food was cheap then and most of the time, by us being raised in the country, we knew how to survive. If we had only one onion, maybe three potatoes, maybe a tomato, we learned how to put all that together and make some soup. With no meat, just soup. And we. We just. I don't know. We just learned how to survive off of little and anything.

YS: I know it was hard for you to stop school.

SM: Yes, but I had to help out with the younger ones and then my sister Sarah died in 1940. I think she died of a heart attack or a massive stroke. I was about twenty at the time. It was devastating. I hope nobody has to go through that.. My sister Sarah worked herself to death. White people paid her five dollars a week and she worked long, long hours. After her death, I was responsible for the children and for my nephews.

YS: That was in Blakely. When did you move to Atlanta?

SM: I moved to Atlanta in 1935. My brother Seymour and his wife wanted me to come to Atlanta because I was old enough to cook and to clean. I took care of the house. Washing, cooking, cleaning. We lived in a small village called Plunketts Town. That's one mile east of Hapeville. You know where Ford and Kraft Foods is now? Well, that was our playground. It was just barren fields with sage bushes. And we also played where the Atlanta Hartsfield Airport is today. That was also all barren fields and sage bushes. Everybody met there and played ball. There were maybe thirty families in our village. We had two churches (one Methodist and one Baptist) and one school, Rosenwald Elementary. I had a great teacher in the third and fourth grades. Her name was Ida Prather. She taught us from the fourth to the seventh. Another teacher, Christine Lewis, taught first through third. I remember I had a supervisor at Rosenwald and she would tell us try not to be a zero. That's what she would say. "Always be a number." That stuck with me. I always wanted to get an education. During the time I was doing domestic work – I retired in 1982 – I would order books through the mail and I taught myself. What I learned from the time I was twenty, I taught myself. I got my education the best way I could.

YS: I want to go back to the time before your mother's death and ask you what did she teach you to value?

SM: All of my people were high moral people, you know. They believed in high morals. We couldn't go anywhere unless it was church or church activities. I had friends and I'd want to go sometimes with them and I remember once asking Mama if I could go and she said, "You see each other at school." She thought that was enough. I'll never forget this phrase she gave me: "Seldom visits make long friendships." That's what she would say and that's true today. My mother was a devout Christian and she was a high moral woman. We were mostly country people. Sharecroppers. My dad was a sharecropper, and they planted corn, cotton, peanuts, cane, vegetables. My mother raised all kind of livestock like cows. We had our own cows and hogs and chickens. As long as she lived on the farm, sharecropping, especially after my father passed away, the man whose plantation they lived on would work them year in and year out raising corn, cotton, peanuts, sweet potato. They would raise cane and in the fall of the year they would take the cane to a place they called the mill. That's where they would grind the cane. The workers would push the cane stalks through this thing, and it would squeeze juice out of the stalks. The juice would go down into a vat, which would hold maybe a hundred or more gallons of juice. The next day, the workers would transfer the juice from this vat to another vat that stood separate from the first vat the juice went in. They would build a fire under this vat and they would cook the juice all day and all night. They kept a fire underneath the vat, you know, and they changed shifts. One person would work, say, eight or nine hours and then that person would be replaced by somebody else. They had to constantly stir that juice so that it wouldn't burn at the bottom. And that's how they made syrup.

YS: Did you ever help them make the syrup?

SM: No, they wouldn't let me. I was about eight at the time and I was too young. They would let children come and stand about ten feet away because of danger of the fire or the hot syrup. Anybody under a teenager was not allowed to get near where they cooked the syrup. But we would always look. It was fascinating to see how juice would go from juice into syrup. Mmmm.

YS: Do you know anything about the landowners your family worked for?

SM: Well, all of them were White. I remember one particular landowner. His name was _____. We lived on his plantation and he wasn't very kind. Maybe because he was young, you know. His father had had a stroke or something and was homebound and he, as the oldest son, took over the whole plantation. He was young and he was eager to show his manhood and what have you. We lived on the _____ plantation for a couple of years and it was there that my mother died.

YS: Did anyone in your family tell you about experiences they had during slavery?

SM: My grandfather's first wife told us about two children being sold. One of the slave masters sold them. That's the way they did. They sometimes would sell the husband and then again they would sell the wife and children, you know, to another slave master. Even in another state. Before my mother died, her sister Flora Porter would tell us about slavery. She was a slave and she was seventeen when Lincoln freed the slaves. She was very wise and an interesting person. She told us about terrible things that happened to slaves in her day. She was a sister from my mother's daddy's first marriage. I remember her telling us stories. I was about five or six, and she would make us sit in a circle around her. She would always play Santa Claus and she would have candy, fruits of all kinds and raisins on the vine. You could get them whole on the vine and that's what she would have.

One time the slave owner's son tried to rape her. She told us a lot about when she was in slavery. She was seventeen when Lincoln freed the slaves. I forget her last name. We called her Aunt Flora, and she was a small statured person. She wasn't as big as I am now, and she told us about how when she got twelve or thirteen, the young son of the plantation owner would get on his horse and ride to the plantation to see who had daughters coming up. You know. Coming into ladyhood. Back then, the White owners would give their son permission to do that. To become a man by raping Black girls on the plantation. And she said they couldn't do anything about it because they were slaves, you know. If they tried to defend their daughters or their wives, they could disappear or be hanged. Back then, some of them didn't have wells in their yard and they had to go eight, nine or ten blocks to get water. There were streams in the fields and that's where the slaves would get their water. My aunt told me about this one time this young buck (they called them young bucks) this young buck caught her this particular evening on her way back from the stream with a bucket in each hand. He got off his horse and tried to force her in the cotton field, to accost her, you know. She told us about how back then the owners had what they called a whip about six feet long and they would ride along and stay on the horse and use the whip on people on the ground. She grabbed the whip. When he wouldn't turn it loose, she grabbed it harder and yanked him off his horse. When he saw he couldn't do what he wanted to do, he got back on his horse. He wanted to beat her, you know. He followed along side her. There was a stream of water they called The Branch and she thought he was gonna jump off his horse and try to drown her in the branch, but she got the best of him. She told us how the slaves were beaten. The men would be tied to a tree and beaten unmercifully by a strong White man.

The slaves could not own any livestock, but some of the brave and smart slaves found a way to own livestock and they outsmarted White men. They would go deep into the woods on the farm and build pig pens and that's where they would raise hogs unknown to the slave owner. Sometimes they would use small trees to make a fence. They would have one big tree for posts and then they would nail the small trees onto the upright posts. They even made a door and you could go in and out of the pens. Different slaves had certain days when they would take what they called slop to the pigs. It would be leftover food from the table. It could be a certain grass that the hogs would eat. It was called pussler. P-u-s-s-l-e-r. Pussler weed. The hogs loved pussler. Sometimes the slaves would put in little bitty nubbins. That's what they called it-nubbins. It would be little bitty and short. They would gather the nubbins and add it to the food. Then they would turn the hogs loose into the field and the hogs would eat and the slaves would throw little nubbins of corn and leftover cornbread in with the pussler. All they didn't eat today, they would throw into the slop. And that's how they raised hogs. That's what we were told. In November or December, they would kill the hogs and divide the meat among family and friends. They would hide the meat in false mattresses on their bed. Cotton or hay mattresses.

YS: Did you have to do any cooking when you were growing up?

SM: Yes. Well my mother started me cooking when I was about six years old. We had this beautiful iron stove, and we had iron pots to cook in. We'd have a pot of peas and some days we would have a pot of rice. A pot of rice would be about a two-pound bag for about eight people. I didn't have to clean. My job was to watch the food. Sometimes my mother got this middling and she would cut off a chunk about four inches wide and about ten inches long because it would be the whole rib of the hog. She would take half a pack of sweet potatoes, wash them and rub lard over the potatoes. They would cook and be smooth and be beautiful. They would go in the oven of the stove. On top of the stove, there might be a pot of collard greens or a pot of turnip greens, a pot of peas, a pot of rice. One of my sisters canned black berries in the summertime, and that's how we would use them to make cobbler.

And we had to wash our clothes and get them ready for Sunday. We went to Sunday school every Sunday. We had to walk what sometimes seemed like ten miles, but it probably wasn't that far.Probably only about three or four miles. Sometime we stayed over from Sunday school in the morning till after evening service was over. And then we had to walk home. Most times, we had what we could say was our time, when those of us who were big enough would go over to the next plantation. And then the next Sunday, they would come to our plantation and play with us. That's how we lived back then. We didn't have toys, we didn't have radios, we didn't have any electric lights. We had the old time lamps, you know, lamps with the kerosene. That's what we had.

YS: Did your mother ever tell you about how she and your father met and how he courted her?

SM: Yes, as a matter of fact, she did. She told me they eloped. [Laughter] You see, what I didn't tell you is that my father is full Cherokee and my mother was what we called Negro then. My father's people did not want him marrying a Negro woman and that's why they eloped. Before they eloped, they would meet at the courting rock. That's what they called it. That was where the young couples would meet, unbeknownst to parents. It was a huge rock between two plantations. It was where one plantation ended and another began. That's where my parents courted.

YS: Were there many Cherokees in Early County?

SM: Well, I don't know, but I know the Cherokees lived in Kola Mocha. I am not sure about how you spell it. I know it was a sacred area for the Cherokees because that's where their ancestors were buried. When we would get there, we had to walk around the sacred burial grounds. I need to check the exact name

YS: When you were growing up, were you aware that you were part Cherokee?

SM: Yes, my mother told me that my father was a real redskinned man and he was a big man, about six feet, one hundred sixty to one hundred eighty pounds and he had long hair that he wore in a pony tail. He was a very talented person. He made musical instruments, like flutes and horns, and he would make furniture. He was very talented. He was a pianist. I guess that's where I got my love for music. I inherited that from my father.

YS: Were there any other ways your Native American heritage influenced your life?

SM: Well, because my daddy was Indian, I knew so many things about herbs. See, the Indians never went to the doctors. They had plants you could eat if you got lost in the woods. You get something sharp. You take all the ground bark until you get to the white part that looks like satin. It has juice, a liquid. You can survive off that if you are lost in the woods. My mother showed me different herbs to cure any sickness. The Weeping Willow. That's where we get our aspirin. Right underneath the bark of the weeping willow tree, that was our aspirin. There were grasses called . . . I can't think of the name. When my mother was living, some days she would take us to walk in the woods and she would show us different herbs and trees.

YS: This is so interesting. You were telling me about your mother.

SM: She had an older sister from her father's first marriage and two brothers. There were just four of them. Aunt Flora, from the previous marriage, made five. My mother's younger sister was the last one of her father's second marriage. In fact, she was old enough to be the mother to her baby sister. People . . . I don't know . . . back then, you know, they skipped all those years and had children. Just like my older sisters and brothers. They are old enough to be my parents. I don't know why they skipped about ten or fifteen years and then they started a family all over again. Anyway, when we moved up around Sasser, my mother thought she was getting a better break on this last plantation that we lived on. And, in a way, it was because we had less work to do. But she passed away. In 1934. She passed away the next year. In March 1934.

YS: So, during what time period were you living in the town where your mother washed White people's clothes?

SM: The last part of 1933 and up until about February 1934. I was about twelve. But she did that work for only a few months. She moved every year. She moved every year after my father died. The White people on one plantation would take everything, and she would move to another plantation. My mother was sharecropping a two-horse farm one time. That's what you call it when you have so much land it takes two mules to plow the land and plant the crop. You'd work one mule to death on all that land. We were poor people and we didn't have that much, and my mother would work a whole year and the boss man would take everything because her boys were teenagers, not men. Back then, Black people didn't have a choice. We did what the White man said, whether we liked it or not. That's why my mother kept moving. She was working hard. She figured one year, if she could clear thirty, forty, maybe a hundred dollars out of all the crops of peanuts and corn and cotton . . . . You know, one owner would promise, "I'll treat you better. I'll give you more. Move to my plantation." So my mother would move from this plantation to that plantation and the new man did her the same way. So that's why we moved around so much, trying to make it better, you know, where the children would have something at least for Christmas. But it never happened. It never happened.

I told my mother when I was about eleven, I said, "When I grow up, when I get to be a big girl, I'm not going to live in the country. I'm not going to do like you do, just work for nothing year in and year out." This one particular Christmas, the stove gave out and my mother went up to Dawson, Georgia and bought the stove. And so my mother bought this stove. It couldn't have cost more than five or six dollars. Back then, when I was a child, everything was cheap because there wasn't any money, except for the White people, you know. They took everything away from Black people. They brought us here as slaves to this country over four hundred years ago, and we worked and we sweated and we toiled and we worked all of the fields the way my mother did. And at the end of the year, she didn't get a thing. Didn't even get a dollar and a quarter to buy her children candy for Christmas.

And so, I told my mother that I would never stay in the country. I said, "I'm leaving the country when I get to be a big girl, when I get grown." I said, "I'm going to leave the country. I'd rather walk the streets and beg than stay in the country and work myself to death." Even as a child, I saw the injustices that my mother went through and I just said that there's got to be something better. There's got to be something better. And I kept looking for it all through my life. I've worked as a domestic all of my life. I worked for the family that owns_____ drugstore. It was _____ drugstore when I was a child. Now it's ___, the big chain that's got drugstores all over Atlanta. I worked for a senator named _____ . I had to cook and clean house and do the washing and ironing and the grocery shopping for his family. You know, I did everything for them.

YS: Were you driving at the time?

SM: Not at that time. You did everything on foot in that day but, on the weekends, like on Saturday, his wife would take me in the car and we would go grocery shopping and vegetable shopping.

YS: Were they kind to you?

SM: Yes, they were really nice. And the mother of Judge _____ that I worked for lived in New York and she knew that I loved music. When she died, she left me a Spinnett piano. She left me that in her will. She was about eighty something and I used to get her up out of the bed and take her to the bathroom and I would bathe her. Wet bathe her. That means bathe her in the bed, not in the tub. Nobody else wanted to fool with her because she was semi bedridden and by me showing the kindness to her, she left me the piano. I worked for them for two years. I was about twenty years old when I worked there.

YS: Tell me how you met your husband.

MK: I was going with a friend to another friend's house to get some collard greens in Pittsburg, right here on McDaniel. This person grew collards, even in the winter time. And when I went there, I met my husband. He was there, too, buying collards. (laughing) He got my name and where I lived. In about two weeks, we started dating and then six weeks later we were married and the next year, we had our son Robert. My husband worked for the Southern Railroad. He was a track man on the railroad, and he worked a second job as a janitor at _____ Baptist Church, a White church, over on _____ Avenue here in Atlanta. On this day, they had some kind of banquet at the church and my husband ate potato salad and developed ptomaine poison, which is what killed him. My husband died the same year our son Robert was born. I met my second husband, John McKibben, when my son was nineteen months old. He was a pipe fitter's helper for the railroad.

YS: What did a pipe fitter do?

MK: They would repair the trains. You know trains were fueled by coal then and the lining of the engine was made of plates of steel. When the trains would go a distance, the coal would get so hot the steel would be damaged. The pipe fitter would have to replace the lining of the engine, and that's what my husband did. He passed away in 1955. He was a good man and he was a good father to my son Robert. My son had such a hard time because he was dropped by the doctor's helper and suffered a brain concussion.

YS: Dropped? In the hospital?

SM: Yes. He was dropped by the doctor's helper at _____, a Black infirmary here in Atlanta. He bled inside for about two weeks, which affected the motor part of his brain. The doctors said he would be a vegetable. Wouldn't talk or walk. But he began to walk when he was about three years old. What happened when Robert was born on a Thursday morning at seven . . . what happened was that the infirmary was using young ladies to help out. I don't know whether they were college students or what. When Robert was born, Dr. _____ handed him to the new girl and said, "Take the baby, clean him and dress him." I didn't know anything until the girl told me later what had happened. She asked me first, "Did they tell you I dropped the baby?" I didn't know. Nobody told me. Nobody told me. She had never seen a newborn and Robert was moving and squirming and she said, "He just slipped out of my hand." They fired her, but she came to my room to tell me what had happened and to beg my pardon. They never told me. They never told me what had happened to my baby. They took Robert to Grady and Grady told them they'd better get out of there. "You can be sued and we are not going to be a part of it." We hired a lawyer and the hospital hustled this girl out of the city and she was nowhere to be found. They searched for months and months, but they couldn't find her. And then Dr. _____ suddenly closed the hospital, which was called _____ Infirmary. She had three hospitals. One in Atlanta and one in some part of Florida and one in New York. She closed all three within three weeks' time. She went underground like a mole. Once a month, Robert had seizures and the doctors said operating would be a fifty-fifty chance of dying or being completely paralyzed. I decided not to let him have the operation. Robert lived to be forty-five years old, but it was like he had cerebral palsy.

YS: Throughout all of your challenges, you have been determined to get an education.

SM: Yes. I started taking GED classes at Dean Rusk Night School. That was in October 1997. And then I took some classes here at John O. Chiles and in 1998 I went to sponsored free GED classes at Atlanta Metropolitan College. I finally did it!! I received my degree on April 17, 1999. And I was granted a $500.00 HOPE scholarship. I am now enrolled in college at Metropolitan College. I was always determined to try.

YS: The theme of survival seems to be in all of your stories. How did you find the strength to survive, to go on in spite of all you went through?

SM: Well, I think, one thing, I think it was our belief in God. We as a people believed that God loved all people. I never did believe that the White people were any better than we were. I felt like they had better, more advantages than I had, but I always loved myself. You got to love yourself and if you can love somebody that you know hates you, then you know you're on the right road, when you can do that. And when you can love people that throw rocks at you and call out, "Hey nigger." Say back, "Hey, White person, I love you." See, they can't stand that and so that's what I say to the children. I noticed there was a lot of rigamarole over at Emory about "oh, he called me a nigger. I saw nigger slurring and stuff on my dorm door." So what? Whenever somebody insults you, don't you insult them back. You just say, "God Bless you. God bless you." I was just born like that. And when I was a young girl working in different homes and called nigger, I said, "Who you talking about. Old beautiful precious sweet me?" You gotta have more sense than the people talking bad to you. If somebody is trying to belittle you, it's something wrong with them, see. See, you gotta, you gotta have enough God in you to be merciful towards that person, because it's like Jesus said on the cross, "Father, forgive them. They don't know what they're doing." Because somebody called you a nigger, you don't have to retaliate and say, "You old cracker." No, you don't do that. You try to live in a way where that person can learn something from you. Like Dr. King. What a mighty man! What a mighty man! He was beaten, he was ridiculed, but did he let that bother him? No. And look today! Did you see the King Memorial Day the other day? On Monday? I was just sitting here with tears just rolling down my cheeks. Tears of joy! I said, "You go, Dr. King. You go." That is the way. That's what we have to do when we are persecuted. You're going to be persecuted, but you have to let that person know that, hey, you're not worth me spending any of my precious time hating. And you have to try to live a life where people can see God in you and they may not tell you this, but they see God in you.

YS: What makes you sad?

SM: Abuse of little children and older people and to see the young Black people throwing away their lives. When I think about what I went through as a youngster, I want them to have a chance at a better life. I want to say to them, "I'm passing the torch to you. Take it and run with it." They don't know what that means. All this energy wasted. I now have a chance to go to school and I took advantage of it.

YS: What makes you happy?

SM: When I wake up in the morning and realize I have another chance at life. I have my health, strength and pretty good mind to do things that I like to do and most of all to please God.

YS: Do you have a role model?

SM: I saw a short clip on Mary McCloud Bethune. Oh, but she was a great leader. All the things she did! And then there was Dr. Carter and Booker T. Washington. All the great educators. I would just wish that I could be like those people. Have a dream and not let it go.

YS: But that's what you did, Mrs. McKibben. You had a dream and you didn't let it go. That's why you have a HOPE scholarship.

SM: Well, yes. In spite of all that I had gone through, I had a dream that someday my day would come and that God would open up a way for my dream to be materialized. In 1997, it materialized and that's when Atlanta Housing and Metropolitan College co-sponsored classes. I wanted to enroll. I passed all seven courses and I had to deal with being laughed at and being called a dummy at my age: "What can you learn?" And I passed with flying colors, at the top of my class. I was selected to bring to the rest of the class an inspiring message and what I said was that you can do it if you put your mind on it. If you can take what the world hands and try to fashion something good out of it and if you know that others don't understand, just keeping on doing what you should. In other words, just do it.

I've had such a hard time, but I know I am blessed. I believe I was a chosen vessel before I was born. The hard experiences I had, God must have had me in training to make me wiser, more loving and kinder than I would have been if I hadn't been a chosen vessel. I cried so many times, thinking about how hard it's been. I've cried about sixty years of my eighty years. I was like Jeremiah the crying prophet. I would say, "Why me?" And then God began to speak to my spirit. And I say now, "Thank you for choosing me. Thank you for letting me be worthy."

YS: What has this experience meant to you?

SM: Oh, it's been fantastic, inspiring, exciting, and I'm grateful to have known such wonderful beautiful women of wisdom. And now I want to tell the whole story. You know, I wonder if I had had a chance, if I had had opportunities, I don't know what I could have done. I might have become a summa cum laude. I could have been great.

MRS. THELMA WILLIAMS MOORE

Atlanta, Georgia
Nurse, Domestic and "Griot of Blandtown"

Let me tell you about the fire in Blandtown. It must have been in March. Let's see now. It was sometime in the thirties. It was real windy and the fire swept all of the houses . It was on one side and then it crossed over to the other side. The fire burned our church and it burned up all the houses on the street. . . . The Salvation Army came out and gave people clothes and other things and people went to live with relatives across the bridge.

YS: O.K. Aunt Thelma. It's Feb 20, 2002, and you and I are sitting in your living room for the first interview for the Spelman project. I'm very happy that we are doing this because you have such interesting stories. You are really a gifted storyteller.

TM: Really? [Laughing] Well, I wrote down some things for you, so I wouldn't forget.

YS: Thank you, Aunt Thelma. This is good, but I want you to tell me your stories. I know you always talk about Blandtown. Tell me whatever you want to share. You were born in Blandtown?

TM: Yes. I was born by a midwife. Granny Everhart. That was her name. I didn't have a birth certificate and when I went to New York and needed one for my job, my sister Louise went to work for a White lady in order to get a birth certificate for me.

YS: How did she go about doing that?

TM: Well, she went down to City Hall. Blacks didn't work down there then, except as janitors who cleaned the bathrooms. Blacks didn't work there. That's where Louise went to get a birth certificate for me. The lady she worked for made one for me.

YS: How many sisters do you have?

TM: Two: Emma Lena and Louise. My mother died when I was nine years old. She died on February 20th in 1936. Her name was Sarah Williams. My father's name was Sedrick Williams.

YS: Today is February 20th, the anniversary of your mother's death.

TM: I know. I always remember that she died on February 20 in 1936.

YS: How old were you?

TM: I was nine. My father married my stepmother in May of the year my mother died. My father worked for the railroad to be there with us. I wanted him to marry because he couldn't braid our hair right and I got tired of having him give me castor oil every Saturday.

YS: Why would he give you castor oil every Saturday?

*Dr. Anderson, a Spelman graduate, is Mrs. Moore's niece. The stepmother whom Mrs. Moore talks about with great affection is Dr. Anderson's grandmother.

TM: He said that little girls needed cleaning out. We would go about four houses down to Ms. Ealey's house and she had a store attached to her house where you could buy candy and other things. That's where we would buy the castor oil. My daddy would give us a nickel to go to Miss Ealey's to buy a bottle of castor oil every Saturday morning. Those days, the streets weren't paved then. There were rocks all around. I would throw the bottle down and break it.

YS: You would deliberately do that?

TM: Yes. And he would say, "Here is another nickel and you better not throw that down 'cause I know what you did." I 'd go back and get it and I'd be just a-crying. When I got back to the house, he'd pour it in coffee. That's why I didn't drink coffee until I was grown and married. Makes me think about castor oil. Oh Lord! I was glad when he married Miss Lucia Mae, but I didn't think she would be nice on account of Cinderella and her stepmother. You had that book, didn't you?

YS: Yes. So you knew your stepmother before your father married her?

TM: They all went to the same church. She was real nice. I encouraged him to marry her because he couldn't braid our hair right and I got tired of having castor oil every Saturday. Oh Lord! People believed in castor oil and in Black Draught and in Rabbit Tobacco. It came from a gray bush that grew out in the woods and the people would get it and boil it and that would be rabbit tobacco. If they hadn't cut the woods down, people would still be using rabbit tobacco.

YS: Tell me about the foods you ate in Blandtown.

TM: Well, our standard was fish and grits on Sunday. During the week, fried green tomatoes. People would get the tomatoes from their garden when they were green and they would fry the tomatoes and that would be just like steak to us.

YS: I want to go back to the castor oil and ask you if your stepmother gave it to you.

TM: Not every Saturday. Just when we needed it. I have so much regard for her because she was really nice to us growing up. She was beautiful. I was pleased with her. When I started going to work, I would buy her nice things. I even gave her a trip to New York. I was nice to her because she was nice to us. She died on August 29th 2002. My father preceded her in death. He died on January 18, 1985.

YS: Do you remember your biological mother?

TM: Yes, I remember my mother. She died from pneumonia. She died that Thursday and they had her funeral that Sunday. They used to have funerals on Sunday back then, but I guess they worked the grave diggers to death, everybody waiting to be buried on Sunday. [laughter] If you died on Monday, they would hold you out until Sunday. Now they did that! You didn't have funerals on a Saturday or a Monday or a Tuesday, you know. Just on Sunday! Back then, people didn't have money, so folks were buried for $250.00. Back then, we didn't have all these flowers. Some people would get crepe paper and make flowers. That's what they would do. And at the funeral, one man would stand at the foot of the casket and another man at the head of the casket, and they would have a hat open. When people passed by to view the body, they would put money in the hats for the family. People didn't buy a lot of flowers because they didn't have any money.

YS: What kind of jobs did Black women have then? This would have been in the mid-thirties and early forties.

TM: They could work in the Black banks but not the White banks here. No kind of way. You could work in the Black banks but you had to be light skinned. The only thing colored girls could do was to work in doctor's offices, in the Scripto Pencil factory, or at Atlanta Life Insurance Co. But you had to know somebody, really know somebody to work at Atlanta Life. It was really hard for Black girls. After I grew up, I did a lot of day work and I made a dollar and a half a day.

YS: What kind of work would you do?

TM: I would baby sit and I would clean house for the White people around The Pond.(Pointing to the tape recorder) Is that thing on?

YS: Aunt Thelma, I am going to hide the recorder so that it won't distract you. We are going to pretend that the recorder is not even here. So you said White people lived by the pond? What pond?

TM: By the Water Works over there on Howell Mill Road. We called it The Pond. I would work over there during the summer, and I would work over there on Saturday. I would cook and baby sit. That was about all that you could do to make a little extra money. White people lived over there. We had two towns back then: Factory Town and Blandtown. Factory Town was over on Marietta Street. Blandtown was at Huff Road and Howell Mill Road. White people lived in Factory Town and Black people lived in Blandtown. All the houses in Factory town were painted white. Did I tell you that Black men didn't work in the factories?

YS: I have to get a map and locate Factory Town and Blandtown. I guess they weren't that far apart.

TM: Huff Road and Howell Mill. That's where Blandtown was. We were between two White communities. Nothing is there now, but it used to be houses there.

YS: When did people start selling their houses and moving away from Blandtown?

TM: Let's see. I went to New York in 1953 and when I came back in _____, it had happened. They called it urban renewal.

YS: I understand why Factory Town was named Factory Town. That's where the factories were located. But why Blandtown?

TM: Blandtown was named after a Black man named Mr. Bland. The White people gave him that land and I don't know how he lost it. Cut that thing off so I can tell you something.

[Recorder is turned off]

TM: Let me tell you about The Hollow in Blandtown. It was a narrow street about three blocks long and it was between the railroad. A lot of things happened in The Hollow. A man took a can of five cents sardines off the shelf and didn't pay the storeowner. Got smart with him. And the storeowner shot the man dead. He left and moved to Chicago before the police could get him. The Hollow was something else.

YS: You'll have to tell me more about things that happened in The Hollow. I want to know about The Pond. You said that was at the Water Works over on Howell Mill Road?

TM: Yes. We would go to the store over there and the White boys would rock you out if they didn't know your parents. It was terrible. They would rock you out.

YS: Rock you out? What does that mean?

TM: They would throw rocks at you. You couldn't go down there unless you had somebody with you. If they recognized whose child you were, they wouldn't bother you. But if they didn't know you, they'd rock you all the way home. They would.

YS: Were you rocked?

TM: Plenty times. Plenty times. Let me tell you about the fire in Blandtown. The lady who caused the fire felt real bad about it. The fire burned our church and it burned up all the houses on the street. On both sides of the street. The Salvation Army came out and gave people clothes and other things and people went to live with relatives across the bridge until the houses were built back and churches, too.

YS: How did the fire start?

TM: I think the lady just left a pot on the stove or something to that effect. She moved to Cincinnati later on because she was so ashamed. Everybody was pointing at her because she caused the fire. It was very windy. One Sunday after church. It must have been in March. I have been intending to find out what year that was. I know I was in elementary school. Let's see now. I finished Washington High School in 1944. So it was in the thirties sometime. It was real windy and the fire swept all of the houses. It was on one side and then it crossed over to the other side.   That was a sad time. Everybody united with each other and everything.

YS: Was there always a lot of uniting in Blandtown?

TM: Oh yes. Everyone was so nice. We had a lot of mamas in Blandtown. If we did something wrong, the women in the community could whip us and somebody at the church could whip us, too. And everybody went to church every Sunday: Sunday school, morning service, BYPU, and night service. We had to go to church. No one would stay home. Somebody was over here the other night talking about how it used to be, how we've lost a lot. Those were happy times.

YS: What made them happy times?

TM: Because we were like a family and a little money could get a lot. We didn't make much money, but it would go a long way. There was a grocery store on Howell Mill Road and we could get so much for a dollar then. We could buy black-eyed peas. We could buy ten cents worth. If you smoked, you could buy cigarettes for fifteen cents a pack and gas cost about eighteen cents a gallon. We could rent a house for twenty dollars a month, get a dress for $1.98 and shoes for that same price. Back then, you could do a lot with five dollars. As things come to me, I write them down to tell you about it.

YS: Blandtown was a small community.

TM: I don't know the population. If I could get the minutes from the meetings, I could tell you just about how many people lived in Blandtown then. We raised our own hogs and livestock in Blandtown. We had outdoor toilets and we didn't think anything about it. And we used kerosene lamps until around the forties. And we didn't have vacuum cleaners like you have now. We would take our rugs outside and we would beat the rugs. That's how we got the dust out. We didn't have vacuum cleaners. I think we had four telephones in Blandtown. You had to go to somebody's house to use the phone. One man made money by letting us use his phone. I think he would charge five cents a call. When you finished using his phone and you said "thank you," he would tell you, "Thank you won't pay the phone bill." [laughter] We didn't have a radio. I remember one time we walked across the bridge to go to somebody's house to hear a Joe Louis fight. By the time we got there, the fight was over. You know, he knocked them out real quick. [Laughing]

YS: You remember so much about Blandtown.

TM: Yes. I loved Blandtown. I just loved Blandtown. I remember a White man would come to Blandtown to collect money on our policies. We called him the policy man. He would sit around in houses in Blandtown and the people would give him cake, you know. And the White man who came to collect rent, people in Blandtown really took care of him. He would come every Saturday and every time he came, he would get so drunk some men in Blandtown would carry him home. They would keep him from being robbed.

YS: How did your father respond to White men who came to Blandtown?

TM: Let me tell you this about my daddy. He was sitting on the porch one day and a White man came up to the porch and said, "Hello, John. Can you tell me how to get to Porter Fertilizer?" And my daddy said, "How you know my name is John?" And the White man said, "I just guessed it." And my daddy said, "Well, you just guess how to get to the fertilizer store." [Laughing] White people always came into Blandtown for one reason or another. Did I tell you about the artists? The White people who came to draw us?. They would come in the summer and they would sit on the hill, drawing us. They must have been studying at some art school in the city. I don't know, but they would draw us and it seemed like they would draw the ugliest of houses. You know what we would do? We would run into the house so that they couldn't finish their drawing. Yes, we would do that.

YS: You felt safe in Blandtown.

TM: Oh yes because everybody was colored there. Everybody. So you didn't have to worry about White people. Now, three White families lived further down the street, about three blocks down the street. My mother sewed for one particular White girl and when she got around twelve years ago, the family moved away. That happened, you know. We could play together until we got a little older.

YS: Tell me about your experiences with Jim Crow.

TM: Well, they wouldn't let you sit on the bus with them. We had street cars, you know. Trolleys. The Whites started off to the front and we would sit on the back. The White kids would come on back to the back, and some of the conducts of the bus would make us get up and let the White kids sit down. We had to stand up. And sometimes when we got off the bus, the White boys would kick us off and even throw eggs at us. When that happened to my sister one day, she pulled that White boy and they fought. The conductor called the police and my sister was locked up. She didn't stay, but she was locked up for fighting that White boy.

YS: Wow! Did White boys bully you everyday?

TM: No, not every day. But that is why we didn't like to ride the trolley. It cost five cents. My father would give us ten cents, five to go and five to come back. That was when we went to Washington High in the forties. I graduated in 1944. A lot of times we would walk back home so that we could use the nickel to buy candy and Mr. _____ used to ride along side us in his car. He was the principal at Washington High School. He would ride in the car along side of us to protect us from the White boys so that nothing would happen to us.

YS: Tell me about your job at the hotel and your father's reaction.

TM: Yes. My first job was working at Hotel Biltmore. I was a chambermaid. I liked that, but I couldn't keep the job because my father said that I got home too late.

YS: I know he had strict rules for you. When did you start dating?

TM: I'll tell you. I was about seventeen or eighteen years old before I started dating. You know what we did so that the boys could come to our house? We would sell candy. They would come to our house to buy candy. [Laughing] It was wonderful.

YS: Did you go to dances?

TM: Oh God, no! They wouldn't let us go to dances. You know the best time of all in Blandtown was Christmas. That was the best time of all. We would go out in the woods and cut down our tree. We would put the tree up Christmas Eve night. We didn't have lights like they do now. We made our own ornaments in school. Rings and stuff. We had lights in the house, but they didn't have any electric lights to put on trees then. That was much later. For Christmas we would get a skull cap, an apple and orange and some raisins. We would be very happy. Later on, we would get a doll. And one of the dolls was made of paper and if it got wet, it would parch up.

YS: Was it a Black doll or a White doll?

TM: White. Black came in later years. Black dolls. We didn't have Black dolls then.

YS: How did you feel about playing with White dolls?

TM: Fine. Fine about that. Much later, much later they came out with the Black dolls. Much later, much much later. We always had a little White doll. I didn't know Santa Claus wasn't real until I was about ten or eleven years old. You know when I told my daddy I didn't believe in Santa Claus, he was upset with me and that year, I didn't get anything for Christmas.

YS: Did you ever travel away from Blandtown?

TM: Oh, yes. See, my father worked for the railroad and he got us passes. We did a lot of traveling. On the weekends, we would ride to Alabama. Sometimes my mother would take us to Washington. After my mother died and my father married my stepmother, we would board the train on Saturday night and go up to Abbeyville, South Carolina. That's where her people are. That is where I know all of those people who grew up there. They all know me and my father. We have a Blandtown reunion every year. See, we just started having family reunions in the last ten years. We would have them every summer. We have a lot of memories there, too. But it is nothing out there now mostly but factories. Everything changed when the factories came.

YS: Where did the people go?

TM: They died out. Most of the people died out or moved to other parts of town. If I could get the minutes from the meetings, I could tell you just about everything you want to know.

What I want is for my niece to come over here and put it like it is supposed to be and paragraph it right.

YS: We can do that later. You said everyone went to church.

TM: Oh, yes. We stayed in church all day. And there was one church near our house and the minister would be preaching and singing so loud, you thought the church was full, but it would be just him and his wife and children. [laughing] We called it Mr. Irvin's Church.

YS: Tell me about schools in Blandtown.

TM: When I was going to school, we would use second hand books from the White schools. That was when I was in grammar school. It was rare that we would get a new book. I went to Washington High School and I graduated in 1944. When we graduated from high school, these are some of the gifts that we would get--a box of stationary, a diary, a box of handkerchiefs, stuff like that. We didn't get big things for graduation. The church would give us something. We didn't get much. That was my most memorable time. When I graduated from Washington High School. When we graduated, we made our little White dresses in home economics class. Yes, that was my most memorable time I remember. When I was going to grammar school, you know they wouldn't let Blacks go to Grant Park. You couldn't go there. The school would take us there once a year. That is what we would do. The grammar school teacher would take us there in a bus. Take the whole class on the bus once a year. That is the only time Blacks could go. We couldn't go to the zoo everyday like they do now.

YS: So what about department stores?

TM: Oh yeah, we didn't eat with the White people. They had a lunch counter downstairs in the basement. I don't believe Davidson's had one, but there were white and colored signs and separate restrooms. They were all in the basement.

YS: Tell me about some the rules for girls growing up in Blandtown.

TM: Oh yes. See, when I was growing, we didn't have cars. We walked with the bus. Girls didn't have cars. Nobody had cars. No young girl had a car. I remember one girl had a car. Her father owned a funeral home. I remember when she graduated from high school, her father gave her a car. There was a preacher named Reverend ____ and he had two daughters and the family thought those girls were better than us. We played together when we were little, but when we grew up, the mother would tell them to learn to class themselves.

YS: Learn to class themselves. I never heard that expression before.

TM: Yes. Learn to class yourself. You know, stay with people in your own class. I remember something else girls didn't do. They didn't live away from home until they got married. Now girls are living in their own apartments. But back then, girls didn't live away from home. I was twenty-seven when I went to New York, when my husband and I got married in my uncle's house.

YS: So what other kinds of things were girls not supposed to do? You said, drive cars, live away from home...

TM: We didn't have cars. I didn't say we couldn't drive cars. I said we didn't have cars. Girls and boys . Neither one had cars except for the wealthy people and even they wouldn't drive cars to school like ya'll do now. And one other thing: girls wouldn't live with boys and marry after.

YS: What about girls getting pregnant out of wedlock?

TM: You couldn't play with that girl. People called her spoiled until she got married. The minister would turn her out of church, but the parents didn't do that. They stood by her.

YS: She was put out of church because she was pregnant?

TM: Yes. And then she would have to join over.

YS: Well, what about the boys? You can't get pregnant by yourself.

TM: I know it, but that is what was done to the girls, not the boys. The girl stayed with her parents until she got married and then, if she got married, she could come back and join the church. That's how it was then. And girls having apartments? That was unheard of. I don't know if that was good or bad. You didn't have the money to go and get an apartment. You really didn't have the money. As things come to me, I write them down to tell you about it.

YS: You have told me about things you did for hygiene.

TM: Soda under our arms. We didn't buy cosmetics. Never used cosmetics.

YS: So how did you make up?

TM: We didn't make up. We would put Vaseline on our lips.

YS: What kind of beauty things did you do?

TM: We used Vaseline for everything. We used to straighten your hair out on a little stove. That is the way we got our hair straightened. The lady whose husband charged us five cents to use the phone? She straightened our hair for years. She had a shop over there on Mitchell Street, but we would go over to her house and get our hair fixed. But you didn't get that done until you were working and had your own money. Before then, you did your hair at home.

YS: Tell me about your husband, Aunt Thelma, and how the two of you met.

TM: We were childhood sweethearts. Yes, George was my childhood sweetheart. He came to New York and we got married in New York in 19____. He worked at the Waldorf Astoria. He was the second cook. I went to school for nursing and then I started working in the hospital so if I got sick on the job, I would be right there. I worked the evening shift and found out that the evening shift was better for me because I had asthma real bad, and if I had an attack early in the morning, then I could get better and go to work. That is the reason why I took the second and third shift I liked working in the hospital. Oh I did. I finished my course there and then worked with the babies. I really enjoyed that. I came out on disability and then I moved here. George died in 1976 and I moved back in 1990, after I retired. I came out before then. I believe it was '89. I came out on disability. Then I retired and moved home. I moved back to Atlanta and stayed with my mother and then I found this place. I have been here in this house for eleven years.

YS: I know how much you love caring for patients.

TM: Yes. I just love it. I just love it. And I love children. I worked in the newborn nursery for thirty years in New York. I would sit with patients because I went through the training of that. But they call that CMA down here. Here you got to have the training and you got to have a piece of paper. And I don't have the paper. I take good care of my patients.

YS: Is there one who stands out in your memory as most special to you?

TM: Yes. The one who was my favorite was a Black lady up in New York. They had to amputate her feet because a rat bit her in the tenement and the bite set up blood poisoning. She was a sweet lady. Must have been about eighty or ninety. So sweet. Ms. _____ I never will forget her." Now when I went to New York, they were just about as segregated as we are here. I went there in 1953. Some of the White people thought they were better than you. Not all of them, but some of them. You know my niece came to visit me once and she was downstairs washing and a White woman asked her, "Are you looking for work?" My niece told the woman, "No, but I am looking for someone to work for my aunt. She lives here in the building." [laughter] You know, I think White people think we were born to take care of them.

YS: I never asked you why you moved to New York or if you liked living there?

TM: Well, really, it was easier to get jobs there. That's why I left Blandtown. It was easier to get a job in New York. At first I worked at the telephone company and then, after I went to school, I started working at the hospital. My asthma was better in New York. I don't know why, but it was better in New York. I liked living there because I didn't need a car. I could get on the train and get off and I would be right at Queens General Hospital, where I worked. And the other thing I liked about New York was going to plays. We would go on Saturdays with a church group. I enjoyed that. But New York had problems too, you know, with the way White people saw Black people.

YS: Tell me about some of your experiences working for White people in Atlanta or in New York. It doesn't matter.

TM: Some were nice. But I don't care how much nice they can be to you, they are never going to invite you to their house. Like _____ here in Atlanta. She is a millionaire, and she gives me all kinds of things. She gave me that Fendi bag over there and that cost four hundred dollars. If she is on the phone when I get there, when I ring the bell, I hear her telling who ever she is talking to, " I have got to let my maid in." She will tell me, "Thelma, Miss _____ is coming over." And she wants me to call her son "Mister _____." Her son and his wife are young enough to be my children. I won't do it.

YS: So what does she call you?

TM: She calls me Thelma.

YS: And what do the children call you?

TM: They call me Thelma, too. If I answer the phone and she is not there, I say, "Ms. " _____ 'residence, Thelma speaking." I let them know that it is Thelma, but I don't say anything about a maid. She would love for me to say that, but I won't. No, I won't say that.

YS: How much does she pay you?

TM: Fourteen dollars an hour.

YS: You always talk about how different kids are from the way you were when you were in Blandtown!

TM: Oh Lord! Back then, you wouldn't talk back to a grown person. You wouldn't talk back to anybody because if you did, they would whip you and then call your mother and you would get another whipping when you got home. No, no, no. The way these kids are acting today. No! When you sit on the bus, they talk about each other's mothers like dogs.

YS: You all never did that. You never told "yo mamma" jokes?

TM: No. NO NO!! When we were coming up, we were breast fed. Now all of this milk and stuff they are giving children, its not even milk. It's something they just make up. That is the reason children are like they are. They are crazy. That is why they are crazy. I believe it.

YS: How did you feel when the Civil Rights Movement started?

TM: Well, I really wasn't living here when Martin Luther King did all of that. I felt good about what was happening. And it was time for us to be treated right. It was time. But you know when they integrated the police department in Atlanta, Black men couldn't change uniforms downtown with the White policemen. And something else. Black policemen couldn't arrest White people. They had to call in for help and hold the person until White policemen came.

YS: Really? I didn't know that.

TM: I have to say that Black people don't always treat each other right. I went down there to Bankhead to pick up my medication and the lady said, "You don't have your old age card." I told her, "No, I didn't bring it. But you can pull it up on a computer because I have been here before." She said, " I am sorry. We just won' t be able to do that." I said, "Look I don't want to be here no more than you want me here." I looked at her in the eye. I said, " I am old enough to be your mother, or maybe grandmother, and I am gonna get my medicine before I leave here today. Somebody is going to give me my medicine." So she went to the back and got that number off of that card. Once, I went down to Grady to get some insulin, and the doctor didn't put needles in there. I said to the lady, a Black lady, I said, "Listen, I need a few needles. How am I going to take this insulin without needles?" She said, "Well, the doctor will have to put it on there!!" Lord have mercy me. I wanted to pull her from behind the counter so bad and tear her up. You know how Blacks can do you sometime. A White man working there put the needles in my bag. Now isn't that something? Sometimes Black people just don't treat each other right.

YS: What has been the best time in your life?

TM: I have always had a good life. I am trying to think of the best time. Let me think. I have always had a good time.

YS: What has been the hardest time?

TM: I think the hardest time is now. Yes, the hardest time is now because I have all of these aches and pains and then I have to go and look for a doctor. It wasn't until the later part of my years that I started getting sick. I have asthma. I am trying to think the best time. What was the best time of my life? I know one of the best things was when I finished high school. I was so happy. I am really going to have to think about that. What was your best time?

YS: In my life?

TM: You have beautiful teeth. Are they all yours?

YS: I had braces. Remember those braces I wore for years? The best time of my life? I don' t know. I feel that I am on the verge of it.

TM: I can't think of the best time. I haven't had any really bad times.

YS: Do you like being by yourself?

TM: NO! I don't like being by myself. It is very boring. I read a lot and I write a lot and when you are lonely, you do things that you shouldn't do. Like, if somebody was here, you get up and make breakfast. Being by myself, I get up and make breakfast around twelve or one o'clock. It gets very lonely at times. But I have lived alone a long time because George died in 1976. I don't like living alone.

YS: What makes you sad?

TM: Young men having to go to war. Leaving their families and going to war.

YS: What makes you happy?

TM: Taking care of people. I am really happy when I do that. I love people. I don't want them to be sick, but I like caring for people. They were so kind to me when I was sick with asthma, growing up, and I want to be kind to others. I love caring for people. That makes me real happy.

YS: What has this experience meant to you?

TM: Oh, it's been wonderful, just wonderful.

MRS. MARY TIGNER

Cobb County, Georgia
Caterer and Entrepreneur

They lynched a Negro in that park [in] Marietta, Georgia. After the lynching, birds came to that park by the thousands. That park is still there. It has seats and in the center is a water fountain, a beautiful fountain. Blacks couldn't sit in the park back then. My grandmother told me that when they lynched that man in the park, that Black man, the birds came by the thousands. That was the curse of the park. Nobody could sit there.

YS: We want to start with some basic questions about your childhood--where you were born and how many children were in your family and . . .

MT: Well, I was born in Cobb County in Marietta, Georgia, and in those days there wasn't such a thing as going to the hospital. You were born at home with midwives. Rich White people had hospitals. I was born in 1917. I didn't have brothers and sisters. I was an only child. And I was mischievous and getting into things, but I didn't have to get many spankings. I can tell you that and I didn't want my daddy to ever get on me. He got on me once and I think I was good from then on.

YS: What happened to cause you to get a spanking and how old were you at the time?

MT: I was about seven years old. It's been many years, but I haven't forgotten it. My grandmother told him he wasn't going to ever hit me again. She did the whipping. My grandmother was my savior. But I didn't get many whippings. I didn't have any brothers or sisters. I was an only child.

YS: Tell us what you remember about Marietta when you were growing up.

MT: When I was growing up, it was White and Black together. We lived right next door. It was that way all over Marietta. We all lived in the same area. Of course, we didn't live where the rich people lived. It was the poor Whites and the Negroes living together.

YS: That's really surprising. In Cobb County?

MT: Our house was on the corner of Henderson and Wright, and White people lived on the next corner. On Wright Street. Their yard came to our fence. Our front yard and their front yard met. That was just the way we lived. You know, I think about that a lot. When I was growing up, White and Black used to mingle. It didn't make any difference to me because I was a child. When you're a child you don't know anything about the hate. That comes in when you get grown. White children love Blacks. They hug them and kiss them. But when they grow up, their parents tell them they're not supposed to do that.

YS: What did your parents teach you about White people?

MT: My grandmother was a young slave, and she lived to be ninety-seven years old and she belonged to Christian people and they didn't have any beating on their plantation, but my grandmother said she used to go to the fence and look over at the other plantation and see them beating slaves. They used to beat the blood out of the slaves. Then they would put salt in the wounds after they beat the blood out. You know, how bad that felt! When you get a little cut on your finger while you're cooking and then get salt in it . Well, now, what do you think about a back that's been beaten. And got welts on it. You pour salt on it.

My grandmother saw that with her own eyes. But her people were Christians and they didn't beat their slaves. You know, there are always some Christian people. The world wouldn't stand if there wasn't. So, my grandmother said the people who owned her had plenty slaves, but they didn't mistreat them. Everybody during slavery wasn't mean. But, then, if everyone had been a Christian, there wouldn't have been slavery.

YS: Did your grandmother tell you anything about the treatment of Black women during slavery?

MT: Well, she told me they would mate the man and the woman. Let the woman be a fast breeder and that's all she had to do. Have babies. That meant the more slaves they would have to sell.

YS: Was she your mother's mother or your father's mother?

MT: This was my father's mother. My maternal grandmother died when I was three years old.

YS: Could your grandmother read and write?

MT: Yes. She could because the White people had a daughter the same age and that daughter would tell my grandmother, "Come on Jane, it's time for the books." So, yes, my grandmother was a good reader and good on arithmetic, too. My grandmother's name was Janie Smith Jones. She lived to be ninety-seven.

YS: Tell us about other members of your family. Did they live in Marietta? In Cobb County?

MT: All of my mother's people lived in Chicago Illinois. Well, my daddy was the baby. My grandmother had Uncle Jimmy, Uncle Willie, Aunt Blondie, Aunt Fanny and Uncle Dave. She had two sisters and two brothers. I didn't know but one. I knew the two sisters because when I was little, my daddy used to take us to see them. They lived in Powder Springs, Georgia. That was a country town at the time, but it's grown up now. I didn't know anything about her brothers until I was nine or ten years old.

YS: Where was the plantation your grandmother lived on? Did she tell you?

MT: No, I don't know where the plantation was. I don't know because when she told me these stories I was a child. But I thank God for my mind. I'm glad you're getting it all.

YS: You are doing fine. You have a good memory. Tell us about your mother.

MT: I didn't really know my mother. She died when I was two and I was eighteen when my father died. My dad moved on back home with his mother. She raised me up. When she got too old, I took over everything. I worked and took care of her. I married before she died. That was her prayer. Every day she'd say, "I could die happy if I could see you married to some good man that wouldn't mistreat you." The Lord gave her wish because I couldn't have found a better man. We may have had disagreements sometimes, but no fussing, never. My husband was a Christian man. That makes a difference. He became a deacon of our church.

YS: How long did you date before marrying?

MT: We dated about five years. I hated him when I met him. That's the funniest thing. Honey, I couldn't stand him. He was older than me. I think that's the reason I didn't like him. I don't know how he won me over. He was a cabman. Back then, they didn't have suburban buses like we have now. They had a streetcar and it ran from Atlanta to Marietta and if you lived outside the bus line, you had to use a cab. That's why I took a cab, and he was the cabman. It took him a year before he said anything to me.
We got married in Cobb County. We didn't have a wedding. We just went to the minister's house and married, but what we did was have a big one-year celebration. We really had a real humdinger of a first-year reception. My husband and me, we lived thirty-three years together. He's been dead now eleven years. I have a forty-four year old son, and he lives in Washington, D. C. I have two granddaughters. That's the granddaughter and her baby. That's my son when he graduated from Washington High.

YS: What did your grandmother think about you getting married to an older man?

MT: She was old when I married. It's a wonder I even got married. She knew my husband was a quiet man. He was a deacon in the church and he didn't drink, curse, or any of that kind of thing. She was satisfied, but he was old enough to be my father, but he didn't act old and he didn't look old. That makes a difference. He had nice skin. He was a good-looking dude. Big! After being married ten years, a son was born. We named him John, Jr. after his dad. My husband was six two. My buddies used to call us Mutt and Jeff. My husband was a quiet man and he didn't talk ugly or mean or anything like that. And he wasn't brutal. I enjoyed him. We had a lovely life together. Almost thirty years. We didn't have any fighting or beating. My husband died on March 10th. If he had lived until the 13th, he'd have died on our thirtieth wedding anniversary. We had been married that long. He was the breadwinner. He was a good provider. If we had an argument, there wasn't anything we couldn't sit down and talk out. He was a good man.

YS: How old were you when you started dating?

MT: I was nineteen or twenty and, you know, I thought I was going to be an old maid. You see, back then, you had to marry at a certain point or they would tell the boy to stop coming.

YS: Tell us what your grandmother taught you about boys.

MT: She really put me onto the facts of life. That's what a young girl needs to know. She needs to know all of the odds and ends young boys use. My grandmother told me. Talk about rough on rats, I was it. They called me snooty and uppity and I strutted away from there because I didn't care. My grandmother told me how sweet and lovely boys can be until they get your gem. Then they go out and talk about it and tell it. Yeah, that was bad. She said never be frisky or say anything out of turn. Just be real nice when you talk to them, but don't let them have their way with you. A boy had to be respectful, you know, from the time he saw you until he married you. In those days, if he beat you after you were married, your daddy would go there and tear up the place. They used to respect you. When they came to see you, it was something, honey. Young people these days don't have any courtship.

YS: Explain what you mean by courtship.

MT: Honey, when you were courting, he would come and sit and talk. On Sundays, he'd take you to the ice cream parlor. That's where you saw all the young people on Sunday. They had these chairs. You all don't know anything about the ice cream parlor. They had round tables, just big enough for two people. Wrought iron. The boys and girls would sit, eat, and talk. That was the only time they could court alone. At the ice cream parlor. When they were courting in the house, honey, either the mother or the father, one would sit in the doorway. Y'all don't know anything about that. When you got engaged to marry a man that would be the only time they didn't watch. That's right. You didn't have any long engagements. When he asked for her hand, he had to hurry up and marry her. That was your joy.

YS: What did your grandmother tell you about getting your period?

MT: My stepmother did that. You see, when my mom died, I was just two years old and my dad married. My mom and dad married when she was going on fifteen and he was fifteen. They were getting boys for WWI at that age and he hurried up and married my mom to keep from going to the army. And after my mom died, he married my stepmother. They had six and everyone of them but one was born dead. That one lived a very short while and she was the prettiest thing you ever did see. That was the first baby I ever saw. God knows everything. That's the reason the children didn't live. They'd been pitiful little children because of the way she turned out. My stepmother wasn't nice. She slapped me one day. I had little whippings, you know, from my grandmother when I was little, but I had never been slapped before. Well, child, that Jones blood flew up and I jumped on her. She never slapped me again.

YS: Did you not know your mother's mother?

MT: Well, you see, I was too little. My mother's mother took me when I was two years old. My mother died when I was two, and her mother died a short while after. They had to give me to my father's mother. My mother's people were in Chicago. When I grew up, you see, I learned that they were there. They contacted my grandmother all the time and then, when I got older, they began to contact me. They wanted me to come for a visit, but I was too small. My uncle got in his car and came down here to get me. He took me all the way to Chicago. I was about eight or nine years old. I was young. He wanted them to put me on a train and the conductor would see me safe. It was a through train, you know, and they thought the conductor would get me safe to them, but my grandmother said, "No." She wouldn't even think about that. That's when he came and got me. He took me to Chicago.

YS: What family members did you have living in Chicago?

MT: Oh, my Uncle John, my mother's brother. Uncle Archer had already died. He was here in Georgia. I had two aunts and one uncle living in Chicago. They just followed me every time I went up there. My aunts lived in their house, and my uncle in his. I had to go here to there to here. If I stayed too long at one, they'd get on the phone, "You gonna keep her over there all the time?" They just fussed over me. I was the only child. They didn't have any. That's the reason I had to go. I had to spend my young life up there with them when school was out. That's where I would go.

YS: So your uncle came to get you every summer?

MT: Yes, when I was little, he would come to get me. When I got big enough, I went on the train. He wanted me to come way before they let me, but after I got big enough, they would put me on the train. Then my uncle would be right there on the train station platform waiting for me to get off.

YS: Before you started taking the train to Chicago your uncle would come to Georgia to pick you up. That's a long drive. Where did you spend the night?

MT: Oh, he drove all night. You couldn't stop anywhere until you crossed the Mason Dixon Line. The South didn't have no place for Blacks. No motels. My uncle and his wife would take turns driving. They drove straight through. They didn't stop. He'd drive then she would. She would get back in the back with me, and sleep. Then he'd get back there and sleep. That's the way they did it.

YS: Tell us about Christmas when you were growing up.

MT: Oh, honey, they went out in the woods and got the Christmas tree. You know that old "timey" tree. Now, we buy these cedars. They went out and got the regular old pine trees. That's the Christmas tree. They used to have candleholders to put on the branches. They'd put the little candles on it. Then they would light those on Christmas Eve. They were real candles. It's a shame that people weren't making pictures then because that was something beautiful to see. They had different little things to put on the tree. And what's that silver stuff?

YS: Garland.

MT: Yes. They put garland on my tree. Like I said, I was a lucky one. Lots of children had a pretty bad time if their mother died when they were two years old. But my daddy was my grandmother's baby. When I got big, my aunts would fuss at my grandmother telling her,

148

"Mama, you do more for Frances than you ever did for us!" See, my daddy was her baby. My grandmother had money because Uncle Dave sent her money all the time. He tried his best to get her to move to Portland. He wanted her to see what he had for her, but my grandmother never would leave Georgia.

YS: Why do you think she wouldn't leave?

MT: I think it was slavery. See, they couldn't leave that plantation. If they did leave, they had to have a written note. And I think that stayed with her. And there is something else I need to tell you about what she told me. See, they had men that drove horses all the time, all through the settlement, to see if any slaves be out without a pass. And they would take the slave and beat him. They may tie him behind a horse and then they just let the horse run through town with him. When they got to the plantation, they'd cut the rope and the body would just roll. Sometimes, it would roll up to the fence. Sometimes, it would stop rolling in the yard. The other slaves would run out to the fence and drag him in. Sometimes, he was alive and sometimes he was dead. This is something I'm gonna tell you. They would go in the house; they all had this homemade lard because the people killed hogs. They would go in and get spoons of that homemade lard. Then they would go to the fireplace and rake up that black soot. That black soot has a gray business, but they didn't get any of the gray. They would get spoons full of that black soot, mix it with the lard, and take it to the fellow who'd just been beaten. His back would be bloody because they dragged him. They would just put this soot and lard that they had mixed up on his back. It was a healer! My grandmother used to grow something in her garden. I can't even remember what it was. It grew green. She took the root part of it. The stuff that she used was White. She made a tea. When I was little, I had stomach trouble. She would make that tea and give it to me, and that hurting was gone. Well, you see, people back in those days were God-gifted. That was the only thing. There were no doctors for them. And, you see, God blessed them with the knowledge of knowing what to grow and use to heal. My grandmother said they had all that stuff. They had something they called "heart leaves." It was a shiny green leaf. It was kinda small. They would take that leaf, chop it up, and make tea out of it. It cured certain things, and it made them well. Now, anyway, what else you want to ask me?

YS: Were there any women other than your grandmother who were influential in your life?

MT: Well, my mother was the oldest child out of four. Yes, I think it's four: Aunt Fannie, Aunt Maple, Uncle John and Uncle Archer. It was five children. My mom made the fifth child, but she died when I was real young. There were four of them. She was named Willie Mae Cowan Jones. Yes, I was one of those Jones girls. Very common name. And, well, let me get back to my aunt, the one who lived here in Atlanta. My home was in Marietta, Georgia. I had an uncle who lived here, too. They were my grandmother's people. I was named after my aunt's daughter, Mary Frances. Mary Frances fussed at me about that until we were grown. I told her don't be fussing at me. I didn't name myself. They lived with us: she and her brother and her mother lived with us when I was small. My dad, Aunt Blondie, her two children and me lived with my grandmother. I don't know when her husband died or when they started living there. As far back as I can remember, we lived together. I wasn't always by myself. Aunt Blondie met this World War I veteran. He moved her out. He bought her a home down here. They married and moved down here. That house is still there. I have been by it.

YS: So your aunt lived with your grandmother until she re-married.

MT: Yes, she married Mr. Harris. I remember him. He was big, oh, God. He was mixed with Indian. He was a good-looking thing. Henry Harris was his name. After the war, he was able to buy her this home. I go by it. That home is still there.

YS: Is the house still in the family?

MT: Everybody's dead now.

YS: Did you have any experiences with family or friends where the term "Black" was used as a put down?

MT: No, I don't remember anybody in my family calling each other "Black". My aunt, my father's sister, was my color. Real dark. My father was just a little lighter than I am. See, my grandmother was pretty. She lived to be ninety-seven. My mom died when I was two, so my grandmother raised me. She was a staunch Christian. Everybody had to go to church. I didn't hear bad fussing when I was growing up.

YS: I noticed that you have the Soap Opera Digest. Which soap operas do you watch?

MT: I just read it sometimes. I don't much look at those soap things. I was addicted to them at one time. Oh, yes, when I was about twenty-five years old.

YS: Did you watch the Amos and Andy Show?

MT: Yes.

YS: Some people had a problem with the way Blacks were portrayed on the show. What about you? Did the show bother you in any way?

MT: No, I didn't hear anybody say they had a problem with the show. It was just taken as good comedy. See, before your time, Blacks were very comical. The only thing I didn't like was the make-up. You see, Amos and Andy weren't ugly men. The way they made them up was ugly. I didn't like that.

YS: Did you ever see a minstrel show?

MT: They had minstrel shows that would come at different times of the year. Now, that's when you had Blacks really dancing. Buck dancing was what men were doing before tap came in. That was all the Negroes knew back in those days. Buck dancing. Tap dancing came in way later when I was in the seventh grade. Now that's when tap dancing came in. We had some Black boys that sure could tap dance. Sometimes the schools would put on different stage shows where you could see the boys tap dancing. Yes, they used to put on things in school. They put on the operetta. I'll tell you, I was hurt because people stopped doing that. Two of my teachers brought the operetta to Marietta. "A Rose Dream." That was what it was and one girl was the center of the show. She's my age and living in Marietta. She was the little girl--in the operetta, you know--who went to sleep on the stage. Everything that we did around her was what she was dreaming. Oh, yes, it had a giant in it. He was the giant that forgot and kept growing. It was beautiful. My class was the roses. They used rose petal net to make our dresses. It had two layers to it. The skirt was petals. Then they had angels and this giant. He forgot. He went out, went to sleep, and he just grew and grew. James Lott was his name. He was the giant. He was a big guy. This little girl, Serena, was dreaming everything that was happening on the stage. She came out, got sleepy, and laid down. Once she went to sleep, everything started. Everyone came on the stage. It was a beautiful thing. The teacher, Mrs. Duncan brought that to Marietta. Nothing like that had ever been in any of the schools, anywhere. They put it in the paper. Oh, gee, we had angels. Oh, I mean, it was so beautiful. I couldn't figure out why they would stop it. That was the prettiest thing to come to Marietta.

YS: I would like to know more about the minstrel shows.

MT: The minstrel show came once a year. It was on the outskirts of Marietta, where they had circuses and things like that. The minstrel show was about the only thing we had where Blacks could go and enjoy themselves. We couldn't go to the movies when I was little. That came about as I grew up. At that time, they put us in back seats. You had to sit in the back or way up high in the balcony. You see, integration came. Martin Luther King brought all this to Negroes.

YS: Were the performers in the minstrel shows White men in blackface or Black men?

MT: The minstrels? This I was never sure. There never were any Blacks that ugly. What they did was make them ugly. They made them paint their faces. They should not have done that. See, that's what I consider abusive to Black people. We have some beautiful Black people. See, you are pretty.

YS: Thank you.

MT: They made up Amos and Andy with black paint on their faces. They had paint around their lips and all. Normal Black men were not ugly. You all should be happy that you didn't come along in those days. We were behind in everything. Even on the streetcars. They don't have any more of those trolley cars running from Marietta to Atlanta, but we had to sit way in the back. No Blacks could sit up front. Even when my child was born, we didn't have integration. Martin Luther King! Honey, God made that man for the Blacks. When he started protesting, that's when integration came about. My child is forty-eight years old and when we would visit Atlanta and take the streetcar, we had to keep walking until we got to the back.

YS: Did you personally know of any people who didn't give up their seats?

MT: No, they would have gotten hurt. They didn't do it. You see, when I was young, the Ku Klux was here. They had parades once a year. They used to come out, take Blacks out and beat them if they had done anything. There were times that the Ku Klux would come after Negroes accused of doing anything to a White person. They'd come, get you out, beat you and leave you somewhere. I heard about a lynching in our town. People talked about it when I was little. There's a big park in the center of the town. They lynched a Negro in that park. That's Marietta, GA. After the lynching, birds came to that park by the thousands. Nobody could sit in it anymore. That park is still there. It has seats and in the center is a water fountain, a beautiful fountain. You couldn't even sit in the park back then. That was the curse on the park. My grandmother told me that when they lynched that man in the park, that Black man, the birds came. Nobody could sit in the park. Birds just came by the thousands.

YS: When did you first realize how serious racism was in America?

MT: I was just about grown. About eighteen. Let me tell you one thing. My dad didn't fear anybody. Black or White didn't make any difference. I was born just like him. I beat up a White girl. She went home bloody. It frightened my grandmother to death. Well, this is what happened. One of my grandmother's friends came to visit with a baby and it was a beautiful little thing. I asked to hold the baby and she let me and Monty, the White girl, was trying to take the baby out of my arms. We got into a fight and she went home with a bloody nose. And when I beat up that White girl, my grandmother thought the Ku Klux was gomma come after me. When my daddy got home from work she told him, "Walter, you gonna have to take Frances to Atlanta tonight. She beat up one of these White girls. I'm afraid the Ku Klux might come." Oh, when my grandmother said that, my daddy got mad. He said some bad words. My daddy went in the closet, got a shotgun, rifles and his pistols and he had plenty of them. He loaded up all these things. He sat posted up near the front door and he would race to the back door. He told my grandma, "Momma, if one of them s.o.b.s come here tonight, we gone see them laid out in those sheets." My dad was just that way. He wasn't afraid of anybody. I'm the same way. I am not afraid of anybody.

YS: Who encouraged you to get your education?

MT: Well, I was determined to get an education. My Aunt Blondie, who lived in Atlanta, her two children graduated from Washington High. Her son took up tailoring. That boy could make a suit of clothes or a pair of pants just like you buy at the store. Her daughter was a seamstress named Mary Frances. See, they named me after her. She was a seamstress and her brother was a tailor. And they were musicians. He played the violin. She played the piano. They played at that big church on Ashby Street. I think about them every time I go by that church. I used to come and visit with them during my school vacations. Well, when I didn't go to Chicago, I would visit them. My aunts and uncle wanted me to spend my vacations in Chicago. They wanted me because they didn't have any children. None of them had any children. I thought that was very strange. Once I got big enough, I'd take the train by myself. The conductor would keep an eye on children riding without their parents. So when I got big enough to ride that train by myself, my grandmother put me on the train with my shoebox. Oh, she had my lunch in a shoebox. I had fried chicken, cake, and biscuits. My grandmother is the reason I went into catering. She did it all. She didn't go to school to learn how. It was God-given with her. That woman cooked the best food and the White people had her doing all that and she didn't go to school. God just gave it to her. That's why I went to catering school To Couch Adult Education. It was on Georgia Tech's campus. That's where I went.

YS: Tell us about some of your experiences as a caterer. Did you cater forWhite people?

MT: Let me tell you one thing I just didn't allow it. You see, a lot of Black people would go in on Monday morning and tell the White people everything that happened in the Negro neighborhood over the weekend. If there was any fighting or any jailing, they would tell it. That was just ignorance. When I first started working, I remember the woman I worked for would hang around me and smile every time I'd get to work. She was waiting on me to start telling her what happened on the weekend. At first, I didn't know what she was doing. Then one day she said, "You know you don't ever tell me anything." She went on to say that, another lady that worked for her always told her if somebody was fighting or something. I just looked at her and said, "I don't have anything to tell you." You know, I had my father's ways.

YS: In another interview, you mentioned World War II and we'd like to know what Black people thought about the War.

MT: I didn't hear much talk about the War. See, war is a thing that, whether you like it or not, you're in it If they call you, you're gone. You have no choice about it. My son is in the Army. I think he did go overseas for a short time. Isn't that funny though? That left my mind. That's something. Well, he did. He went overseas. I forgot where he was. I'm gonna ask him. When he calls me again, I'm gonna ask him. He went overseas and that liked to have killed me. Oh dear Lord! Wait a minute. Korea. I believe it was. Yeah, that's where he went. He went to Korea. Let me tell you one thing. He almost married a girl over there and I would have died. Oh, God, I'm telling you the truth. When he told me that, I just lost it. Yes, I did. Oh, child, you know one thing? See, my son, he wasn't used to girls much. I knew when he lost his virginity.

YS: You did! How did you know?

MT: He didn't know I knew, but I knew. I could tell. See, when you have a boy and he becomes a man, you can tell. He changed. He was entirely different, and I told him about it. He didn't deny it. That's when I got on him. I said, "Let me tell you ." His daddy was sick then. See, my husband got sick when John was just past a year-old. John had finished high school when his daddy died. I was the one that had to tell John everything about life. That's when I told that boy about girls. I said, "Don't you bring shame on the family, on me and your dad or any of our people." I told him. Oh, I embarrassed him to death. I had to tell that boy a lot of things that his father would have told him, but my husband was sick for seventeen years. I had to be man and woman. My son is forty-four years old, and he doesn't know to this day that I would cry when I whipped him. I really did. It hurt me worse than it did him, but I had to do it because a boy is harder to raise than a girl. I just had to tell him the facts of life. I had to tell him what to do and what not to do with girls. I told him, "Don't you bring any shame on me or that girl's family." And he didn't. Thank God for that. He was married eight years before my first granddaughter was born.

YS: What's your favorite dish? What do you like to eat?

MT: Oh, Jesus. You know, I don't know. I don't know whether I have a favorite. You know I cooked so much food until eating is not important. It is important because I have to eat to live, but I have cooked so much different food I don't have a special dish. See, I catered twenty-eight years. I have cooked every kind of thing that you can think of because I catered for those people out in Buckhead. Rich White settlements in Sandy Springs, Buckhead and Gwinnett County. When you're catering, you have so many different things to fix. See, I was out there four years at Couch's. That's where I learned. That was a four-year program. Some people didn't go that long. See, I went for a purpose. I wanted to know more about food, finer foods. They taught you how to plan a meal and how to buy the foods. Sometimes I'd cater cocktail parties with three or four hundred people. I had maids and butlers.

YS: How many people did you employ?

MT: It would depend on the party size, but I had three regular girls. They wasted all their time and money going to catering school. They didn't do anything with it. They would help me. They should have gone on out for themselves.

YS: When you were growing up in Marietta, did you think segregation would ever come to an end?

MT: Discrimination is bad, you know. I don't know if it is over or not. At least, Blacks have better opportunities than they had years ago. I am sure about that. We have better jobs than we used to have. And Black women can hold office. When I was young, I never heard of a Black woman that was holding an office like they do today. That's mainly because education has changed. See, education is so much better for Blacks. Blacks have come a long way. Blacks got better jobs now. When I was small, all a Black man could do was dig a ditch. Now, Black men can get the education to be almost anything they want to be. That's the thing now. See, Negroes can be whatever they want to be. Of course, I feel sad about those who are not using the opportunity. You know, since we've got opportunities Negroes never had before, but some of them are not doing like they should.

YS: What can we do as young people to be sure we are taking advantage of the opportunities that we've been given?

MT: You young people are something! When you come out of college, decide before you come out what you want to do. Make up your minds. Make up your mind you are gonna be somebody. Don't waste this time in college. Come out and be somebody. I'm gonna tell you, Black people have risen up. They used to be under the feet of White people. Before it's over, we're gonna have a Black president.

YS: You think so?

MT: Yes, we are going to have a Black president, whether it's a woman or a man. It could go both ways. We got some smart women. We gonna do that, but I bet I'm not gonna see that. But it's gonna be. Blacks have just come up. We would have been up long before now, but they held us down. Of course, God put a man here to get us out. He had to die.

YS: Are you referring to Dr. Martin Luther King, Jr.?

MT: Martin Luther King. He was put here for us. He had to die, but he did it. He fixed it for the Blacks. To think that a man died to give us a better way. I figured one day segregation would end. God stands for something! I didn't believe that He put Blacks here to be under the feet of Whites. Martin Luther King came into this world to free us and lose his life.

YS: You use some strong language when you talk about Whites in the old days. How do you feel about Whites now?

MT: Well, my grandmother told me and my daddy and my aunts told me, "Don't hate them. Don't hate them. God takes care of all that." That's what I tell my son now. "Don't hate White people. Just let God take care of them, which He will." I never grew up hating. My grandmother said that if you hate them, then you're gonna be just as bad as they are. She said, "Don't hate them. Love them." You know, that's kinda of a hard thing to do, but you ask God to strengthen you and you can do it. He wanted everybody to be together, and that's good. It's better than what it used to be because the lynching and that kinda stuff has stopped.

MAMA DAVIS

LaGrange, Gerogia
Evangelist and Nurse

You have to get to yourself and when you get to yourself, you have to get quiet. It's called silence. When you sit in silence, you'll get something. See, the Spirit will come. The Spirit will talk to you and you'll get something about yourself. And when you get it, you'll be a different person because Spirit talked to you. Do you believe that?

Bonding with Mrs. Alberta Jackson "Mama" Davis
The Wisest of the Wise 2002-03

Shacara Johnson

I made the decision to become to become a Young Scholar in Spelman's Independent Scholars (SIS) during a Senior Class meeting Fall 2003. I wanted to be involved in a learning experience that would further my development as a critical thinker and make me proud of what I had already accomplished in life. At the first meeting, I was in awe of the students who had participated in SIS last year and of their mentor who spoke with a great deal of enthusiasm. She seemed to love what she was doing and she was very proud of the students in SIS. At the end of the meeting, I waited in line to sign my name to the list of interested students. I liked the fact that students in SIS are not called students or Spelman women. They are called Young Scholars.

SIS has been one of the most significant learning experiences in my life. As a Young Scholar I conducted informational surveys, assisted in organizing a campus-wide Marching for Black Colleges, and journeyed to Newtown, where I learned what environmental racism really means. Because of SIS, I have a greater sense of myself as a young woman who will achieve.

The highlight of my SIS experience was my bonding with Mrs. Alberta Jackson Davis. She is the reason I have a clear vision of myself doing something in the future that will have a positive impact on humanity. I call her "Mama Davis" because that is the name she prefers. I was new to oral history and I didn't know what to expect. I had attended SIS seminars, but I had no idea what was about to happen in my life.I remember being so nervous that I was quiet as I drove to Mama Davis' house with Lauren Teague and Kira Lynch. Like me, they had asked to interview Mama Davis. We were impressed by the fact that she is an evangelist. We also were curious about talking to a woman who was ninety –four years old.

We left Spelman's campus on February 17th at 2:15. The day was sunny and humid, and there was a beautiful and serene feeling in the air. The directions were easy, especially because Dr. Jackson, Mama Davis' daughter-in-law, had told us to look for a White church. That was our landmark, and from there, we would have no difficulty finding Mama Davis' house. We found the church. We walked up to the front door of the house. Mama Davis was waiting for us. Actually, she was sitting near the window watching for us. After that first interview, she watched for us each time we would visit her. She called us her "daughters," and we liked that.

It was my third interview with Mama Davis that truly touched my heart because I had experienced so many hardships that I had begun to question many aspects of my life. Setbacks had caused me to doubt my ability to succeed. Mama Davis's wisdom and faith healed me. When asked about a fear she had had earlier in life, Mama Davis replied "Oh, yes. There was a fear I had to get rid of. There's nothing you can do until you get rid of it. Because like in the Bible, anything that bothers you, it makes you fall." My life changed in that instance. I knew I would never give in to fear. I knew that I would achieve what I wanted to achieve and that I could handle any hardships that might come my way. When I graduate in May as a math major, I will take Mama Davis' wisdom with me and I have no doubt that I will accomplish my goals. There will always be a place in my heart for Mama Davis. She believes in me, and she taught me to believe in myself. .

EXCERPTS OF INTERVIEWS WITH MRS. ALEBRTA JACKSON BROWN DAVIS
Conducted by Shacara Johnson, Kira Lynch and Lauren Teague

[With Assistance from Mama Davis' Daughter-in-Law, Dr. Joycelyn Jackson (DJ),and Grandaughter, Ms. Jennifer Jackson (JJ)]

YS: We were told that your father went on medicine shows.

MD: I don't remember them.

YS: Your father didn't do medicine shows?

MD: He'd take a glass of water and tell people things. I remember seeing him one time. I was a little girl. About seven or eight. After being out of school for fifteen years, I went back.

YS: So you didn't finish high school until years later. Is that what you are saying?

MD: Fifteen years later. Yes, I did that. So, after school, I taught kindergarten with the children. I liked that. They used to be mixed. White and Black. But I don't see Whites down there now. Nothing but Blacks. I don't know what happened to it. It was a real nice school.

YS: You were telling us that you went to different high schools and that you didn't get to finish. What happened?

MD: Well, I finished high school at Washington High.

YS: And then you went to Grady?

MD: Yes. Grady Hospital. While I was in high school, I wanted to be a nurse and Grady Hospital was taking nurses. And so, that's how I got in. When I went to Grady Hospital, I used to bathe people and some of the people had false teeth. But, of course, coming up, you know, I got used to that. I would take care of people after they had passed. We had to take care of them just like when they were living. We had to clean them up. I got over that. I got used to it. I worked there for six months. White dresses and blue aprons. After we'd been there for six months, they put us on night duty and I got used to that, too.

YS: You told us last week that you worked at Harris Memorial Hospital. Did you work there before you worked at Grady?

MD: Yes.

YS: Was Harris Memorial a hospital for Black people?

MD: Yes. It was across the street from Washington High on the old Hunter Street, and I worked there for about twenty-five years.

YS: And you were telling us that you met your husband at Grady.

MD: He would come and stay as long as 10:00. He was coming to see somebody else. That's how I met him. He was a young man. We both were young. I think we might have been about the same age. We had Wednesday nights and Sunday nights for courting nights. We had to be in by 10:00. They had night watchmen to watch the building.

YS: You were living in a dorm at Grady?

MD: We signed when we got in and when we came out. We had four beds in a room and we had our own beds. We had bathtubs across the hall, I think. And then we had bowls we used for washing up.

YS: What happened if you didn't come back by 10:00. Were there some girls who came back after 10:00?

MD: They were kicked out of there.

YS: They were kicked out of the program?

MD: Yes, if they didn't have a good excuse. One girl ate something one night and she didn't come back. Her daddy was a chaplain at a school in Gainesville. I guess she wanted to get married. I was married on a Sunday night. I didn't see him all that day. That's the way they did during that time. [Laughing] They believed it was bad luck to see the groom.

YS: When you and your husband married, where did you live?

MD: We had an apartment. Somebody named Fanny. He knew her. That's where we stayed and I had to cook but I didn't know how to cook.

YS: That was your first husband.

MD: Yes. My name was Alberta Brown. I married Jonathan Jackson. And then I married Robert Davis some years later.

YS: Where did you meet your second husband, Mr. Davis?

MD: I can't remember that. It was in Atlanta. He had a good job at Lockheed.

DJ: I know they were married in 1960 when I first met Mama Davis. Jonathan and I married. Right, Mama? You just can't remember when you met Daddy Robert.

MD: Not really. I had been working for White people and meeting him.

YS: Mama Davis, when did you receive your calling into the ministry?

MD: I was going to a little church out on . . . I can't think of the name of that street. I used to go out there and I enjoyed it. I got to be a preacher out there.

YS: What denomination was the church?

MD: It was what you call a surrogate church. We had classes every Tuesday night and a woman taught us the Bible and we had a book that had everything in it and we studied out of that book. A spiritual book. I wanted to know all about it, so I just kept on studying. Then after that, I went to Detroit and Chicago and I went to Cleveland, too. And I worked at churches, too. Just moving around.

DJ: You are an evangelist, aren't you, Mama?

MD: Yes.

YS: What is the difference between an evangelist and a preacher, Mama Davis?

MD: Well, you go to different places to teach. If you do a good job, they want to pay you.

YS: Did they pay women evangelists the same as what they paid men evangelists?

MD: They didn't really pay. They gave you a donation. Sometimes you would get a nice donation and sometimes you wouldn't.

YS: Depended on the church?

MD: How big a crowd the church has. They feel. That's what they call feeling the Spirit.

YS: Where did you stay when you went on these trips?

MD: We stayed at hotels, and then we would stay at the preacher's house or somebody's house. It was quite interesting.

YS: Were you allowed to go into the pulpit?

MD: Yeah, I preached from the pulpit. I didn't tell you about the lodge. I'm in the Elks and the Eastern Star.

YS: Is it true that men go higher than women in the Eastern Star?

MD: They are higher. I don't know too much right now about them, but they can go higher.

160

YS: Do you have all your colors and your stars and your badges and your gloves?

MD: Oh, yes.

YS: When we were talking last week about women who gave birth, you said that some women were counseled about having children. What happened to the women who didn't want to have children?

MD: They had counseling at Grady.

YS: You mean like counsel to give birth or do you mean counsel to give up the child after birth?

MD: I mean counsel to give birth when they didn't want to give birth to the child at all.

YS: Was there any mention of abortion then?

MD: They do that now, but they didn't do it when we were coming up. Sometimes they would have to do it to save the patient.

YS: They did this at Grady?

MD: Yes. I had a friend at that department. They would do it if you were in school.YS: Did you ever know women who would become pregnant and try to abort at home and then come to the hospital with problems?

MD: Sometimes they would have to have [the abortion].

YS: If they didn't go to Grady, where would they go? Would they do it at home?

MD: They would come in at night. They would go to the fire station and get medicine. I don't know too much about it.

YS: Were the women who were able to have abortions White women or Black women?

MD: Black women, mostly.

YS: Did women have birth control then?

MD: They were supposed to have it. Yes, they used to have birth control.

YS: It was probably really expensive, though. Was it a pill or something else?

MD: I think it was probably condoms and some probably would take a pill.

YS: Did your mother or your grandmother talk to you about women's issues when you were growing up?

MD: Naw. You couldn't even bat your eye. They didn't do things like they do now. If my mother had talked to me, I would've been a little brighter. She didn't tell me. I remember the first time. The lady next door told me and that's how I knew about women's things. People wouldn't tell their children things like they will tell y'all now. They want y'all to be smart and know.

YS: How old were you when you had your son Jonathan?

MD: Twenty-two. He was a Depression baby.

YS: How many years were you and your husband married?

MD: I don't know. It was a long time. I suppose it's on our marriage certificate. It's old now. He died when he was young. He died at the hospital.

YS: Tell us about the Depression, Mama Davis?

MD: It was bad.

YS: How did it affect you and your husband?

MD: As I said, my son Jonathan was a Depression baby, but we made it. I tell people I went through the Depression and they don't believe it.

YS: Did you have to work two jobs to make ends meet?

MD: I worked at Harris Memorial. We got food to eat. We couldn't get much, though. And my husband, he worked at a recession store and he called that a good job. When integration came, we walked out of Grady. They weren't going to stay there.

YS: White people walked out?

MD: No, the Black ministers.

YS: When did Grady begin training nurses like you? Do you remember when that was year? Was it after you moved into this house? Did you work at Grady when you were living here on Highland Avenue?

MD: I don't remember the exact year. But I was living here.

YS: Is that where your apartment was when you were working at Grady? How long have you lived here?

162

MD: Since 1955 or 56. It's in the safe deposit box. . . .Back during our day, we didn't have bathrooms like here in this house. We had to go straight out back to what we called outhouses. And we didn't have washing machines, so we would wash our clothes on a scrub pan and we would use lye soap.

YS: Lye is strong, isn't it? Would it mess up your hands?

MD: Naw. It would clean your toes. Get the dirt out. All those things are real old.

YS: Whose well did you get the water from?

MD: I don't know, but the well was in the yard. We would use it and it was good water, too. We would draw the water from down in the well and I don't know how we did it. That was years ago.

YS: Now, this was in LaGrange?

MD: Yes, in LaGrange, Georgia. You remember I said that, didn't you? I remember the time I was a little girl and I wasn't even thinking about anything. [Everyone laughs] I said I knew that these are things they might want to hear. Oh and here is a nice black hat that I had. See I found this nice black hat.

DJ: She was getting it out of her closet because we were cleaning up.

YS: You liked to wear hats?

MD: Well, I don't wear hats anymore.

DJ: We found this one in the closet.

YS :Wow, Mama Davis. You wore stylish hats.

DJ: There was one made of leopard skin and she didn't want to keep it, but I thought it was fabulous.

MD: I had them in hat boxes, but I haven't seen those hat boxes in years now.

YS: Wow! So when you went out, Mama Davis, you didn't go without your hat and gloves?

MD: Oh no. I wore my hats when I was dressed up. Ann. I gave her the leopard hat. She wore it.

DJ: Oh, you did? Good!

MD: Yes, that leopard hat. She wanted it.

YS: I know I would have to have on a pair of high heels if I were wearing a hat like this.

MD: Yes, we had high heels. I wore my high heels. I wouldn't be complete without high heels, I had all kinds. [Laughing]

YS: Would your heels be as high as some of the ones women wear today?

MD: No They wouldn't be that high. [Laughing]

YS: Is this high enough [pointing to the heels she is wearing]?

MD: Ooooh. I don't know how you wear them. We didn't have any that high but we had high heels. I'm not sure if I am remembering everything.

YS: You are doing fine. I have a question, Mama. I know some churches today don't regulate women's dress and so women can go to church without stockings and they can go to church bare-armed. How do you feel about that?

MD: Well, some churches don't, but my church . . . See, my pastor hasn't said anything about it, but the only thing he says is that for the summer and the spring you don't have to wear hose.

YS: I couldn't go wearing jeans?

MD: Well, yes. You can wear jeans.

YS: Really?

MD: It's not regulated on dress, but you have to be dressed.

YS: No short skirts?

MD: No, you can't wear that.

YS: How do you feel about the dress young people wear today and about some of the music we listen to? The popular culture. How do you feel about that?

MD: I don't care for them myself but they are all right..

YS: The other day you said you watched a movie on the Black church.

MD: The Black church. Yes.

YS: Was it the Shrine of the Black Madonna?

MD: No not that church.

YS: Do you mean the Black Hebrew Israelites? Is that the church you are talking about?

MD: Exactly. It might be that. Well, I went there.

YS: What did you think?

MD: Well, I went just that one time. It was too much guilt and hurt and people's attitude . . . reflecting on oppression in the U.S. There were some like that at the hospital. They had real strong emotions.

YS: It was quite an achievement for you to become a nurse and an evangelist at a time when women were not welcomed in those roles. Where did you get the strength to do this?

MD: Oh my strength? I got it from God. He gave it to me. Everyone doesn't get that strength. You have to get to yourself and when you get to yourself, you have to get quiet. It's called silence. When you get in that silence . . . See, we had classes every Tuesday night called SILENCE. We had prayer and a song and then we would sit in silence. When you sit in silence, you'll get something. See, the Spirit will come. The Spirit will talk to you and you'll get something about yourself. And when you get it, you'll be a different person because Spirit talked to you. Do you believe that?

YS: Yes ma'am. We believe that.

YS: Was that a form of meditation?

MD: Uh uh.

YS: It was like a conversation with God?

MD: Yes. You talk to him. See, you talk to the Master. The first time that happened to me, I was at this lady's house, I had this jug that looked like a little hog and it suffocated me. I went up to the top of the house. I really did. Different things happen to you with Spirit. Another time something happened to me. We had these, see, I went to all the different meetings. This man, his name was Papa Richardson, and this arm [touching her right arm] would give me trouble and so I haven't had trouble anytime since then and that was many, many years ago. Haven't had any troubles since then. But you have to have faith. You got to believe. If you don't believe, then you won't be healed. You have to have that faith. You got to believe in it. And it don't come to you all at once. It takes years. It took me years and years to get the feeling like that. I used to burn a lot of candles. I don't do that now. Jocelyn, you don't see me do that anymore. I used to burn candles all the time. I thought I had to have a candle to do everything. And I thought if I didn't have a candle burning, nothing would happen. But when you get close to the Spirit of God, everything works. I'm not sure how it works, but it works. You want to know some more about it, don't you? You will get that feeling and it will heal. A lady called me last night. She had to go to the doctor today. She used to work with me. She finished nurse training and after she finished nurse training, she took up being a preacher. What you call evangelist. She is

Reverend Mabel Calhoun. She got her calling. It's a wonderful thing if you know how to take care of yourself and don't have to be afraid.

YS: Why were you afraid then?

MD: I been scared all my life, but now I'm not quite as afraid. It's just that I don't have that feeling like I used to. Do I, Jocelyn?

YS: Have you accomplished all you wanted to accomplish?

MD: I think I have. Now, I jotted down some things that I could remember to tell you. I don't remember real well, so I will be just talking like to one of my ladies in the choir. She stops in sometimes. Her name is Dorothy James. She's from Florida and went to college somewhere here in Atlanta. She is also a college graduate, so I told her about y'all and she said, "I don't know what you are going to tell them since you don't tell nobody nothing." Then she said, "You won't even tell anybody how old you are." She said, "You got a lot of things you can talk about, you won't tell them." So I said, "I will tell them this year since you all so worried about it."

YS: Everyone always wants to know how old you are and, yes, you did tell us.

MD: I did?

YS: Yes. You are ninety-four. You were born on September 8, 1908. Did you do any traveling as an evangelist?

MD: Yes. I would go to meetings at different churches. I would go to Chicago, to Detroit, Michigan. I have even been to New York and so people have me come into their houses. And I would come in and bless the house. I would come in and clean it up and bless the house and the people would be blessed, too.

YS: Did you learn how to do this in your spiritual classes or was that also something that just came to you?

MD: You have to learn to get that. See you got to get something to help you. The Spirit. The Spirit works for you. It will work with you as long as you read your Bible. The Bible will talk to you. And what other things I would do? I would fast every Tuesday, every Friday. I would fast. That will give you strength. You can do things that will help your spirit.

YS: So, when you fast. . . .

MD: When you fast, you take nothing into your body. No food. No water. Nothing in your mouth for hours. I would fast. I wouldn't eat from 6 o'clock in the morning till 12 o'clock noon, timing it. You have to time it for your prayer to go through. Your prayer won't go through if you don't time it. The timing. Your prayer is like anything else; you have to time it. You have to pray on it.

166

YS: What advice would you give young women today about becoming connected to Spirit?

MD: Well, I put some things down for y'all. I couldn't drive a car and I wanted to drive a car. So what I would do? I lived in an apartment upstairs so I would go down and sit in my car. And I would sit there and cars would stop. See at that time, we had streetcars. We didn't have what you have now. So I waited till the buses stop running and the streetcars stop running and that would be about twelve o'clock. And that's how I learned to drive. I did learn how to drive that way.

YS: Are you saying you taught yourself?

MD: Yeah.

YS: So how long did it take you to learn how to drive?

MD: Oh, it took me a long time. But after I learned, see, I fell and I been kinda scared about walking around in here because I fell coming in, but I go all around this house now. It tells you immediately. The Spirit comes and takes that fear from you. I find myself way over there [pointing toward the lamp and table across the room]. I didn't used to go over there. So, I'm doing better. It all comes to you.

YS: What else do you have for us on that paper?

MD: So much down here. Half the time, I don't remember what I put down. I told you I'm mother of the church at East Lake United Methodist, and I enjoy it. I told the lady, "Well, I'm the mother of the church" and I say, " I can go wherever I wanna go." I can go to any meeting. We had Men's Day Sunday, and I had donated the church a piano in my son's name. And the piano sounded good.

YS: Do you believe in the saying that you get wiser with time?

MD: Oh, yes. It'll come to you, honey. It's going to come to you. You'll be surprised. You know, the lady at your school called me "The Lady of Wisdom" because I'm an old woman. [Laughter] Well, we were going to this school once a week and we talk to the children and they loved us. Something about old people that you get that you . . . . The Spirit is going to work with you, going to use you and you will do things you've never done before. Did you have something in your life that you wanted to do?

YS: Well, right now I'm trying to graduate from Spelman and I want to go to grad school, but I'm a little nervous.

MD: How long, how long before you all graduate?

YS: In May. So, I'm trying to get ready for grad school and it's something . . .

MD: You want to graduate and you have good marks?

YS: Well . . .

MD: Do you feel like you going to get them?

YS: Well, not quite. I'm going to graduate with a BS.

MD: Well, you need to have your mind made up.

YS: I want to go to medical school, but right now I have to go to grad school.

MD: Well, you're like me. I've been going to school all my life. I stay in school. See, I go to a senior citizen school. [Laughing] I always have something to keep my mind elevated, keep it going, you know. You have to think with your own mind.

YS: Is that something you would tell those of us who are about to actually leave college and go into the world?

MD: You need something to help you. My daughter, she likes for me to go to school. She is a school teacher and she wants me to go to the senior citizen school and if I don't go, she gets disappointed. She teaches older people. You know? Grown people? And they like it because she helps them. That's what my son did. He taught grown people.

YS: You have a daughter.

MD: Yes, that's my daughter [pointing to Dr. Jackson, who is her daughter-in-law]. She sees about me. She sees about me. She and my granddaughter are good to me.

YS: You said earlier that you had many fears.

DJ: Mama, what did you fear? Was it people or things you didn't know? What was your fear about? Have you ever thought about it?

MD: Well, I'm not as afraid?

DJ: But when you were?

MD: Oh, yeah. There was a fear I had to get rid of. There's nothing you can do until you get rid of it. Because, like in the Bible, anything that bothers you, it makes you fall. It doesn't bother me like it used to. The Bible says anything that bothers you, it makes you fall. It doesn't bother me like it used to. I didn't know how to drive. This is the way I learned how to drive. I had a candle burning at my house and when I got in my car, I put everything in the back of the car. You don't understand why I put everything in the back, do you? [Laughing] I prayed and I put nothing but good in my car. All good things and

168

that's how I learned to drive. [Laughing] What we call it? The good Spirit. The good Spirit has to be with you, but you have to know how to handle it. When you say your birthday is?

YS: My birthday? [Shacara]

MD: Yeah.

YS: January 12.

MD: Yours in January. And yours?

YS: May 13 [Kira]

MD: You are the burning bush.

YS: I'm the burning bush? [Kira]

MD: And you?

YS: July the 7th. [Lauren]

MD: That's good. Mine is in September.

YS: On what day!

MD: Eighth. Jocelyn's in June. Last of June. My aunt had a birthday in January and she liked ice cream. You like ice cream?

YS: Yes [Shacara]

MD: My teacher in the Spirit would take us to different churches and try us out, you know. I say, "You talking to me?" You heard of people giving readings, have you?

YS: No [Shacara]

YS: What do you mean "giving readings" [Kira]

MD: Reading and talking to somebody.

DJ: From the scripture or . . .

MD: From your mind. I asked you what your birthday was? May? [to Kira]

YS: Yes [Kira]

169

MD: And what did I tell you?

YS: You said "burning bush." What does that mean?

MD: Well, Christ had a burning bush. There's a whole lot of things you will learn when you are in Spirit. You have a good spirit. All of you. All three of you have good spirits. Sometimes when I feel like it, I'll give you a message, but it's not in my mind now. Because it helps you to know whom you dealing with and who you with, who you have met. Looking inside, you can tell what they are, who they are, whose they are, and what they can do. You'll learn a whole lot of things because the Spirit will tell you. The Spirit will work with you. You'll learn things and your mind will be opened up. And it will come to you. It will talk to you. I'm not trying to scare you. [Everyone Laughs]

YS: You were talking earlier about spirits and cleaning up people's houses and blessing the houses and you were also talking about how you started driving and the good spirit in your car. :Did you ever have experiences with bad spirits.

MD: I didn't.

YS: So, when you were cleaning or blessings houses or even when you would meet people, did you ever feel negative energy in them?

MD: Oh, yes. I'll know it. I feel it. But you accept nothing but the good. And the lady I told you about? The one that live out by Hairston? [turning to Dr. Jackson]. What's her name?

DJ: Ms. _____]

MD: Yes, that's right. Ms. _____. She from over the water and I can hardly understand what she saying. Her husband is from the British Kingdom. They from back over there across the water. Well, he's afraid to catch the plane, so they put him to sleep to keep him quiet. She came to see me yesterday. I don't know she says she loves me, but she did. She is from those people over in Decatur. They are spiritual with their minds open. So, she came to see me. You want to say something? [speaking to Kira]

YS: No, I'm fine. I'm just listening.

YS: Actually, I have a question. It's a little bit off the topic of what we are talking about. [Lauren]

MD: Well, just anything that I can answer.

YS: What do you remember about the Civil Rights Movement and Martin Luther King, Jr. [Mama Davis hands us a bulletin of the Martin Luther King, Jr. Celebration at her church. She seems prepared for us and we are surprised.]

YS: Well, you are ready for us. [Lauren]

170

DJ: Mama lived across the street from the King house, and she and Jonathan knew the King family well.

MD: That's his picture. That's just an old writing and I had nothing to write on. But that's his picture. When I was at the dinner out there to the school on Sunday that day, I sat next to . . . What's her name, Joycelyn?

DJ: Christine. [Dr. King's sister]

MD: Yes, Christine.

DJ: Mama, tell them about Jonathan growing up with A.D. [Dr. King's brother]

MD: Oh, yes. He was good friends with A.D. Did you know him?

DJ: I don't think they were even born. He died in 69.

MD: At the dinner, she didn't know he was my child and she asked a lot of questions about my granddaughter Jennifer and where she lived, Christine did. They have a nice church. That's a little card. You see that little small card? I saw a lady at the Center and she gave me a church card. She helps with elderly people and doesn't charge them anything for all that she does on the card. Like going to the bank and taking care of the wash or whatever.

YS: Mama Davis, what are your feelings about the upcoming war in Iraq?

MD: It looks like it's going to be. We don't know what's going to happen. I think it's about pride. We had an incident when we had to get out of the building, talking about terror. It was a birthday party and the security guards come in. And you know I always cut up and they said, "Y'all get out of here. Get out of here right now. Leave everything." And I had my little dinner and I had my little walker and I couldn't hardly get out of the building. They supposed to train us how to get out of there. What you call it? Combat? We had, you know, nothing like that, but they need to teach us how to do that to get out of there.

DJ: Do people at the Center talk about the war?

MD: That's one thing about the Center is that they get different people to come in and talk to us . . . tell us things. Somebody came and talked about the war and the President last Thursday and told us what was going on. And that day, I was the President [everyone chuckles] and I told them, "Y'all have to do what I say do because I'm the President." And that was our fun. I am the secretary and they come in there and they wouldn't say my name. They would say, "Hey, Ms. Secretary." I've been secretary for fifteen years. It's good to keep your mind abreast of things. It makes you think and nobody can make a fool out of you. As long as you are aware, people have to watch what they are going to say.

YS: Do you think people try to take advantage of the elderly?

MD: They don't try. They do it. They teach us that at the center. People call me on this here telephone trying to get me to buy stuff. See you got to be on your P's and Q's. Be alert. That's what you call being alert. And if you are alert, no one can fool you about what's going on.

YS: They should know that they can't pull anything on you.

MD: We play bingo at the Center. You see that little flower cup. A man that comes over to help me. Well, I had that cup full of candy and I gave him some. He comes over to help get what needs to be done and he almost ate all the candy up. At my old age, I think I'm doing fine and I like my old age. I am what you call a senior citizen. Isn't that right, Jocelyn? Y'all have someone or something that you hope to be like or have in your old age. A young lady talked to me the other day and she sent me the card you see up there. Don't you want to say something Jocelyn?

DJ: No, ma'am.

YS: Mama Davis, do you vote?

MD: Oh yes! I vote!

YS: How do you feel about people not voting, especially people in the Black community?

MD: They should vote. They don't vote but they should vote. The people at the center love to vote. It is part of their living and then they take us to Kroger's once every other week. You know they take us to Kroger's. Older people live in high rises, you know. High rises are like these homes. They stretch out and those that live in high rises, they are able to move around. They have about four or five rooms and they like it, but the owners won't take you if you can't take care of yourself. You have to know how to cook and clean.

YS: Mama Davis, how do you feel about women's rights?

MD: Women's rights? I was reading this article in the newspaper . . . I like to read . . . something talking about women's rights. And we should definitely have them.

YS: What do you say when people argue that women should be preaching or teaching in the church? What do you say?

MD: I don't say anything. They say we not supposed to do it, but we do it anyway. Some of them don't want women to preach in the church.

YS: So what do you say to people who believe a woman's place is not in the pulpit?

MD: A woman brought the word, didn't she, because she birthed Jesus. That's what they tell me.

DJ: Have you ever had any opportunity to say that to someone who asked about a woman's right to be a minister or a preacher?

MD: I sure have.

YS: So men have actually said that to you?

MD: Yes.

YS: Have you ever been at a church that has not allowed you in the pulpit or wanted you to speak from the floor?

MD: Well, when I went to churches, I was invited. When I went to Cleveland, I was invited and this was a man's church and they carried on a revival for a week when I was thirty. It is wonderful work and you know it. [speaking to Kira] You don't have to be one but when you feel like . . . You like it a little bit, don't you?

YS: Yes, I do.

DJ: Do you think that Jonathan went into theology because of you or do you think it was by your example and others that brought him into it?

MD: I don't know but he did it, didn't he? [Everyone laughs] He went to a lady, Mable Butts with Unity, somewhere on Ashby Street and she taught him. Taught me. We had Unity lessons with her. She told me, "You have to know it to believe it," and that's what started me. I started it and I liked it.

YS: Is Unity the name of a church or a particular way of worshipping?

MD: Unity. It is a church and a Christian movement. I've been to some in Chicago and when I was young, I took charge and went to all these different places. That's why I was skinny but I don't try to do it now by going to all these different churches. Anybody, churches or things, that come to town, I would be sitting there as one of the first ones there. I enjoyed it and it helped me help my mind. It is good to know things. Know how to master. See what you can do to master yourself. Know what I'm saying? When you master yourself, you get along with yourself because you are in charge of yourself.

YS: When you were talking earlier, you said that if you read your Bible and talk to God, your mind will be open.

MD: That's right. See, you've got to open up and when you open up, you'll get it. Your mind has to open up.

MRS. MARYMAL DRYDEN

Richmand, Virginia
Policy, Planning and Development Executive

Well, to me, [being a feminist] means believing that a woman has a right to a career and equal opportunity in that career. It also means believing that she has a right to independence of thought . . . that she is not an appendage to her husband. That was really what women of my generation were supposed to be. Appendages. And many many women saw themselves that way. I am not an appendage. Can't be.

YS: Mrs. Dryden, I want to begin by asking you biographical questions. And, of course, if there is any question you do not want to answer, just tell me to move on to the next question. Are you a native of Atlanta?

MD: No. I'm originally from Richmond, Virginia. I moved to Atlanta in 1967. I have a long history in Atlanta because my father's family is from Atlanta. I have an ancestor who finished Spelman in the class of 1887. Her name was Cornelia Porter, and my grandmother was named Mary Cornelia in her honor because she was the first woman in our family out of slavery to get a formal education. She went to Spelman at a time when Spelman was a normal school, somewhat like a high school. But in those days, a few years out of slavery, going to a normal school was quite an achievement.

YS: And I'm wondering about your name: Marymal. It is such a different name. I know there is a story here.

MD: Mary was my paternal grandmother's name and my mother's mother's name was Malvina. That is an old "Southern" name. My mother actually named me Mary Malvina, but when I was an infant, people would call me Mary and she didn't want them to call me that. Malvina is on my birth certificate. It is one word, but my mother dropped Vina, so my name became Marymal: M-a-r-y-m-a-l. It's an interesting name that makes for about five minutes of conversation.

YS: Are you an only child?

MD: No, I have a brother who is deceased. He was four year younger than I am.

YS: Tell me what it was like being the older child in the family.

MD: It was interesting. My parents lived separately from the time I was about eleven. There was a family by the name of Scott that lived on the same street we lived on in Richmond - Tenth Street - and the woman just fell in love with my brother. He was a very beautiful child. Almost chocolate brown with curly hair. Because they didn't have children of their own, this couple asked my mother if my brother could stay with them. I think what happened was that they would take care of him while my mother was at work. I don't really remember how it actually happened because when I knew about it, it was already an accomplished fact. He lived with them until he went to college. He claimed later that he would have been a much stronger person if he had lived with my mother. The Scott family quite simply spoiled him because he was such an adorable child.

YS: Tell me about your parents. What were their names and how did they meet?

MD: My mother's name was Florence Peyton James Morgan, and my father's name was Henry Tasca Morgan. He was a native of Atlanta, but he went to high school in

Tuskegee. You see, there was no high school for Blacks in Atlanta at the time and so he went to Tuskegee Institute. It might not have been called Tuskegee Institute at the time, but that's just how I knew it. And after finishing there, he studied at Atlanta University, which was an undergraduate school at the time. He was trained at Tuskegee in brick masonry and when he went to Richmond, where mother was living, he was able to get a job as a teacher at a trade school— teaching brick masonry, of course. He also worked as a salesman for the telephone company. This was during the late 20's and early 30's when phone service was just getting started and salesmen would go door-to-door selling the service. I think that's how my father met my mother. They stayed married a long time, perhaps fifteen or twenty years. They separated when I was eleven, but they stayed married until the day he died.

YS: What do you know about your grandparents?

MD: My grandmother on my mother's side died when I was a child, maybe about two or three. My maternal grandfather I remember as a shadowy figure. When I say "shadowy figure," I mean that I remember him visiting the house and my mother telling me that was her father. But I never had a relationship with him. He, too, died when I was a young child. It was quite different, though, on my paternal side. My father's mother was the core of my life because I spent my summers with her. She was married to my step-grandfather, who was really the only grandfather I ever knew. His name was Reverend Moreland, and he was a Baptist itinerant preacher and he had three rural churches. I remember that one of them was in Rockmont, Georgia, one in Cedar Town and one in, I think, Rome, but I'm not sure about Rome. Later he pastured at Macedonia Baptist here in Atlanta. My brother and I would spend summers with my grandparents, and I enjoyed going to church with my grandfather. I remember that after the service, there would be a feast. There would be table after table after table covered with food and everybody would want my brother and me to eat at their table because, you see, as the pastor's grandchildren, we were pretty special. Just the other day, a friend and I were talking about this ritual--because it is a ritual--and my friend remarked that she couldn't eat at these church feasts because of all the flies. I really don't remember the flies, but I do remember that the ladies had fans. I guess they were fanning away flies. [laughter] It was just such a wonderful time for me that I never saw the flies.

My grandmother on my father's side--her name was Mary Cornelia--spent a lot of time with me. She went to Spelman for a short time, but the family was so poor she couldn't stay in school. Mary Cornelia was an entrepreneur, and she was named for her father's sister, Cornelia Porter, who attended Spelman Seminary and graduated in 1887. Cornelia Porter was the first person in my father's family to receive a formal education after the end of slavery.

I named my only daughter Cornelia in her honor. Now my paternal grandmother, Mary Cornelia, as I was telling you, was an entrepreneur. She owned restaurants in Atlanta. The first one I remember was in downtown Atlanta. The Georgia Power Company had a large office building in downtown Atlanta and one part of it faced Marietta Street. My grandmother's little restaurant was in a little alley behind a building that faced the main street. This was during the days of segregation and White people would send Blacks to my grandmother's restaurant to get food. This is an interesting little sideline. Not too long ago, my present husband--Charles Dryden, a Tuskegee Airman--wrote a book entitled <u>A Train: The Memoirs of a Tuskegee Airman.</u> Last year, because of the book, he was invited to speak at the Veterans' Day Celebration for employees at Georgia Power Company. During the program, they showed a film my husband is in called Birds of a Feather. I had a chance to meet the President of Georgia Power and in our conversation I told him that I had a unique linkage to Georgia Power Company. He said, "Explain it to me." And I said, "My grandmother used to have a restaurant right across the corner, right in this little alley way where the old power company offices were, and the Georgia Power Company employees, Black and White, would buy breakfasts and lunches from her and I added that the money she earned helped me attend Spelman.

She was quite a remarkable woman. She saw the potential for property and she bought a house on Simpson Street in the immediate vicinity of the Georgia Dome. Do you know where the stadium is? Where the Georgia Dome is? The property extended from one corner to the other and on one corner there was a hill and at the base of the hill. My grandmother built a building that was large enough to have a grocery store on one side and a restaurant on the other side.. When he wasn't preaching, my grandfather ran the grocery store.

And I must tell you that my grandmother was an excellent cook. I remember when I was at Spelman, I used to sneak off the campus to visit her, much to her dismay. In fact, I lived with her one semester, but that didn't work out. I was seventeen. Turned eighteen in October. And, you know, you're full of vim and vigor at that age, and I was falling in love. My grandmother must have said to herself, "Oh no, no, no, no!" Living there was a problem for me because I had to be on campus for chapel at eight o'clock in the morning. I just couldn't make it. My grades were okay, but back then at Spelman if you missed a certain number of chapels, you lost quality points. And so, I lost quality points because I didn't go to chapel in the morning. My grandmother said, "This is not going to work," and she made immediate plans for me to live on campus! So when the next semester began, I moved to campus. But, you know, I never could make up those quality points because there was no summer school at that time and Spelman didn't have mid-term graduations. As I result, I spent an additional entire year at Spelman. When I tell people that I was at Spelman from '44 to '49, it sounds as if I might have been retarded.

YS: Now, you said that you enjoyed going to church with your grandparents. Would you say that you grew up in a religious family?

MD: Well, my grandfather was a Baptist preacher, but he also ran the grocery store and I remember that men would come to the store and stay all day sharing their stories and listening to my grandfather share his stories. He always had a story to tell. His preaching on Sundays was more like an avocation. I never thought of my grandmother as being a serious religious person. As a matter of fact, what I remember is that she was not active in the church. She worked in her business all of the time. However, she was a very spiritual person who inspired others and had very strong principles of life. My mother was not that active in church either. When I was fairly young, I was attracted to the Episcopal Church, and my mother allowed me to go there. In fact, she would drop me off at my church on the way to her church, Ebenezer Baptist, in Richmond.

YS:	Tell me some of your fondest memories of living with your mother in Richmond.

MD:	Well, we lived in an upstairs apartment in a two-story house and we had one bedroom and a living room and a kitchen. My mother and I slept in the same bed. And there was a very small room that she let me make into whatever I wanted. It was my playroom and I made it into a classroom. I always liked to play school. Also I liked playing with my dolls. They were paper dolls, and I made them.

YS:	Did you have any dolls other than the ones you made?

MD:	Yes, I remember some dolls. They were "White" Shirley Temple dolls and "baby" dolls, but paper dolls were my favorite.

YS:	Did you watch a lot of television? You know now that is what kids do. They watch television and play video games.

MD:	Oh, no. We didn't do that. In fact, television hadn't been invited. We lived on Tenth Street and we played games in the middle of the street. We played hopscotch. We played hide and seek. We played jacks. That's what I remember. And then, of course, I played a lot of school inside. You see, my mother didn't like me to be out in the street, so most of the time I would be in my room with my imaginary friends. You've heard the expression "It takes a village to raise a child." Everybody on the block knew my mother and knew she worked during the day and so they watched me when she was not at home. She would tell me, "Now you know you're not supposed to be doing such and such because everybody's watching you and they'll tell me when I come home." Every now and then, I would go outside and play in the street. I never will forget that I did not like to do housework.

YS:	Did you have many friends when you were growing up?

MD:	Not many. I was somewhat of an introvert, in part because my mother worked. My mother had to work. Before she got the job as a city jail matron, she worked as an elevator operator in a residential senior citizen high-rise for well-to-do White people. She was very likeable. I remember so well there was this wonderful dining room in the Chesterfield Apartment and the head cook, a lady by the name of Ida, knew that my mother was raising me by herself, and Ms. Ida would give my mother enough food for both of us. That is how I learned to eat certain delicacies like creamed sweet breads, filet mignin, and Smithfield ham. Because of Ms. Ida, I didn't grow up eating soul food. I didn't learn to love "soul food" until I got to be an adult and moved to Georgia. But I remember that so fondly because Ms. Ida would always see to it that my mother brought enough home for the two of us. That's what they called "toting privileges". You probably never heard of that. Well, some Blacks who worked for Whites had the privilege to take food from the working place. They were were "privileged," in a sense, to "tote" things away.

YS: A survival motion for Black people during the era of segregation.

MD: Well, Richmond was segregated, but the segregation was not nearly as harsh as segregation farther down South. I think we couldn't try on clothes in department stories, but my mother made all of my clothes and she did such a great job that I always looked nice. She was an excellent seamstress. I remember that my mother had a friend, a White woman, who sold shoes in a store in Richmond and that woman would fit me with shoes, so I grew up wearing very good shoes all my life. And then my mother had a friend, a White woman, who worked in the yard goods department. If there were a fabric my mother wanted, the woman would put the sale price on the fabric so that my mother could afford to buy it. My mother made those kinds of little individual connections with people in order to survive. She was a very resourceful woman. We moved from the housing project to a house because she was so resourceful.

YS: You lived in a housing project in Richmond?

MD: Yes. Gilpin Court, it was called. Now this was in the early 40's and it was prestigious at that time to live in a housing project because you had to undergo a lot of scrutiny in order to be accepted as a resident. Housing projects then did not have the same image they have now. You see, initially, public housing was designed to provide temporary housing for upwardly mobile people. You could live there until you saved enough money for a house. After my mother saved enough money, she bought the house on Garland Avenue.

YS: I gather that you and your mother were very close.

MD: Yes. We were very close, but early on I developed a streak of independence. She wanted me to be a teacher, but I did not want to be a teacher. She was very anxious for me to marry a young man called Oscar because his father was the first Black to be a manager at a post office. She wanted me to finish Spelman, return to Richmond, teach school, and marry Oscar, who would be employed at the post office. My mother was very disappointed that she could not program my life. When I finished Spelman, I went to graduate school because I was able to get a fellowship. You see, in the 40's, because segregation prevented Blacks from going to the University of Virginia, we could go to a Black school and the difference in tuition would be paid by the State, and transportation would also be paid by the State. Actually, this enabled Black southerners to go to any school we wanted because our parents could put up the difference. So when I came to Spelman, you see, part of my tuition was paid by the State of Virginia. When you think about it, that really worked for us.

YS: A positive side of segregation. So was your mother satisfied with the path you chose?

MD: You know, I don't know. I had this independent streak so I didn't marry Oscar. I married George and though she wasn't displeased with him, she wasn't all that pleased either. We divorced and I married my second husband. He was a very handsome man, but he was a gambler. He came from a family that was well-to-do, and they set him up in the funeral business. When I met him, he had been elected to the City Council of Cleveland. My mother didn't dislike him, but she was not that happy that he was ten years older than I was. She realized that I tended to marry older men and was probably kind of like looking for a father figure, but I didn't think of them in that way. I thought of them as being exciting people because they were more worldly. I married two like that, and I had four children--three by my first marriage and one by my second marriage. The advantage was that I had a good education. And that's what my mother and my grandmother always stressed. They would tell me, "You need to get a good education so you don't have to take any stuff." They would add: "so that you don't have any stuff from any man." So I was armed with a good education.

YS   As you recall your years in Richmond, what kinds of jobs did Black women have and what was an older Black woman in the community who was a role model for you?

MD: In my mother's circle, most of the women were waitresses, nurses, small business owners, and elevator operators. Some were school teachers and post office workers, and, as I can recall, those were the highest paying jobs.

YS: Let's go to college. [laughing] I know you have hundreds of Spelman stories you could share with me, but I'd like you to choose one, just one, that captures the impact that Spelman had on your life.

MD: Marian Anderson used to come to Spelman and she claimed Spelman girls as her little sisters. When she was in concert, we were allowed to sit in the orchestra section. That was the only time that the concert hall was integrated. That was such a privilege to go to the city auditorium and if it wasn't the city auditorium, then it was the Fox Theatre. We wore our gloves and our hats.

YS: Professionally, you have been very successful.

MD: Yes. Social work, which was my chosen profession, was very lucrative at the time and because my area was community organization and policy and planning, I was on an executive track. I've always had secretaries, always had administrative jobs. That's why I don't type today because I've never had to type. I've had all kinds of fascinating jobs in the community. Each one was a step up. And let me say this. Even though I was married three times, I did not marry men who were slouches. They were well respected and they made a name for themselves, but my second husband was into horses. The point I am trying to make is that my mother wanted me to have a life that was ideal or what she thought was ideal. When I married these people and the marriages didn't work, she wasn't sure whether it was me or them. If I had just gone on and married Oscar and taught school in Richmond, Virginia, then I would never have gone through what I did go through with these marriages. The good thing is that I had an advantage in that I was well equipped educationally, so no matter what circumstance my marriage was in, I could always get a job and I could always be independent. Actually, I think independence might have created havoc for my marriages because after a certain point I realized I didn't really have to take anything that I didn't want to take! Even with four children, you know.

YS: You were independent before independence was popular for women. You graduated from Spelman in 1949 and you went from there to graduate school?

MD: I went immediately to the Atlanta University School of Social Work. Forrester B. Washington was Dean at the time. Actually, he made the AU School of Social Work into one of the finest schools in the country. I went into the community organization tract, which put me on the executive path. I was an Urban League Fellow, so I was able to go to an Urban League placement in Pittsburgh. Let me tell you a funny story about my first placement. It was in Atlanta at what was called the Atlanta TB Association. Now it is the Atlanta Lung Association because they have broadened the scope of service to all kinds of lung diseases. Back then, in 1950, it was just tuberculosis. It was located in a large building on Piedmont Avenue in one of those older houses. The Association converted the house into two units: one was the Black unit and the other one the white unit. A Black lady cooked lunch everyday for Blacks and for Whites, but we ate on our side and Whites ate on their side. The house had one large bathroom and rather than have us share a bathroom, the Association cut that one large bathroom into two and gave the larger section to the White people and the smaller section to us. Actually, there were only four of us: two students, our Supervisor Mrs. Lucy Cherry and her secretary. Four Blacks. The White unit had a large staff of at least 10 people. Well, Mrs. Cherry couldn't use our bathroom because she had very wide hips. The Black bathroom was so small she couldn't get in through the doors.

YS: What did they do?

MD: They had to give us the larger bathroom. All the White folks had to use that tiny little bathroom. We thought that was so funny.

YS: That is one of many stories you have about living with segregation and, in an earlier conversation, you told me you weren't really affected by segregation.

MD: Yes, I was, but I was saying that our families shielded us from the harsher realities of segregation, but there were some things you couldn't avoid. I grew up in Richmond and it didn't seem to me that segregation was nearly as mean-spirited. For example, we didn't have segregation on public transportation. I guess that's because we were so close to D.C. I do remember that when I was in high school, I wanted to go into fashion and there was a program at our school that put students as interns in their area of interest. I wanted to be a department buyer. You started out as a clerk and you were paid and then you moved into team management, but they wouldn't let me make that move, so I had to stay at the clerk level and learn how to put tags and things on the clothing rather than be out on the floor. I knew it was because of my race that I was not given the opportunity to have the full experience. I think they said something about not having facilities for colored. That's what we were called at the time. Colored. This was in the '40s.

And then there was my experience with "college board." Students who were headed to college could work in a department store as a member of the college board and sell clothes. I applied, but I was not selected because of my race. Well, they didn't tell me that, but the fact is there were no Black kids on the college board. So, really, this is why I didn't get into fashion. I simply was never given the opportunity.

YS: Were you bitter against White people?

MD: No. On an individual basis, I knew good White people. As you will recall, my mother worked at one point as an elevator operator in an apartment complex where a lot of older rich White people lived and when they learned that she was a single woman raising two children, they gave her tickets to cultural events. And they gave her expensive clothes their grandchildren had outgrown. Really, I didn't run into nastiness until I got to Atlanta, and that was on the Jim Crow streetcars.

YS: Tell me about your response to the Civil Rights Movement.

MD: By the time the Movement got into full swing, I was married to a Civil Rights lawyer and living in the North. He was an avid supporter of the Movement and I was active in the NAACP. I wasn't as active as I wanted to be because I was busy being "barefoot and pregnant." I was busy rearing children during the early years of the Movement. Some of the marchers slept at our house. They would come with their backpacks and we would let them sleep on the floor in the living room and dining room. I marched on a couple of occasions when we lived in different parts of Ohio. I had been in school with Martin and his sister Christine and his brother A.D., so I knew them personally. By the time he got to Ohio, Martin had become well-renowned.

YS: You were at Spelman while he was at Morehouse?

MD: Christine was the oldest and Martin was the next oldest and then there was A.D. As I recall, the three of them were in college at the same time. Christine and I were classmates, and A.D. was a freshman.

YS: The brown paper bag test. Did you hear about that when you were growing up in Richmond?

MD: That is something I remember quite well. I have to admit that my grandmother - bless her soul - had a thing about dark-skinned people. My first love was a very, very dark and very, very handsome man. My grandmother referred to him as "blue." She thought he was too dark. His color didn't matter to me. It's interesting that most of my husbands are brown. Chuck and my first husband are about the same complexion, and my second husband, my daughter's father, was about my complexion. I will tell you this: almost all the queens the Morehouse men would elect would be high yellow. Dr. Mays would say,

"Give our brown-skinned girls a chance." That's what he would say to his students. The color thing was based on the plantation mentality. And of course, he was always against the plantation mentality. The plantation mentality was with Black men especially. There were girls who looked almost White and they had long, flowing, straight hair. That was one category. And then there were other girls, like myself, who were in between. I'm not real dark and I'm not real light either. Really, I'm browner than I am fair. And so there was us and then there were the very, very dark girls. I don't recall a very, very dark girl ever getting elected as Morehouse queen. That was a tradition there then. I don't think it changed until we started saying, "I'm Black and I'm proud." I remember that I had moved to Atlanta and I carried my kids down to the stadium to see James Brown, and all of us were standing up shouting, "I'm Black and I'm proud!" James Brown was the one who started that slogan. That was the age of SCLC and SNCC and the afro, so that's when everybody was really displaying their Blackness. It was kind of interesting, too, because the students were saying, "You can talk Black, but if you sleeping White, then you're not really a brother." That created a lot of dissention because some of the fellas, who were very ardent Civil Rights leaders, were married to White women who followed the movement, especially in Mississippi. That happened more with SNCC than with SCLC. I created this conference called "Women in the Civil Rights Movement" while I was at Georgia State and I consider it one of the high lights of my professional career. It was to bring together grassroots activists and scholars to discuss the role of women in the Civil Rights Movement. They undergirded the whole movement, but you only knew men. In fact, maybe I can ask you this question. So the point was that we needed a conference that really focused on the role of women. It was the first time it was ever done, and it ended up being a book, Women in the Civil Rights Movement, Trailblazers and Torchbearers.

YS: Tell me about your first job.

MD: My first job was with the Frederick Douglas Community Center in Toledo, Ohio. That's where I met my first husband, George Bingham, who was graduating from the University of Toledo Law School. That was sometime between September and May of 1951. He was very, very brilliant. He passed the bar at his first attempt. George needed money for a refresher course that was gonna be $1,000 or maybe more and since he knew how to paint, I arranged, through my social work contact, for him to get the contract to paint some of the rooms in the YMCA. After we were married, he decided that he wanted to be what he called the big fish in a small pond. We moved to Portsmouth, Ohio, where they were building an energy plant. I had my first child in Portsmouth. It was just a charming little community, but it could not support a lawyer. We went there because the atomic energy plant was supposed to bring a whole lot of people to the town, but the people who came were transients. However, before they could continue the construction of the plant, the atomic bomb became obsolete, which meant that they dropped construction of that bomb and moved to something else. So we moved to Manfield, Ohio, which had a strong industrial base and a fairly large population. George was still holding on to the idea that he would be a big fish in a small pond. I had my second baby within fifteen months after we moved there. I told you I was barefoot and pregnant. My first boy, George ["Bingie"] was born August 10th in 1953 and Anthony ["Tony"] was born December 31st of '54. I didn't work very much then. My first job I remember was between babies. I didn't have time to work between Bingie and Tony, but I had a two-year period between Tony and Kenneth ["Kenny"]. He was born in '57. I was working as a caseworker at an agency in Mansfield.

YS: Were you ready to have kids?

MD: I didn't have any choice. They just came and I took a deep breath. That's really where some of our marital difficulties came up because he was very enthusiastic and did not believe in doing anything other than bragging about his babies, but not in terms of helping me around the house. He said, "No, I'll just get you a housekeeper." He wasn't about to be part of picking up and keeping things straight. I just was overwhelmed. That's when I became interested in flower arrangement and table design. I had always loved flowers. When I was a young girl, my mother would send me to the market to buy stuff and I'd always buy a bunch of flowers for twenty-five cents from the ladies who would come up from the country. I loved to buy zinnias. That's my favorite flower today. I organized a garden club in Mansfield and exhibited at the Mansfield Botanical Garden and, as I recall, I was the first Black woman to exhibit and the first to win ribbons.

YS: That's very interesting. So how long were you married to your first husband?

MD: Ten years. We were married in 1952, I think, and we were divorced by 1962, and I became a single mother with three little boys. It wasn't a nice divorce. I left him. If you read that chapter in that book, you'll see why I left him. I won't tell you. You'll just have to read that chapter! One of my friends, who read the book, said, "I don't know if I would have said all that." I told them, "That was my life, you know? If you want to know my life, you have to know what I endured." When I left him, the only thing I carried with me was that picture of Rosalind on the fireplace in the family room. That's when I wrote that little chapter about Rosalind, my alter ego. I'd look at her and I'd say, "You know, if that lady could survive on a tenant farm in Alabama, I know I can survive even though I have three children. I can survive." That was when I left him. Kenneth was an infant at the time. Being a single mother was a challenge but, you know, I was up to the challenge. The divorce was ugly, but he's devoted to his children. With the visitation, we kind of learned not to be hostile. It took me three marriages to know how things are supposed to be.

YS: Your third marriage was worth the wait.

MD: Yes! We were older, too. When I married Chuck, he was 50 and I was 49. He gave me a "Foxy 50" party. Let me say: I think that women are entitled to enjoy intimacy. I think they have to understand, though, that their sex is not a bargaining chip. I think men are now more realistic abut women because it used to be that a man would want to sleep with you but wouldn't want to marry you. I have been told that Dr. Mays would ask the students at Morehouse, "How many of you want to marry virgins?" Almost all the men in the chapel would raise their hands. Dr. Mays would then say, "Leave some." My mother would say, "When somebody makes an inquiry about you, you want them to be able to say, 'she's a lady. She carries herself well'." So that's how I've carried myself, and I'm very proud that I have done so.

YS: I know that you married Colonel Dryden later in life, but have you had any experiences as the wife of a TuskegeeAirman?

MD: I jokingly say that I didn't go through the horrors, but I'm enjoying the benefits. At a panel on "Her Story" held last weekend on the lives of Tuskegee Airmen wives, two women, a wife and a daughter, shared their experiences and, actually, it turns out that the Airmen had a fabulous lifestyle. Wherever they went, they had maids and people assigned to the family. But the daughter said constant changes were difficult for her. She never had the same doctor. She never had the same dentist. She never had the same teachers. She was always making new friends. She said the one thing that she wanted to do when she settled down was never move and she hasn't. She came here and she's been here since.

YS: You are a mover and a shaker in a lot of different arenas.

MD: I think what happened is I have a kind of presence, and I don't know where I got it from but I guess it's because my grandmother and my mother told me that I was absolutely fabulous. I always thought that I was pretty fabulous and didn't realize I wasn't that fabulous until I got to Spelman where there were a hundred other girls just as fabulous! [laughter] That was good for me because I didn't need to have that much ego. It was good in another way because it confirmed that I was okay and that has served me well. I think what happens is that when you have a kind of presence, people assume that you know a lot more than you may know and, as a result, you are invited to serve on boards and I think that's kind of what happened with me. However, I will admit that when I moved to Atlanta, I had been head of a project in Cleveland that was one of the forerunners of what they call "Community Development Project" programs. This was back in the 60s. I earned the MSW in 1951 and at that time an MSW was like an MBA or what an MBA used to be before the market crashed twice. My area was Community, Organization, Policy Planning & Administration, which put me on an executive track. I knew that I didn't want to be a teacher, and when I went into social work, I knew I didn't want to be a caseworker. It seems as if my personality fit being in community organization. So that's how I got into community organization.

YS: One thing that comes through in all of our conversations is that you are a strong advocate for women. Do you consider yourself to be a feminist?

MD: Oh yes! But I didn't know that I was until the 50's.

YS: What does being a feminist mean to you?

MD: Well, to me, it means believing that a woman has a right to a career and equal opportunity in that career. It also means believing that she has a right to independence of thought and that she is not an appendage to her husband. I am not an appendage. Can't be. I have never been comfortable with women's organizations that are called women's auxiliaries. I don't see myself as an auxiliary or an appendage.

YS: What makes you happy?

MD: I think what makes me happy now is the contentment I have in my life. I'm very proud of my children and their adult lives. I'm very proud of the relationship I have with my husband. I'm really enjoying my grandchildren. This is the glorious sunset of my life! It's nice to have contentment and to be respected by your peers and to be seen as a woman of wisdom by young people. However, because you are older does not always make you wiser. I know some older fools. [Smiling]

YS: If you could speak to a group of Black women of my generation about being focused and empower women, what would you say?

MD: I think the main thing I would say would be that you should be respectful of yourselves and then you are able to control your actions as they relate to your body, to activities with people of the opposite sex and to your professional development. Secondly, I would suggest that they learn to value friendships with other women and not view them as competition and that they should be supportive of issues and causes that relate to women.

YS: What has this experience with the SIS project meant to you?

MD: It has been very fulfilling and I think the key is that you are such an interesting young lady. I am impressed with your intelligence. The experience itself, the experience of journeying into memories, has been a meaningful one for me. You know, when you look at your life over a period of years, you value your experiences and you come to fully appreciate how important and interesting your life has been, and continues to be. This is what the SIS project has done for me.

DR. ANNA HARVIN GRANT

Jacksonville, Florida
College Professor, Scholar, and Administrator

It was hailing, and Daddy came to back door and said, "Baby, come help me get my boots off." My Daddy worked outdoors at a wood and fuel company and so, on the surface of his face and his arms, he looked to be about your color. I started pulling his boots off and before I knew it, I was trying to cover his feet with my dress. I said, "Mama, Daddy's White. They're going to take him away from us!" You know, back in those days, children didn't see their parents' naked feet.

EXCERPTS OF INTERVIEWS WITH DR. ANNA HARVIN GRANT
Conducted by AeuMuro Lake

YS: This is my first interview with Dr. Anna Harvin Grant, and my name is AeuMuro Lake. We have with us Dr. Grant's daughter Donna, who says of her mother, "She is my heart." Dr. Grant, I have a particular interest in interviewing you because I am a sociology major.

AG: Oh, that's lovely!

YS: Also, I have heard so much about you as a scholar. I'd like to know how you became interested in scholarship.

AG: I got sick as a child in high school with what they called "juvenile tuberculosis." My sister had died of it. She was in her early twenties and working as a maid at a motel. We're from Florida, and when I got sick, I spent two years on "bed rest" in a hospital. My physical activities were limited after that. I couldn't play with the other kids or go to school, so I began reading everything. My godparents who lived across the street had a library, a room full of every kind of book you can imagine, and I just read everything. I just wanted to find out all I could about everything and that was the way it went.

YS: Do you remember your sister being sick with tuberculosis?

AG: I didn't see her much because she was in a sanitarium. Tuberculosis ran through one family after another in our neighborhood. Back in those days, life was pretty finicky, pretty finicky.

YS: When you were on "bed rest," did your friends visit you?

AG: Yes, two friends who are still my friends. Clessie and Dena. They were the only ones who came but they could only come to the window. Someone would push me out on the porch and I would wave at Clessie and Dena.

YS: Do you know what developments there were at the time for the treatment of tuberculosis?

AG: All they knew was rest and artificial pneumothorax. That was a procedure that would push your lungs down with air. My right lung stayed down until I got sick when I was in school at Washington State University. I was taken to the hospital and doctors tried to get my lung to expand, but it never fully expanded. I made it, though.

YS: Were White people affected by tuberculosis as much as Black people?

AG: Not as much, but I'm sure they caught it because they had Black people who were sick working for them. Some of the Black people worked until they collapsed.

YS: You grew up in Florida?

AG: Yes. Jacksonville, Florida. My mother came from a large family. She said her daddy had thirteen wives and thirteen children by each wife. Every time he got to thirteen, he'd change wives and say bye. When one wife would die, he'd get another and start out all over having all those children. He'd give the children away. People used children in those days like servants. The family where they lived would take the children and work them to death. Somehow my mother's brothers and sisters kept in touch with one another. She had a sister Rebecca who lived down the street from us. Rebecca was adopted. They called it adopted but there was nothing formal about it. Rebecca was adopted by a schoolteacher named Ms. James. But for some reason my mother's sisters and brothers kept in touch with one another. Even the half brothers and sisters kept in touch with one another. Uncle Ben, my mother's brother, would come and get me every Saturday and take me to his place. He was considered one of the successful ones. Apparently, I was supposed to be smarter than he was. He'd come and get me every Saturday and take me over to his place so his friends could meet his smart little niece. And I'll never forget the first Coca-Cola I ever had. My uncle stopped at this store and introduced me to these people and they offered me a Coke. That thing almost took my head off. People said that Coke has changed, and I believe it. They claim that Coke used to have cocaine in it, but I don't believe them. I know that it was something.

YS: Did you have a large extended family?

AG: There were three of us—my brother Herman Samuel, my sister Elizabeth Adie, and myself—and my daddy's two children by his first wife, a boy and a girl. My mother had a sister who had only one son. She had two brothers. As far as I can remember, none of them had any children, except for stepchildren. At one point my mother lived with her aunt, and her aunt had a daughter named Ruby who was just a few years older than I was. I'll never forget Ruby wouldn't go to school without me. The first grade teacher was our neighbor. Here Ruby is, seven-years-old . . . seven or eight . . . and she wouldn't go to school without Anna. So I started school at four-years-old. At four-years-old, I talked the teacher into letting me go. That girl would not go to school without me.

YS: You started kindergarten or first grade when you were four-years-old?

AG: First grade.

YS: Goodness!

AG: My mother's foster mother put her out. So that's when she went to go live with Aunt Sue. Aunt Sue was really mean to Mama. Treated her like a servant. I remember, I was this little thing, and I'd say, "That's alright, Gina." My mom's name was Virginia, and I thought it was Gina. And I'd say, "That's alright, Gina. You don't have to take this. We can find us a place of our own." Aunt Sue would get so mad: "You little heifer!" It was so funny because as fate would have it, Aunt Sue and Ruby had to come and live with us.

YS: Tell me about your grandparents.

AG: I don't remember my grandparents because my mother was an orphan. Back in those days they didn't have orphanages for Black people. Black orphans were just sent to families of relatives or anyone that would take them in and use them as servants really. My mother went to live with a lady named . . . My father, who was really my stepfather, was old enough to be my mother's father. His wife had died and left him with two children and he married my mother so he'd have someone to take care of his two children.

YS: Do you remember your mother telling you about growing up as an orphan or growing up in different homes?

AG: Mama always said that she could've been a singer if she had the encouragement. Nobody encouraged her, not even her aunt, because she got pregnant with me by her foster mother's son. Her foster mother didn't think she was good enough to be a daughter-in-law, so she put my mama out. That's why my mama went to live with her biological aunt, Aunt Sue, who treated Mama like a servant. My mother's name was Virginia and I thought it was Gina. I said, 'That's alright Gina. We don't have to stay here. We can move.' It was an interesting thing. Before life was over, Aunt Sue and Ruby, her daughter, had to come live with us. Isn't that something? Life has its sense of irony.

YS: So what did your mom tell you about getting pregnant by the foster mother's son?

AG: She never talked about it. When I grew up and felt that I had achieved something, I thought my biological father would have been proud of me. I can't remember anybody from that side of the family ever making themselves known.

YS: When did you learn that your father was your stepfather and not your biological father?

AG: I was a little girl when they married, but I always knew he was my stepfather.

YS: I'd like you to describe the neighborhood in which you grew up in Jacksonville.

AG: We lived on the corner of two streets-Jesse Street and the other street where the so-called upper-class Blacks lived. They were mostly professionals such as teachers and doctors. All Black people lived in the same neighborhood. You knew everybody. It was interesting. I remember they had two grocery stores in our neighborhood run by Whites. Other than that, everything was Black. I remember the non-Black family that lived across the street on the corner. They had one little girl that played with us until puberty. I guess back in those days you never dreamed of real integration. We thought it would stay that way forever.

YS: Was integration something you hoped for?

AG: I don't think I hoped for it. I just thought it would never happen. I belonged to the junior NAACP back in those days. I don't think they even have a junior NAACP anymore. I did a whole lot of things that my parents thought was dangerous. But I did them anyway.

We'd go on the bus and sit in the front seat. It was always children that did that because Whites were less reluctant to strike out at children than at adults.

YS: Tell me about your father.

AG: My father was one of the most intelligent, intellectual and curious people I've ever know. He did not go that far in formal education, but he read everything he could get his hands on, and I think that's where I got my interest in reading. The interesting thing is that back in those days, White people called Black people by their first names, but I never knew anybody, Black or White, who called my daddy "Herman." His name was Herman Harvin. White folks called him "Harvin." I remember when the company he worked for changed ownership and the new owners came looking for my daddy one day, and they asked for "Herman." Nobody knew who they were talking about. I said, "Herman?" Suddenly, it hit me that my daddy's name was Herman Harvin and here are these crazy White people! I said, "Are you looking for Mr. Harvin." Those were the days

YS: So, did your father make sure people called him by his last name?

AG: No, that was the thing. They just respected him like that. That's the way Daddy was. Even White people called him Mr. Harvin. They wouldn't call him Herman.

YS: I'd like to hear more about your father.

AG: I'll never forget the day my daddy stopped to have drinks with some of his friends before he came home. It was hailing, and Daddy came to the back door and said, "Baby, come help me get my boots off." He was just soaking wet. My Daddy worked outdoors at a wood and fuel company and so, on the surface of his face and his arms he looked to be about your color. I started pulling his boots off and before I knew it, I was trying to cover his feet with my dress. He said, "Baby, what you doing?" My Mama heard and she said, "What's wrong?" I said, "Mama, Daddy's White. They're going to take him away from us!" You know back in those days children never saw their parents' naked feet. I looked at his feet and then I looked at his face, and that scared me to death. Scared me to death! My sister was a little lighter than me. My brother and I were the same color. It had never occurred to me before, but to see my Daddy's white feet scared me to death! It was something.

My daddy was very firm. Very firm. If you made new friends, he would ask fifty million questions about them and he would want to know who their parents were. He insisted that he meet the parents. And we couldn't go to anybody's house until he knew their parents. There was a rule in our family that when another's family started dinner, you came home. No matter how hungry you were or how tasty looking the food is, you'd say 'no thank you.' That was the rule in our family. Now, other children would come to our house, and he wouldn't do that to them. It was something else. My daddy was old enough to be my mother's father. His first wife died and left two children. Then he married my mother. My auntie said he married Mama so that she could raise those children. My daddy was something else. That was the way life was in those days.

191

YS: When did he and your mother let you start dating?

AG: Late. You know, all of my friends married right out of school. I didn't. I just kept on going.

YS: You went on to college.

AG: Yes.

YS: You didn't feel that you were missing out on partying or going out?

AG: No. Kids thought I was crazy. Girls would sit around in college and talk about their sexual exploits and I never had anything to say. I didn't know what they were talking about. I didn't even know what people did when they have sex. I think I was retarded sexually. I had a sister and a brother and we all slept in one room. So my sister and I slept in the same bed and my brother slept by himself. Every time we'd look up, one parent or the other was pulling the cover over on us. I didn't know what people did when they had sex.

YS: Are you serious?

AG: Yeah. I didn't know.

YS: And you were in college at the time?

AG: Yes.

YS: Did you have any friends who were as serious about studying as you were?

AG: Yes. I had one friend. Dina. I'll never forget Dina. The only word I would use to describe her was smart. Dina was the only girl I knew who was smart. Now, I was the smartest then in everything except math. That Dina! Dina was something else. Now that I look back, I realize that Black people had a color complex. Dina was dark, real dark. Nobody pushed Dina, and she was the smartest girl in the class. She worked her whole career through the military. Nobody said, "Dina, you ought to go to college," or "Dina, you should do this." Nobody pushed her, but everybody was pushing me. Don't let anybody tell you that Black people aren't color-conscious . . . because they are. If you were my color, you were hopeless. One boy said, "She's smart, but I can't take her home to my Mama." That's something, isn't it? You'd be surprised at how awful people were in those days about kinfolk. Lord have mercy!

YS: How did you react to things like that?

AG: I was busy doing my school work.

YS: You mentioned something about your brother being a stowaway, and I didn't quite understand what you meant.

AG: Well, my parents kept an eye on him. They really did. They called my brother one of those "bad boys." He was something else. Jacksonville is a port city, and many young Black men would leave home by stowing away on ships. That's what my brother did.

YS: He ran away?

AG: He stowed away in a ship. He couldn't have been more than fourteen or fifteen when he did that. He lied about his age. When he retired, he had been everywhere on the globe. Everywhere! Those were the days.

YS: I guess he didn't like to read and study as much as you did?

AG: Oh, no. He liked the physical stuff - - climbing trees and all that kind of thing. I could barely keep up with him. I thought I was going to break my legs trying to keep up with my brother. I remember thinking there was nothing he could do that I couldn't do.

YS: But you were studious at a very early age. I know you have degrees from several institutions and I'd like to hear about your educational path.

AG: I went to a two-year college then located in St. Augustine, Florida, called Florida Normal and Industrial, which was close to Jacksonville. Because I had tuberculosis, my mother didn't want me to go far from home. So, she let me go there, and that's where I started college. They called it "Florida Normal" and from there I went to Florida A & M and from Florida A & M to Fisk University in Nashville for my master's degree. When I was at Fisk, two White men (one was on the faculty at Vanderbilt and the other on the faculty at Peabody College) came to Fisk to give seminars. They told me about a university in Washington State that had scholarships for Black students. Well, you know how many Black students there were in the state of Washington! I became interested because southern White colleges were still segregated. I applied, I was accepted, and I was given a scholarship to Washington State University. I thought my daddy was going to have a fit when I went way out there because he said, "Why is it that everybody else's daughter decides to go to school at home except ours?" That was my first experience traveling away from home and meeting people from all over. Through the years, I have traveled all over the world on assistantships and scholarly grants. I almost got arrested for putting my foot over the line into Russia! Thank God, the border patrol let me go. I just wanted to say I had put my foot on Russian soil.

YS: What time frame was that ? When you went to Russia?

AG: In the '50s, I think, because I finished college in the late '40s and my master's in 48 and I worked as a probably in the early '50s because at the time I was on the faculty at Grambling College in Louisiana. I always enjoyed traveling and interacting with other cultures, but I didn't like traveling in groups. I wanted to find out stuff on my own. Once when I was traveling in India, I got away from the group . . . went out on my own . . . and had an interesting experience I will never forget. A little Indian boy saw me and looked up from playing with another little boy and said, "Look at that tan girl!" He said, "My sister ought to see that; all she does is burn!" He had no idea that I had anything but a tan. It was interesting to me to find out about everything. Some of the White people in the group thought I should have been insulted by what that little boy said, but I wasn't. I dated an Indian guy for several years. He said, "I'm not getting married," I said, "We can't live in India and you don't want to live in the USA."

YS: Why was that?

AG: He wouldn't have fit in! He would've been miserable, abandoning his culture and I wouldn't have been comfortable living over there.

YS: Oh goodness!

AG: You know, I learned a long time ago that when you're young, you don't give the elders the benefit of having superior knowledge. It's fine to have relationships, but they were right about not mixing cultures. When you think about a family and bringing up children, you have to look at the rules of society. Otherwise, you are making problems for yourself and for your children. You don't want to do that. Life is hard enough as it is.

YS: Were you really involved with him?

AG: Yes. It was one of the most beautiful relationships I ever had. I knew that it couldn't go on forever. It was like a Black and White relationship with two different cultures. That is even a greater risk, you know. It's funny that in comparison to skin color, Blacks are closer to them. The only distinguishing feature is really the hair. But it's interesting. It's really interesting.

YS: Of all the places you have traveled, which culture and which countries stand out to you the most?

AG: Oh Lord, I don't know. I tell you one thing. You learn to appreciate America with all its faults because in some of these cultures, everything is just too final and there is no possibility for upward mobility. If you are downtrodden in one culture, why would you want to stay there. I understand why people migrated to America and to other free societies.

YS: Tell me what you think about the impending war in Iraq?

AG: One thing that I have never been able to understand is why people would want to destroy one another. I don't understand that. We're supposed to be superior. Why can't we spend all that energy trying to find ways that we can get along? If we spent the amount of energy trying to work out ways to get along as we do trying to find out ways to destroy one another, we'd be so much happier.

YS: And in all your studies of sociology and society, you've never really come up with any kind of reason?

AG: I don't understand why one group of people feels the need to prove that they are superior to all other groups of people. Why? Why? My father . . . oh boy . . . I remember we were walking down the street in Jacksonville, and I'd never seen a White person begging before. I reached into my pocket . . . I might've had thirty-five cents . . . and started to give some of the change to this beggar. My father slapped my hand and dragged me off. I said, 'Daddy, why did you do that to me? He's poor and hungry." My father said, "He has been free all his days." I will never forget those lines "He has been free all his days." He didn't say any more. You know, it's a funny thing, my father was obviously part White, but he didn't talk about it. He was my stepfather. I'll never forget that he used to say, "You're good as anybody, but better than a whole lot of folks."

YS: How did you meet your husband?

AG: I was teaching at Grambling College, and I owned a car. I was one of the few Black women who did. I took my friend, the college nurse at Grambling, home one day to some little town in Louisiana. Thomas was there because he had brought her sister home, and he had driven her sister's car and was going to take the bus back. My friend said, "Well, Anna, Thomas only lives only sixteen miles from Grambling, so he can ride back with you and take the bus from there." We talked, talked, talked all the way back to Grambling. He asked me if he could come see me on the weekends, and I said sure. He was teaching up in the country. That's how we got started, and next thing you know we're getting married. My husband was light-skinned. In fact, he reminded me a lot of my daddy.

YS: Your husband wasn't color conscious?

AG: No, his daddy was dark. His mama was like your color maybe, with Indian features. I'll never forget White people trying to get all the Black people to sell their land because they wanted to develop it. They had intimidated a lot of the Black people. One day they were coming to talk to his mama about buying her land and she got her rifle and sat on her front steps. When the white people arrived, she said, "What you want?" She cocked her gun. They said, "That's alright, Clara. That's alright. Never mind. You ain't no nigger no how." They were one of the few Black families that were lucky enough to have their own land, and she had inherited it from her White ancestors. You could tell she was racially mixed with Caucasian and Native American.

YS: When did you and your husband decide to get married?

AG: I remember one night when we were dating, we were driving around, and we got horny. He stopped the car and he said, "We're going to have to get married." [laughs] We married in an Episcopal Church in Nashville.

YS: Had you been a member of the Episcopal Church?

AG: I joined the Episcopal Church when I was out in Washington State. My daddy didn't go to church at all except for special occasions. New Year's Eve he would go to the midnight services. They'd pray and pray until midnight. Then he'd come home. The church was just a block up the street from my house. He'd come home and shoot a gun up in the air. I don't know what that was all about.

YS: You and your husband married in An Episcopal Church?

AG: Yes. We must've invited about six people, and about sixteen to twenty showed up. We just went by the prayer book. There are certain things you read and say. Just go by the book. Everything is a ceremony in the Episcopalian Church. Everything you would ever do is written down from dirt to dusk. Everything is written out. Everything.

YS: Is baptism?

AG: Everything. I was baptized when I was about twelve-years-old in the Baptist church of my godparents. See that red book back there [pointing to red book]? I think that's it. That's the prayer book. Is it?

YS: It's the Book of Common Prayers. So you were telling me about your godparents?

AG: They were Baptist. They went to what they called Simple Baptist Church. It was downtown. I'll never forget once we were going to an eleven o'clock service and I saw these White people coming out of the church. I said to my godmother, "I didn't know White people went to church."

YS: Why didn't you know why they were going to church?

AG: Because I thought they were so mean! What were they going to church for? Lord have mercy. I didn't know White people went to church. I thought Black people went to church to get away from all of them. I thought White people had everything, so why were they going to church?

YS: Were you baptized in an Episcopalian church or the Baptist church?

AG: I was baptized in a Baptist church. Once you are baptized, you're baptized, as far as Episcopalians are concerned. I guess I like the Episcopal Church because it makes sense when you think about it. My mother, I think I told you, was an orphan and she grew up in the Methodist church, the AME church, African Methodist Episcopal church. So we were normally associated with churches that made noise. I would go to church on Sunday with my godparents. It was a Baptist church, but they didn't have all that hootin' and hollerin'. My brother and I would go to the sanctified church, as we called it, just to see if he could clown around. One of the members finally told my mother that my brother and I were coming and making fun of them. I never understood that. There's nothing about religion that struck me to have to get up and hoot, holler, shout, dance, and all that kind of stuff. It was something else. It was entertainment for us.

YS: Was there ever a point at which you questioned your religion or your faith?

AG: Oh yeah. I'm not the textbook believer. In fact, I don't believe in God as a concept. So that makes me different. You have to be careful who you say that to because people will judge you. I don't know why people feel the need to judge. You try to explain things that you don't understand, and sometimes you just can't do it. I don't worry about it. I don't worry about it. I have this little granddaughter who is three-years-old. She is something else. She will make you think about things that never occurred to you before.

YS: Were there any people in your life growing up who sort of caused you to question or to look into an Episcopalian church?

AG: I had godparents, who were Baptist. They lived across the street from us. They were one of the few Black families that owned a car. My godmother was the only Black woman I knew who drove. I would go to church with them. My mother wouldn't go to church because she said she didn't have anything to wear.

YS: You have two daughters?

AG: Both of my daughters are adopted. I knew I would have to adopt because I had to have surgery when I was out in school in Washington. The doctor told me, "You'd better go ahead and have children because you won't be able to have children for long." He wanted to do a hysterectomy, but he didn't want to do it as long as I wanted children. He said that he wasn't even sure that I could carry a child to full term. My children are both adopted.

YS: What did that mean to you, when you learned you couldn't have children natural?

AG: I don't know. I don't think it bothered me that much.

YS: So did you adopt your children when they were infants?

AG: Yup. They were the children of my girlfriend's teenage nieces. They came home to me from the hospital. At the time, I didn't have a husband. I enjoyed being a mother.

YS: You didn't have a husband? Is that when you moved to Atlanta?

AG: Well, he didn't come home one day. His mother's house was like sixteen miles from where we lived in Grambling, and he didn't come home. I thought that was strange. So the next day I went to see what happened. He said he didn't want to come home. I told him I don't want to stay in Grambling, a little country town, the rest of my life. He said just give him a couple years. Next thing I know, a couple years came around and he hadn't moved. I moved to Atlanta. Next thing I knew he showed up on my doorstep. As they say the rest is history . . . I suspected that he wanted children and he just didn't know how to say it. So he fooled around and had two children out of wedlock.

YS: You said your mother had a hard life so she lived with you? When did she begin living with you?

AG: After I got married, I had her come stay with me. I left Fisk after awhile and went to Grambling. That's where my husband was from, a town close to there. I told him I didn't want to stay in a little country town. So he said, "Well, Anna, let's just stay a couple years and then we'll move." A couple of years came and went and he didn't want to move and so I moved on to Atlanta. I remember my mother died. Next thing I knew, he showed up on my doorstep. Been here ever since.

YS: Were you satisfied with Atlanta?

AG: I love Atlanta.

YS: Dr. Gayles tells me that you have a W.E.B. DuBois story to tell.

AG: I remember that I wanted DuBois inducted into Phi Beta Kappa and they didn't want him because he believed in communism. I said, "What does that have to do with Phi Beta Kappa? That's about scholarship, not politics." He accepted and came all the way back to America from abroad for the induction. He asked somebody how did he get it and they told him that I had influenced the decision. He took me to dinner and I will never forget that I caught myself saving the napkin. He had a napkin that had on it 'W.E.B. DuBois,' and somehow I must have put in on my plate when I was through with dinner. I lost it. That was the thrill of my life to go out to dine with W.E.B. DuBois. He was something else.

YS: So what was it like trying to get him nominated and what exactly did you have to go through?

AG: It was just that they thought he was a Communist. I told them that this is scholarship. This has nothing to do with politics. There were more White people opposed to it. Most people in the Phi Beta Kappa chapter at Fisk were White. Next time they accepted him.

YS: How about your own induction into Phi Beta Kappa?

AG: I never understood how it came about because I was at Washington State at the time getting my degree in Sociology. None of the departmental faculty were members of Phi Beta Kappa. I was a Psychology minor and that's how I came to the thinking of people outside of Sociology. Later on I was inducted. It was really something. I never understood why it came about.

YS: You were one of the first African American women inducted into the chapter right? Or were there other African Americans?

AG: I don't know. This is a memory now, but somebody told me that years before a Black woman in nursing made it. I don't know if anybody ever looked that up because back in those days you weren't ever supposed to know who nominated you . Mama didn't know Phi Beta Kappa from a hole in the ground. She just thought it was nice that I was an honor student.

YS: I was just informed that I have made Phi Beta Kappa.

AG: Oh wonderful! Wonderful! Congratulations.

YS: Thank you. What advice do you have for young African Americans who are either in school or not in school right now about achieving their goals and living a meaningful life?

AG: Just be yourself. Don't ever think that what you want to do is beyond your reach. If you have the ability to do it, go after it. Don't let anybody tell you what you can or cannot do. Just go ahead and do it. You just have to have confidence in your ability whether you win or lose. You just have to work at it. That's my advice to them. Just go for it.

YS: Are you a feminist?

AG: No, I'm not a feminist. I think people ought to do what they can. I think that sometimes women are put in situations where if they don't move forward and take control, then things are going to fall apart. I don't think women have to sit around and wait for some man to take care of them. You do what you have to do and you strive for personal fulfillment.

YS: [looking at plaques in her den] So this was made by Morehouse College in a tribute to you for "thirty-five years of outstanding dedicated service." It has the Morehouse College seal. "National Consultant. Scholar. Writer. Lecturer. Trailblazer." This is a letter from a Fulbright Scholar, Dr. Ingrid and this is from a Dr. James Irving and this one is the Committee of Education and the Workforce from the U.S. House of Representatives. It's a long letter. The person says, "I have fond memories of my association with you." This is from Charlie Moreland on behalf of the Alumni Association . And this is from the President Emeritus of Morehouse, Dr. Hugh M. Glosters . These were tributes at your retirement

AG: Yes.

YS: So what did you do as soon as you retired?

AG: Rested.

YS: Is there a story associated with your name?

AG: I was named for my maternal grandmother, Anna Augusta.

YS: Did you have a nickname when you were growing up?

AG: That's the thing that bothered me. I thought people didn't like me because nobody ever gave me a nickname. I was just Anna. All the time, Anna.

YS: If you could have a nickname, what would you like it to be?

AG: I don't know.

YS: What did you hope for your two daughters when you were rearing them?

AG: I wanted them to fulfill themselves, and that's what I want for them. That's all I want.

YS: What is the fondest memory of your childhood?

AG: I'll never forget that when Daddy would go to work, Mama would come and get me and put me in the bed with her. My sister, my brother and I slept in one room. My sister and I slept in the same bed. My brother slept in a bed in the same room, by the window. When my mama would come to get me and put me in the bed with her, you couldn't tell me nothing.

YS: She would wake you up from sleep?

AG: No, she would just come and pick me up. I'd pretend to be asleep sometimes. Those were the days.

YS: What makes you sad?

AG: What makes me sad? All this war is driving me crazy. I cannot understand how any human being, who has a mind, cannot sit down and use his mind to figure out how to get along, or how to fill the earth's resources. War is something else. I just simply do not understand. I can't understand what makes numbers of people feel they are more entitled than other people. I can't figure out why we can't work out a way to fill the earth's resources without killing each other. It does not make sense.

YS: What makes you happy?

AG: Oh God, that's hard to tell. I don't know. I enjoy my husband and my children. I especially enjoy my grandchildren. I have a little granddaughter who is four years old.

She is very intelligent. She'll make you think about things you never thought about before. She'll come up to me and say, "Nana, come out of the bed and come up here and talk with me." Not to her. "Talk with me."

YS: Have you ever asked yourself what is the purpose of life?

AG: I don't remember ever wondering about that.

YS: What do you think it is?

AG: Sometimes I think . . . I think we're just a part of it. If I accepted the reality of God, I think I would have to say that he was frivolous-"Well, let me see what happens if I did this." I don't think that life is frivolous.

YS: What has this experience meant to you? Being interviewed and talking about your life?

AG: Well, it's nice to know that somebody thinks of us. I thought everybody had forgotten I ever existed. So it's nice to know that somebody was interested to know what I had to say.

YS: You have a very remarkable life. You have done so many wonderful things and I am just honored to be in your presence.

YS: Who do you think should read your story and why?

AG: I don't know. I don't know. I guess I enjoyed reading biographies and stuff. I was the kind of student who would come to the library to read one thing, and I'd do everything but that one thing until I realized I was about to run out of time. I don't know. I guess people just interested in reading other people's experiences. It's always interesting to read about other people's experiences and to wonder what you would have done.

YS: I was wondering what your granddaughter calls you.

AG: Nana.

YS: That's a nickname?

AG: For Grandma.

YS: So you do have a nickname.

MRS. EDITH JOHNSON

Greenville, Kentucky
Certified Professional Secretary
Award-Winning Quilter

I have the coal miner's hat Daddy wore. It has a lamp in front, and I remember that the lamp would click into the hat, in the middle, in the front of the hat. Carbide burned in the lamp. Miners needed the lamp because when they went into the mine, they would go into the very bowels of the earth. . . . It was a hard life. . . . My parents would tell us, "When you get old enough, get out." They wanted us to leave Kentucky and get an education so that we would have a better life.

EXCERPTS OF INTERVIEWS WITH MRS. EDITH JOHNSON
Conducted by Natane Eaddy

YS: When we were told in class that you are a quilter, I knew I wanted you to be my Woman of Wisdom. So
I want to thank you again for serving as my mentor.

EJ: Well, I'm honored that you chose me.

YS: I will not take more than an hour of your time at each interview.

EJ: My time is yours.

YS: Thank you. I want to begin with biographical details. Are you a native of Atlanta?

EJ: No, I was born in Greenville, Kentucky.

YS: Is there a story associated with your name?

EJ: There was a young lady who lived up the street from us. Her name was Edith and she was a very nice
young lady. My parents named me after her. My middle name is Victoria.

YS: So at birth you were named Edith Victoria.

EJ: My maiden name is Simons.

YS: Do you like your name?

EJ: Yes. I went by Vickie for a long time. I thought it sounded more sophisticated than Edith. But, yes, I like
my name.

YS: Tell me about your family.

EJ: My father's name was Roy Gerald Simons. My mother's name was Lizzie Nall Simons. Daddy was a coal miner and Greenville was a very small coal-mining town. He had two sisters. I think his father lived in another part of Kentucky, so Daddy had to help out with his family's expenses. He started working in the mines when he very young and that's why he didn't finish his education. His mother was what we now call a single parent. He worked in the mines to help the family.

YS: Did she work in the mines?

EJ: No, she worked in White homes.

YS: What did she do on her job?

EJ: Everything. Cooking, washing, ironing, cleaning. Everything.

YS: How many children did your parents have?

EJ: There were five children: three boys and two girls. brothers are now deceased.
        I was the middle child. My sister and two of my

YS: Tell me what life was like in Greenville.

EJ: We were all hard working people. My parents and all of the children. We were never
        hungry. We had chickens and hogs and a garden. Everybody worked in the garden. We
        had a cow for milk and hogs for meat. The men would go fishing and hunting, so
        sometimes we ate rabbit. Hunting was for a sport for the men, especially my uncles who
        had guns. I lost contact with my uncles. They left Kentucky and went to West Virginia
        and to Chicago. They went to big cities. Daddy was not a gun person. Mama's family, I
        guess, was a step higher than Daddy's because there were eight boys in her family and all
        eight of them went to work in the coal mines. Eight men in my mother's family brought
        in money, but only one in my father's family. Daddy was the only son. I always felt that
        Mama's family always had enough. In fact, I don't think my grandmother on my
        mother's side worked for White people because the boys went into the mines. They were
        good looking men and hard workers.

        Daddy was a little man, but he was a hard worker. People called him "Little Roy" and
        they would say that he could dig more coal than some of the big men. People would say,
        "Little Roy can dig a lot of coal." Daddy wasn't educated. He couldn't go to school
        because he had to help his mother and his two sisters. He was very active in the church
        and he became a steward.

YS: Tell me about the community you grew up in Greenville.

EJ: Greenville was a very small town. The population was 2500. It was a racially mixed
        town, but most of the people were White. There were different sections in Greenville for
        Blacks and different sections for Whites. There were White people [and that's what we
        called them: White people] who lived a rock's throw from us. In fact, I remember going
        to get water from their cistern. That's an underground reservoir for rain water. You know,
        we had the well and sometimes the well would run dry. So, we would go to the White
        neighbors and get water. The White woman would eat at our house, but we would never
        eat at theirs. It was a closed thing. White and Black. We called them Miss So and So and
        they called Mama "Lizzie." They called Daddy "Roy."

YS: Did that bother them?

EJ: They never talked about it. That's just how things were. As far as I can recall, there were
        no bad feelings. Remember now, this was Kentucky in the late thirties.

YS: Yes, I have to keep that in mind. How far away from stores and schools did you live?

EJ: We were right at the edge of city limits. That means we were in the country, but we never considered it that way. The sidewalks ended about half a block away from where we lived. Actually, we were on the highway. We considered ourselves to be in Greenville, but we knew that we were past city limits. There were Black neighbors around us. You didn't find a Black family in the midst of White people. We lived close to an AME Zion Church and we could hear the Sunday school bell ringing at 9:30. We had to hurry so that we wouldn't be late. We walked everywhere. There were few cars in Greenville. Even when it was very, very cold [and Kentucky gets real cold], we walked. Daddy would clear the snow so that we could walk to school. Tractors would clear the highway, but, remember, we lived past the city limits, so Daddy had to clear a path for us. All over town, children walked. There was no other way. Sometime in the 30's, we had a car. The closest store to us was "Miss Boyd's" and there was everything in the store from soup to nuts. It was within walking distance. And there was a phone at Miss Boyd's and that's where we made all of our phone calls and that was where people called us long distance. We didn't have a phone at home until the children were about grown..

YS: Was Miss Boyd White?

EJ: Oh yes!!! There were no Black stores near us for a long time. There was one Black store in the middle of town and the man who owned it must have had White parents because he looked half White. There was a dance hall not far from where we lived and people had to pass our house to get there. At lot of time we could hear sounds coming from the dance hall. You know, they did a lot of drinking and rowdy behavior there and the women who went there were called "loose" women. There were no jobs for women in Greenville except working in White people's homes.

YS: Tell me about schools children attended.

EJ: Well, you know, the schools were segregated. There was a "colored" school not far from where we lived and, of course, we would walk there. It was built of wood and it burned to the ground. There was a potbellied stove in the school [and we had a pot-bellied stove at home.] Sometimes it would get so cold in Kentucky that by the time we walked from home to school, our arms would be real cold. I remember that we had a lovely teacher and we would put our hands under her armpits or run them through her hair to get them warm. That's a good way to warm your hands. And we would gather around the pot-bellied stove so that our feet and our hands could thaw. We were somewhat lucky because we didn't have to walk as far as other children.

YS: Where did you go when your school burned down?

EJ: We had classes downtown in an old theatre and then we got one of the Rosenwald schools. It was a little brick square schoolhouse. Rosenwald was a White man who gave money to Black schools all over the South. There was no library for Blacks, and we couldn't check out books at the White library. We couldn't do that, but we had a little library at school. My grandmother would bring home books that the White people she worked for threw away. Sometimes the book would be my Christmas present. One of the books she gave me is a first-edition book and I have kept it all these years. It is in my library here. I think the name in the book is the name of the White child who owned it.

YS: Tell me more about the work your mother did.

EJ: In Greenville, women cleaned for White people. We would say, "cleaned kitchens," but it was the whole house we took care of. That's the work my mother did. She cleaned a Presbyterian church and she also cleaned the minister's house. We would go with them sometimes to help clean the sanctuary and the house. I remember that very well. One of the things I liked about the Presbyterians was their work in foreign fields. As we were dusting and cleaning, I would see pictures of people from different cultures. And of course my father also worked in the coal mines.

YS: Tell me about your father's work in the mines.

EJ: Daddy left home for work at five in the morning. Somebody would pick up all the workers and they would go where the mines were. They left at five and they returned to the community right before dark. We wouldn't eat until Daddy came home and we wouldn't eat until Daddy had had his bath. When he came home, he was covered with black coal dust. We would have water heating on the coal stove and we would have hot water in the tin tub. Daddy bathed in the dining room because it was close to the kitchen, which made it warm. The tub had handles on both sides and two of us would carry it out. After Daddy had his bath, then we would sit down and eat as a family.

YS: You had dinner after your father's bath?

EJ: No. We had supper. Supper was the last meal of the day. We had dinner on Sunday because we ate earlier in the day. During the week, when Daddy worked, we had supper because he came home in the evening and we always ate together as a family.

YS: Now I know the difference between dinner and supper. Did your father wear special clothing and carry certain tools for his work?

EJ: I have the coal miner's hat Daddy wore. It has a lamp in front, and I remember that the lamp would click into the hat. Right in the middle, in the front of the hat. Carbide burned in the lamp. Miners needed the lamp because when they went into the mine, they would go into the very bowels of the earth. Coal mining was the only work Daddy could do because he didn't have schooling and he had to work to help support his family. It was hard work and dangerous work. Tragedies did happen. Sometimes there would be explosions in the mines. But it was good pay for the times and it was regular work. Daddy would tell us that sometimes the miners would actually wade in water in the mines. It was a hard life, a very hard life. I think there were unions that helped families if a worker got hurt.

YS: Did working in the mines affect his health?

EJ: Yes. I think it affected his eyes. Daddy went to Memphis for surgery on his eyes and when the children left home and moved to Indianapolis, Daddy was almost blind. All that dust and stuff in the mines and no medical care. So, in answer to your question . . . yes, working in the mines affected his health? I must tell you that we coal mining families in Kentucky thought we were better off than Georgians. [laughter] We lived in a border state and that put up a few steps up on the rung, over Georgia. I guess it's because Georgia is in the Deep South and Kentucky isn't in the Deep South. That made us feel that we were better than Georgians.

YS;   You mentioned that adults went to dance halls. Tell me what children did for fun and entertainment.

EJ: All of our fun was connected to the church. The pastor and his wife would have socials at the parsonage. We played croquette and we ate ice cream. [laughter] But I wasn't that interested in the socials. People would say about me, "She's somewhere reading a book." That wasn't meant to be a compliment. I was bookish.

YS: How did you become interested in books?

EJ: My parents were interested in education. They didn't want us to stay in Kentucky. They would tell us, "When you get old enough, get out." So, they stressed education, and, I don't know. I just loved books. When I was very young, I loved books. And our parents wanted us to love books. They wanted us to get an education. They didn't want us to stay in Kentucky. Daddy did not want his sons working in the mines and his daughters working in White people's homes. Mama didn't want that either. So, they wanted us to leave Kentucky and get an education so that we would have a better life. I remember one time working in a White beauty salon and Mama would come and help me mop. I had to take rollers out of White women's hair and I had to clean up all the hair that had fallen on the floor. I will never forget the owner telling me one day that when I finished my education, I could always come back. I think about her sometimes and I smile to myself because I got out before she did.

But not all of them were that bad. I worked for one White woman who had a library and she would let me take home a book this week and return it to the next week. I worked I think one day a week. I dusted. This was in Indianapolis, Indiana. She had feather dusters for her lampshades. When it was lunchtime, she would fix the lunch and her sister and I would sit down for lunch. She would send me out in the back for blackberries. I remember that. I would pick a few blackberries and she would make a pie. And when the lunch was ready, I would put the iron down and have lunch and then I would wash the dishes. That was a good experience of working, but it was only five dollars a week. I worked for one lady who would have me eat lunch on the basement steps. And that's when you really have to say, "I don't have to do this all the time". Daddy and Mama always told us they wanted us to leave Kentucky. "When you get old enough, get out." All of us left, one by one. One brother went into the service. Another stopped in Louisville. The rest of us went to Indianapolis to live with this cousin who was in nursing school. She was an only child and, really, I didn't like her because she was snooty and I have written to apologize to her for the way I felt about her. There we were, country bumpkins living in her house . We had done what Daddy and Mama wanted us to do. We had left Kentucky.

YS: How many years did your father work in the mines?

EJ: Let me think. How many years? Well, we grew up with him working in the mines. When my parents married, he was working in the mines. When he left the mines, Daddy worked as a janitor at a White school and my mother worked there as well. The children would go there after school and help

YS: You said that your father had eye surgery in Memphis. Would you tell me what medical care was like in Greenville?

EJ: Well, it was all White in terms of professionals. I guess he might have had to go to Memphis because that was where the mines had their policies, you know. You have to remember that the town was small.

YS: Were there any Black doctors in Greenville?

EJ: No. All the doctors were White, including the ones that delivered us.

YS: Do you remember any home cures that people used? For example, when you and your siblings caught cold, what treatment would your parents use?

EJ: Mama knew about such cures. You know? This root and that root. I don't remember what they were, but I do remember that she would put things around our neck and she would rub our chests with something that she had put together. You just didn't go to the doctor all the time. I remember that we drank teas when we were sick. Sassafras. We didn't go to the drug store and buy medicines as people do today, except for castor oil, which was a nasty cold medicine. There were things growing out in the woods and we would walk there and Mama knew what to use. People would come to "Miss Lizzie".(that's what they called Mama) for cures and roots and things. She was known for that. When I was in college and thought I was different, I would write her and change her name to Elizabeth. She did not appreciate that and she told me, "That's not my name. My name is Lizzie."

YS: Tell me about the role of the church in your upbringing.

EJ: It was the center of our lives. We went every Sunday. The church wasn't too far away. We could hear thechurch bells when they rang. AME Zion. I have a picture of the small church in my mind. Mama sang in the choir and my sister and I sang in the Youth Choir.

Daddy was a Trustee. I would go to meetings with him. I was really a Daddy's girl. The church would have big picnics in the summer and at different times of the year there would be socials in the church basement. Methodists had youth conferences and that would give us a chance to travel away from Greenville. I remember going to Madisonville, Kentucky. It was like a retreat. I remember we didn't have money to stay in the dorms, so we stayed at the pastor's house and Mama sent food, so we didn't have to pay for individual food. When the preacher came to Greenville, he would stay at our house.

YS: Was there an adult woman in the community you looked up to, other than your mother of course?

EJ: Yes. The undertaker's wife. She and her husband, both of them, had good voices. We would go to her for information beyond what Mama and Daddy could give. The whole town was 2500. You knew everybody. You knew all Black folks and some White folks. If a stranger came to town, we would know. The undertaker's wife was kind of fancy and plump with pretty hair. Light-skinned. She sang and directed the choir and taught at the school. She knew everything about everybody. She had all the contacts. If you needed special information, you could go to her. She kinda stood out in the community. She was different, and very influential. And there was another woman who saved all of her magazines for us. We couldn't afford magazines, so she would give them to us and I had the prettiest scrapbook from cutting out pictures in her magazines.

YS: What were you told about being a female?

EJ: There was a great deal of emphasis on reputation. On being a moral girl. There were certain boys you didn't go out with, you had to come home at a certain time, certain places you didn't go to, certain houses you didn't enter "because their mamas let things happen." I was told, "Don't let a boy get you into a car." And when I had company, Mama would yell from the back of the house, "Tell them to go home or I will." I wasn't a popular girl. Boys weren't knocking my door down. I didn't date early in high school. Greenville was a small town, you know, and there was no public transportation.

YS: When you entered puberty, what were you told?

EJ: First of all, don't have sex with anybody. They always told us, "Don't let little boys get in your pants. Just don't have sex," and I didn't. Mama said that was bad, bad, bad. I didn't want to be a bad girl.

YS: Did you know of any instances of teenage pregnancy?

EJ: Yes, there were girls who had babies out of wedlock. It was considered a disgrace and there would be a lot of gossip, you know, "So and so got pregnant by . . ." Nobody was ostracized, but they did not seem to blame the boys, just the girls. There was a lot of talk, but nobody was ostracized.

YS: What kinds of chores did you have?

EJ: The boys didn't have to do any housework. We did the house and they did the yard. We always had a garden and they would work in the garden. Mama liked flowers. The boys did that. We could work in the garden if you wanted to, but it was the boys' job.

YS: Describe a typical summer day for you when you were growing up in Greenville.

EJ: We cleaned the house. Made our beds. Washed the dishes. We didn't cook. Mama did all the cooking. Our job was the dishes. Set the table. We played hopscotch and hide and go seek. We had a big front yard. No movies. This was a small country town. We didn't have electricity until I was ten. I'm guessing that I was ten when we got electricity. We had a battery radio. We had a piano and Mama played the piano. We took lessons, but we didn't become proficient.

YS: What did your parents teach you about race relations?

EJ: That there were good White folks and mean White folks. They had captions: good and bad. Mama would work for some who were good and some who were mean. Before I left home, I worked for several White folks and some of them had my mother doing things that she shouldn't have done. Do this. Do that. Come here. Stay long. Yes ma'am to all of them. One of my first experiences was washing dishes for a family that Mama worked for. When I was in Indianapolis, in order to get money for college, I worked for a woman who would not let me sit at the table. Not with them. She gave me a sandwich and I sat on the top step going to the basement. The funny thing is that she was poor and in much worse shape than I was. That was when I was in college in 1947. That was in Indiana. I did summer work in Indiana. The Urban League would send us out on these jobs. I remember that the person in charge was good and she would give me places in good locations. She picked some nice places. One White woman I worked for was poorer than I ever hoped to be. There are certain parts of Indiana that are like any place you could go to in Mississippi. I thought that the farther North you went, the better it would be. But that wasn't necessarily the case.

YS: Your parents wanted you to leave Greenville?

EJ: Yes. Daddy didn't want his sons working in the coalmines and Mama didn't want us working in White people's homes. That's why we went to Indianapolis. All of the children eventually left Greenville.

YS: What year did you leave?

EJ: I moved in 1943 right after finishing high school in Greenville. That was during the war, and my first job was in a war assembly plant that built bombs. I made more money than I had ever seen in my life.

YS: And you attended college in Indianapolis?

EJ: Well, actually, I left Indianapolis and went to Nashville to attend Tennessee State. I stayed there for two years and then I returned to Indianapolis and finished college there. I graduated from Indiana State University in 1949 with a Bachelor of Science in Business Administration. I married in that same year. I was twenty-four at the time. In 1965, I earned a Master of Business Education from Georgia State College.

YS: I know quilting is your art. What is your profession?

EJ: I am a CPS.

YS: That stands for?

EJ: Certified Professional Secretary of the National Secretaries Association..

YS: What influenced you to become a CPS?

EJ: I could type and write shorthand. That has always been my interest, which is why I majored in Business Education. One day, I saw an ad in the newspaper about Certified Professional Secretaries, and I said, "I want to be that." I applied and showed up for the test. It was given in downtown Atlanta, across from Macy's [Davison's at that time] in a small business school and we had to bring our own typewriters. There were just two Black females taking the test. There was a closet, like a little book closet, and it had paper over the window, and they said we could take the test in there if we wanted to, but we could not take it with the other people, with White people. Things went well, until noon. We had a break and we went to the bathroom and it was then that we realized the other ladies were pretending that there was no room. They were just standing there. The point was they didn't want to share the bathroom with us. So, eventually—I am sure we used it right after lunch—the director of the program, the owner of the school, called the two of us into the office and told us we had to leave because they could not have a racially mixed group. I am sure he said Negro. He couldn't have said Black. So, I called my husband and told him to come to pick me up. I couldn't go home by myself, not carrying the typewriter, and it was a manual typewriter. The place was upstairs at that. After I made the call—I don't know where I made the call from—I went downstairs and waited on the first floor. The other Black woman stayed. It is my understanding that she finished the exam there, but I did not.

We had a friend at Indiana University. He was a professor in the Business Education Department, and we called him. He knew the person in charge of the exam and we talked to a man [I think he was Dean of the school] who asked if I would be willing to go to Knoxville, Tennessee, and finish the exam there. They would finance my trip. I went, but I did not pass then. After my experience—and I do not know who facilitated this—no exams were given in that place anymore. It had to be given where everybody could participate fully. After that time, it was given in the Red Cross Building downtown. I took it the next time it was given, and I passed. Even after I had my own business, people would challenge the CPS after my name. They just took for granted that I could not do it. I have all of the papers. I was certified. I am certified.

YS: I am going to give you a name or a phrase and I want you to tell me the first thing that comes to your mind. Don't filter anything. [laughter] Anything goes. Whatever comes to mind, please share it with me. Rosa Parks.

EJ: A very strong, very strong woman.

YS: Work ethic.

EJ: My parent believed in work. As you know, my father was a coal miner. Mama was a seamstress, and she did day work. Sometimes, she would take us with her, her two girls. I remember going to White folks' houses with Mama. In high school, I worked for White folks. I think we got a dollar day for washing dishes, cleaning up. I did that work when I was fifteen or perhaps fourteen. I worked, and I never minded working at a good job. I started out doing menial labor and, as a child, I would get 50 cents. Well, 50cents would buy a little bottle of lotion. Neither one of my parents went to college. Mama finished the eleventh grade and Daddy went to the third grade, but they wanted us to have a good education.

YS: Children.

EJ: I have two, and they both did quite well academically, and they didn't have to work outside the home. Cindy, the older one, is a lawyer. She earned her law degree at the University of Iowa. Pam is a computer systems analyst. She earned her degree at Purdue University. I enjoy being a mother.

YS: Tell me your fondest memory as a mother.

EJ: Well, I guess the fondest was the birth of the first child, my daughter Cindy. I had been married seven years before the first child. My husband was in school at Indiana University so that was why we kept delaying. Cindy was born in Bloomington, Indiana, which is a small college town, because, as I said, my husband was in school, and I was working on campus. We lived out in the city . . . renting a home rather than living on campus. My husband was graduating and I couldn't attend the service because I was in the hospital with Cindy. After he finished, we moved back to Indianapolis and I had Pam a year and half later. That was as joyous as becoming a mother the first time. They were both easy to manage.

YS: I was informed that one of your quilts was exhibited during the Atlanta Olympics.

EJ: I'm very proud of that. It was the Georgia Quilt Exhibit and the 1997 Calendar carried a picture of my quilt, "Homeland." The back of the calendar carries a story I wrote about being a coal miner's daughter.

YS: What influenced you to quilt or maybe I should ask who influenced you?

EJ: Well, my mother quilted. She would make a quilt to work to work on during her spare time. I started looking at them and I thought, 'I can do that.' Mama had a quilting bee, but I like to quilt alone. I don't want other people working on my quilt. [Laughs] If we are doing a project maybe for a church or something, and we want to get something out, I'll probably accept that. But otherwise each is different, you know, different. I don't think you would want someone else sitting in your dress, would you? Well, that's the way I feel about quilting with a group. The quilt is my expression. It's my expression. So I guess I'm pretty selfish about that. If I am making a quilt for a particular person, I try to bring them in, but I don't like for anyone to tell me what to make. It has to be my design. I might look at a picture and try to replicate that, but I always feel free to change anything I want to. That's their quilt. This is my quilt. It's such a relaxing thing. I can't imagine not doing it all the time. I quilt all the time. Sometimes I stay up late.

YS: Where do you get ideas for your quilts?

EJ: Sometimes I look at books. I have a lot of quilt books that people have given me as gifts and sometimes I take a design as I see it. Other times I change it to suit my own taste. I wish I could read and sew at the same time. If I could do that, I think I would be complete. I can't sing. I can't dance. But I can sew.

YS: Do you think quilting is a Black art form?

EJ: Not necessarily. There are many more Whites at quilting exhibitions than there are Blacks. It doesn't mean Blacks are not quilting. We are just not exhibiting. It might have been Black in the beginning, but now as an art form? No.

YS: Is it a woman's art form?

EJ: Not really. There are men who are quilters. You know, for so long, quilting was about comfort. It was a necessary thing. It was to keep you warm. And that's really the big difference between a quilt and a comforter. A quilt is about design, and the design is about colors and shapes. A comforter is about warmth. The emphasis is on the inside. For the quilt, the emphasis is on the outside. Usually, a comforter doesn't have a thousand little pieces. A quilt is designed to have a thousand little pieces. Comforters are functional. Quilts are art. They are like a painting. The artist uses a paintbrush. The quilter uses a needle.

YS: It must be a wonderful feeling to see a finished quilt. I mean, how do you feel when it's all done.

EJ: Good. But I look back and become a very critical of it. Those stitches were a little big over there. That square was not really a square. It's a relief when you put that last stitch in. When I sew my name tag in, it is finished. It's done.

213

YS: And then? What do you do with the quilts?

EJ: I give them away.

YS: You give them away!!!!!

EJ: Yes. My quilts are gifts. I have done them on commission. When someone is buying, you have to be more commercial. And other people have too much input into the design. It's too commercial.

YS: If you could speak to a group of young Black women in their early twenties about preparing for the future, what would you say?

EJ: I would say try to make a plan for your life. Do something to make a contribution. Do something for the environment. Something. I would tell you to feel that the world is a better place because you are here. Train to have something to contribute, because in order to have something to contribute you have to be trained, you just can't come from the country or little town, and automatically have something to contribute.

YS: Tell me about challenges you have had as a Black woman.

EJ: I guess I haven't really had anything getting in my way. I had a business that didn't last long. It was good while it lasted but financially I had to give it up. I enjoyed teaching at Blayden Business College here in Atlanta. When we came from Indiana, with the two children, and my husband would travel, I was alone with them a lot and I applied for a job as a typing teacher and I got it! I enjoyed that. I would take the girls to Auburn Avenue, and I guess that's where I got the idea that I could run a business. It was located in the West End in a two-story building at 1065 Gordon Street. I offered personalized professional secretarial service (PPSS). The teaching of typing and shorthand was one of my very best experiences. That was beautiful. That was really, really rich. Let me show you the pictures. That's when I left Marta [pointing to a picture]. A friend told me about a post at Marta. I was secretary to the director. I worked there in the late seventies. I was honored when I was named "Employee of the Quarter." Let me share this with you.

YS: [reading from Marta Transit Times, August 1, 1978]: "A positive person, Johnson says she sees herself in the teacher role." It's clear that you enjoyed your work because of what you say: "I'm doing what I like."

EJ: Yes, that was a very positive experience. I left Marta only because the Presbyterian Church asked me to come with the national office here in Atlanta. I worked there as administrative secretary until my retirement.

YS: Have you ever traveled outside the States?

EJ: Yes. I traveled to Ghana. Where else did we go? I went to South Korea. I said Ghana, but I went to other countries as well, so I guess I should say West Africa. And oh yes, to the

214

Philippines. That was one of the hardest I believe in terms of standard of living. All of my traveling was related to the Presbyterian Church, U.S.A..

YS: What makes you sad?

EJ: When people hurt each other.

YS: What makes you happy?

EJ: Is that different from what I enjoy doing?

YS: Well, yes, but it need not be.

EJ: What makes me happy is helping someone, you know, as the song says, "If I can help somebody along the way. My living will not be in vain." Knowing that I am helping someone makes me happy.

YS: What has this experience meant to you?

EJ: It made me examine my life up to this point and evaluate my life to see whether or not the fact that I am here has made a difference. It's important that we make a contribution when we walk this life. The question we have to ask ourselves is would it have mattered if we had not been here. So, talking with you has made me examine my life and ask myself that question. And it has also brought back so many happy memories of my parents. They were special. And this project has been special. I consider it an honor to have been involved. My mother would be proud. Thank you, Mama. Thank you, Daddy.

DR. ELLA PEARSON MITCHELL

Charleston, South Carolina
Author, Scholar, Theologian, and Preacher

He said to me, "Now you can preach from down there on the lectern, but don't extend the invitation." So I preached. . . . By the time I had finished the sermon, he was nowhere to be found. I extended the invitation and seven people joined that morning. I remember White women always wanted me to preach about how it feels to be Black in the midst of all of this trouble. I don't have the problem of race.

YS: Rev. Mitchell, we are really honored to have this opportunity to talk with you. We know from what we have read about you in a number of books that you were born in Charleston, South Carolina.

EM: Yes. I was born on October 18, 1917.

YS: Were your parents natives of Charleston?

EM: My mother was born in Charleston, but my father was born in Walterboro and there is a street in the city named for him. It was the street he lived on after he retired.

YS: Do you know how your parents met?

EM: Yes. Papa [that's what I called him] was principal of a school in St. Helena Island, and he was called to be pastor of Olivet Presbyterian Church in Charleston. Let's see. That must have been in 1907. He finished Johnson C. Smith University in 1900 and he got his divinity degree in 1903. Yes, that must have been 1907 when he became pastor at the church. My mother was one of the members. They married at noon on Christmas Eve, and they journeyed forty miles to Walterboro, where they spent their honeymoon. And they lived happily ever after. Papa died at 94 and Mama at age 90. They were married for 64 years.

YS: Did either of your parents tell you about grandparents or great grandparents who were in bondage? I ask because you really can't study slavery without reading about South Carolina.

EM: Mama and Grandma didn't talk about that. Even my oldest sister didn't talk about that. She didn't even want to publish Mama's death. So, no stories were passed down, but I remember that my maternal grandmother was a very light-skinned woman with blonde hair. I never could understand why Grandma Hannah had those features. I later learned that she was the product of the master and the slave. She actually had her wedding in the big house.

YS: That was in Charleston?

EM: No, that was in Walterboro. That was on the Frazier Plantation. My paternal grandparents were married in the big house. I tell you. It blows my mind. They were married in the big house on the plantation and they left immediately and went back to the Pearson plantation. They had fourteen children.

YS: One of whom was your father? What was his name? And your mother's name?

EM: Joseph Richard Pearson. Jessie Lugenia Wright Pearson.

YS: You grew up in Charleston during the 1920's. Tell me what were some of the games you played as a child growing up in Charleston?

EM: Oh! One of them was hopscotch. You know that one? And we played the juggling board. That was a lot of fun. An unusually interesting game. The board was suspended between two posts. The other thing we played most of the time was tag and hide-n-go-seek. We didn't have advantage of anything like radio or television. No, radio came in when I was about ten. We got our first radio . . . I think I mentioned this in the book . . . from the neighbor, Mr. Waters. He was a Navy man, and he allowed us to come over to his house and listen to the radio.

We had to put on headphones, so only one person could listen at a time. We'd take turns. You have no idea now what that was like. You've seen the pictures of the little dog Atwater Kent Radio. Have you ever seen that? Anyway, there was a big round speaker on top of a rectangular box and there were earphones. And you couldn't listen unless you had the earphones on, so we had to take turns listening to the radio. That was in the early 20's . . .about '22 or '23. I was a very young girl. It was so much fun because he did allow us to hear the radio.

YS: Mr. Waters?

EM: Right. Waters. A Navy man. He was the first in our neighborhood to have a radio. It was an Atwater Kent radio. And they were the most sociable ones in the whole neighborhood. The Waters lived there, the Breauxbreoaux lived on the front and they were German. B-r-e-a-u-x-b-r-e-o-a-u-x. The Shermans were the Jewish people, and the Lessermans on the other side were German. Across the street was a huge mansion that had an elevator, and that's where the Jantz family lived. And whenever one of the six daughters over there got married, they always threaded curtains through the steel bars of the rod iron fence so that no one could see in on the huge yard. But we used to prop ourselves in front of the door so that we could see them come down very high steps that led to the yard and we would see the procession. Now, their cook and housekeeper was a woman we called Aunt Janie and she supplied us with so many goodies. All we had to do was go over to Ms. Janie's. There was a huge stable in the back where they kept the horses and buggy. People didn't have cars. Can you imagine what it was like without cars? We could go through the stable to the kitchen and the living quarters for the maids and servants. Sometimes, when no one was there, we would go through the entire house and see all the beautiful paintings and the furniture and . . . Jantz was a very rich man. The others in the neighborhood were middle-class.

YS: You said your father was a pastor. What did other Black people in the community do?

EM: There weren't any other Black people in the community for blocks around. I don't know how we happened to be there. I have never found out but my father built that house. He actually built the house. The church was there and as I told you it was previously pastured by a White minister. Our social life was spent with the members of the church and they lived maybe about four blocks away on what was called Short Street. The Coaxums, the Baileys, the Bryants, the Haywoods and our playmates from school lived in this area. One of the most historical places was The Jenkins Orphanage. It is mentioned in the book, Slaves in the Family.

YS: I know about that book but haven't read it. I intend to, though.

EM: Now, getting back to the neighborhood, as I said, all of our social life was in the neighborhood. We did not have movies, we did not have tapes, we did not have CD's, we did not have any of those things.

YS: Did you hear about or witness any racial violence in the community? I ask because this was in South Carolina in the early twenties and . . .

EM: I didn't witness or hear about racial violence in the community. Not in the community. Behind us there was an alley and there was always a lot of fighting and cursing. We weren't too far from Catfish Road, which was the setting for Porgy and Bess. We knew Porgy as a child. He rode around in a goat driven cart. My mother worked at Legeton Bookstore . She was an arts and crafts expert in the store, and Porgy used to sit outside the bookstore in his cart. He would park the goat cart behind the store and sell pencils and little trinkets. If we were rude, he would give us a tongue-lashing and our mother would give us a spanking.

YS: Why?

EM: For being rude. Legeton bookstore was a White bookstore but because my mother was so talented in art, they let her have classes for White and Black alike. But in the stores, we had to be really careful. Whites watched us like hawks. They were always right on our necks as if we were going to steal something. And in the stores, we couldn't try on clothes. No, we had to buy it according to our measurement and many times we had to have things hand sewn. I always did my own sewing. Mother taught us how to make all of our clothes and everything. It's odd, though, that we could try on shoes. I always wondered about that. We could try on shoes but we had to have on ankle socks. I used to save my money to buy the silky one, you know. I remember my first year in college we got nylons. Ah! What a change! All those other times, we had cotton stockings like you're wearing now . The colored ones with patterns, but nylons were expensive. They cost seven dollars a pair.

YS: So when you were in high school in Charleston, did you work?

EM: No, I didn't. One time I planned to go to work and I went for an interview and they asked me my name and I said, "I think you've got it on the record. It's Ms Pearson?" And then they said, "I don't think you can work for us," so I didn't get to work. I used to volunteer at Charleston Hospital and Roper Hospital. I did a lot of singing and so my Sundays were always very well engaged. I didn't get a chance to stop at just one church; it was usually two or three. Later on, I learned to play the pipe organ and I played for several churches. My major was music.

YS: Tell us about the hospitals in Charleston. .

EM: The hospitals were segregated. Roper had a segregated ward. Charleston was the all-Black hospital. We were called Negroes in those days. We had not come into the term "Black." The term "Black" came in the early sixties.

YS: You talked about going away to college. Where did you go?

EM: We had exposure to a large number of teachers from different colleges. I don't remember any teachers from Spelman, but I do remember them from Fisk and Talladega, from Clark, from Atlanta University. There were three teachers from Talladega and they were always telling me that's where I should go and I got a full scholarship to Talladega College. I entered in 1935. That was my first trip away from home. My father got an older girl who was going to Talladega College to accompany me there and set me up. You students have parents or friends who come and set you up in college; we had none of that. But I did ride in a Pullman car. That's how I went away from home. Now in my first year, I did not go home for Christmas. In fact, I didn't go home until my senior year in college. In my first year at Talladega, I suffered from severe lack of vision. In fact, I was utterly blind for a period of time. I had to have someone help me dress. I had to have someone help me get to classes. I was stricken during my first week on campus. My father took me to Washington, D.C. to the Eye Nose and Throat Hospital. I had polyps in my Eustachian tubes and blood could not reach my eyes. I'll never forget my father conversing with the doctor in Latin. Latin. That was the only language they had in high school. Momma had taken it, too, but Papa had it in high school and in college. So I had an operation, and I never knew what was going on. Any way, I went back to school after the operation, and I finished with my class in time that year. I sang in the choir and had anticipated being a voice major, but I developed an interest in sociology. Actually, my main interest was religion, but there was no religion department at the college at that time. There was in my senior year and the professor in the department was from Gammon, which is now a part of ITC. I took twelve courses and those courses qualified me for graduate work in religion, so I had a real break. I was the only student in the class. I was chapel assistant at the college and because I could sew, I was able to make all of the drapes for the pulpit and the communion table. I really had a great time.

YS: Both of us are from Africa and we don't know anything about Talladega. Where exactly is it located?

EM: In Alabama, about 125 miles from Atlanta. Talladega College was started by the American Missionary Association and at the time it was highly rated for producing Ph.D.s. Almost everybody coming out of Talladega went on to earn Ph.D.s and other graduate degrees. Talladega and Fisk were very highly rated Black colleges. Lincoln in Pennsylvania, my husband's alma mater, was the first of the Black colleges. I finished at

Talladega in 1939. It is still a functional college but, like most of the Negro colleges, it is going down financially.

YS: Tell us what it was like growing up as the daughter of a preacher.

EM: We were restricted. We could not dance. We could not play cards. We couldn't drink. I am sure my sisters did.

YS: I am sorry. I should have asked you early on if you had siblings.

EM: There were four of us and I was the third daughter. There were no boys. Four girls, and we were four years apart. I don't think my parents had planned that at all. It was just the way we fell. My oldest sister died in 99; she was eighty-nine when she died. My youngest sister this weekend on the twenty-ninth would be eighty-two. I'll be eighty-six in October.

YS: A family of four girls! And you were the third daughter! I am sure your sisters gave you a wealth of information about womanhood.

EM: Not too much. As I said, we were four years apart and so we didn't really grow up together. Actually, my father was the one who did all the instruction on how I was going to transfer into womanhood.

YS: Your father?

EM: Mother was very, very reluctant about telling us about sex and life. In fact, one of the things we hold against her [laughing] is that she said, "After all of these years we have been married, Papa has never seen me in the nude." She was so Victorian. Henry and I laugh about that all the time. Papa died when he was ninety-four. Mama died when she was ninety. They were eleven years apart so it spanned a long period of time. Jet magazine in 1997 had a spread on the Pearson sisters, and at that time we had been married a total of two hundred and twenty-seven years to the same husbands. Somebody must have taken the magazine because we have not been able to find it around here.

YS: Why did you decide to become a preacher? A minister?

EM: Papa was a preacher, and I enjoyed so much being with him—riding around the community on the handlebars of his bicycle and going to visit the sick and the shut-ins with him. When we went to different houses, people would give me goodies that I could take home and share with my sisters. I was interested in the ministry from childhood.

YS: I am just a little curious about what your dad told you about womanhood.

EM: Oh, one of the things he told me (and I still practice this) was, "If you really want to enjoy life, smile." He would have me stand in front of the mirror and smile. Not a thin grin, but a genuine smile. And as he had me doing, he would say, "You are large for your age." At twelve, I weighed a hundred and thirty-five pounds. I was short and chubby. And my father would say to me, as I was standing in front of the mirror smiling, "When you go down the street in a certain neighborhood, men are going to whistle at you and call you and try to attract your attention, but you go on as if you don't hear them. Just guard yourself and don't get in any kind of position in which you could be raped." The other thing he said was, "Always have a very positive answer for people. Don't let them cup you in anything that would involve you in a negative way." I have lived on that all my life. My father told us, "Don't say anything to anybody if it has to be negative. Rather than be critical of people, just don't say anything at all." Another thing that he told us was, "Worry is the most devastating thing in all of life. You don't have to worry about anything." My husband doesn't believe I know that because right now I am thinking about our financial condition. He says, "There's enough, Ella. Just don't worry about it." Yesterday, he took me to the bank and I moved money from savings to checking so that I wouldn't be worried. Papa said, "Worry is the most futile thing in the world. It can destroy you."

Now with regard to sex , he did not do too much talking about the birds and the bees, but he did tell us, "When you're in "that" condition, be careful to protect yourself and to be very clean."

YS: That condition being your cycle?

EM: We did not have the advantage of Kotex or Tampax or any of these modern things you have today. We had large baby diapers. And you had to wash them almost as soon as you wore them because the blood would stain them. My mother used to tell me, "You must be a very calm person because your menstrual pads wash out so clear and so fast." They never had any stains; that must have been my life. I tried to be calm.

YS: Do you remember when you had your first period?

EM: I do remember so well. I was sitting in the living room in our house and I felt this strange feeling come down my panties and I called to my grandmother-- she was about seventy-two at the time--and she told me to come up to her room and she told me these periods would be once every twenty-eight days for years.

YS: Your grandmother?

EM: I don't think Mama was there at the time, but I would have gone to Grandmother anyhow. Mama was so inhibited.

YS: Tell me about your first pregnancy.

EM: My husband was Dean of the Chapel at North Carolina Central and we were living in North Carolina. In Durham. He was a candidate for a position at Friendship Baptist Church here in Atlanta. I was speaking in Jacksonville, Florida and I came back after my afternoon speech to meet him in Atlanta. We believe I became pregnant on our return from that Atlanta engagement. He did not get the church. Maynard Jackson's father got the church. We left North Carolina and moved to California. Because I was pregnant, it wasn't safe for me to travel to California and it wasn't wise for me to go to Charleston to have the baby. That was at the time Ernest Just had just died in South Carolina, because they would not let him into the hospital because he was a Negro. My husband said, "No, you are not going to Charleston. You are going to Ohio to my parents." He took me to Ohio and he went on to California to start his service there. He was going to be a missionary responsible for building new churches in California. The war industries had brought many people to the state. This was in 1945. We married in '44.

I'll back up a little because this is very funny. The first month after we were married, we were at the dinner table. It was on a Sunday, and I told my husband, "My period has come on, so I am not pregnant." He cried. We were living in North Carolina at the time. The next month, he got so sick he couldn't teach his classes. I had to teach for him. And one Sunday, he was not able to go to chapel. We had guests for dinner that Sunday and he had to be excused to go to the bathroom because he was so sick. So we called the doctor. The doctor came over and after he examined my husband, he said, "Have your wife come to the office tomorrow." I went to the office and that is when the doctor told me I was pregnant.

YS: Oh! Your husband got sick for you?

EM: Yes, and he was sick all the time. [laughing] I had to teach his classes because they were at eight in the morning. He had morning sickness for about a week. People tell you when you are pregnant, you are going to lose a tooth. My husband lost a tooth. I didn't.

YS: I'd like to hear more about your pregnancy.

EM: I went to Ohio. My husband's father was a mail carrier, but he had a garden on the railroad crossing and every afternoon we would walk up there. I had to walk because that's one of the things you have to do when you are pregnant in order to have an easy delivery. I can tell you this. Before we married and I took the test, the Wassermann test for venereal diseases like syphilis . . . Anyway, Dr. Mae Chinn was my doctor and she was a very famous doctor in New York. At that time, I was in seminary and I had gone to work in the Church of the Master in New York City. Dr. Mae Chinn said to me, "You will never have any problems having any babies. You have very large groins. Your pelvic bone is very well suited for delivery." The doctor in Ohio told me I would have no problems, but it would be difficult for me if the baby were large. I went into labor about six o'clock in the afternoon. I was in the worst labor pains. Mother Mitchell took me to the hospital and she walked up and down the halls saying to the nurse, "Do something! Do something for her! She is having such labor pains. Do something!" Anyway, I delivered at about one in the morning. My baby was nine pounds and two ounces and twenty-inches. I had to have twenty-three stitches. It was really rough.

YS: Were the labor pains that intensive for all of your children. How many children do you have?

EM: I'll tell you about all of them. I have three children. Our son is now deceased. He was huge and he grew to be 6'2. When he was seven weeks old, we went to California, and because I was nursing him, I didn't have to take the formula bottles and everything. We flew overnight from Columbus, Ohio to San Francisco in a propeller plane. It took almost eight hours. Now it takes only four by jet. He was a great baby; he slept all night on the plane. The next baby was born two years later. Two years later, in April, our first daughter was born. She was eight pounds and six ounces. What a difference! She was born as they were taking me from the labor room to the delivery room. The third child was seven pounds, thirteen ounces. She was born in the labor room. We didn't even get to the gurney. I remember calling the doctor. In fact, I was on my way to take the two older children to the nursery school so that they could be cared for. My husband was across the way at the garage working on our old car. He was rebuilding the motor. He is just that kind of person. So I called to him on the way, "I am going to the nursery to take Hank and Muriel to school." I didn't get down the street five minutes before I was doubled up in labor pains. I mean I doubled up like going to the ground. Our son Hank went across the street to the garage and he told Henry, "Mommy is having trouble. She can't walk." The baby was born in the labor room.

YS: You remember your deliveries in such detail. May I ask your position on abortions?

EM: If it's a medical problem, a woman should have an abortion, but I don't favor having abortions because you just don't want the child. One time I had to supervise a girl who was on study leave at Spelman. She was pregnant and was going to have an abortion. I asked her what her parents thought about it and she said, "My mother died when I was fifteen and my father doesn't care what I do." And when she went to the clinic and put up her visa card, my jaws just dropped. You know, pay for an abortion with a Visa card, but that happened. One of my high school classmates came to my wedding, and she died on her way back to Charleston as the result of an abortion. As I said, I am in favor of abortions for medical reasons. I don't think anybody should suffer. I don't believe that you are destroying a life if you have an abortion. Life does not really come into a child until the child is delivered. As long as it is in the womb, it is not a full life. There are a lot of people who believe that it begins when the sperm unites with the egg, I don't believe that. I must have aborted one of my pregnancies between the oldest child and the second child. We were trying to put a mattress on the top of the car. I must have been at least two months, but I didn't realize I was that much pregnant. So there I was helping to put a mattress on the top of the car and my water broke. I started bleeding, and I just expelled. It was frightening to see such a tiny little thing. I don't think women have to fight for their rights. Whatever comes, is going to be the word of God, and the way women in ministry do it is just frightening to me, because you never win a battle when you are fighting for it.

YS: Tell me what you taught your daughters about womanhood.

EM: When they arrived at age twelve, I read for them from the Bible the story of Jesus in the temple when he was discussing with the elders and his parents had not been able to find him. I told them that it was a change in life. That they were leaving childhood and going into their teens. I did that for my son as well. Both Henry and I did. We always sat them down together so the children could hear it from both of us at the same time. After the discussion, we would ask them if they had any questions. We gave them all the details-- well, as much as we could about what was going to happen. I remember Elizabeth saying, "Oh, my goodness! I don't have any help any more." She was so startled about going into thirteen. We tried to tell them, each one of them, that they were responsible for their own health and sex and everything from here on. "You are in charge of your affairs," we told them. "You are an adolescent." God knows some of those teen years are the worse years of all in our lives. Oh, they had trouble. They had lots of trouble. I don't think Muriel had any trouble. I do remember Hank asking for help with a young woman he had impregnated, but she did not want help. She wanted to have the baby, and the family was satisfied with that.

And my daughter Elizabeth was accosted when she was in Boston in law school. Elizabeth is the one in the top picture over there. She is five feet tall. She is working on a doctorate at Columbia Seminary now. She was in law school in Boston when she was beaten and robbed. I don't know the extent to which she was beaten. We asked her did she want us to come up and take care of her, and she said she was going to be all right. She was the one who got the bruises. One morning, she was fixing breakfast and her husband had just left to take the boys to school. Somebody broke into her back window and stole her purse right off the table. She turned around to reach for something and she cut her hand in two places. I had to rush her to the hospital. She always seemed to be having trouble like that. They found the purse up the street and, of course, it was empty. That was fine. I just didn't know she was going to cut her hand that badly. She never seemingly wanted to have any help. She's always been independent. She worked in the White House with President Carter, scheduling appointments. She went to Paris to study voice. She took a Paris Opera course. A young man who went over to Paris from here asked her to marry him. They have been married now for twenty-two years. She is something else. Independent. A little feisty. The older girl, Muriel, is a teddy bear. Her daughter is the one in the picture there.. She is a pilot for United Airlines. She stays with us when she's not flying.

YS: I keep thinking about a parent's role to protect their children, and at a certain point not being able to offer protection.

EM: Every tub stands on its own bottom. You cannot live for them. I'd love to. I am an awful mother because I try to get into everything. You can't live for your children. Right now, we are in quite a worry about our granddaughter the pilot. She is planning to be married in August, and they are trying to find a place to move to. Our garage is full of her things. Her room upstairs is full of her things. Our daughter Liz has a place over there across the street that has three bedrooms and two baths. We would love for them to stay over there. In fact, originally she said, "We would like to be close so we can take care of you older folks." We told them that we would help with the rent if they would take care of us. They could come over here every now and then and do the things that need to be done or, like on Saturday, they rushed to the airport with the medication we needed because they were in the house. But they have found a place in College Park that they love very much. The rent is four hundred dollars cheaper. So, I think we've lost them. When I get too anxious about that, I remember Papa saying, "Worry is the most futile thing in the world. You don't need to ever get stressed about anything." There is a song that says, "Jesus walked this lonesome valley, and he had to walk it by himself. Nobody else can walk it for you. You have to walk it by yourself.

YS: I have not finished your book, Rev. Mitchell, but I have read most of it. It's really interesting! I find it extremely entertaining, especially the story of how you met Rev. Mitchell and the—shall we call it—courtship. I thought that was all so interesting and so very different from most courtship stories. You were the one to propose and then you took your proposal back.

EM: [Laughing]. He thought I was serious and I was kidding.

YS: I thought you were serious. As I was reading the book, I honestly thought you were serious, but that you thought better of it.

EM: It was leap year. If you don't make your proposal on leap year day, then you have to wait another four years.

YS: It was therefore imperative that you ask the question as quickly as possible. I understand. [laughter] I remember reading that when he proposed, he said he wasn't madly in love, but he believed you were whom God sent for
him.

EM: That was right. My answer was, "If God is for us, who could be against us?" That's the way it's been for all these years coming up to fifty nine now.

YS: I'm a little jealous because Yomi has read the story and the rest of us haven't. So I was wondering if we could get a little taste of exactly what happened. Yomi keeps telling me, "Oh! You've got to read the book!" Could you explain a little?

EM: Henry and I met sixty-two years ago on an elevator in seminary and we were going up the tower to the third floor where the library was. The library was access to Hastings Hall, which was a dormitory for male students. So he went through the library to go to his Hastings Hall. We didn't speak to each other on the elevator. You see Papa told me never to speak to strangers. It was a little elevator, self-operated, and just the two of us were in there. So when we got off the elevator, I said, "I'm matriculating here this year." He says, "Are you planning to study this year?" And from then on, it's been fun. I sat beside him in the library. We had cubicles, you know. My name ended with a P and his with an M. I used to work in the library and he would come in the evenings and get his books out. But he was engaged to Charlotte Pinket. So on the day he was going to get the ring, . he asked me to go with him. And I told that I had promised to work on Saturday for someone who had another engagement and I said, "Be sure to come by and show me the ring when you come back." Well, he purchased the ring and showed it to me and went through with the engagement, but Charlotte's mother said, "No, you can't marry a poor Baptist preacher." She came from a wealthy family. Her father was a bail bondsman and they owned lots of property in Washington D.C. and her brother was married to Pearl Bailey, the actress. They were that kind of family. She said, "No, no, no, you're not marrying him." So the engagement was broken. That Christmas, my intended came up to New York to bring me the engagement ring. He was a senior student at McHenry Medical College. I was working as a church worker and he said, "You might as well be married to the church." And I said, "You're right." So he left. Well, my mother thought I would be heart broken, but no way! He married a woman who was a socialite and they had two sons. He's been dead since 1957. He died of alcoholism and I hear that his sons didn't go to his funeral. I learned this from his sister, who was my very good friend.

YS: We were wondering, how did you become a minister at a time when women were not accepted onto the pulpit?

EM: Well, as I said, I had prepared for it. I was in the seminary. I had worked as a Sunday school missionary in South Carolina and I was establishing Sunday schools in different places. We'd have one under a big oak tree, say, at four o'clock in the afternoon. Mayesville, South Carolina, is where I got acquainted with Mary McLeod Bethune. And that's what I did actually for a living. I sold my car and decided I was going to seminary. I applied at Yale, and they said in New England, there is fieldwork experience only for men. They suggested I apply to Union in New York City, and I got a student assignment that Henry and I went to apply for the same night. We sat there and talked while they were in the meeting and then they called us in one at a time. Henry went in first, but he said he would wait for me so that we could leave together. At that time I never thought anything about getting on a subway at 11 o'clock at night. Not a thought. No one would ever bother me. But Geeez! I don't even want to go to New York now. But think about it. That was in the '40s. The early '40s. And I had to pass the Apollo Theater when I went up to my apartment. Never thought anything about it. From my childhood, I had been with my father in his parish work there. So there was no question at all when I went to college to ask for a religion major.

YS: Were you accepted into the pulpit?

EM: Not at all. Not at all. In fact, they didn't even have women in parish ministries as a preacher. It was always religious education. You could be director of religious education or minister of religious education. That's what I was doing when we got married. I was director of religious education. I also worked with camps during the summer. I remember one Y camp in Beach, Virginia, where I was the chaplain and I had to take all kinds of responsibilities for the services and everything. All the way from my years of childhood, I wanted to be in religious work. I'd gotten into it in college and then after college into missionary and then into seminary. According to the record at Union, I was the second Black woman to get a degree in their one hundred year history.

YS: That's quite an achievement. Do you think women ministers still face barriers?

227

EM: Tremendous barriers! Yes. I was talking to Sue Jay Johnson, who is president of the ministers' conference in Hampton. She is the first woman in the hundred years of the conference to be president. And she called me the other night and she said she was here in town and she had wanted me to preach at the Green Pastures Church. She's always called me "the Mother of the Movement" because she thinks that I'm . . . well, I am that old. I told her that it was thirty-five years from the time I was licensed to the time I was ordained. That's a lifetime for most people, but I've really had a rough time. Time and time again, I could not go to the pulpit. I had to preach from the floor, which was all right. I can preach from the chair, if necessary.

YS: So they didn't allow you to actually preach from the pulpit?

EM: No. Women sat on the front bench and if you were going to preach, you would walk up to a table on the side or to a lectern , something that was set up for you. I remember very well. There was a man in a church in Oakland. He said to me, "Now you can preach from down there on the lectern, but don't extend the invitation." I said, "Alright." So I preached. My sermon was: "We have this treasure in earthen vessels." By the time I had finished the sermon, he was nowhere to be found. I don't know how he got out of there so fast! He must have gone out of a back door or something. I thought, "Well, I have to extend the invitation. He's not here." Oh my goodness! I extended the invitation and seven people joined that morning. There were more men then women. There were five men and two women. Through the years, it has not really been grievous. It has not been a sad experience for me because I had tremendous opportunities. I remember White women always wanted me to preach about how it feels to be Black in the midst of all of this trouble, you know. I don't have the problem of race.

YS: Since you mentioned that, I wanted to ask you what is the most pressing issue or problems that African Americans face today?

EM: In the ministry?

YS: In ministry and in general.

EM: Well, somehow we have mistakened our values. We have misplaced them. Our priorities are not with deep moral and religious thought. We've been attracted to things that are making us beautiful even from pressing hair, which came in my time with Madam C.J. Walker. We have been trying our best to look White. You know that? We imitate White women in almost everything that we do unfortunately. We aren't thinking about our grandmas, who had the pressure of slavery and who did such wonderful things with children, although they were enslaved. The almighty dollar has taken over our lives too much so. We're trying to live like White women, although we don't really sense that is what we are doing. We don't say, "Well, I want to be White," but almost everything we do is an imitation.

YS: I have a list of names, places, periods in time and I was wondering if you could give me tell me, briefly, in one word or one sentence, what comes to mind when you hear them. I shall start with Martin Luther King Jr.

EM: Martin Luther King Jr. was really a memorable person. He was concerned not only for our race, but for all people.

YS: Malcolm X.

EM: Malcolm X at first was selfishly Muslim. Then he turned to embracing everybody; accepting people for what they were rather than putting a label on them and identifying them by that way.

YS: Sojourner Truth.

EM: Sojourner Truth. Well, I am so proud to be on that same picture with her [indicating the cover of a book with Rev. Mitchell and Sojourner Truth and others]. There she is over there and Ella Mitchell is on the other side. Only two women. We visited her place. It is quite a memorial to her. A brave woman. She said to Frederick Douglas, "Is God dead?" He was trying to make some point, you know, and she said, "Is God dead? Frederick, you don't have anything to worry about."

YS: Ida B. Wells.

EM: Ida B. Wells. I did not get to know about her until I was in my sixties. I had not heard too much about her before, but she was a brave woman. Very brave writer. A pioneer.

YS: George W. Bush.

EM: A man out of his time.

YS: Condoleeza Rice.

EM: I think she sold her heritage for a "mess of pottage."

YS: Howard Thurman.

EM: Howard Thurman was a mystic. A man who would enjoy having people dig into what he was saying. We knew him personally. In fact, I was at his wedding when he married Sue Bailey.

YS: Africa.

EM: The continent? Africa?

YS: Yes, the continent.

EM: Oh. Been there twelve times. The different cultures have really intrigued me. I don't think I would want to go back to Africa now, with all the turmoil and everything there. One of my most exciting experiences was in Kenya. Then we stayed a longer time in Ghana and Nigeria. I did not go to South Africa until I was 80 years old. I asked to go to South Africa for my birthday. I had wanted so much to visit the embassy and meet the U.S. Ambassador and, you know, I talked my way into getting into the embassy. Got to the Ambassador's office and looked and saw pictures of a program Henry and I were directors of, a program for travel to Africa to study our religious roots. Just as we walked out of the office, going to the elevator, I heard someone calling out "Henry and Ella Mitchell!" Ambassador Jim Joseph was coming out of the elevator. He took us back to the office, and we sat there for at least twenty minutes. I was eighty years old.

YS: Rosa Parks.

EM: Rosa Parks, the mother of the Civil Rights Movement. She's a gracious lady right now. She's ninety.

YS: The Black Madonna.

EM: That was a drawing. A picture. Let's see. Finch talks a lot about the Black Madonna. Isn't that true? Yes. I learned a great deal from him about the Black Madonna, especially in Eastern Africa. I think we ought to keep more of those alive.

YS: Spirituality.

EM: It's what you live. The testimony of your life is your spiritual life. A lot of people pin it onto you, but it's what you do everyday of your life. If you're not spiritual, you're something else. It can be worship of God. It can be worship of things. It can be worship of persons. Whatever your spirit leads you to do is the way you behave. That's true, isn't it? What you want to do, you do. What you enjoy doing, you do it.

YS: Motherhood.

EM: Motherhood is great. To think that a child is in your body and you have the opportunity of taking care of the fetus for nine months. I was told very early on that it would be very easy for me to have children because I have such a broad pelvis. I approached motherhood with a great anticipation. I enjoyed it and I'm still enjoying it.

YS: Young, Black women.

EM: [Sigh] We have not been kind to them in the way we have forced them to live and grow. We have misplaced a number of the real priorities that they should have had. So I blame our generation for stumbling into that. Black women have had real opportunities. They've had so many openings, so many opportunities. We are still tripping into somebody else's pattern, and selling our souls for . . . I wanted to say that about Condaleeza Rice.

230

[laughter] We knew her when she was a young woman. She grew up in a church in Palo Alto.

YS: Finally, I would like to ask who your she-roe is.

EM: My she-roe. That would be very hard for me to say. One? Just one? The older people I've had in my life are hard to honor. They have passed over. I would say my mother was a very, very , but she was not an outstanding person who would have done anything remarkable. It's very hard for me to narrow it down to one person. I've had a lot of great influences in my life. Are you disappointed that you asked me that?

YS: Oh no! Not at all.

YS: What would you like us to say about you when we write the story?

EM: Gee, what would I like you to say? Well, maybe the one thing I would like you to say is I'm a God-fearing woman who is trying to live what she believes. I've really tried awfully hard. I believe that God is the creator, the sustainer, and the leader of my life. I really do. I think, as I said to somebody just this past week, I understand why a minister said he could not ordain me. I know that he was limited and maybe not taking his direction from God. Then the one who did ordain me said to me, "If your life has not said all the things about you in these thirty five years that I have known you, then I can't ask you a question that you couldn't answer." There wouldn't be any questions. You see what I'm saying? You understand? That if my life has not been a testimony by the way I live, nobody can say anything about the answer that I would give because you couldn't really judge me if you hadn't seen it.

YS: Thank you so much, Reverend Mitchell.

EM: I appreciate the fact that you had those names. I'm sorry I can't come up with a she-roe.

YS: Oh no! That's fine. We have your mother.

MRS. RUBY NEAL

Atlanta, Georgia
Teacher, Administrative Assistant, and Community Volunteer

I had just started at Washington High School and my brother was working at a shoe shop down in Five Points. We had streetcars then, not Marta. Well, when I would take the streetcar down to Auburn Avenue, I would be busy trying to wave at him when we passed the shoe shop and he would be busy wiping his lips trying to tell me that I had on too much lipstick. We had a beautiful relationship.

EXCERPTS OF INTERVIEWS WITH MRS. RUBY NEAL
Conducted by Michaela Warren

YS: Mrs. Neal, I want to thank you for giving me the honor of interviewing you for the SIS Oral History. And you are making it so convenient for me by letting me interview you here on campus.

RN: Well, I am here on a regular basis volunteering in the museum and I thought if I could save you the trouble of leaving campus, that would be better for you. I know how much work Spelman students have to do for their classes.

YS: Thank you. Now, during the interviews, Mrs. Neal, if at any time I should ask a question that you would not like to answer, just let me know and tell me to go on to the next question.

RN: That's fine.

YS: Alright. Would you tell me your full name?

RN: Ruby Davenport Neal. My maiden name is Davenport.

YS: You don't have a middle name?

RN: Yes, it's Marie, so my full name is Ruby Marie Davenport Neal. And when I was growing up, they called me "Sis." That was my nickname: Sis. My sister Lillian gave me that nickname and I never heard her say why , but they called me Sis and they called my younger brother Bill.

YS: I know you live in Atlanta, but were you born here or did you come here as an adult?

RN: I'm a native Atlantan. I have lived here seventy-eight years. [Laughing]

YS: So, you were born in Atlanta! Tell me what you remember about growing up in Atlanta.

RN: Well, My father worked as a laborer. He was more or less a mechanic, and my mother was a housewife. She didn't work away from the home. My father was the one who worked and when he got off work, he would came home. My daddy was always around. I had a very wholesome relationship with both my parents, and I was close to both of them.

YS: What are some of the things you remember you and your parents did together?

RN: There was no television and we didn't have all the modern things we have today, but I remember my mother used to read the paper a lot and she would tell us different stories. She would tell us about different events that had happened in history. I never shall forget the sinking of the Titanic. That was one of her favorite stories.

YS: Before the big movie?

RN: Yes, my mother told us about the Titanic. Some of her other favorite news stories were the kidnapping of the Lindberg baby, the Lindberg's "Lone Eagle" flight, and the Scottboro case. We attended church services together and revival meeting.

YS: What was the family's most special time together?

RN: Christmas was the most special. My brother always found the perfect little Christmas tree, and we decorated the tree as a family. That was fun. I can remember the multi-colored lights. If one light went out, it seemed that we would spend hours trying to find the defected bulb. It was quite frustrating, but that was a part of Christmas. My sister and her friend made Christmas cakes, lemon cheese was my favorite. We had a delicious dinner on Christmas day.

YS: Was going to see Santa a part of your Christmas celebration?

RN: No, I didn't go to see the real Santa Claus, but each day, at 5:00 p.m., my neighbor invited me to her house to listen to the Santa Claus program. We didn't have a radio at that time, and Santa would come on the air, and he would talk to the little White children about their Christmas wishes. I would sing along with them the favorite Christmas songs.

YS: Oh, This is the Way of Christmas When Santa Claus Comes to Town and Jingle Bells and of course Rudolph the Red Nose Reindeer. I would go to bed as dust fell because I didn't want Santa to find me awake. Would you believe that I did not realize there was no Santa until I reached the 7th grade? I would hear other children saying that there was no such thing as Santa Claus, but I just did not want to let go of the fantasy. Davison displayed in their show window a big mechanical Santa who waved at everybody passing by. I loved Christmas when I was growing up and also when my children were growing up. I think Christmas in Atlanta is just wonderful for all ages. When my children were growing up, we would take them to Rich's to ride "The Pink Pig" and to do their shopping at the Secret Shop. And when they were growing up, there was a Santa for Black children and a different Santa for White children. The highlight of their visit downtown was having their picture taken with Santa Claus.

YS: You mentioned your brother and your sister. How many siblings do you have?

RN: I had two sisters and one brother. My brother was named Walter after my father. His nickname was "Bubber," and he made sure that his little sisters were conducting themselves as ladies. He was four years older than I. He kept a watchful eye on all of us, including my bib sister. Many times when she went to the library to study, my mother would have him go along with her. If my younger sister and I were invited to a party, he would always appear and he would interrupt us if he thought we were dancing too close to a male partner. I can hear him now: "Sis, get back. You are dancing too close." Of course that embarrassed me, but that was his way of protecting his younger sisters. Let me share this story with you about my brother's protective behavior.

234

When I entered high school, I thought I had arrived [laughter] and I started wearing makeup. Mainly lipstick. At the time, there were no trackless trolleys in Atlanta, so our means of transportation was the street car. En route to my high school – Booker T. Washington – the streetcar would go down Edgewood Avenue by the shoe shop where my brother worked. I will never forget this particular morning when I was waving at him from the window of the car. What do you think he did when he saw me?

YS: He waved back?

RN: [Laughing] No, that's what I wanted him to do, but instead of waving at me, he began wiping his mouth, trying to tell me that I was wearing too much lipstick. I think if he could have stopped the cat and gotten on, he would have wiped it off himself. [Laughing] That was just his way, you know. He never wanted it said that his sisters were conducting themselves anything less than as ladies. He was a good brother and a good son, who never caused our family any tears or headaches. He was always proud to tell people that I was his sister. Even on his last days on earth, when visitors would go to see him, if I were there, he would raise his frail body up and say, "That's my sister."

YS: You loved him very much.

RN: Yes, and I loved my sister, too.

YS: Tell me what it was like being a middle girl.

RN: Well, sometimes my younger sister and I would fuss and fight about hair rollers. [laughter] We didn't have real rollers then like the kinds you buy in the store today. We made our rollers out of brown paper bags. And my younger sister and I would fuss about the rollers. She would say I took her rollers, and I would say she took mine. Other than that, we got along fine. And my older sister was the biggest influence on my life. Her name was Lillian. She's deceased now. She passed in 1980. Lillian would always encourage me and always compliment me and she would always correct me when she thought I was wrong. She was ten years older than I was. She was my role model.

YS: Tell me about the neighborhood you grew up in?

RN: Well, it was a very good neighborhood of professionals and homeworkers. School teachers, college professors, postal workers, railroad men, janitors, maids, preachers, chauffeurs, and cooks. Most of the homes were occupied by owners, but there were a few rental homes in the neighborhood. Ours was among them. But whether you were owner or renter, you took pride in your home. People would sweep their yards and the sidewalks in front of their residence. That was a way to get the latest gossip in the neighborhood. [laughter] Everybody attended church and the children attended Sunday school. My family lived in a modest home. It was nice, but I wanted to move to the housing project. That was when they had just been built. They were new to us.

235

YS: The housing projects? Why would you want to move from a house to the projects? I thought it was supposed to be that you moved from the projects into your own house.

RN: That might be the case now, but then it wasn't. Housing projects had more than many houses. They had the luxury of an electric refrigerator, gas stove, steam heat . . . They had much more than most of the homeowners had. So, I wanted to move to the housing project, but my mother wanted no part of the housing project. [laughter] This was during the Depression.

YS: And times were very different then.

RN: Well, during the Depression, people were on what they called relief. I guess it was similar to today's food stamps program. Many fathers were out of work, and that meant that a lot of children didn't have decent housing or clothing. It was a difficult time. People didn't enjoy any of the luxuries we enjoy today. And when Roosevelt became President, he implemented a lot of programs that put people back to work and he was the President responsible for public housing, which we call housing projects. Before then, people who were having a hard time lived in little shacks. I grew up in the Depression, but it didn't affect me too very much.

YS: I've heard people say that Blacks didn't have as hard a time during Depression as Whites did. Do you agree with that?

RN: That was true of some people, but not everybody. My daddy worked at Fulton Bag Cotton Mill. He didn't make money, but he had a job. I want to tell you about the time I saw President Roosevelt. It's on Boulevard, N.E, and there are loft apartments now where the company used to be. Now let me tell you about the time President Roosevelt came to the city. I believe that was in 1936, but it had to be 37 or 38 . And and he came to Atlanta and he went to the appointed spots where housing projects were to be constructed. There was such vacant land there. I don't remember how old I was. I remember going to the dedication of the first housing project for Blacks ever built in Atlanta. That was University Homes.

YS: You were telling me about how neighborly your community was. That they would sweep the front porch and have conversations on the sidewalk. What did the children do?

RN: We played in the street. We didn't have playgrounds, so we played in the street. We would play baseball in the street and we would play hide and seek. We would hide behind different houses, you know. We played hopscotch. In later years, we had a playground opened at Young Street School (that was the elementary school I attended) and we would go there in the summer and play. I remember that we would have sack races and different contests. We played Jack Stones. Have you ever heard of Jack Stones? I spent many happy hours playing Jack Stones. My mother would call me, "Come wash these dishes," and I would respond, "I'll be there in a few minutes."

YS: Did you like going to school?

RN: Well, I liked getting lessons, but I enjoyed recess because you could meet with all the children. We didn't have a cafeteria.

YS: Really?

RN: No. We didn't have a cafeteria. I remember we had a little lunchroom and we would go there and get a bottle of milk and little snacks. That's when we would get a chance to talk because our teachers were very strict. We couldn't talk in class, but at recess we were very relaxed and we could talk among ourselves. It was nice.

YS: You said teachers were strict then? What about your parents? Were they strict?

RN: No, I don't think they were strict. My mother had her rules and we had to abide by them. We had to go to Sunday school every Sunday. We could not stay out late. Eight o'clock was considered late. We had to study our lessons and go to school every day. And we had to practice "The Golden Rule": treat others like we would like to be treated.

YS: Did your mother have the same rules for your brother?

RN: Oh, yes!

YS: Really?

RN: Now my brother could stay out later than we could. He could stay out maybe until ten, but we had to be home at eight. I would visit a friend who had a dollhouse in her backyard, and I would be watching the clock to be sure that I would get home by eight.

YS: What did he teach you about relationships with boys?

RN: Well my mother and older women in the community taught us to be very careful. We were taught not to let boys touch us. We weren't supposed to have sex until we were married. Believe it or not, my oldest sister, the one I told you was my role model, taught me this. My mother never did too much talking about sex, but my older sister, who was ten years older than I, taught me so many things. That was one of those things.

YS: Growing up, did you have many adult women friends in the neighborhood that you would go to when you needed to talk?

RN: Yes, there was a lady who lived next door to me. In fact, she taught me how to make a bed. Her name was Miss Sarah Carrington and she taught at Clark College. She had a little boy and I used to go over and see her during the day because, during that time, we hade double sessions in elementary school. We went from eight to twelve and then we went from twelve to four. When I wasn't in school, I'd go to see Miss Carrington. She taught me how to make a bed and how to tell time. She was a French teacher and she taught me this song, Freres Jacques. And I had another lady who lived across from me;

she was a mother at our church and she enjoyed baking for other people. She baked a lot of cakes. I would go over to her house after school to scrape those pans. Those women were more or less like mentors, but my sister was my main mentor. My oldest deceased sister, Lillian Johnson.

YS: What is your fondest memory of her?

RN: When my sister finished college – Old Clark which was Southeast Atlanta – and people didn't have cars then. My mother dressed us up to see my sister graduate. And then when my sister married and I had a brother-in-law, I thought that was so wonderful. I really remember when she graduated from college. I was so proud of her.

YS: She must have been a big help when you started your cycle. Do you remember how old you were and what you were doing?

RN: Yes. I remember it well. I was almost fifteen years old. It started in February and I was going to be fifteen that March and let me tell you, I was so ashamed. All of my friends had started their cycles and I hadn't and I would pretend, you know,. that mine had started because I wanted to be grown-up, too. All of them started before I did. They would come to school and go to the clinic because they had cramps. I wanted to be like that so bad. I remember the day I started because that was the day we moved to a larger house. It was just across the street from the small house we lived in. That was the day my period started! I think I was just so excited that we were moving to a larger house that I got my period. But I was almost fifteen years old! Most of my friends started when they were twelve or thirteen. It looked as if mine would never start. I was overjoyed!

YS: What were you told about getting your period?

RN: The main thing was not to let boys get near you. After I started my period, I tried to remember what my sister taught me about staying my distance from boys. She always impressed upon me what the consequences were. And during those days, to have a child out of wedlock was just awful! Now it seems to be a way of life. That was one of the things I thought about. Being careful not to become a mother before I became a wife. I wasn't afraid of the cramps!

YS: You mentioned how awful it was for a girl to have a child out of wedlock. Did you know any girls who did?

RN: Yes, I knew of two girls in my class who became pregnant, and they weren't allowed to come to school anymore. They had to go to night school. I tell you . . . then, it was just a moral sin to have a child out of wedlock. Everybody talked about those girls. We grew up being told, "Don't walk around with her; she's too fast."

YS: They were ostracized.

RN: Yes.

YS: They had the baby rather than have an abortion. What did people think about abortion during that
time?

RN: It's kinda hard to say. It was a mortal sin when a girl became pregnant. They didn't encourage abortion, but getting pregnant was a mortal sin.

YS: What is your position on abortion?

RN: Well, I think if pregnancy is going to injure the woman's health, I think it's okay, but if not, I don't think it's right to kill an unborn child.

YS: Tell me about dating conventions.

RN: I think I was about seventeen when I started dating because my father would not let me date until my younger sister was sixteen so that we could date together. I think I was about seventeen and, you know, I remember my very first date. I met him in high school, in the eleventh grade, and his name was Eddie Lomax. Back then, when we dated, we would go to the movies and we would go to parties. There would be parties in different homes. We would have record players at our homes and our parents would let us invite friends over. And there was a place called the Top Hat, which was changed to the Royal Peacock. It was over on Auburn Avenue, and that's where everybody had their dances. See, during my day, people had social clubs, and the clubs had dances at different places : at the Royal Peacock and the Sunset Casino and the Sky Room at the City Auditorium,. which is now a part of Georgia State, and also at a place on West Lake where the Job Corps Center is now.

YS: Where were social clubs?

RN: I guess young people today don't have social clubs. Well, when I was growing up, a group of girls would get together and organize a social club. In fact, I'm a member of a club that I've been in since I was eighteen years old. It's called the Starlets, and we had about twelve members who were seniors when we were in high school. When you have a social club, a group of girls would get together and organize . Elect a president, a secretary and other officers. One Sunday out of a month, we would meet. The Starlets still have monthly meetings, but so many of our original members have passed.

YS: Did you have special colors? A motto?

RN: Yes. Our colors, for The Starlets, are pink and White. Our motto is: We strive to better the best." Our club song was "I Surrender, Dear." There were other social clubs: The Regals. The Chesterfields. The Yumphs. The Crosonstantanians. There were just groups of social clubs and this is the way we socialized.

YS: Do you think having social clubs made it easy for people to meet and get to know one another?

RN: I don't know. That's a hard question to answer. Atlanta was much smaller then than it is now. You could connect better with people then. Now Atlanta is so large, and I think that makes it a little difficult to meet the right people.

YS: Did you ever wish you could move to a different city or a different state?

RN: No! I love Atlanta, Georgia. I have done a lot of traveling. I've been to Europe . . . to London. I've been to Los Angeles several times. I've been to the Bahamas. I've been to Hilton Head , to New York and New Jersey. My daughter went to school in New Jersey, to Rutgers, so I've been up there quite a bit. I've been to Washington. I've never been to Philadelphia. Oh, yes, I've been to Texas and to Florida. So, I've had a chance to travel a good bit. My oldest daughter worked for the airlines and that made it real convenient for me to move around quite a bit. But after a week of traveling, I'm ready to come back home. No, I have never wanted to live anywhere, but Atlanta, GA. [Laughing]

YS: I want to know how you and your friends would get to the Top Hat.

RN: We walked. We lived within walking distance. Occasionally, a boy would have an automobile or we would catch the streetcar. A group of us would catch the streetcar together. But we usually walked.

YS: Those were the fun days, huh?

RN: The things you never had, you never miss. We didn't have Marta so we could not miss Marta. There were tracks in the street then that the streetcars ran on and we just had a good time. We knew everybody at the dances because we went to one high school: Booker T. Washington. We just had a good time.

YS: What jobs were available for Black teenagers during this time? Now we have fast foods and Six Flags and . . .

RN: Most of us had some type of job. Even as early as my elementary school days, I was in business [Laughing]. I set up a lemonade stand in front of my house. Each day, I would sell my lemonade to the many peddlers who came down our street: the Peach Man, the Watermelon Man, the Vegetable Man, the Ice Man, and the Block Man. A cold glass of punch for just two cents on a hot summer day was like heaven to them. On Saturdays, I would add sandwiches to my menu. Incidentally, Rev. Martin Luther King, Sr. and his family would stop at my stand and sample my lemonade. [Laughing]

When I was older, I worked as a clerk in a five dime store on Auburn Avenue. The store was owned by a Greek man named Paul Maloof. This job gave Black teenagers a great sense of pride. Baby-sitting for White people and working as waitress at different hotels were also jobs we could get. My first job as a teenager was working as a maid in an all-

White beauty salon. My job was to pick up the hairpins and the bobby pins off the floor and wash them out so that the operators could use them again. I also had the job of going to the store for customers in the shop. You know, they couldn't go because they were . . . well, you understand. It was my job to go to the store and get them what they wanted. There was a delicatessen at Peachtree and 10th. I never shall forget it: Jacob's Drug Store. It was downstairs and the beauty shop was upstairs. Well, I was more or less like the little maid and the errand girl for people in the beauty shop. I would go to the store to get lunch for the different clients, pick up rollers and hairpins, wash them, and sweep the floor. If the customers got their hair cut, I would get the broom.

YS: Tell me what you remember most about Jim Crow in Atlanta.

RN: I remember the signs on water fountains: "For Colored" and "For Whites." I remember separate restrooms. Going to the basement in Rich's Department store to get lunch. Going to the side window to be served at eating places. Having no hotel accommodations when we traveled. I experienced this injustice on my first trip to New York City.

YS: What happened?

RN: We had to park beside the road and sleep in the car because there were no hotels or motels for Blacks.

YS: I don't know how we dealt with all of that and maintained our dignity. What was it like to go on a date during the Jim Crow era?

RN: Well, it was not easy if we went to see a movie at the Fox because we had to go up the back stairs. I remember my first time going to the Fox. My date had promised to take me there and I was really excited because, back then, you really did rate if your boyfriend took you to the Fox. Of course, when we got there, we went to the side door and I will always remember being faced with three flights of steps.

YS: Three?

RN: Three. I said to my date – and I really meant this – "I can't walk up those stairs." You know what he did?

YS: I can't believe this.

RN: He picked me up and carried me all the way to the top.

YS: He carried you up three flights of steps?

RN: Yes, I will never forget him. At that moment, he was my hero. Jim Crow was a way of life for us. Our first name was "boy" or "girl" and many times "nigger." When I worked at Grady Hospital as an admitting clerk, I witnessed White policemen abusing Black people. Those were difficult times for Black people. Thank God for Dr. Martin Luther King, Jr.

YS: What did your parents teach you about race relations? I mean, did they tell you how to greet White people and where not to go and how not to act?

RN: They always told us to respect White people, sit where you are supposed to sit and do what they told us to do. They were trying to protect us because there was so much racial violence during that time. In other words, we were taught to stay in our place in order to be safe.

YS: Did you hear of or know about any incidents of racial violence?

RN: Yes. They had something called The Racket, similar to numbers. They would have little books of numbers. They would make extra money for their families. If police caught them, the police would beat them. And I saw that happen more than once. Just think. Now the lottery is legal.

YS: Were you angry at Whites? Bitter? Did you think segregation would never come to an end?

RN: I don't know. I never gave it a thought. I'll be perfectly honest with you. That you've never had, you never miss. I never thought about it, but I was so proud and happy when it did go away.

YS: Were you aware that women also dealt with restrictions? I have learned that there was a time when women couldn't get credit in their own names. Do you think women had a hard time because they were women?

RN: I'll tell you one thing. Black women could not teach school if they were married. That's one of the reasons many women became old maids. Women could be nurses and secretaries. Most women were cooks and domestics.

YS: When you were growing up, did you see adult Black women bonding with one another? Tell me how you saw them through the eyes of a young girl or a teenager.

RN: I know my mother used to bond with our neighbors. If she needed a cup of sugar, she could go next door, and our neighbor came to our house. We had a neighborhood club and the people would bond through that club. They went to church together and the children grew up together.

YS: You told me that you have lived in Atlanta all of your life and that means you met your husband here?

RN: I had finished Read Business College and I was working at a mortuary school. Reed was located where the Atlanta University Center is now on the corner of - -what at that time, was Fair and Chestnut Street. There was a Yates and Milton Drug Store on the corner and the school was upstairs. Between classes we would go to Yates and Milton. [Laughing] That was like a hangout for us. When I finished Reed, I got a job at the mortuary school. It was on the corner of Brawley and MLK . . . well, then it was Hunter Street. That was right after World War II. Before then, we would have only eight or nine students because of the War. But when the War ended, there was the G.I. Bill for veterans to get an education and so we had about seventy students to enroll. My husband happened to be among them. I was a secretary at the school. I would be sitting at my desk, you know, and he would come up to me and ask if I had any relatives in California. At that time, California seemed as far away as Europe! [Laughing] I said, "No, I don't know anybody in California". And he would come in everyday and tell me I looked like a girl he knew in California. I never shall forget; he said her name was Frankie. I don't remember her last name. Well, one day he brought a friend in to see me, and he asked the friend, "Doesn't she look just like Frankie?" Finally, we started going to lunch together and that's how we got to know each other. The mortuary school stayed there a good while. It was demolished, but I had somebody take a picture of it for me and I have the picture in my family album. That's where I met my husband. My husband attended the college of mortuary science, but he never took his apprenticeship, so he always did hotel work. He was a banquet captain at the Hyatt Regency when it first opened. He was in charge of banquets for twenty-one years until he became ill and couldn't work anymore.

YS: Three questions: how long did you date, when did you marry, and did you continue working after you married?

RN: We met in 1945. We married in 1947. I continued working until I was five months pregnant with my first child. I stopped work and looked up and there was another baby. I didn't go back to work until Cindy was six months old.

YS: What is the fondest memory of your life with your husband?

RN: Well, the fondest memory is when I first met him and when our first child was born. He showered me with flowers. We were so very happy.

YS: I'd like to hear some of your stories about childbirth.

RN: Well, I was just overjoyed when my children came into the world. I have five children: Pamela, Obbie, Jr., Lillian, Kathy, and Cynthia. I can tell you about the birth of one of them, my middle child. I was having false labor frequently, and my husband took me to the hospital at least six times. [Laughing] Every time we went, the doctor said, "It's not time." I guess I was over anxious and I wanted her to come on. Every time I felt a little funny, I'd wake my husband up and we would go up to Grady. That's one of the unique stories I had about false labor pains.

YS: And you had your children before you came to Spelman. Would you tell me what it was like to return to school as a mother with children?

RN: Well, I left Spelman in 1942 and went to business school. After business school, I got a secretarial job and, as I told you, I met my husband. I went back to school in 1971. I always wanted to go back to school. I stayed focused on graduating from Spelman. I will never forget that I was sitting in my office at Morehouse . . . that's where I was working at the time. Watching kids go back and forth to class, and I turned to my boss and told him, "I wish I could go back to school." He said, "You can, Mrs. Neal. I went back." That was very encouraging! So I immediately started getting my credentials together, and I enrolled in a sociology class here at Spelman.

When I first got in the class, I felt so awkward. I sat there and all those children were sitting around me and I thought to myself, "What in the world am I doing here with these children?" [Laughing] After a few days, a lady came to the class who wasn't quite as old as I was, but she was definitely an adult. That made me feel a bit more comfortable. In those days, all the kids were wearing afros, so what I did was I wore an afro and started wearing my jeans to class and I began to blend in with the children. And before I knew it, they were asking to study with me and we were studying together. [Laughing] They were asking me questions and it was fun!

Then that summer, I took a course in psychology at Atlanta University and, of course, there are all ages in summer school. I enjoyed that class. And I think that next year, I had to take a break because my children began to grow up. They were in so many different things that I had a lot of activities to go to, so I had to put that Spelman education on hold. But I never let go of my determination to graduate from Spelman.

When my husband passed in 1987, I decided I wasn't going to sit at home and cry myself to death. I was going to channel those tears into the degree, and that's when I returned to Spelman and stayed. I didn't stop. I took courses at Morehouse, and it was fun because some of the students I knew as work-study students, and they were in class with me. You know, when some of the boys would sleep in class, I'd hit them on the head and tell them to wake up! These were some of my work-study students. [laughing] Also, my grandson and I were in a class together

YS: Now that must have been interesting.

YS: Well, we didn't let anybody know that we were related. He'd sit way on the other side of the room. College was hard work for me because I chose English as my major and I had a lot of reading, a lot of writing and a lot of going to the library, back and forth . A lot of work. But it was worth all of it. Sometimes I'd go to the library when I would have liked to be at lunch with some of my friends, and I'd say to myself, "What in the world am I doing here, sacrificing like this?" And then something would say, "You've got to get it! You've got to get it! You can't stop!" So I just continued and I finished. I got my degree at age sisty-eight. I finished Spelman in 1992. I was a member of the class of 1942. I stopped school, got married, reared a family, and returned to school. I received my degree fifty years after I first entered college.

RN: I was always determined to graduate from Spelman.

YS: Tell me in what ways Spelman was different when you returned in 1992.

RN: When I came back? Well, the children were different. As I told you, the younger generation was so much more relaxed than they were when I was here. I just took one class and I was an off-campus student. The way they dressed was different. And some of them acted a little bit different than the way we did. Remember, I was in school in the '40's and this was in the '70's, so there was quite a time change, but they all held Spelman in very high esteem.

YS: What did you do after you earned your degree from Spelman? Did you continue working at Morehouse?

RN: Yes. I was a secretary in the Education Department for twenty-seven years and I enjoyed every minute of my work. And when I retired, I was determined that I would not sit home everyday. I was going to stay busy. And that's when I started volunteering.

YS: Where do you volunteer?

RN: I volunteer at the Carter Center. I conduct tours for school children. And then I volunteer out at Southwest Hospital in the Human Resources office. I answer the telephone and take messages. I also volunteer at the Darnell Multi-Purpose Center at the information desk. I also play cards there on Friday; I love to play bridge! And of course I do some volunteer work here in the museum. Sometimes I think I stay too busy. [Laughing]

YS: In one of our earlier conversations, you said that you wanted to become a Delta. Would you tell me why?

RN: Yes I had an aunt who was a Delta, but my oldest sister, Lillian Johnson, was a Delta. And as I told you, my sister was my role model and I just wanted to do everything she did. I thought about becoming a Delta when I first graduated, but sometimes . . . I don't know . It just doesn't matter too much now.

YS: In your opinion, what is the most pressing problem in our nation today?

RN: I think poverty is the most pressing problem. There are so many people who don't have places to stay and don't have food. It's so very sad. And education is a pressing problem because we have so many drop outs. So many young people just never finish school.

YS: If you were in a position to change something about Atlanta that affects Black people, what would it be?

RN: I guess it would be the practice of hiring. Many times, we are not the first ones considered for jobs and I'd like to see that change.

YS: What would you like to see happen nationally for Black women?

RN: I'd like to see Black women play a more important role in politics and government. I'd like to see more Black women in positions like Condoleeza Rice.

YS: How do you feel about the man being the head of the household?

RN: Well, I think the man is supposed to be the head of the household [Laughter], but I guess I was an exception. I was the head of my household. When my children wanted to do something, my husband would say, "Go ask your momma". It's different today, isn't it? [Laughter]

YS: Well, no, not really. My dad says, "Go ask your mom", but he's really the head of the household. It's that my mom is more into what can and can't be done with the kids.

RN: That's right. That's the way it was. My daddy went to work everyday and my husband went to work everyday - of course I worked too - but I didn't go to work until after I had given birth to my fifth child. My husband would always tell them, "Ask your momma".

YS: Tell me what you remember about growing up during World War II?

RN: My boyfriend fought in World War II. I never shall forget that he was at my house on Sunday night when Japan bombed Pearl Harbor. We were listening to the radio and they announced that the Japanese had bombed Pearl Harbor. He went into combat.

[Mrs. Neal and young scholar are riding in her car. This is the trip through her neighborhood that she talked about in several conversations.]

RN: This is the section of Collier Heights. At one time, this was a wooded area. All of this was woods. In fact, this house that we live in, my family's house, was the fourth house on this street. A Black man named Mr. Porter wanted to build nice homes for Blacks because we'd never had homes like this before. They built one house at a time. Some of the original residents are still living here today. I'm the only one who represents my family. We had a doctor who lived nearby. Dr. Shepard, who passed away. These houses were built during the late 1950's. Before then, this was nothing but woods. The streets weren't paved. All of this was dirt. It's been a wonderful experience seeing the area and the city grow. Collier Drive is the main thoroughfare and on the left is an elementary school called Collier Heights, which is getting ready to relocate to Harwell Road. The school was an incentive for a lot of people to move here. This is the Collier Heights Park with facilities for tennis, baseball and other activities. As we enter Harwell Drive, you will see where St. Paul of the Cross Church is located, the elementary school that my children attended and also the parish that we attend. This is also the church where all of my children married. We have Mass twice on Sunday at 8:30 and 11:30 and once on Saturday at 6:00 in the evening. The building was recently sold to Atlanta Public Schools. We had nuns then, but we don't have them any more. My children received their early training in religious experiences here.

YS: Were your parents Catholic?

RN: No, they were Baptists. I'll show you the church where they attended when we go across town.

YS: When did you become a Catholic?

RN: I became a Catholic in 1958 or 1959. I was a member of Wheat Street Baptist Church. This was formerly Drexel High School and then Atlanta Public Schools bought it and they are getting ready to change it to something else. This is where my oldest daughter finished high school. The school closed as a result of desegregation and we couldn't attract White students to come out here, so as a result we had to close the school and the children had to go to St. Joseph to high school. That's another example of desegregation. They refused to come out here, so we had to close Drexel down. This is the Northwest section of the city. I just wanted you to see some of the neighborhood. These homes originally sold for about $14,000 -$18,000, but today they are worth much more. Many of them need renovations. This is Skipper Drive and one of oldest attorneys in Atlanta lives on this street. Have you ever heard of Donald Hollowell?

YS: No.

RN: He was a Civil Rights lawyer. This is Eleanor Terrace and this is where my girls embraced adulthood. This is where we were living when they married. These homes are in a different price range. A lot of professional people live in this area. My daughter Cathy's childhood friend lives on this street. *** Now, this is where we used to live: 930 Kings' Grant Drive. Cindy was only six years old when we moved here and they were so excited because they had never lived in a house with an upstairs, so they would go up and down the stairs all day long and they did it so long that I told them we were going to move back to our old house! This is where we were living when they got married. When we moved, they were heartbroken. They actually said to me, "Momma you don't need to move out of our house".

YS: I would understand why. They lived there for so long and got married while they were there.

RN: They didn't want me to move even though they all were gone. Well, my husband had heart problems and he couldn't go up and down steps so that was why we decided to move into the family home. We are about to enter Hamilton Holmes Drive, which was originally called Hightower Road and was changed a few years ago. Hamilton Holmes was the man who integrated the University of Georgia.

YS: When did the name change?

RN: It changed about four or five years ago. At one time, White people lived in these homes. Now this is where we were living, when my youngest daughter Cynthia was born. This is the first home we ever bought and it had only three bedrooms and we had five children. There was a lady on the corner who had eleven children when Cindy was born. We didn't have enough space for seven people. We had three bedrooms and one bathroom and in the mornings my husband would be trying to get ready for work and all the girls would be trying to get to the bathroom, so we moved to Kings' Grant to have more space. I still have a lot of friends over here. This is Mrs. Bridges house, the lady with the eleven children. It was amazing how they were able to take care of all of them. They had a vegetable garden and everything. Have you ever been out this way before? YS: I have been on Collier Drive before, but that was it. I have never really explored Atlanta.

RN: This is Radcliff Presbyterian. A lot of Spelman people attend that church. To your left is Douglas High School where I do some substitute teaching. The children are very well mannered there.

YS: Are they mostly children who live in Collier Heights?

RN: Yes. This is MLK, but at one time this was Hunter Street. It was the most fashionable street in the city for Blacks.

YS: Fashionable as in . . .

RN: This is where most of the homeowners lived. This is Mosley Park, and we were not allowed to go here. It was for Whites only. We only had one little park and that was Washington Park. We used to ride by Mosley and watch the White people out there in the park and wish that we could go. This street was Mosley Place. Back when I was a girl, the houses out here were so pretty, we would ride out here on Sunday evenings just to look at them. My friend's mother had a car and we would ride and look and claim the houses that we liked. This is my high school, Booker T. Washington High School.

YS: Did you ever come back and substitute here?

RN: Yes, I did some substitute-teaching here a couple of years ago. The principal is a graduate of Spelman. They've made some additions, but at one time this was a USO for servicemen and they renovated it to make a gym for the high school. This street was called Sea Street then and they changed the name to Whitehouse Drive. A very prominent musician lived on this street. His name was Graham Jackson. I don't know if you've ever heard of him. He used to go to Warm Springs to play for President Roosevelt. You know about Paschal's, Michaela?

YS: Yes, ma'am.

RN: They used to have a little place right across the street before they moved over there and they sold good fried chicken. You could get a fried chicken sandwich for a quarter then. Have you ever been to the Herndon Home?

YS: No, ma'am.

RN: It's one of the tourist attractions in the city. My first job with Atlanta Public School System was at E.A. Ware School. I worked as a secretary. I started in 1963. Have you ever been to Friendship Baptist Church?

YS: No, ma'am.

RN: That's it over on the right. Spelman was founded in the basement of Friendship Baptist Church.

YS: Oh, yes. I knew that.

RN: Years ago people didn't do too much flying. They rode the train and this is where the terminal station was located. Another station down farther was Union station. Atlanta had two stations. Flying is so popular now that we don't use either station. All of these are government buildings. I think that's the Hurt Building and at one time it was the tallest building in Atlanta. My mother used to go there every Saturday to pay her insurance.

This is the fourth ward. We'll go down Decatur Street. Now you wouldn't believe it, but this used to be nothing but a slum area. There was a restaurant down the street called the Metropolitan and a red light district where prostitutes hung out. It was a very dangerous area. Georgia State took this over. I used to come over here to the library when I was in school and study at Georgia State because so often the library on campus didn't have the books that we needed.

YS: That's so true.

RN: This is Grady Hospital. Have you ever been there?

YS: Yes, I have.

RN: Well, as I told you, we used to have two hospitals -Black on one side and White on the other side. I experienced a lot of segregation at Grady when I worked there in the late 50's and 60's. We didn't have the opportunity to serve White patients, but the Whites served Black patients. In other words, we were supposed to stay in our place. Grady Hospital was the first place that I worked when I entered the workforce and then later I went over to Hughes Spaulding. It's now a children's hospital. At that time, it was a private hospital and a lot of Black doctors practiced there. We couldn't go in the White hospitals.

This is the curb market on Auburn Avenue where my mother used to come everyday to get collard greens. This is still the fourth ward. I lived on Gartrell Street.

YS: Did you walk to school?

RN: Yes, we walked.

YS: Is Boulevard in the fourth ward?

RN: Yes. That's Ebenezer Baptist Church. This is Wheat Street Baptist Church where I was baptized when I was seven years old. I used to teach Sunday school here, sing in the choir and serve on the junior usher board, but I finally decided to go to the Catholic Church because my children were all going there and I wanted our family to be together. That's New Horizon, have you ever been there?

YS: No, ma'am.

RN: You should go there. They have beautiful services over there. These are some of the row houses that were here when Martin Luther King was alive and that was his home. They've preserved all of these houses. This was the King community.

YS: Is the house you grew up in still standing?

RN: No, that was back on Gartrell Street; it's no longer standing. They tore all of those houses down and built apartments. I wished they were still there. This is John Hope School, which is newly renovated. That's where my older sister, my role model, taught the first grade.

YS: What does your younger sister do?

RN: She doesn't do anything now, but she used to teach. She's retired now, but she's just two years younger than I am. This street has been changed from Houston Street to John Wesley Dobbs. John Wesley Dobbs was the grandfather of Maynard Jackson, our first Black mayor.

        Now we're going to the Varsity to have lunch. In one interview when you asked what did we do for recreation as children, I forgot to mention that I liked to skate. I used to roller skate and ride bicycles all day long. Now lunch will be on me.

YS: What four possessions, or characteristics, do you think most represent you? If you could put them on an altar, what would they be?

RN: I'd like to have my character placed on the altar. I'm a person who loves other people and I practice the Golden Rule. I'd like to have attributes like that placed on the altar. And I would like to have it said that longevity is a beautiful thing and I'm very grateful to have enjoyed the golden years of my life and the blessings I've received. That's what I'd like to have placed on the altar.

YS: What makes you sad?

RN: What makes me sad? To see so many single mothers. That saddens me.

YS: When I write about you in the oral history volume, what would you like me to most tell the readers about you?

RN: I would like for you to talk about my determination, my perseverance, and also my love for Spelman College. I want you to emphasize that age has no limit on what you can accomplish in life. I would like my story of returning to school fifty years later and earning a college degree at age sixty eight to be a lesson of inspiration.

YS: What makes you happy?

RN: To see young women like you moving forward to become leaders. That makes me very happy.

YS: If you could speak to a group of young Black women in their early twenties about being Black women, what would you say to them?

RN: Well, I would tell them how important it is to respect themselves and to love themselves and to be models for other young women. I would also tell them to make education one of their priorities. And I would encourage them to continue to go to school and learn as much as they can so that they can make a difference.

YS: This experience has been wonderful for me, Mrs. Neal. What has it meant to you?

RN: I think this is an important project because it's the history of an area that I lived in. It has brought back many pleasant memories of my life. I have relived those experiences, and that has brought me much joy.

MRS. ALICE HOLMES WASHINGTON

East Point, Georgia
Pioneering High School Counselor
Recipient of Spelman College Spirit Award

When we left [the Bottom], my father said, "Baby Doll, I want you to remember always to speak up and to be nice to everybody you see because you don't know whose two dollars put the shoes on your feet". At that time, one or two dollars was the going rate for doctor. That's how I've tried to get other people to understand that ownership is something else. That philosophy has been a guide for me, and it was a gift from my father. It came from a man of Cajun background in Louisiana.

EXCERPTS OF INTERVIEWS WITH MRS. ALICE HOLMES WASHINGTON
Conducted by Danielle Phillips

YS   Let's begin with your full given name, as it is on your birth certificate.

AW: My name is Alice Cary Holmes. Cary is spelled different according to the woman who named me.

YS: The woman who named you? Who was she?

AW: Mrs. Alice Dugged Cary. She was one of the professors at Morris Brown College and she taught Greek literature. At one time, she was acting president at Morris Brown and later became the first Black librarian for the Atlanta Fulton Library System. She was a good friend of my parents and when I was born on Saturday, October 23, 1919. She announced to the students at Morris Brown that Alice Cary was born today. My parents did not change the name because Mrs. Cary had said who I was.

YS: How did she meet your parents?

AW: My parents were supporters of Morris Brown and at that time Mrs. Cary was in her senior years and they just sort of adopted her and she adopted them. Mrs. Cary lived in the dormitory at Morris Brown because she had no family at that point, so our family became her family. She wanted to name my brother Alfred, William Alfred Fountain Holmes for Bishop William Alfred Fountain, who was the head of the AME Church, but my parents would not use the name William, but the rest of the name they kept. My brother's name is Alfred Fountain Holmes. So there was peace in the valley with Mrs. Cary and with my family. [laughing] That was the beginning of our friendship with the Fountains as a family and Mrs. Cary and all of the Morris Brown students who lived in the dormitory and who took care of her. We would give them a box of candy or a dollar or a hamburger and other gifts to thank them for taking good care of Mrs. Cary. We enjoyed Mrs. Cary and she liked us.

YS: That's quite a story. Mrs. Carey lived in the dormitory at Morris Brown. Was she from Atlanta?

AW: Mrs. Carey came to Atlanta from the Indian country down below Macon and she settled over where the King Center is now located, on the corner of Boulevard and Auburn Avenue.

YS: Tell me about your family. Do you know where your parents were from?

AW: Yes. My father was from Louisiana, from Cajun country in Louisiana, and my mother was from Pittsboro, North Carolina, but she spent much of her childhood with relatives in Raleigh, NC. My father didn't speak anything except Cajun dialect until he was a teenager My father's name was Hamilton Mayo Holmes and my mother's name was Pattie Lee Reaves.

YS: You mentioned in our first phone conversation that you were born in East Point, Georgia.

AW: When my father was graduating from medical school in Raleigh, NC, where he met my mother in the spring of his graduation year, he came to the Atlanta area, as you children would say, scoping out the territory. He came to see where he might settle.He chose East Point because there was no doctor in the area at the time. That meant that he was the only doctor for East Point, College Park, Hapeville, Palmetto, Fairburn, and all of the South Fulton area.

YS: He was the only doctor?

AW: He was the only Black doctor. He had an office in South Atlanta, not too far from where the Spelman campus is now, and he practiced in East Point. My father would make house calls in those areas. I was born in East Point. In fact, all of the children were born in East Point. I have my mother's wardrobe trunk downstairs and I am going to give it, maybe, to the East Point Historical Society because it has her name painted on it: Mrs. H.M. Holmes, East Point, GA. No address. No zip code. None of all that. Just her name and the city. I'm sure she brought it to East Point on the train with her. Times have really changed! We lived on Randall Street in East Point. When I worked at South Fulton High School, I could see the house in which I was born and, years later, I watched as the house was torn down and another house built on that lot.

YS: Can you describe the house for me?

AW: It was just a small cottage, but it had a porch with a swing and there were big cement flowerpots on the porch, all of them filled with flowers. We took those flower pots with us everywhere we moved. One thing we did not move, because it sort of vanished, was the marble stone that had the name and house number engraved in it. We would stand on that stone to get to the buggy.

YS: And you were born in that cottage?

AW: Yes. I was born at home. In the days of horses and buggies, this friend of my father who came down with him to help determine where they would practice was supposed to deliver us, but he never made it, so my daddy had to deliver all of his children.

YS: Wow! Your father delivered all of his own children! Why didn't his friend make it?

AW: The buggy was slow or they didn't leave in time or the children were impatient and didn't wait for him to arrive. Dr. C. W. Powell was his name.

YS: Did you hear any stories about your mother's experiences when she was carrying you?

AW: Well, one of the things that I think is most important is that she was living in the country. You see, East Point was country then. There was a galvanized pail or tub that had water in it for some purpose and my oldest brother, Hamilton, Jr., was walking around and fell over into that tub. For all practical purposes, he drowned and died. Well, my mother was a graduate nurse. But she was not working as such, and she said, "I cannot sit back and see my child die." So she took it upon herself to do all of the things her training and her mother wit taught her to do, or had her to do. She massaged my brother and rubbed him and held him upside down and did all of those things. She brought him back to life. The only impact of that incident was that he developed a stammer. We felt as a family that was a little something to pay for having his life.

YS: That is an incredible story. Where did your mother get her nurse training?

AW: She trained at St. Agnes, which was on the same campus where my daddy took his medical training: Leonard Medical School in Raleigh, North Carolina. The complex included a nursing school, a medical school, and a state school/center for the deaf. Shaw University now occupies the grounds where Leonard was located. It was always a treat to see Daddy's sheepskin diploma and the class picture, which was of poster size, of students and faculty. Most fascinating was a picture of students with "Mr. Bones," a skeleton used in instruction. The Atlanta History Center has exhibited those artifacts. Historical references by graduates, faculty and school supporters credit Leonard as the first to provide medical training for "colored" people. My father graduated from Leonard in 1910, and he and my mother married in that same year.

My mother was what was called in those days a graduate nurse, and while she was in school at St. Agnes, she became affiliated with a group of Black nurses you would call activists today. They became chartered, and they encouraged other Black trained nurses to join them in advocating for improved working conditions and pay increases for nurses. And this was needed to change conditions because when Black nurses worked in hospitals with White doctors, they were subjected to being called Mary or Susie or Lillie or Girl or whatever. They wanted the respect and the dignity that went with their training and the money that went with their training.

YS: Your mother was truly an activist.

AW: Yes, she was one of the founders of the Negro Graduate Nurses Association, organized before 1910. It disbanded in 1946 or 47 because it appeared that conditions were better for Blacks. My mother was invited to New York to what they called the 'dissolution luncheon' where there was a ceremony to dissolve their charter. Lena Horne was the speaker, and the luncheon was held at the Tavern on the Green in New York. And because Lena Horne was from Georgia and my mother was from Georgia, she—Lena Horne—made a big to-do over my mother and wanted her picture made with "the lady from Georgia." So that was one of the highlights of my mother's nursing career.

YS: That's quite a story. Did your mother ever practice in East Point?

AW: Oh, no. She would take care of neighbors who came by and wanted little reassurances that they were going to make it and, of course, she took care of us, but she did no formal nursing.

YS: You also mentioned in the phone interview that East Point then was different from East Point today.

AW: Yes, we had our side of the railroad track, and it was interesting because we had to walk from what they now call Main Street straight down Cleveland Avenue to get to the Black side. Or we could go up to Central Avenue where the streetcar would go up, cross the railroad tracks, come down Bayard Street, and reach what we called the Black side. When I went back to East Point to work in the late forties or early fifties, Mr. O.J. Hurd had a bus line that would pick up the passengers on Cleveland Avenue and Main Street, very much where the buggy works is, and bring them down over to what we call 'Blackville'. It has been quite interesting to see, as has happened in Atlanta, that Blacks are now living all over East Point.

YS: Did your father ever encounter any racism when he was practicing during that time?

AW: Well, it's interesting. When he made his visit to determine that East Point was where he was going to settle, he made the rounds of drug stores and that is when he met these people who operated the drug stores. This was in the spring of 1910. Well, a young White couple saw my father on Randall Street and they told him that the wife was ill. It was an emergency, and the pharmacist said, "There's a new doctor in the town. He's Black." The couple said, "We want to know where we can find him." At that time, it was against the law for Black doctors to treat White patients. My father said, "Now you know this is against the law, but I have just taken an oath to serve where I must serve." And the young woman and her husband both agreed that they would take their chances with him. When I tell this story to various groups in and around East Point and other places, I always say, "And things went well. Otherwise, I wouldn't be here." [Laughing]

And that was how my father got his first patient. The interesting thing is that when my father died, he called me from his office at about ten or eleven at night. He was about to pack up and come home. That late hour wasn't unusual because then doctors didn't go home at the end of the afternoon—you know, go for lunch and stay and have a siesta and have the night off. He called and he said, "Baby Doll," because that's all he ever called me, "I want you to know something." And he proceeded to tell me that the last patient he had seen that evening was a White woman who had voluntarily found him. He said, "It's legal now for me to help her." He left his office right after that. It must have been about 10:00 or so. At one or two in the morning, he got up, went to the bathroom, put his robe on, tied his belt, and died. That was in 1965. So his first patient was a White woman, and his last patient was a White woman. That's something I have remembered, and will always remember.

Among other things that I remember about my daddy is a bit of philosophy. I would always ride with him whenever I could. When we moved into Atlanta, we lived on

Chapel Street, right at Fair and Chapel. It's called Northside Drive now. We would take the turn either to go down to University Homes, the housing project, or to Fair Street to what we called The Bottom and go straight up Chapel Street to the Spelman campus. The Bottom was a bad neighborhood then. Well, one day I was with him when he went down to The Bottom and I was slow speaking to someone. When we left the neighborhood, my father said, "Baby Doll, I want you to remember always to speak up and to be nice to everybody you see and to be kind to everybody you see because you don't know whose two dollars put the shoes on your feet". At that time, one or two dollars was the going rate for doctors, and that's why he said "whose two dollars put the shoes on your feet." You know, my father didn't chew me out in the presence of people. He got me off where no one could hear. And what he said soaked in. I have told this story to people as they try to claim ownership of a building and I try to tell them, "You don't know whose two dollars put the brick next to your brick to build this facility or whose two dollars put a book next to the book you bought in this library or whose two dollars did whatever the circumstances might have been". That's how I've tried to get other people to understand that ownership is something else. That philosophy has been a guide for me, and it was a gift from my father. It came from a man of Cajun background in Louisiana.

YS: Did you ever travel with him to Louisiana?

AW: We went one time when the boys were big enough to help drive and we went down to see where he used to live. Just that one time. We went quite often to North Carolina because that was closer to Atlanta, and we could get in a car and drive there; or if we had to get on a Jim Crow coach, the trip was not as long as the trip to Louisiana. Just that one time we went to Louisiana.

YS: Can you share any memories that you have about that one time?

AW: Well, we met my daddy's extended family. His father was a Baptist preacher and had several wives, each one younger than the one before her. [laughter] My father was so moved by the way his Louisiana family was living that he just packed them up and brought them to Georgia: his half sister, her husband and their children. He brought them here so that they could be closer as a family. That was one of the major benefits of that trip. It gave us more relatives.

YS: Did they live with you?

AW: No, they had a house that they bought, but in my daddy's declining years he lived with his sister in her house because she was available to do the things that he needed to have done. I was off at the time and working with children and could not give him the care he needed, so he lived with his sister in his declining years. He died at 82, but now that is not a declining age. I'm 83. Actually, my father was in good health and had started playing golf. In fact, on the day he died, he had been to the golf course that morning and later in the day he went to his office to see patients. He always said that being on the golf course where he had to walk from one hole to another instead of using the carts that they have now gave him time to think clearly without interruption about what he might do next to help "Mrs. So-and-So with her gallbladder," or whatever ailment he was treating. It cleared his head and helped him think about the next treatment he would try. That was how he justified to himself and others the time that he spent by himself on the golf course, walking from one hole to the next.

YS: I am sure the community held your father in high esteem.

AW: I am still seeing people who tell me that their parents told them that my daddy was their doctor. And I have one friend from a White family in Hapeville who said that when they were all sick, my daddy went to their house to treat them. He went with his horse and buggy and brought them back to the land of the living. I know this later, and she never called me anything but Alice Mae. She would tell me, "You are from the time when they gave girls double names." It was Elsie Mae or Susie Jo or some such, not just Mary or Danielle. My name was Alice Carey. But she said I just looked like I should be an Alice Mae, so she called me Alice Mae and I called her by her name [that I won't say]. Twenty years after my father made a house call to her family, she told me that her neighbors later said how sensible it was for them as a family to find a doctor who would come to them. She wanted me to know that she was living because of my daddy.

YS: Did you ever go with him when he made house calls?

AW: Yes.

YS: What was your most memorable experience on a house call?

AW: Sunday afternoon was our usual time as a family to go out with him, not as he made calls as such, but as he made social visits to the families of some of his patients. We enjoyed that because it gave us a chance to meet people.

YS: I'm sure you have special memories of times you spent with your mother.

AW: Well, my momma was the person who was at home all the time, and she would always have a yard full of children playing with her. She grew up Methodist in North Carolina, and my daddy grew up Baptist in Louisiana. I think I told you that his father was a Baptist preacher, so we went to many church activities. Well, we went to Baptist activities and also to Methodist activities: Sunday school in the morning and BYPU in the afternoon and Young Methodists. We always had activities associated with church. My mother helped to organize a club in East Point of women who wanted to do service for others. We would tell her, "You were taking care of the homeless before it became politically correct to take care of the homeless." They had their own Habitat for Humanity back in 1912 and 1914 because the ladies built a house for a homeless man in the neighborhood. The man's name was Joe. Now how I remember Joe's name was interesting. As I matured, I was invited to join the club. It was a sewing circle. In a practice held every May, every member of the club had to model a dress or a garment that they had made. They did embroidery and had to show off all the handicrafts that they had made. One day, while I was talking with them, they told me the story of Joe and the house.

YS: I'd like to hear about school experiences you had in East Point.

AW: My youngest brother and I were not of school age when we lived in East Point. So we came to Atlanta and started kindergarten and school here. I started kindergarten at Chadwick Home, which is over on the campus at Spelman. Ms. Chadwick had a little kindergarten for the girls who lived in her home, and that's where I went to school.

YS: The school was on campus?

AW: Yes, right there in the building that was torn down maybe ten years ago.

YS: Wow! What was the name of the building?

AW: Chadwick. It was the Leonard Street Orphan Home, then Chadwick's Orphanage. It was taken over by Spelman and called Chadwick Hall. It's in that little corner by the wall across from Read Hall.

YS: I didn't know that.

AW: That's where I started and finished on Spelman's campus.

YS: Oh, so you started at Spelman at a young age.

AW: It's interesting that when I started at Spelman as a freshman, Mr. Kemper Harreld would take me up the hill everyday because he had to get the music lined up for the organ and all of that. Mrs. Harreld was in New York with their daughter Josephine, who had just graduated from Spelman and was studying at Julliard. My momma would fix his breakfast every morning and he would walk back a half a block to his house and get his car warmed up and by the time he got back up, I was on the sidewalk ready to ride to Spelman. So I think maybe the reason I have a record of never being late is that Mr. Harreld was always there early to get the music out and practice a little bit.

I always knew what we were going to sing. That was my acquaintance with Sisters Chapel as a Spelman student. But when I was in school at Washington High, our teacher would take us to Spelman to various lectures and concerts in Sisters Chapel. In those days, there was one high school on the west side of Atlanta and later, on the north side, there was David T. Howard. I went to David T. Howard as a junior high student. We would see the boys walking across the campus with Rayford Logan, and that was very inspirational to us and made us want to do what they were doing.

YS: What is your fondest memory of a concert or a lecture in Sisters Chapel?

AW: We had Marion Anderson to sing. We had DuBois to speak. Rayford Logan led a talk in the University system, but he was still at Howard, I imagine. He helped us understand the meaning of Black history. They called it Negro history in those days. In high school, we had a separate course in Negro history, and we used Carter G. Woodson's book as our textbook. The book that was later used over at many of the colleges and is being reprinted this year . . that is the book we used in high school.

YS: Wow! That's interesting.

AW: I finished high school in 1934. My class was the largest in the history of the school. There were almost eight hundred in my senior class.

YS: Did you always know that you wanted to go to Spelman?

AW: No, not really because in those days I don't know that children had much say so about college choices. We honored our parents in where we were going and what we were going to do. I think we just did what was expected of us or did as we were told. The one thing that I wanted to do that I did not get to do was to go to the Homer Phillips Hospital in St. Louis to study hospital dietetics. My parents put a foot down on that. [Laughing]

YS: Do you know why they did that?

AW: Well, I went to Spelman when I was fourteen years old and graduated when I was eighteen, and they felt that, at eighteen, I was too young to go that far away from home. You'd think nothing of it now, but at that time it was a different story.

YS: Was that the usual age to go to Spelman? Fourteen?

AW: No. Ordinarily it was eighteen.

YS: How did you get there so early?

AW: Well, because I got an early start at Chadwick's nursery school and in those days the standards and regulations weren't as strictly observed as they are now. Also, in those days, you were skipped or double promoted. I was able to skip several grades, and that put me at an early age to finish high school.

YS: Since you were so young coming to Spelman, did you have older mentors at the College?

AW: In those days, members of the junior class were big sisters to members of the freshman class. I talked just last week with one of the girls who was a big sister to me. They did all of the work in helping us make the transition, and I think it worked out well because they were just a little older. They had been at the College, and they knew which way to go. One of the things that I remember about my freshman year at Spelman was that for the first time in the history of the school, boys and girls were able to dance together, looking at each other instead of being to the side or some such.

YS: I'd like to hear about that.

AW: We had as our activity a dance to inaugurate the new power plant. We had a tunnel in the power plant, which is the sculpture facility or the fine arts building now, I believe. We were able to dance up to the dining room. As a class, we joked that we broke the barrier! That was our contribution to Spelman: to bring dancing to the campus.

YS: Tell me about some of the dances that were popular then.

AW: The regular fox trot and some other stuff. It was a matter that you could dance. I don't know that we did any Lindy Hops and throwing all over heads and dances like that. We just did the two-step, the fox trot, and whatever they used to call the other things.

YS: Tell me about attire you were required to wear at Spelman activities.

AW: White for Founder's Day and special occasions. Of course when we became seniors and put on our cap and gown for the first time, you couldn't tell us a thing! We wore the cap and gown once a week, always on Sunday. We had to get that robe pressed and that collar pinned down. One thing we did at Spelman was to take two examinations. We had to go through Mrs. Ludie Andrews and the nursing staff at McVicar to show that we could make a bed and tuck the corners—miter the corners—like a hospital bed. And we had to go through an examination on ironing. We had to iron a tablecloth and pillowcase and the sheets to the satisfaction of the person in charge of the laundry. I can see the little lady, but I can't remember her name. Those were scheduled examinations that we had to pass before we could graduate. And of course the P.E. testing was done by the P.E. teachers. We didn't have swimming back then. My children had the swimming test when they came along. In those early days, when you lived on campus, any appliances you had had to be checked by the housekeeping department. If you had a radio, an iron or whatever, it had to be checked. One of the things that I had was a wind-up victrola. We would wind it up and put records on, and our housemother would come running up the steps thinking she was going to catch us with a radio. And as soon as she would get down the steps from seeing the victrola, we would put the radio on and listen to the Sunday night 10:00 jazz program. That was one of the cheating things that we did! Then, of course, the bells would ring, letting us know that it was time for the young men to leave the campus. They had to leave at 5:00. We had bells that rang five minutes before chapel. I don't know it they still have bells, or if the bell tower works.

YS: No, not as much.

AW: At that time, the fountain was as far as we could go. That was our boundary.

YS: The fountain? Where is that?

AW: In the middle of the campus.

YS: So you're saying the campus wasn't developed past the fountain?

AW: Yes, it was, but we couldn't go past the fountain. You had Giles Hall there and that walkway, but we didn't go behind Giles Hall. We just had what we called the center campus and the fountain was boundary. We were free to walk to class or to the dormitory, but we couldn't sit and visit with young men past the fountain. We couldn't do anything past that area. We did our entertaining in the living rooms of the various dorms, but somebody was always sitting there as a chaperone.

YS: Oh, really? [Laughing]

AW: When you left the campus in those days, the streetcar came to the upper end of the campus, which was between Sisters Chapel and the driveway that goes to the gate that is locked now back by the computer lab. If you went to town, you had to wear your hat and your gloves, and you had to go with at least two people. You never went anywhere by yourself.

YS: Tell me about friendships you developed at Spelman.

AW: The friends you make at a school like Spelman are your best friends, and you stick with them through thick or thin. I have one that I talked to last week. I talked to someone today just before you came who was a friend of a friend who sent a message to me. That's a joy you can't just throw out the window.

My best friend was from Atlanta. Other friends who were in our group have all died. She is still living. One other person I consider a friend of long standing is also a graduate of Spelman. What happened was that by the time I skipped grades, I left my original friends and class behind. So I had friends in one age group and friends in another age group. I remember a teacher at Morehouse telling us that he went to a White preparatory school and a White high school and a White college, and he never had the luxury of going to a town and calling a classmate to say, "Hi, I'm in town." He said that once they said hello, that was it. There was no such thing as going back and forth to the weddings of the children or any other special occasion because there was a different kind of association. Because of his experiences, he wanted his children to have the benefit of Black culture for future friendships, life and happiness. That's one thing that we remembered and were able to pass on to our children – that your friends are always your friends.

YS: Did you meet your husband while you were at Spelman?

AW: No. I met my husband after I had worked and come back to school.

YS: I'm sorry, but I'd like to go back to your studies at Spelman. When you were describing the examinations you had to take, I became interested in the courses.

AW: All of us had freshman biology and English. We had history and, whether you wanted to or not, you took P.E.. I was a home economics major so I had extra science classes to take. We had an economics course to take, and my instructor for that was John Hope, Jr. Home economics majors had a minor in science, so we had physics and chemistry . Not of the same intensity that science majors or pre-med folks took, but we had chemistry. Electives were pretty much what you have now. I chose speech and drama as an elective one year. We had a nine weeks grading period and, in those days, if you weren't doing well, the students who worked the reception area there in the big hall in Rockefeller would come across the campus and bring a little note from the Dean. We had the fear of getting a note as an incentive to do our work. Going back sixty-five years is not that easy. That's really going back.

YS: Did you have a favorite professor?

AW: Yes, I had several favorite professors, but Dr. Nathaniel Tillman, who was a professor at Morehouse [we were able to take some classes there], was among my favorite professors. I guess it's because of individual personalities. Back when I was coming along, sixty-five years ago, they didn't have school counselors, per se. I became a school counselor and was in the first class that Atlanta University graduated. And I was among the first counselors hired for schools in the state of Georgia. I think Dr. Tillman was a teacher and a counselor, and that was the first time somebody just sat down with me and said, "Now let's see where you are and where you want to go." I think that makes a difference in how you respond to a question like the one you just asked me. "Who's your favorite?" You like folks who like you. And Dr. Tillman liked me and I liked him, so he became my favorite.

YS: The last time I was here to interview you, I noticed this beautiful painting of three African women. I know there is a story associated with this painting. Would you share it with me?

AW: Yes, that is one of my prized possessions because one of my former students did that for me. His name is Howard Nicholson, Jr., and he did that when I was serving as counselor at Headland High School in East Point. "Faith, Hope and Charity" is the name of the painting. He always thought he needed another little touch of Black in one of those corners to make it suit his fancy. The frame was done by students in the industrial arts department at Headland. They felt that kind of rough framing would do better for the matting that Howard had done and the colors he had chosen. So when I see that, I am reminded of my 33 years as a school counselor. That's one of the joys you get from teaching. You don't get money, but you have other things that help you remember pleasant times.

YS: Did he ever say why he decided to paint these three women?

AW: He was not even in art class, but this is something that he enjoyed doing. I imagine he had seen that painting done somewhere, and he painted a copy of it. As you can see, it was painted in April of 1980.

YS: When I saw the painting, I just thought about Black women in general, and I started thinking about our conversation last weekend. You were telling me a lot about your childhood experiences in East Point. Could you please elaborate on your memories of Black women in your community?

AW: It's interesting because all of the artwork that we have is of women. Two photographs have fallen: one of my mother and one of my mother-in-law. One reminds me of my daughter as a child. The other is a wood carving of an East Indian woman who looks like family. The other that you see behind you (and I'm coming away from your question). was a gift to me in appreciation of my kindness to the people who operated the Chinese laundry in the West End where the Wachovia Bank is now. They had to close down because Wachovia wanted that space for a West End branch. I would go in and take my laundry, and we would have all kinds of conversations. The owner had his sister over in China to transcribe this, and that's how I know the characters are good luck, happiness, good health, and love.

One of the nicest women that I ever knew was a schoolteacher in East Point. She walked every morning, that mile or mile and a half, to catch the streetcar to come into Atlanta to work. Her last assignment to work in Atlanta was maybe three or four blocks from where this house is. Her name was Ann Chunn. She took good care of me. When she went on vacations, I went on vacations. My first trip to Washington was with her, and that was at the time when the White House was open to visitors, so I had a chance to meet the sitting President. I went to Chicago with her. I went to New York with her and had a chance to sit on the lions outside the New York Public Library. She was what was called in those days a spinster or an old maid, which is not at all like today's liberated female who chooses not to marry. Her interest was in traveling and she would take me with her. Now, to me, she was a symbol of young Black womanhood with some strength. There was an old wives tale then that if a man were the first to take a newborn out of the house, that child would have characteristics in keeping with a man. When it was time for me to make my first move out of the house, people jokingly said, "Don't let Honey take her out because she will never stay home." Her name was Rosabel Murray, but that was a mouthful, so I called her Honey and everybody else called her Honey as well. Honey Murray was a member of the club I think I talked to you about that did embroidery work and crocheting and things of that nature. I think I still have some towels and washcloths that Honey put fancy trimmings on. They are extremely worn, but they are priceless and precious to me. The trimmings are the only thing left. All the middle is worn out, but I still hold on to the strings that were crocheted gifts from Honey Murray.

Then there is a woman whose life is tied up with Spelman because she lived on Westview Drive, just across from Woodruff Library and at the corner that's adjacent to the Fine Arts building. She was a member of the Maxey-Austell family, and she was principal of a school out in East Point. Where people would use bells or vocal commands to summon children into the building, Mrs. Maxey used classical music. I have it written somewhere that her daughter has a tape going back to those olden days that she wants played at the graveside service for her funeral.

I have met some very strong women in my life, and I guess one of the most highly regarded is my mother. She is the one who insisted that we do for others, that we volunteer, that we should not look to be paid for everything we do. You know, people say now that service is the rent we pay for being on this earth. My mother didn't use those words, but that's what she had us to understand.

And in Atlanta there were two strong women with Spelman backgrounds who had an influence on me. One was Sarah Fisher Brown, and she was a graduate of what they called the teacher-training program. Sarah was a good friend of Cora Finley, a graduate of Spelman who lived in the house with us. She was a spinster or old maid (whatever you want to call it) who was interested in traveling. Later she became a Jeannes Supervisor in her hometown. There is one thing you have to remember. When these women were employed as teachers, it was understood that they could not marry. You could not marry after you became a teacher.

YS: Why was that?

AW: They wanted the teachers to give undivided attention to their students. One of my friends, Mary Hughes, who died a month ago, filed a suit against the Fulton County School System because of this restriction. Miss Cora Finley enjoyed life to the fullest. She wrote a letter to the President of the Southern Railway Company complaining about the discriminatory treatment of Black soldiers. And she was one of the persons who filed a suit against the Atlanta Board of Education for equal pay for Blacks. Coming out of a segregated society, you had lots of things that were done to Black folks; lots of things that were done to Black women. You had threats placed upon Black men who were the supporters of their families. It was not the easiest thing to step out and file a suit against the people who signed your check every month, but Cora Finley did that and, with the help of the NAACP, won the suit. She was active with the NAACP back in the days of DuBois and Walter White, and she attended some of the first NAACP conventions. She helped Mrs. Selena Sloan Butler found the Black PTA, which was called the National Congress of Colored Parents and Teachers. Mrs. Butler was a Spelman product. Now Mrs. Butler did all sorts of political things. And, you know, when I was doing research for an organization, I discovered a quote from Mrs. Butler in a state textbook. That was quite something else. Mrs. Butler petitioned and won for Blacks in the City of Atlanta the right to have night school.

YS: You had to petition for night school?

AW: Yes, and Mrs. Butler was in the forefront of this effort. And she worked with the night school, which was over at Yonge Street School. During the War, she went to Fort Huachucha, Arizona, with her son, who was a physician, and she did for folks on the Army base all of the things volunteers do: write letters or read the mail for soldiers who were not literate. Her picture hangs in our State Capitol. Black women who have influenced me? I could go on and on and on, but I think I'll stop.

YS: That is so interesting. Was it common for Black women during that time to be unmarried and activist at the same time?

W: Yes, because there were some people who knew that the only way that we were going to make any progress would be for them to get out and make a difference, and they did. They had time because they didn't have home responsibilities. But the main point is that they were committed, and they were courageous.

YS: What was the line of work of most Black women in your community?

AW: When I was growing up, it was not a major concern to me what people did to earn a living. But when I think about your question, I would have to say that many of the women were domestics and some were teachers. There were Black women insurance agents. I remember two families that operated funeral homes in East Point. The man did some of it, but the women were the ones who sort of put the smoothing touches onto the business. And then women earned a living by selling food to workers on the railroad and to train passengers. You see, we couldn't eat in the dining car or in restaurants in the city.

The thing that I remember was that my mother never worked away from home, but she always had her own little spending money. She would gather the eggs from the chickens she would raise or she milked the cow, and we would go with her to deliver the milk and the eggs. When people said they had their milk and egg money, that's how she had hers. My momma was a very thrifty person, and I guess it was good for us that she was because my daddy spent money faster than he could make it. He thought that was what money was for—to be spent.

Speaking of thrift, when our house was built in Atlanta, my mother signed all of the checks for the construction work. I don't know if I've told you this before, but at this time women could not get credit. My mother had her own little money because she sold chickens, eggs, milk, and vegetables. She would tell us, "Always have your own money." The other thing she would say was, "Always have enough money to get back home," whether it was by train or bus or car or whatever.

YS: Where did she learn to milk cows and take care of chickens and ?

AW: Necessity is the mother of invention.

YS: Do you know what your paternal and maternal grandmothers did?

AW: They were probably housewives. Nothing special as I remember. They were deep in the country and by the time they took care of their own families, they probably didn't have time for gainful employment. They were mothers and housewives from sunup to sundown. From "can to can't," as they used to say. No employment that I've ever heard. My paternal grandmother was a Baptist minister's wife. We were talking about her the other day, and its shameful that I don't know her name..

YS: Did your mother ever talk to you about her mother?

AW: Yes, and the one thing I do remember was the discussion about where my mother would stay when she went to nursing school in Raleigh. The decision was that she would stay with Aunt Lizzie. So she stayed with Aunt Lizzie until Aunt Lizzie located suitable accommodations for her on the campus. My mother had a brother whose name was Prince, and he would always meet us when we would go on the train to Sanford, North Carolina. When I was quite young, maybe three or four, he would pick me up off the step of the train coach. And he would have a cigar in his mouth and one time I was burned on my cheek. People have said that was the beginning of the mole I have right here. That could have been the case, or it did not have to be. But that's what I have always heard. I've believed it and had no reason to question it. So be it.

YS: Tell me about your experiences with Jim Crow.

AW: Back in those days, parents sheltered children from the ugly side of life. They had to undergo lots and lots of trials and tribulations, but they never bothered, my folks didn't, telling me what they were struggling to accomplish. They took the positive side and took us where we could go without problems. When I was growing up, we always had streetcars that had seating from back to front for Black folks and front to back for White folks. And when you got to the point of needing a seat in the middle, then the person who was Black stood up or moved back. The streetcar turned around in front of our house because they would change the connection and the conductor would go to the other end of the car. The streetcar would go down Fair Street to where the Morehouse gym is now located. I would get on the streetcar and ride with the conductor to that end. When I was older, I would sit with a Jewish woman who operated a grocery store about a block from my house. We would ride to where the Richard Russell building is now located because that's where I would have to change cars. So we lived with segregation. My daddy bought a car exclusively for my momma to use, and he had a student drive her where she had to go so that she would not have to deal with segregation. The fathers of two of my friends worked at the post office, and they rode bicycles from home to work in order to avoid segregation. I had a brother who would walk from my house to West Fair Street and he took pride in saying that he walked almost as fast as the streetcar ran. Sometimes we did this to avoid dealing with segregation, but it was also to have the streetcar fare to spend for something else. [laughing] We tried to find a way to get around segregation, but we tolerated it for just so long until we were like Fannie Lou Hamer who said, "I'm sick and tired of being sick and tired." Then we did something about it. My family filed and won the first major Civil Rights lawsuit in the South to open golfing facilities to everybody. My father and two of my brothers and two of our family friends filed that suit.

YS: Mrs. Washington, in our last interview, you mentioned that you were a high school counselor at Headland High School in East Point. Tell me when and how did you start working there?

AW: It's interesting how I went to Fulton County to work. I was working at the Atlanta Daily World as a reporter and taking classes at Atlanta University just for the fun of going to school. After I did a class, a school principal came to me and said, "You're going to be my counselor". And I said to him, "I am?" And he said, "Yes, you are". So that is why I always said to Fulton County, "You asked me to come. I didn't ask you." I began working the first year that Fulton County employed counselors, and I worked for thirty some years. I was in the first class of counselors that Atlanta University graduated. I was employed at South Fulton High School. I need to clarify when I say "first" because White schools had counselors.

YS: Black schools didn't have Black counselors?

AW: They didn't have counselors, period. You see, there was always the homeroom teacher or somebody to help guide folks, but not with the title, Guidance Counselor.

YS: Do you know what brought about the change?

AW: I think it must have been a sign of the times such as what we are seeing now. It was a way of helping young people think through their futures.

YS: I'd like you to describe a typical day at South Fulton High School as a counselor?

AW: Well, in those early days, counselors were treated as teachers, paid as teachers, considered as teachers. Therefore, you had to have some classes to teach. You didn't have anything like a full-time counselor all day with nothing else to do. You had classes and counseling services. I was given permission to teach physical education without any real preparation other than what I had been taught at Spelman by Ms. Callahan and Ms. Dupree and Ms. Simon and others. And when I was certified in social studies, I taught that and PE and home economics. We also had to score and grade all of the standardized tests students took. That was the counselor's responsibility. And I have to give accolades to Dr. Oran Eagleson, my teacher at Spelman and at Atlanta University, who saw to it that we learned statistics.

I always was given homerooms that had some big bad boys. And when I say "bad," I mean bad in terms of mischievous, not bad as in the 2003 interpretation of "bad." I always got the homeroom that had the football players. And when they weren't in school, I had a standing permission to go to their homes and wake them up and say, "Come on. Let's get to school." You see, there was a policy that you couldn't participate in extra-curricular activities if you weren't in school and on time. Many of the students said later in life that the reason they got to school and graduated was that somebody made them get up and get to school. There was a standard joke at the school: "Where is so-and-so?" Answer: "He's asleep because he caught chickens."

YS: He caught chickens? What did that mean?

AW: You see, the poultry houses would come to the neighborhoods out in the rural areas of East Point and get a truckload of children to go to the chicken farms at two and three in the morning to get chickens ready for market. So, understandably, the children would be tired and sleepy and could not do their homework because they were working at the chicken farm. There were many young people whose income from these night jobs made the difference in eating or helping momma pay the rent or buying clothes or whatever. They didn't work at the farms to get spending money or money for a car. They worked to get money for necessities like food and housing. Well, you can understand that, at the end of the day, we counselors were very tired. We were busy throughout the day. And then, after school, we attended extra-curricular activities. We ended our day way over in the night, and then we started all over again. Early.

YS: What issues did female students face in high school that male students did not face?

AW: In the early years, I worked in a city school and then I worked in suburban areas. I would say that the one common thread (now that you ask about a commonality) was that the girls did not have high expectations for themselves. They had not grown up thinking that they could do this, that or the other. They had to be pushed into higher education. You had to push them into thinking, "Yes, I can play basketball; yes, I can sing; yes, I can do some of the things that others do." So that was one thing. One of the benefits of a school like Spelman was the opportunity to see alumnae who did well in many, many areas.

YS: In high schools today, there is a high incidence of teenage pregnancy. Was that common during the time you were teaching?

AW: No. In those days, an unwed mother had to go home and stay. She couldn't put her feet on the street. I remember a conversation I had with a superintendent about pregnant girls coming to school or going to an alternative program. I think I must have been about the oldest of the counselors. My position was that the young woman who had a child out of wedlock with no strong support system needed education as a support system. That should be one of our thrusts, I told him. "We must do what we can for the young people who really need us." His eyes stretched and he said, "Well, you know, maybe you've got a point there". I pride myself that maybe my conversation with that gentleman that day, when nobody else had nerve enough to say to him what I said, might have made a difference at some point to change his thinking because shortly after that we did have alternative schools. They put one on each end of Fulton County. It was not as convenient as going to school just across the street, but at least the girls were able to go to school and they even added daycare or childcare to support her. Or if she had delivered, then her child could be in daycare while she was in school. That may have raised the educational level and moved some people out of poverty.

YS: Roe vs. Wade. I'd like to know your position on this Supreme Court ruling.

AW: I am with the pro-choice, and I am pleased that many of the younger men are now saying that a woman's body is hers for certain decisions. We're going to need more younger men to be able to speak out instead of the older men who have the idea in their feeble brains that women should do "what I tell them to do." And affirmative action. I am just as happy as I can be that there were young people from all walks of life in that demonstration. I do believe that my granddaughter was there in front of the Supreme

269

Court building. I think I saw her. Maybe I was just so hoping that I would see her. I am very pleased because I know what it takes to open doors.

MRS. HATTIE MAE WELLIGNTON

Stokestown, North Carolina
Student at Spelman College, Recipient of HOPE Scholarship

One time I went to work for a lady who had never washed dishes. Every pot, every pan, every plate, every knife, every fork and spoon was dirty. And then you couldn't even look out her kitchen window, it was so dirty. That was the thing I hated about Virginia. I worked hard so that my kids would finish school. I wanted them to have a better life. And they do. They do!

HW: There were seven children in my family and I am the third youngest because I had a brother and a sister under me. I grew up in a place in North Carolina called Stokestown. That's what my books say. I was born in Stokestown, North Carolina in 1931. From the time I was five years old, my father and mother were farmers. The first house I remember we lived in was back up in the field, and they called it "the house in the field." Both my father and my mother drank whiskey. I was the baby of seven kids. My mother and father had five daughters and two sons. I think she had one that died and a couple of miscarriages. But when I was a child growing up, I remember my mother and my father working real hard. We used to wear hand-me-down clothes from the White people. My mother used to work helping White people after we finished our crops in the fall. She would bring home clothes that were torn. We grew our own vegetables and everything. Right? The house we lived in was okay, but I remember that the back steps were broken down and to me nobody should live like that. I was a child. My oldest sister used to cook for us when my mother was working. The sister who was next to the older sister was real mean. [Laughing]. Do I need to go all the way through when I talk about my family? Are you going to stop to give me another question or should I just keep going?

YS: No, I won't stop you. I want you to continue as you wish.

HW: We moved a lot because we didn't own our own farm. We went from farm to farm and from house to house. We just moved, moved, moved and there was nothing you could do back then because you didn't own your own house. You moved to where the White man had the farm, and you farmed. That's what you did. You farmed. A lot of times they would let you profit and a lot of times they wouldn't.

YS: You were sharecroppers?

HW: Yes. We moved and moved and moved

YS: What crops did you farm?

HW: Tobacco, corn, cotton. Tobacco, corn, and cotton were the major crops and then peanuts. White men would own the farm and then lease it out to someone. You farmed under the White man's jurisdiction. You would lease the farm the way you lease an apartment. You know what I'm saying?

YS: Yes. So, you would harvest the crops and then give the money back to the owner?

HW: Well, no, it didn't work like that. You worked. You shared the crops. They got their share and you got your share. A lot of times it didn't work like that either. Sometimes the man that owned the farm, the owner, would get his money. If you owed a debt, like, say, fertilizer [you had to buy your own equipment], he would cheat you. It was just like slavery. Farming was just like slavery. We were angry about it, but what could we do? Farming was just like slavery.

I remember my daddy's first new car, which we got when my brother was seventeen and my daddy would let my brother drive the car. One night, my daddy had been drinking [my mother always had a lot of bad headaches and I would always lie down with her because I loved my mamma]. Well, this night, when he came home, I was in the room with my mamma and I could see a blaze of fire coming out of the car. Someone had set the car on fire. We tried to put it out, but we couldn't. And so, we had to move from that farm. We went back to Stokestown. That's why I wrote my book about Stokestown. There was so much chaos.

My mother went to church, but I don't ever remember my daddy being at church. My mother and I sang in the same choir together. I don't ever remember seeing my father in church, but he could sing. I think he was supposed to be a preacher. You know the Bible talks about many who are called but few who are chosen. I think my daddy was called to preach, but he turned it down, so it fell on my brother.

But anyway, the life of a child growing up in the country and being raised by two people who drank whiskey was kind of bad. People now snatch kids and carry them away and kill them and that could have happened to my brothers and me and to my nephew. But it didn't happen. I remember some weekends we would be home all by ourselves. Our parents would leave on Friday and come back late Friday night. They would leave on Saturday and come back late Saturday night. We would be home by ourselves. My mother had a friend and she would keep us until my mamma came home.

Back then, we didn't eat a lot of meat like people do now . . . steak and pork chops and all that stuff. We only ate what back then they called killing hogs. You know about that? That's where you get your pork chops and your spare ribs and all that goody stuff. But we ate a lot of vegetables and fruits. I remember when I was going to school, I had only two dresses. Two dresses. I wore one for two days and the next one for two days and my mother would wash and iron the other dress. I remember one time she brought me a pair of shoes you couldn't shine. They were so hard you couldn't shine them. Another time I remember wearing shoes that were boy shoes the White people gave to my mama, and I remember those shoes hurt my feet real bad. But I had to wear them. I had no choice.

My mother only got to the second grade. She was the oldest of her siblings and her father kept her out of school so that she could work on the farm. I thought that was awful. That's why she wanted me and my brother and sisters to get an education because she didn't get it. I don't think my daddy went to school at all. He couldn't sign his name, but he could count.

I think all my sisters left home young and got married young. I think that was because of my father. He drank and he was very abusive. He was very abusive, mostly with his mouth. You know what I'm saying? They left home early and left me and my baby brother and my baby sister and my nephew. My mama raised one of my sister's child, a son.

We worked real hard. I remember in the country when we went to school, we had to walk. People think it's cold now. It's not cold now. It's not cold like it was when we walked to school. I remember when the ditch, the water in the ditch, would freeze and my brother and I walked to school and when we got to school, our feet would be so cold. Our socks would be wet. And we would pull off our shoes and then our socks and sit there until they dried. I remember one day when we arrived at school, I was sitting up close up under the pipe [I should have shown you that picture] to get warm. Well, the pipe came out of the wall into the heater. It was a long pipe, and I was sitting too close to the heater. The pipe fell loose and hit my nose. It burned my nose. I had a scar. It might still be there.

We had every class from the first grade to the seventh in the same room. Just had them sectioned off. You could see everybody. That's the kind of classroom we had. Yep, at school we had one room with all the grades. I'm going to bring you a picture next time we have a session. But it was fun. It was fun because we made up our own games. It was fun.

We had fruit trees at one school. I remember this school. Poppy Hill they called it. We had fruit trees across the road and the teacher would let us get fruit from the trees. It was really enjoyable going to school because then we had cooks. The government started giving the schools food to cook so that the children could have a decent breakfast. It was fun, until I would go home and my daddy would be drinking and he would be all over my mom and, you know, stuff like that. I made a vow that my children would grow up in a happy home. But guess what? I married a man who drank liquor. I still made my mind up that I was going to raise my kids up so that they would finish school. My life wasn't that bad in a way , but my dad was very abusive to me and to my mom.

YS: Did your mother or father ever tell you how the two of them met?

HW: No, I really don't know where they met. No, I really don't. No. But we can choose the wrong mates. We don't know it, but we choose the wrong mates. If we do it ourselves, we choose the wrong mates. I think if you pray and ask God to send you the right person, I believe God will do that. He doesn't want us to be abused. He didn't make women or men to be abused. My life, you know, marrying my husband? All that's behind me. When I think about it, I laugh. I don't get sad because I am at a point in my life where I am happier than I have ever been. You know what I mean? I'm doing some of the things that I've always wanted to do. I went back to school. I didn't know I could draw or paint, but I always did write poetry. I write poems. Right now I'm pretty good. I'm stable in my mind. You know what I'm saying?

YS: Yes, I understand. Tell me about going to school when you were growing up on the farm.

274

HW: Well, in school I was happy. I can't really remember, but I think we had to be there by eight o'clock, which means we had to wake up at seven or seven thirty because it took thirty minutes to get to school because we had to walk. And I rode the school bus, too. I rode my first school bus when I went to Poppy Hill School. My teacher's name was Ms. Dupree. We put on minstrel shows. We made a lot of money and we used the money to buy our first school bus. And then when I went to the ninth grade, I rode a school bus. In the eighth grade and the ninth grade, I rode a school bus. And I loved to study spelling. My brother and I were in the spelling bee. We used to sit everyone down, and then we would sit each other down. Sometimes he would out spell me, and sometimes I would out spell him. We laugh about that now. That was my favorite subject, spelling. Yep, I loved spelling. We studied spelling, math, reading, and English.

YS: Did you have chores to do when you came home from school?

HW: We had chores on top or chores. I know in the fall of the year, we had to have the heater ready to burn to keep us warm. My brother and I had to do that. My daddy would cut the wood and put it on the porch so that if we needed wood at night to put into the heater, we could go and get it off the porch. As I said, my daddy and mama were farmers, so we'd come home from school and have a stack of tabacco from here to there. We had to tie it up in bundles. We had to do that. Yes, ma'am. And we had to keep the yard swept. We used what we called a yard broom. Sometimes he would sweep the yard and sometimes I would sweep the yard. We didn't have to draw any water because we had a pump. I remember getting up early when I got older because I had to cook breakfast before we went to school.

All my older sisters left home young. Right? I think I was about nine and my mama would wash up the collard greens, cabbage, or whatever and put it in a container in the icebox. She would cook her meat early in the morning because she had to work in the fields. So, she would cook her meats and fix the cornbread and have it ready to go into the oven. She'd send me home from the fields about eleven o'clock. She'd say, "Louise, go home and stir the pot and my food will be done when I get there." One day, my mother and father had gone to see her brother in this little town, and I told my brother, "I'm gonna make us a cake." He said, "All right, Mama's gonna get you." When I finished the cake, I gave him a slice, my baby sister a slice, and my nephew a slice, and I took a slice. Then he looked down the road and said, "Here come Mama and Daddy." I took the cake and put it under the house. You know, back then, on the farm, houses were built on stilts and you could put things under them. My brother told on me. He said, "Ma, Louise made a cake!" She said, "Did you make a cake, girl?" And I said, "Yes, ma'am." And she said, "Go get it!" I had to go under the house and get the cake. [Laughing] That was funny. She tasted it and said, "Mmmmm. That's pretty good." That's when she told me, she said, "Since you planning on cooking, I'm going to teach you how to cook and from here on out, you're gonna do the cooking." That's how I learned how to cook. I would cook breakfast and after I cooked, I had to walk a third of a mile to get to the street to get the bus.

But it was fun. It was fun. I remember my mother teaching me how to wash. And that's another thing that she did. She washed for the White people. I hated that she had to do that. I remember there were times when she didn't feel like going the day she was supposed to be going and she'd send me. The White people always had a table in each room. This table had a watch, some money and I don't know what else on it. I'd see it in one room and then when I go in another room, I'd see it there too. I said to my mama, "Those people got a lot of watches and money." She said, "Louise," she said, "They carry it from one room to the other to see if you want to steal it."

I learned how to sew. My mother didn't teach me because she couldn't sew. One fall, my brother, my sister and myself went out picking cotton to get money for a sewing machine. So we got a sewing machine. One day—I don't know where Mama was--I said, "I'm going to learn how to sew today." Girl, you should see some clothes I made. I used to make all my girls' clothes. People thought I got those little outfits from the store. And guess what? I made them with my hands until I got a sewing machine.

I was real close to my mother. She'd get her hair fixed. I'd get my hair fixed. She'd take me with her to the beauty shop. She'd go fishing. I'd go fishing with her. She'd go to church. I would go to church with her. I thought I would never leave my mother. Isn't that something? I never told her I'd never leave, but I thought that in my spirit I would never leave because in my spirit I was so close to her. Life has not been that bad for me.

YS: On the farm, how close did your neighbors live?

HW: Oh, we lived close. See that tree?

YS: Yes.

HW: Okay, this was the man that owned the farm. He and his wife lived there. They were White. And then down the road lived my mother's best friend, named Laleeta. We had pretty good close neighbors and they were nice neighbors because the lady that lived close to us, she would ask me to cut the grass. She would ask me and my brother to cut the grass. She would say that if we cut the grass, she'd give us fifty cents or a quarter. We would take the money and go to the store and buy candy. I remember one day we said, "We'd better save our money because when it comes Mama's birthday, we can give her a birthday party. Buy her some grapes and some appalies and Coca Cola." That was when we had those Coca Cola bottles. And we would put everything into the room and when she came into the room, we would sing happy birthday to her. It was that we loved her. She was amazing. Wonderful.

My mother stood about four feet and four to five or six inches. She was real short. She was real dark skinned, but her hair came round here. She was real petit. I don't think she weighed 120 pounds, if that much. But she was really strong. Very intelligent. She could make anything from nothing. She was very intelligent and I learned a lot from her. One thing I learned was how to be clean. She used to tell me if you have one dress, wash and iron it and put it back on. Keep your hair combed and your teeth clean. I have all my teeth. I'm seventy-one and I had eleven babies. They always say when you have all those kids, your teeth get bad. You lose teeth. I haven't lost one. My mamma had a way about helping us. She was very intelligent but, as I said, she only got to the second grade. I think she was smart. I thought she was the sweetest, the little prettiest thing I had ever seen in my life. She was nice. I just hate that she married my daddy.

YS: Do you think she was happy?

HW: No, I don't think so. She loved her children, but I don't think she was happy. She might have loved my daddy, but she wasn't happy with him. You know what I'm saying? But she was a very intelligent woman. She only got to the second grade. When I got married, she didn't want me to get married because I got married real young. I got married at seventeen. She said, "Louise, you are too young to get married." My name used to be Louise. When I got my birth certificate, it said Louise, but I changed it to Hattie Mae because I always used the name Hattie Mae. So I just changed it to Hattie Mae. She always wanted me to finish school and go to college. I had an aunt who wanted to send me to college, but I got married. She didn't speak to me for three years after I got married, she was so angry with me. She wanted the best for us. But you can't have the best if you are with somebody who is a drunk, a gambler, a woman chaser, a number player . . . My daddy and mamma got into liquor on the weekends. Other than that, though, I'd say she was the best mom and the prettiest mother in the world.

She taught me how to take care of myself. She always said, "I don't care where you go or who you meet or what they are doing. You are just as good as they are." That's what I told my kids. She said, "You are just as good as anybody in the world." She used that word to me. That's what I used on my kids. I told them, I said, "I don't care where you go. You are just as good as anybody in the world. And don't think you are not." That's what she taught me. I was proud of myself.

YS: What did she tell you when you entered puberty? Do you remember how old you were?

HW: My mother told me I was to keep myself clean and stay away form boys. Let's see now. I was twelve. It really wasn't' scary because my mama had already, you know, alerted me. I was picking butter beans in the garden when I started. [Laughing] And you know, we used white rags then. [Laughing] White rags.

YS: Tell me about some of the do's and don'ts for girls when they were on their cycle.

HW: Let me see. Let me try to think. No, we didn't get in the bathtub. We didn't take whole baths. We washed up with warm water and soap. Mama said your organ is open then. And she told me not to have sex with boys because I could get pregnant.

YS: In your community, did girls have babies out of wedlock?

HW: Yes. A lot of times when a girl got pregnant, the mother would keep the girl in the house until she had the baby or the mother would send the girl away. I don't know where. I think mostly rich White people did that. Sent daughter away. Abortion was really very secretive then. You know what I'm saying'?

YS: When you were growing up on the farm, what was your favorite holiday?

HW: Christmas. I loved Christmas. My mother used to put oranges and apples, candy and nuts and raisins in a bag and put our name on it. I always did love fruits.

YS: Did you celebrate Xmas at home or at your grandparents'?

HW: No, no. We celebrated it at home. I don't remember going to their house on no holiday. I did visit my step grandmother on my mother's side. I don't remember my father's father and mother or my mother's mother at all. When my mother's mother died, I think I was two. But we spent most holidays at home. Now Easter, I would say Easter was my favorite holidays because we used to have Easter egg hunts at the church. It was nice. Yep.

YS: Tell me more about your church.

HW: It was small. Small. There might have been a hundred members. That's all. As I told you, my mother and I sang in the choir together. I remember she would lead the song and I would be standing right beside her. It was really fun for me. Our church wasn't integrated. It was all Black, and it was in the country. There would be dinners at the quarterly meetings, every third Sunday, and the people would spread the food out. Most of the people in the church were everybody's family. People would come from another country to come to this church. We had wooden floors and wood heaters. Didn't have air-conditioning. Only fans.

YS: And about your best friends?

HW: Okay. I had one friend named Margery Coley. She lived down from the school I went to and her father   and mother owned their own property. They owned their own house and their own land. I used go there mostly on the weekends to keep away from my daddy because he would be fussing at me when he would be drinking. Her daddy had a car called a T model Ford and he would take us to town. Another thing, they used to cook a big ole fish. It was good. I enjoyed being there with them with her dad because her daddy would never fuss. We went to the same school. There were two Hattie Maes and two Jessie Maes at the same school. I don't think Margery went to the same school I went to in North Carolina. Hattie Mae and Jessie Mae were my good friends when I was in school. If we had twenty-five cents, we would divide what we bought. Most times we would divide hamburgers because hamburgers cost fifteen cent at the school. We would get a hamburger and divide it three ways. They were really good friends. Jessie Mae and Hattie Mae and Margery Coley were the only friends I remember having.

But I was real close to my brother James Earl. He's the pastor of a church in Kenson, North Carolina. We were real close. My daddy always said to my brother and me that we would never be anything. I don't know why he told us that. I think he was being used by the devil. He told my brother he was a sickly SOB. He told me I would be a ho in the street. My brother is doing beautiful. He can do anything with his hands. He can build anything in the house. He's great. That's my favorite brother. He dropped out in the eighth grade. I didn't do much better. I dropped out in the ninth grade and got married.

YS: Why did he drop out?

HW: He had problems with his head. The fuss would always bother his head, and my mama wouldn't let him go any more. I think it came from my daddy being the way he was. The stress made my brother have headaches. He also had problems with his stomach.

YS: Tell me how you met your husband.

HW: I was fifteen. I was going to the mail box. We lived back up in the field, right? So I was taking all my family's mail to give to the post man and the list of some new people and he saw me coming. I was skipping and I was in his yard. "I'll take that from you," he said. I said, "No, you won't take it from me." He was mannish. You know mannish? You know how fresh some boys act? That's mannish. He said, "You're gonna be my wife." I said, "Boy, nobody's gonna marry you." So I went back on skipping down the path. After that, he started coming to the house. He was a big liar. He would come and sit and make my mama and my daddy laugh and make my nephew and my sister laugh. So we started dating. We dated for about two years. He was seventeen or nineteen and I was fifteen. His father and mother were farmers like mine. Farmers. He was a farmer. He dropped out of school before I did and he stayed at home and farmed with his father. Yep.

YS: Why did you drop out of school?

HW: I just wanted to marry young. I have an Aunt. I think she must be about ninety five now. She never had any kids, and she always begged my mother for me. She said—my mama's name is Rosa—she said, "Rosa, let me take this one and raise her and I'll send her through college." She wanted to send me to college, but I told my mother I didn't want to finish high school. I was going to marry young. I said, "When I finish high school, I'm gonna get married." But the main reason for me leaving was because my daddy was abusive. We moved in with my husband's parents and we worked in the field. In the hot sun and the cold. I was used to it because I came from a family of farmers. I went to a family of farmers and I came from a family of farmers. We lived in a room that had two beds. When we had company, they'd sleep right along side us. I got along with my husband's father, but not with his mother. She was kind of arid. Rea light. And they called her White Indian. She had real long hair and she said one day that all her sons had married nappy headed ugly girls. And I said to her, "They marry who they want to marry." That stopped the conversation right there. But I got along with his daddy. The fact about it was, his father was better to me than my own father was. I found a father figure in him. You know. He was a good man. A real good man. I loved him. He was wonderful. He always saw something good in me. My daddy never saw anything good in me. I overheard my husband's father say one night, talking to his son, he said, "Boy . . .

279

[back then, they didn't call children by their name]. . . Boy, if you mess up, you're gonna mess up something good. You got a good little wife." I could talk to him about anything. I couldn't talk to my daddy about anything. I don't remember having a conversation with my father. And that is really sad for a child. But I got over it. Things happen to you in life, but you got to push them out of your mind and out of your spirit and get on with your life.

YS: Tell me about childbirth experiences for women who lived on the farm?

HW: We had the babies mostly at home. And midwives delivered them. You would go to the doctor when the baby was about to be born and the doctor would send for the lady. The midwife. I never asked my mama where we were born. Probably at home. Yes, probably at home. She told me childbirth was scary. A lot of women died and the babies died because doctors didn't have the knowledge, you know, as they do now. Not even when I had my babies. You know what I am saying?

YS: Were you working on the farm when you became pregnant?

HW: Yes. I was eighteen. I was working in the field and I fell. I guess I got too hot. I fell.

YS: When you told your family that you were pregnant, what was their response?

HW: My husband was happy, but his mother didn't believe the baby was his when it was born because the baby was dark. Real dark. And being pregnant was terrible. The first one was hard.

YS: Did you continue to work in the field while you were pregnant?

HW: I still worked in the field. Yes.

YS: For how long? Up until how many months?

HW: Maybe until about the seventh or eighth month.

YS: And was your baby born at home?

HW: In the house. With my husband's mother and father. In fact, my first three children were born in that house. The first one was bad, real bad. The second one wasn't that bad. The first was bad because it was my first, and the last one was bad because I had had so many and I was older. Childbirth is not that bad and it's not that good either. I didn't have morning sickness like some people had because I was good and healthy. With the first one, I was in labor for maybe ten or fifteen minutes. I was fast.

YS: Tell me how you felt when you saw your first child.

HW: Honey, I was happy. I was happy it was out. [Laughing]. I was happy it was out.

YS: You said your mother taught you a lot about working and about being proud. What did she teach you about race?

HW: About race? You know, that is a good question. Well, maybe I started learning when I was younger, but it just went over my head. The kids used to call me nigger. I would walk to school with my brother and the White kids on the school bus would call us nigger and spit at us. I didn't think it was just me. Child, I thought that was normal until we moved to Alexandria, Virginia. That's when I really found out that prejudice was alive and well.

YS: What happened there?

HW: One day I was coming home from work and some young men threw something White toward me. And I did like this to keep it from getting into my face. I don't know what it was. I didn't see prejudice that much in the country. Really didn't see it until I moved to Alexandria, Virginia. That's really strange, isn't it? When I moved to Alexandria Virginia, I was thirty seven, maybe thirty five, and already married. I used to work at this cafeteria, this restaurant. It was owned by three brothers. They had two cooks—a head cook and a cook right under her. Right? And I was the dishwasher. We always had to get to work at five o'clock. Be there to cook and have the biscuits ready by 5:30. So you got the milkman, the paper man, and people who go to work that early. This was in the fifties. And one morning, a White man hollered out to us back there in the kitchen, and he said a really bad word: "What are you doing? Get them GD biscuits ready. So I set my head through the window and I said, "I really don't want to hear that word come out your mouth any more because we are working as hard as we can." We couldn't go to the front to eat.

The hospital was like that. The room in the hospital wasn't even as big as this room. It might have been from the end of that thing to right along here. You had this bench and everybody breathing in your face. Whites were treated better than Black people.

YS: Were the schools the same way?

HW: We got hand me down books, honey. We had to walk. Whites could ride. The schools were much better for the Whites. Oh my God, yes! School bus. New books. All the books they were finished with were handed down to the Black kids. That's terrible, isn't it?

YS: When you were growing up on the farm, what dreams did you have for your life?

HW: I really wanted to become a WAC in the army, but my mother didn't want me to go. I wanted to do that. Then I wanted to become a singer, a blues singer. She didn't want me to do that. Then I wanted to be a dancer. She wouldn't let me do that. But I could dance and sing. My baby sister was a dancer. I think she out danced everybody. They said she'd out dance everybody out of twenty seven schools. They said she danced so hard she danced out of her new dress.

YS: When your children were growing up, did they work in the fields?

HW: Yes they did. They didn't like it but they worked. They started working when they were twelve or thirteen. Maybe nine or ten because the work wasn't hard. And I always took them to work with me even when I was cleaning White people's houses. They learned how to do it. They learned real fast and I would send them off by themselves to work with somebody I thought I could trust.

YS: That was in North Carolina?

HW: Yes. We moved to Virginia when I was in my thirties.

YS: Why did you move?

YS: Why did you leave North Carolina? The first time we farmed with this lady and her son, we profited. I don't know how much money, but we profited. But when we went to another man's place and farmed, we almost starved. The man was real mean. And the next year, we went back to the people we had farmed with and they took everything we had. They took all our crops.

YS: What do you mean they took the crops?

HW: They just took it. My husband had what you called a big tobacco selling, which we call tying. He and his brother took the tobacco to market to sell it. I was working when they came home that afternoon. I was sitting in what you call the pack house. That's where you grade the tobacco - first grade, second grade, third grade. You put the light by itself. And then the dark. Like that. So he came in looking real sad. I said, "What's wrong with you?" He said, "Hattie Mae, you can't believe it." I said, "Can't believe what?" He said the lady who we farmed with [I'm not gonna say her name] He said, "She gave me 20 dollars and told me she was gonna take the rest of my crop to pay our bills." He said, "We haven't had any bills." I said, "I know we haven't." He said, "Well, you know what I'm gonna do? I'm gonna kill them." I said, "You can't do that." At that time I had six kids. I begged and I begged and I cried with him. He had to find him a little job doing something. So, he worked with a man doing what they called cutting the ditch banks. It's like a canal, but it's a ditch, and you weave on each side. He went and did that, and I went and picked up in order to help him out. I would work in the morning and I would take my kids out to farm. We made it. After that, my husband said, "I'm not gonna farm anymore." I said, "What you gonna do?" He said, "We're going to the city." And we moved from there to the city.

We kept moving. We moved to a little town called Stoneberg. You heard me say it a while ago. A young guy told my husband, "Hattie Mae, you and them kids gonna starve because Hattie Mae can't work with all those little itty-bitty kids." But I never was a quitter. I started working for a little White girl. She had been in an orphan's home, but her husband was rich. She was rich. And I started helping her out. That's how we left the farm. We went from Stoneberg to a little town called Wilson and from Wilson we went to Alexandria, Virginia.

And when we got there, my husband worked at a sawmill. He worked at a sawmill, and I started working at White people's houses trying to help him feed the kids and buy clothes for them. When I say the people took our money, I mean they took everything. See, when you farm, you write down how much fertilizer you got to throw on your crops and how much groceries you buy at the store. The people at the store put all that down on a piece of paper and take the paper to the man you farm with so that he can check it out. But what was wrong is we didn't make a list. We just trusted them too much. That's how we got messed up. That's why we left the farm and moved to Virginia.

YS: What year was it when you moved to Virginia?

HW: I would say 1966. Yep. Wait a minute. No. No. In Wilson, he worked at a sawmill, but in Alexandria he worked at a hospital. He worked on different jobs. Custodian. Cleaning. Scrubbing. Cleaning . He worked for a construction company, for the sawmill, and he also worked for the army in the service department, the NCO Club, and that's when he got real sick and he had to quit. He had sclerosis of the liver. Yep.

YS: How was living in Alexandria different from living in Stokestown?

HW: Well, I didn't like Alexandria because of the tension of prejudice there. But I liked it because all my children, except one, finished school in Alexandria. They did well. That's the part I liked. Yep. In Stokestown, I had to work in the hot fields, but I didn't do that in Alexandria because I worked in White people's houses, not in the hot sun. For me, that was better. It was just better. I made more money in Alexandria than in the country because, as I told you, we were farmers. And I had good neighbors. I didn't have bad neighbors in the country, but they weren't that close to me. I had real nice neighbors in Alexandria, Virginia. And I could go to Washington, D.C. on the train. Go and come back. I went maybe about once a week because my husband's older brother lived there with his family. I liked going on the train. Sometimes I took the children. Sometimes I didn't.

YS: And what did you like the least about Virginia?

HW: That I worked in so many different people's houses and they didn't appreciate me because I was Black. They didn't care about how much work I did. One time I went to work for a lady who had never washed dishes. Every pot, every pan, every plate, every knife, every fork and spoon was dirty. And you couldn't even look out her kitchen window, it was so dirty. That was the thing I hated about Virginia. I washed clothes, ironed and sometimes I cooked and, if they had a child who wasn't old enough to go to school, I took care of the child. Some of them were nice, some of them weren't. One family in particular was real nice. The _____s. Their kids act as if they loved me. They were rich. The husband owned a car company. I worked for them for three years. Then I started working for this girl, _____. One day when she came in, I was on my knees getting something off the dining room floor. See, she had four kids. She looked down at me and said, "Where is my husband?" And I looked at her and I said, "Excuse me, _____?" She said, "Where is my husband?" She bought my uniform, right? This is going to be funny. They buy your uniform so you wouldn't work in the clothes you brought from home. I guess they thought you had germs on your clothes or something. I looked in each one of the pockets on my uniform and I said to her, "_____, your husband's not in either one of my pockets and I didn't eat him." She made me mad because to me she was inferring something. So the next week I sat in her dining room and I talked to her and told her I wanted to quit. I worked hard so that my kids would finish school. I don't want them to do what I did. I wanted them to have a better life. And they do. They do!

YS: What was your greatest challenge when you were raising your children?

HW: Keeping them clothed. I knew how to sew and how to do hair. So I kept them neat, but keeping shoes on their feet was hard because there were so many of them.

YS: You taught your children a great deal about life. Is there anything they have taught you?

HW: I've learned a lot from them because in a way when I was growing up I wasn't as wise as my children were when they were growing up.

YS: What do you mean when you say they were wiser than you were?

HW: Um, let me see. Well, for one thing they finished school and they didn't get married as young as I did. They went to college. You know what I'm saying?

YS: What brought you to Atlanta?

HW: I had a daughter who was already here and she was establishing a ministry. She needed some help. My husband had been dead for years, so I just moved down here to help my daughter. That was in 1995. I lived with her for maybe one month and then I got my own place. I got my GED in 1995 and that's when I decided to go to college. I want to be a mature Christian woman here in the school and try to encourage young people to stay in school and to love God.

YS: What has been the most important achievement in your life so far?

HW: Raising my kids. Seeing them get grown. And seeing my grandkids grow up and my great grandkids. Would you consider being healthy an achievement?

YS: Oh, yes.

HW: Well, that's the main one. I am able to take care of myself. Yes ma'am

YS: What makes you happy?

284

HW: What makes me happy? You want me to tell you the truth. What makes me happy is to see young people happy. I raised eleven kids. I raised a grandson that made twelve. And I like to see young people happy. That just brightens my day [Chuckling]. To see them smiling like you are smiling now.

YS: What makes you sad?

HW: What makes me sad? To see young people get mistreated and abused. There is more than one way to being abused. There are many ways. That makes me sad. You know young babies are killed and young ladies are molested. That makes me sad. I cry a lot about that when I watch it on TV.

YS: Is there something you have wanted to do with your life but have not done?

HW: I started but I haven't finished writing my autobiography. I'm going to finish that. That's one thing. Some places that I've wanted to go and have not seen yet. I've always wanted to go to Africa and Israel. I haven't done that yet. And I want to have my own business. There are a lot of the things I haven't done yet [Laughing].

YS: When I write about you in the volume, how do you want me to describe you? What would like me to tell the readers about you?

HW: You want me to say it?

YS: Yes.

HW: A woman that never gave up. When you read what I showed you, you'll know that's the way they describe me. Raising my children was a great challenge. It was also a great experience. I loved it because I was strong. I always did love children even when I was a young child myself. Raising children was a joy because I always liked to see children dressed up and cleaned up and I liked to teach them things. You know? That was my joy.

GRATITUDE FROM YOUNG SCHOLARS

Bonding with Mrs. Diana Anderson
by Radia Turay

love Mrs. Anderson. I remember the first time I went to her house. That was when SIS had just been launched. Do you know that Mrs. Anderson served a full-course dinner, with dessert, to all of us in SIS? She was just up and going the entire time. Actually, she had more energy than many of us in SIS. Dr. Gayles said that we need to challenge cultural assumptions about women who are our seniors. Mrs. Anderson taught me a lot that night. She is very involved in volunteer service. She takes care of bills for a blind person She takes care of one of her neighbors. I don't know how she does it . Taking care of that big house, caring for herself and doing service things for people around her. And we complain about our schedules!! No more of that after our work with Women of Wisdom.

After each interview, I would say to myself, "She's an utter lady." She doesn't internalize the negative. She just moves on. Just as you said, Yomi. She is too busy doing good things to have time for the negative. That's what we mean at Spelman when we talk about women who are in charge of their lives. During my first year here, I tried to fight fitting into the image of the "Spelman Women" that was pushed on us. After my bonding with Mrs. Anderson, I am now saying, "If this is what a Spelman woman is supposed to be, then show me how to become one."   Thank God for Mrs. Anderson! No more frowns, Yomi. No more worrying. Mrs. Anderson does not frown and she says only kind things about people and positive things about life. I love Mrs. Anderson.

Bonding with Mrs. Nadine Bryant
by AueMuro Lake

I would leave campus in the afternoon to drive approximately ten blocks to the Fulton County New Horizon Senior Center to interview my Woman of Wisdom, Mrs. Nadine Zora Bryant, the proud mother of six children and six grandchildren. She always greeted me with a tight hug and with a laugh After the first visit, I knew to expect a warm embrace from Mrs. Bryant and to hear her sound my name with laughter. She told me that, as a young girl, she would go to her grandmother's house after school and immediately change out of her school dress into her play clothes. She would then tend the garden, a plot of land in her grandmother's back yard. Sometimes she would begin the cooking or the washing. Mrs. Bryant learned as a child that her grandmother expected her to be responsible. She shared many stories about her life, but one in particular captures her integrity and nobility. It was a Wednesday evening when Mrs. Bryant was working diligently to clean a room a rentee had just vacated. She opened a drawer and found a roll of ten one hundred dollar bills. Shocked and nervous, she slammed the drawer shut and walked around the room. She sat on the bed and turned on the television as she contemplated what to do with the money she had found. "I could see my grandmamma's face," she told me, "saying, 'That's not the way I raised you'." She said to herself, "That's somebody's hard working money. They came here and left and you have to turn the money in." Listening to her grandmother's voice, which was her conscience, she turned the ten one hundred dollar bills into the hotel manager. Weeks later, the money had not been claimed. The hotel manager and the director of property management rewarded the entire sum of $1000.00 to Mrs. Bryant and they wrote her letters of commendation. This is only one of the many instances in which Mrs. Bryant showed her capacity for honesty and caring concern. She is an exemplum of integrity and hard work for my generation. Thank you, Mrs. Bryant.

Bonding with Mrs. Harriet Chisholm
by Jamie Chatman

I turned into the driveway next to the brick mailbox that bore the numbers _____. I turned off the ignition, got out of the car, walked to the front door, and nervously rang the doorbell. I waited in anticipation. Soon I heard the sound of a lock turning. The door opened, and I was face to face with my African American Woman of Wisdom, Mrs. Harriet Chisholm. She welcomed me into her home without fanfare and with naturalness I would later come to associate with her. I had no reason to be nervous because Mrs. Chisholm made me feel at home immediately. We walked from the front hallway to the back of the house to the den area. The room was bright, colorful and homelike. A perfect place for our conversation. We sat at a table that was in full view of a backyard of tall trees. I relaxed, sat back in my chair, and the interview began. I was ready to listen because I knew I was in the presence of an empowered and interesting woman. In that first interview, I learned that Mrs. Chisholm is an honest woman who shares her ideas with candor. Mrs. Chisholm's home is like a museum filled with family artifacts dating back to the 1800's: her grandfather's spectacles, family baby pictures, wedding invitations, court documents, and shelves of photo albums she has put together. She told me in one of the interviews that her mother kept everything and she does so as well. She showed me engraved wedding invitations and invitations to social events dating back to the nineteenth century. She showed me a directory of Black businesses on Auburn Avenue in the first decade of the twentieth century. The directory belonged to her grandfather. I was surprised when Mrs. Chisholm told me that she was born in a hospital owned by a Black woman physician. I never felt that Mrs. Chisholm was rushing me to end an interview, and I believe she enjoyed our time together as much as I did. When I asked her if there is anything she wants to do but has not yet done, she said that she would like to write a book. I told her that she has four books in her stories. I hope she writes them.

I did not think that meeting Mrs. Chisholm would have a lasting effect on the way I look at the world, but it has. After the formal interview was over and often when the tape recorder was turned off, we had candid conversations about school and about life, conversations about college, independence, and my goals for the future. Mrs. Chisholm's advice not to grow up too fast and to live within your means, and not the way others might think you should live, has stayed with me. Mrs. Chisholm constantly reminded me to be myself regardless of the pressures of the world. She is a special person and, although she has retired from the school system, she continues to teach and to positively affect people's lives. Thank you again, Mrs. Chisholm.

Bonding with Mrs. Marymal Dryden
by Shayla Griffin

I remember being nervous as Dr. Wade Gayles drove me from campus to meet my Woman of Wisdom, Mrs.Marymal Dryden. What would she think of me? Was I dressed appropriately? Were my questions open-ended enough? Dr. Wade Gayles only exacerbated the anxiety I was feeling. Although well-meaning, she "tested" me en route. "What will you do if she answers a question with a 'yes' or 'no'?" Although I had known what to do in every possible hypothetical situation an hour earlier, my mind suddenly became blank. As we pulled into a curvaceous driveway, my heart was beating fast and I began to sweat, all the while thinking that sweaty underarms and palms will hardly make a good first impression. The driveway took us to the back of Mrs. Dryden's house and to her flower garden, a variegated field of pink, yellow and blue flowers. Suddenly, I laughed out loud. At the entrance to the garden was a life-size placard of a woman's backside covered with ruffled white red and white polka dot bloomers. At that moment, I realized what would later be confirmed time and time again: Mrs. Marymal Dryden, a sophisticated woman with class, has an infectious sense of humor and a childlike sense of mischief. On one of my visits, she would appoint me her accomplice in hiding dirt stains in the back of er husband's car left by large bags of soil and fertilize—bags he had specifically instructed her not to load into his new car. I could not have known as I drove to her house for my first interview that I had chosen as my mentor an easygoing, light-hearted, fun-loving, accomplished, and yet humble woman. I knew that I would hear Spelman College stories—Mrs. Dryden is an alumna—but I could not have known that I would hear such interesting stories about achievement, about independence, and about "disobedience," which has been fundamental to her empowerment. Mrs. Dryden is an excellent role model for me. She is confident, self-assured and serious, and yet she is lighthearted, easy going and humble. She spoke of her achievements (and they are many) in a very casual, matter-of-fact way. During my time with her, I learned the importance of staying focused through all of life's ups, downs and in-betweens. In the process of learning from Mrs. Dryden, I fell in love with her.

Bonding with Mrs. Evelyn Dabney
by Dabney Jalylah Burrell

will always remember the winter and spring of 2002 in Wednesdays. Chilly then progressively warm Wednesday afternoon brisk walks to John O. Chiles senior high-rise in between English classes at Spelman. After buzzing me in, Mrs. Dabney would stand at the front door of her second floor apartment ready to greet me in her sweet lilting voice with arms wide open poised to embrace. I represented a new relationship, a distant generation and for the first time two eager ears intent on listening to a women much of whose lifetime was spent "listening to other people's problems." Our SIS mentor had armed us with strategies and confidence for these very moments, but I was frequently overwhelmed by Mrs. Dabney's generosity of spirit, easy-come memory and rich stories. I liked listening to Mrs. Dabney. I enjoyed the twist turns, double back and leaps in her life story that memory dictates, but I felt that I was failing as a oral historian. I wasn't extrapolating her story. I was trying to shape the interviews, to artfully direct the tributaries that were her experiences into the river that was her life. In most of the interviews, my tape recorder and I followed the tributaries to their ending points, expansive oceans, varied ponds, tiny brooks and streams, but even these shallow waters ran deeper than I could ever have expected. Mrs. Dabney lost her young son in a tragic accident, but she offered her heart and home to young families. A church-going philandering polygamist betrayed her, but she "didn't pass up romance." Her aspirations to write and act were cut short by a dubious drama teacher thieving her story and her studies at Morris Brown College were ended by a prolonged and intense illness, but Mrs. Dabney is joyous, dramatically so, and she writes with her words in stories she generously shared with me. Each Wednesday, we ran a few minutes over our prescribed hour and I ran back to my class at Spelman trying to ensure I wouldn't rack up too many tardies. She always left me with "I love you", words of thanks, a warm hug a little more intense than the one with which I was greeted, dainty trinkets that now grace the countertops and windowsills of my Brooklyn apartment, a composition book, a tape, and a mindful of stories.

Bonding with Dr. Anna Harvin Grant
by AeuMuro Lake

On the back of an internet printout of directions to Dr. Grant's home, I wrote out the directions my mentor, Dr. Gloria, had gone to the effort to show me the neighborhood route. Surface streets rather than the expressway. I started out on Ralph David Abernathy, a long street that eventually turns into Cascade Road. I was glad to find so many restaurants along the way! Once I arrived at Dr. Grant's home, I entered another long, treasure-filled road, the road of the memory and experiences of a pioneering Black woman scholar, a sociologist. She is an inspiration to me, and that is why I caption journal notes of my time with her with these words: " A Love for the Life of the Mind: Dr. Anna Harvin Grant, the Person, Scholar and Teacher." Her works and achievements are many. For thirty-five years, she served Morehouse College as scholar, writer, lecturer, trailblazer, chair, consultant, and teacher. The tributes she received upon her retirement from Morehouse tell the story of her impact on the College and on the lives of young men who have achieved, as she encouraged them to do.

All of my interviews with Dr. Grant were inspiring and heartwarming, but one interview remains most memorable. We were talking about religion, and I asked, "What do you think of organized religion and worshipping God?" In the balance lay my curiosity and my own ideas on the correct way or ways to practice religion. Dr. Grant responded easily, "I don't worry about it. Loving God has never been a worry to me. I just pray and try to do good things." Her answer freed my thoughts. I left the interview that day feeling comfort, hope and the ability to sing a little more.

In another memorable interview, Dr. Grant told me the role she played in the induction of Dr. W. E. B. DuBois into the Fisk Chapter of Phi Beta Kappa. She nominated him and challenged those who didn't want him inducted because of his politics. She still remembers that he took her to dinner after the induction and that she saved the napkin on which was printed, "W. E. B. DuBois." She said, "He was something else." I have no napkin bearing the name "Dr. Anna Harvin Grant," but I have this volume that contains highlights of my time with her. To me, a young Phi Beta Kappa Scholar and sociology major, Dr. Grant is "something else." I thank her.

Bonding with Mrs. Edith Johnson
by Natane Eaddy

A classmate, friend and fellow SIS member, AeuMuro Lake, introduced me to SIS. She came to one of our Sociology classes with a picket sign and a poll regarding the War in Iraq. Later in the day, I saw students in SIS walking on campus with picket signs and conducting polls on the War. These women were conscious, active, and tangible agents of change. I knew I had to be involved in SIS because students were serious about doing something to bring attention to political, cultural, and social issues. I later learned that two of my best friends were members of SIS, and one of them, Shacara Johnson, told me that SIS would be conducting oral history with African American Women of Wisdom— WOW, as the women are affectionately called. It was at this point that I immediately went to speak to the faculty mentor, who responded to me with such warmth that I knew SIS was something that would meet my intellectual and political needs.

I asked to be assigned to Mrs. Johnson when I learned that she has received recognition as a quilter. I was unprepared for my first interview with Mrs. Johnson. I could not find the Faculty Mentor to ask for last-minute assistance, and I could not cancel the interview "just because." That is something we will not/cannot do in SIS. I sought the advice of my friend Lauren, another SIS member, who told me to begin with one simple statement: "Tell me about yourself." I arrived at Mrs. Johnson's home, which sits on top of a hill with a beautifully lush garden and tall trees in her front yard, a bit more relaxed. Mrs. Johnson met me at the front door. She invited me into her home. Our conversation began with ease. Mrs. Johnson, so small in stature and so calm, has accomplished so much that she inspires me. She earned her bachelor's and master's degrees in Business Education at a time when Black women were denied educational opportunities. She co-founded and operated a Certified Professional Secretarial School near what is currently Clark Atlanta University. And she received recognition during the Atlanta Olympics as a talented and accomplished quilter. I could tell in the first interview that Mrs. Johnson's experiences and wisdom would help me stitch a quilt of accomplishment at Spelman. At the end of that very first interview, for which I was so unprepared, Mrs. Johnson gave me one of her quilts. A handmade quilt by my Woman of Wisdom!!!! It will be an heirloom that will be passed from generation to generation in my family, along with the wisdom Mrs. Johnson gave me in each interview.

Bonding with Mrs. Darylne Killian
by Takkara Brunson

t was my first interview, and I was nervous. "I should have left earlier," I thought. I threw an extra pair of batteries into my bag with a tape recorder and fled down the stairs of Howard Harreld Hall. I ran past McAlpin Hall to meet Mrs. Darlyne Killian at the back gate of Spelman College. She never came. After ten minutes, I knew something had gone wrong. I began looking for her, first in the Cosby building and then at the parking lot. Soon I had what seemed like half the staff of Spelman College calling and radioing on a campus-wide search for Mrs. Darlyne Killian, my African American Woman of Wisdom mentor. I found her in the upper concourse of Alma Upshaw Dining Hall. Seated in a comfortable chair with her hands resting on a wooden cane and her grey hair neatly pulled back into a bun, Mrs. Killian was watching Spelman students rush past her as she waited for the student who would interview her for the SIS project. No longer nervous, I sighed with relief that I had found her, unperturbed and patient. I smiled and introduced myself.

We went through the food line together and walked to the faculty lounge, where the interview would take place. Thus began my journey into memory and wisdom with Mrs. Killian as my guide. Each interview would be interesting. There would always be something Mrs. Killian would say that would make me laugh and, of course, make me think. Mrs. Killian and I shared many meals together, during which we traced her family history from the Trail of Tears to her love affair with art and her many years of teaching in the Atlanta Public School System. She told me about growing up in Texas during the era of Jim Crow and attending Spelman during the era of strict rules. Mrs. Killian is a talented storyteller and a very good teacher. Each interview was like a seminar in history and culture. She talked, I listened, and I learned. I learned about the culture of the West End Atlanta community during the 1940s, integration at the University of Georgia, and the richness of Bluebell Ice Cream. I listened and I learned about Mrs. Killian's love for teaching, her belief in students, and her role in pioneering changes that took place in Atlanta Public Schools. Mrs. Killian helped developed the middle school program and she helped create what was called Future Studies, an innovative program that provided creative outlets for children labeled mentally challenged or gifted. During her thirty-four years as an educator, she was what we now call "multi-tasked," balancing well the responsibilities of educator, wife, mother, student, caretaker, and artist. She loved each role, and she succeeded in each role. Today, she is no less active and no less dedicated to education. In addition to taking art classes at a community center and giving support to various activities at Spelman College, Mrs. Killian is conducting research on the history of her family. I consider myself privileged to have heard some of the stories she has discovered in her research. I consider myself privileged to have been her SIS mentee.

Bonding with Mrs. Mabel King
by Taneya Gethers

My senior year, at a class seminar early in the fall semester, I heard about a new learning experience called Spelman"s Independent Scholars in which students would interview Black women elders and transcribe their stories for inclusion in an anthology. At the end of the assembly I rushed to the front of the auditorium and handed the Faculty mentor of the experience a self-made sign-up sheet with my name and contact information. In my senior year, I would have the chance to do something I always wanted to do: learn from African American women elders! I was paired with Mrs. Mable King, the mother of Spelman's newly welcomed provost, Dr. Joyce King. Mrs. King and I were a perfect match: both dwellers of East Point, Georgia; both originally from the West Coast—the "California Pair," and both soft-spoken, yet full of surprises. She and I instantly jelled. . What I remember most about our visits are the lunch dates that we had at the senior citizens center in East Point. On those afternoons at HJC Bowden, I felt like Mrs. King's honorary granddaughter—as if there were photos of me in her wallet next to her other grandchildren, as if I were one of her grands whom she bragged about to the ladies at the center. She introduced me, her "little friend," to everyone from the cafeteria staff to her computer instructor to the director of the Center. "We're working on a special project," she said proudly, never boasting. That wasn't her style.

I wanted to listen to her stories more than I wanted to eat, but Mrs. King always insisted on our lunch dates that I have something—a glass of sweet tea, a slice of pie, a side of salad. And in between our exchange of stories and laughs, she would give me wisdom that is priceless. I've been extremely fortunate to know Mrs. King, yet more blessed to love her and be loved by her. She has a quality about her that is refreshing, similar to the renewed feeling that you get when lotioning up after a hot shower or a long soak in a tub of fruit-scented bath salts and bubbles. You just want to hug her all the time, to be in her company. She's more than wonderful. She's a reason to celebrate. Umi. Mother. Mommy. Ma'dear. Nana. Mama. Mom-mom. Grandmom. Grandma. Granny. Ma. Madre. Grandmother. Queen Mother. Abuela. Bubbie. Big Mama. Beloved. Most Beloved. The Grandest of them all. A precious treasure.

Bonding with Mrs. Mignon Lewis
by Brandi Lee

Mrs. Mignon Lewis, a conversational, energetic, friendly, and feisty woman captured my attention, and my heart, immediately. She was the first Woman of Wisdom my fellow young scholars and I met. She was the only Woman of Wisdom we interviewed as a group, and we did so before we were assigned our individual mentors. I am sure there was a reason Mrs. Lewis was chosen to make this important contribution to our learning experience. Only someone like her—empowered and very smart—could have turned one of our early training sessions into the best experience ever in SIS. We sat in one of the circular classrooms on the third floor of Cosby literally entranced by her energy.

Mrs. Lewis amazed me with her storytelling ability. She knows how to paint scenes and describe people. She remembered vivid details about childhood experiences and she recreated them for us so well that we felt as if we had been with her all the time. In that group interview, I knew immediately that I wanted Mrs. Lewis to be my mentor. Her talent as a storyteller and the fact that she was originally from my native state, Oklahoma, made her the mentor of my choice. For all of our interviews, Mrs. Lewis met me on campus. She's thoughtful like that. I live on campus and I don't have a car. Since she was on campus on a regular basis volunteering at the museum, we held our interviews in Cosby. She always came on time and she always came with a muffin and she always gave me advice that was helpful to me as I was finishing my last year at Spelman. There was never a dull moment with Mrs. Lewis. I was laughing as I was learning. Her tales of being rebellious are very humorous. I was proud when Mrs. Lewis and I were asked to speak at the dinner for new scholars and new Women of Wisdom. Although we were quite nervous, we pulled it off by sharing wonderful memories of the time we had spent together the previous year.

Mrs. Lewis showed me that seniors live active and eventful lives. They are independent and they are in charge. She taught me so much about life and achievement that I now understand why young man should seek their elders' advice. She also taught me that education and achievement are not new to African American women. The history books don't tell the story the way it should be told. But Mrs. Lewis did. I was very lucky to meet Mrs. Lewis before I graduated from Spelman!!!

Bonding with Thelma Moore
by Alita Anderson*
(With additions by Young Scholars)

She is a woman full of warmth and fire with a laugh that can lift a ton of sadness and soothe a bitter pain. A deep, clear well of life she is, holding a spirit as cool and refreshing as summer's light rain. A wise woman. Thelma Moore, is her now name; Thelma Moore after taking the name of her child hood sweetheart, George, in marriage. Before, when she was a young girl, dropping castor oil on rocky roads and selling sweet candies to neighborhood boys, she was Thelma Williams, the younger of two girls born to Blandtown, Georgia's Deacon Shed. When you see Aunt Thelma, you see a woman who lives fully. She loves music, food, people, and clothes. Oh, clothes! She is the best dressed woman in any place. Her closet, a textile museum. Silk, Cotton, Linen, Fur, Poly and Ester all gather there to be admired and worn. She is an energetic and entertaining woman of simple elegance who takes you to her bosom and holds you there with an indisputed honesty. It is easy to love Aunt Thelma because Aunt Thelma easily loves people with whom she is connected: her family, her friends, members of her church, and patients to whom she gives excellent care, for whom she wishes excellent health. She has never forgotten the care and concern she received from people when, as a young girl, she suffered with asthma. Remembering the gifts, Aunt Thelma wants to give back. She says of her work caring for patients, "I just love it. I just love it!"

We salute her as the Griot of Blandtown because her memory of that place and that time in Atlanta's history is encyclopedic and detailed. Indeed, Thelma Moore is so talented a storyteller that no place in her stories is unfamiliar to us and no person is a stranger. Something there is about her laughter and the punctuation of her stories with "and let me tell you" that transports us five decades in time to a place that no longer exists. We watch the raging fire move from one side of our street to the other, destroying our community, or we run fast from white boys at The Pond who want to "rock us," again. We walk across the bridge to hear a Joe Louis fight on the radio, only to get there after the fight is over." And we throw back our shoulders in refusal to identify ourselves as "the maid" for white people whose houses we clean. We didn't earn much money, but we knew how to make a small sum go a long way. That's how it was when we were living in Blandtown. Thelma Moore is a gift to oral history not only because she is a gifted storyteller, but also because she knows what history is and what it means. And what's more, she has an eye and an ear for culture. Ours. You will meet her here, and her words will tell you more about her spunk, her zest, her honest and generous heart. Listen. Listen softly and you will hear the tinkling, the ever rippling of the life giving spirit in her deep well.

*Alita Anderson, who earned a B.A. from Spelman College and an M.D. from Yale University, was a guest researcher during the birth year of Spelman's Independent Scholars. Alita is a visual artist and a published author.

Bonding with Rev. Dr. Eleanor Pearson Mitchell
by Radia Turay and Yomi Adesanya

I remember that when we set up the appointment with Rev. Mitchell, I was struck by the message on her answering machine: "You've reached Ella." A man's voice says "Ella." The message continues, "And Henry." A woman's voice says "Henry." I thought to myself, "How adorable." I learned later that they are called the love couple, which made me want to meet Reverend Mitchell and her "Henry." When we arrived at the house, I was struck by the fact that Reverend Ella Mitchell and Reverend Henry Mitchell were dressed alike: khaki trousers and black sweaters. And I thought again, "How adorable." The dress was symbolic of the close relationship they have. Both are ministers, and they are not in competition with each other. Reverend Mitchell is a very accomplished woman. She is a preacher, a theologian, and the author of a number of books. She wife, mother, author, preacher, activist. Actually, Rev. Mitchell is a pioneer and this is what made us feel so privileged to be in her presence. She is a pioneer because she challenged gender restrictions in the church without becoming hostile or bitter. In fact, what strikes you immediately about Rev. Mitchell is a calmness that nothing can disturb. She is a regal woman.

Our interaction with Reverend Mitchell was most interesting because four of us sat in on two interviews with her: Radia, Yomi, Ife Finch (who had just finished high school), and Megan Kemp (who was starting the eleventh grade). Rev. Mitchell made all of us feel welcomed and she connected somehow with each of us. She had actually taught Megan's father at ITC. She was friends with Ife's parents. Ife was actually "promised" to one of Rev. Mitchell's grandsons. Talking with Reverend Mitchell made me rethink a lot of assumptions I have had about so many things. For example. I would never think that a father would be able to talk with a daughter about something as personal as entering puberty. Well, I threw away that assumption after talking with Reverend Mitchell because it was her father, not her mother, who guided her through that experience. And when we asked her what kept her going, she talked about her father's advice. He told her to stand in front of the mirror and smile--a real smile, not a fake smile—and that would make her feel better. Thanks to Reverend Mitchell, every day when we wake up in the morning, we go to the mirror and smile a good, genuine smile.

Bonding with Mrs.Shirley McKibben
by Mia Everett

In late January of 2002, I prepared to leave campus for my first interview with my assigned elder, Mrs. Shirley McKibben, who lives in John O. Chiles High Rise. I had more than a small dose of anticipation. I worried about winning the trust of a woman who came from a generation entirely different from my own. I was particularly anxious about my ability to extract the nuances of Mrs. McKibben's inspiring story about achievement against the odds. I met her at her apartment in Chiles after she had celebrated her eighty second birthday.

As I timidly knocked on the door of Apartment _____, joyous voices seemed to serenade for me. After a third knock, the door opened, and Mrs. Shirley McKibben, small of stature with beautiful salt-and-pepper hair, greeted me with a warm hug and an illuminating smile. Smartly dressed in a gray silk shirt and a gray skirt, she welcomed me to her apartment and introduced me to the sources of her joy: her niece, her nephew and a neighbor whom she called her "Sister in Christ." I knew immediately that my mentor in SIS had the spirit of a warrior.

In today's world of expected or searched-for instant gratification, we rarely see the kind of determination and love that Mrs. McKibben has threaded into the garment of life she wears with such dignity. We collapse in the face of an unexpected challenge. If we find hurdles in our path, we make detours or we turn back. Mrs. McKibben never gave up on her dream of being educated and she never became bitter about her losses and her difficulties. Mrs. McKibben, having completed only the third grade, returned to school at the age of seventy-nine to earn her General Equivalency Diploma. After a stellar graduation from the GED program, she was awarded a HOPE Scholarship and began working toward a bachelor's degree at Metropolitan College. Although health challenges forced her to leave college, Mrs. McKibben maintains an intellectually and socially active life. She is still studying and it is her intention to earn that college degree. I have no doubt that she will!

Bonding with Mrs. Ruby Neal
by Michaela Warren

The first SIS meeting that I attended was wonderful. Students from the previous year talked to us about their experiences with women of wisdom and told us what we could expect from being involved in SIS. I have always wanted to talk with women who are my seniors, and this project gave me that opportunity. I consider myself fortunate to have been assigned Mrs. Ruby Neal as my Woman of Wisdom. My first interview with Mrs. Neal took place on campus in a sitting area near the museum in the Olivia Hanks Cosby Academic Center. As soon as I met her, I knew that being mentored by her would be extremely beneficial to me as I completed my last year at Spelman and as I plan for a meaningful life. What gave me comfort in each interview was that Mrs. Neal has very motherly qualities. She is kind and caring. She was always patient with me. When I didn't phrase a question as clearly as I wanted to, she answered as if I had put everything just right. She was never abrupt with me and because she was not, she helped me develop self-confidence. I don't know whether or not Mrs. Neal realized that having her as my mentor helped me stay focused and motivated. She would tell me how proud she was of Spelman students, but what I want her to know is how proud I am of her. At a later age in life, after rearing her children, Mrs. Neal returned to college. She had always dreamed of graduating from Spelman, and she let nothing keep her from realizing that dream. Her story is a lesson about determination and empowerment. It is a lesson all of us as students need to learn.

For our last interview, Mrs. Neal gave me a tour of the different places where she has lived in Atlanta and places that are a part of historic Black Atlanta. She drove and she talked, and I learned. I was transfixed throughout the tour. When the tour ended, Mrs. Neal took me to lunch. As my mentor, she gave much more than I could have expected to receive. When I turn the tassel at graduation, I will count her among the teachers who taught me at Spelman. Thank you, Mrs. Neal.

Bonding with Mrs. Mary Tigner
by Hatshepsitu Tull

How delightful that I had an opportunity to interview someone who enjoys food as much as I do! Mrs. Mary Tigner, the African American Woman of Wisdom who would serve as my SIS mentor, is a retired caterer and businesswoman. I looked forward to hearing about her life and how she overcame obstacles she might have faced because of her color and her gender. When the SIS assignments were being made, I decided to work with a partner so that I would feel more at ease in the interviewing sessions. What luck that Wanda Cannick wanted to work as partners. She is a senior applying to med schools and finishing up senior projects. I am a junior attacking my most difficult math classes yet and participating in various activities. We were relieved that the SIS mentor agreed that we could pair up in our research.

On Thursday afternoon (February 6, 2002), Wanda Cannick and I walked from Spelman to John O. Chiles Apartment Homes on Lowery Blvd for our first interview with Mrs. Tigner. We took the elevator up to the ____ floor and we rang the doorbell at Apartment #_____. Mrs. Tigner greeted us with a warm smile and a feisty personality. She was ready to begin! Her positive attitude and her infectious energy of enthusiasm put Wanda and me at ease. In the first interview, Mrs. Tigner gave us biographical information like her birthplace, her education, her career. We did not ask Mrs. Tigner when she was born, but she volunteered the information. We learned in one of our SIS seminars that asking a Woman of Wisdom her age, or any adult woman for that matter, could be too invasive and might be seen as disrespectful. After Mrs. Tigner gave us biographical information, she began telling us some amazing stories. She is quite a storyteller—or should I say, a "raconteur." Wanda and I learned that her grandmother was enslaved, but because the owners were "Christians," her grandmother was not whipped. This same grandmother helped her son raise Mrs. Tigner after Mrs. Tigner's mother died. She also influenced, or nurtured, Mrs. Tigner's love for food by letting Mrs. Tigner begin cooking at the young age of seven

Also in the first interview, Mrs. Tigner told us how she met her husband, her relationship with her only son, and her successful career as a caterer. I was surprised to hear her talk about a Black community in Marietta, in Cobb County. That's where she was reared. Now when I drive on 285 to get to Marietta, or Cobb County, I will remember that Mrs. Tigner made the trip without the benefit of an expressway. It took her then an hour to make the trip that takes us fifteen minutes. In the first interview, Mrs. Tigner taught us a great deal about changes in the Greater Atlanta landscape. Now Wanda and I can participate in SIS seminar discussions of first interviewing experiences. I find these discussions important because they give all of the Young Scholars an opportunity to share touching stories our Women of Wisdom share with us and also an opportunity to express our fears about asking questions on sensitive issues like racism and discrimination. I was anxious to say at the seminar that Wanda and I were lucky to have been assigned Mrs. Tigner because she is energetic, entertaining, informed, and passionate. In just one interview, I had grown in knowledge about African American women and how they were empowered by family. I can't wait for my second interview. Thank you, Mrs. Tigner.

Bonding with Mrs. Hattie Mae Wellington
by Takkara Brunson

At the end of my first interview with Mrs. Hattie Mae Wellington, I asked her how she wanted to be known. She thought for a second and looked at her fingers. She looked up. "As the woman who never gave up," she responded. At the time, I didn't quite understand what she meant. How could I, not having heard her incredible story about challenge and achievement. However, over the next several weeks, I learned so much about Mrs. Wellington's life that there could be no more appropriate way to describe her than "The Woman Who Never Gave Up." She is a woman of incredible strength with an incredible story of triumph. She told me about her mother, who stayed in an abusive relationship in order to support her family. Years later, Mrs. Wellington found herself in the same situation, living with an abusive husband whose depression led to heavy drinking. Because she and her husband did not earn very much money as sharecroppers, Mrs. Wellington often worked extra jobs to help feed her family. She prided herself on the fact that she kept her children clean and well dressed [She made all of their clothes] and that she encouraged them to build a better life for themselves. Nothing came easy for her and yet, amazingly, she speaks about her challenge as simply a lived experience. When I heard about her many difficulties, I never heard self-pity or despair. This, simply put, was her life. Where did she find her strength? She found strength in her relationship with God and her children. Mrs. Wellington decided to work toward a bachelor's degree. With a HOPE scholarship, she began her studies at Spelman. Often I would see her in between classes, wheeling her backpack from one building to another, and always chatting with other students. Mrs. Wellington is an inspiration to me. She continues to create new goals for her life and she continues to realize her dreams. She is definitely a woman who never gave up . Who never gives up. Her determination inspires me to believe that I, too, can do anything I set as a goal and that, like Mrs. Wellington, I should never stop dreaming.

Bonding with Mrs. Alice Carey Holmes Washington
by Danielle Phillips

I had become acquainted with her voice over the phone. It was a gentle, yet inquisitive voice. I remember imaging the person who was speaking to be a woman filled with good southern wit and humor. What I thought would later prove to be correct. When I went for my first interview, I thought I was climbing Mount Everest. Mrs. Washington's lovely home sits on a hill that gives her a view of passers-by and a view of parts of the Atlanta skyline. I was committed to making the climb to reach the woman with the gentle voice, the woman who would become my newly adopted grandmother. With each step, I wondered if she were actually different from what I imagined her to be. I remember knocking on the door, not really knowing what to expect. A woman with good Karma opened the door and said with a smile, "Hello, Miss